Archive Books
Igor Zabel Association for Culture and Theory
ERSTE Foundation

Extending the Dialogue

**Essays by Igor Zabel Award Laureates,
Grant Recipients, and Jury Members, 2008–2014**

8 Introduction

Piotr Piotrowski
12 **Peripheries of the World, Unite!**

Jelena Vesić
28 **The Annual Summit of Non-Aligned Art Historians**

Edit András
52 **What Does East-Central European Art History Want?**
Reflections on the Art History Discourse in the Region since 1989

Tímea Junghaus
78 **Our Beloved Margins**
The Imaginings of the Roma Transformative Subject and Art History Scholarship in Central Europe

Fouad Asfour
98 **A Letter**

Raluca Voinea
122 **The Tranzitory Garden**

Maja Fowkes and Reuben Fowkes
140 **Cracks in the Planet**
Geo-ecological Matter in Eastern European Art

Klara Kemp-Welch
164 **Autonomy, Solidarity, and the Antipolitics of NET**

Daniel Grúň
188 **The Case of Milan Adamčiak**
Visual Music between the Acoustic Process, Performance, and the Autonomous Sphere of Writing

210 — Sabine Hänsgen
Polaroid – Link – Means for a Series
Three Performances from the Videotheque of the Collective Actions Group: Dedications to Inspection Medical Hermeneutics

240 — Ekaterina Degot
Russian Art at the Rendezvous
Post-Soviet Russia at the Venice Biennale

266 — Karel Císař
Modernology
Art after Postmodern Art

286 — What, How & for Whom / WHW
"There is something political in the city air"

308 — Alenka Gregorič
Cultural Jetlag
Fact, Curse, or Opportunity?

Kirill Medvedev
322 Live Long, Die Young

Miklavž Komelj
336 Partisan Art Revisited

Keti Chukhrov
368 On the Violence of the General

Lev Kreft and Aldo Milohnić
380 When the Avant-Gardists Go Marching In

408 Biographies

Introduction

Every two years since 2008, the Igor Zabel Association for Culture and Theory and the ERSTE Foundation have presented the Igor Zabel Award. Named in honour of the distinguished Slovene curator, essayist, and art critic Igor Zabel (1958–2005), the award recognizes the achievements of curators, art historians, and art theorists whose work deepens our knowledge of visual art and culture in Central, Eastern, and South-eastern Europe. A no less important part of the award programme are the working grants that are presented to deserving scholars and curators.

The present book brings together texts by nearly all the award laureates and grant recipients since 2008, as well as several past jury members. The contributors come from twelve different countries and represent a range of disciplines and interests: their number includes art historians, philosophers, cultural theorists and activists, critics, curators, and poets, with most of them falling into two or three of these categories. All have made important contributions to contemporary art and cultural production, art history writing, and critical thought within, and sometimes far beyond, the region once known, problematically, as "Eastern Europe". The book thus offers a collection of urgencies and agencies in art history, art writing, and art and cultural production from across this cultural and political geography. It is a survey of the pressing issues that stimulate these authors' scholarly, curatorial, and cultural investments and so provides a referential, if fragmented and incomplete, picture of current conditions of art and culture in the region.

Given the diverse backgrounds of the contributors, it is hardly surprising that the works collected here express such a variety of concerns and approaches. While most (but not all) the texts deal with the visual art and culture of Central, Eastern, and South-eastern Europe, some look at specific countries, others at the region as a whole; some are more concerned with work produced under the former socialist regimes, others with the situation that has developed since their collapse, while yet others trace significant connections and continuities between the two periods. A few look further back, to the period of World War II and, earlier, to the avant-garde movements of the first decades of the 20th century. A number explore the relationship between the region and the so-called West, the use of post-colonial theory, and related questions about national and ethnic identity. A lively exchange thus emerges as similar issues are examined from sometimes very different perspectives. And while most of our contributors couch their ideas in the more or less traditional genre of the critical essay, a few take a different approach, with texts in the form of a dialogue, a letter, and a poem.

With the choice of topic, approach, and form left to the writers, the editors were faced with the question of how to present such diverse contributions in a coherent way. While we decided against arranging the texts in discrete thematic sections, certain natural groupings soon became apparent.

The first of these groupings – with texts by Piotr Piotrowski, Jelena Vesić, Edit András, Tímea Junghaus, and Fouad Asfour – addresses issues

Introduction

in art history and theory from a critical geo-political perspective. The question of the centre–periphery relationship in writing about Central and Eastern European art is enriched by perspectives from other "peripheries" and discussions about competing global, regional, and national views, including questions about the impact of rising nationalism in Europe. Feminist, post-colonial, and minority positions also come into play as the matrix of power in art writing, art history, and art education is critically examined.

In the second (and largest) grouping – with texts by Raluca Voinea, Maja Fowkes and Reuben Fowkes, Klara Kemp-Welch, Daniel Grúň, Sabine Hänsgen, Ekaterina Degot, Karel Císař, WHW, and Alenka Gregorič – we move from broader questions of definition and identity to critical examinations of specific art phenomena. Several of the essays apply comparative and horizontal art-historical methods to reposition Eastern European art within the global context. Critical environmental concerns are also represented here. In many cases, the artworks under discussion were developed outside official institutional structures, often as ephemeral manifestations; hence, the artistic and performative potential of documentation and archives also becomes a prime concern. Other essays, meanwhile, reflect on the conditions of contemporary cultural production in the region, critically examining the role of cultural institutions in the struggle for access to knowledge, and in national representations, and ponder the future of the public art museum at a time of renewed political pressures and reduced state funding.

The last grouping of texts – by Kirill Medvedev, Miklavž Komelj, Keti Chukhrov, Lev Kreft and Aldo Milohnić – deal with the intersection of politics and art, specifically with the region's (utopian) legacy of revolution, socialism, and communism. But they do this from very different, sometimes contrasting perspectives, presenting a mix of scepticism and idealism, philosophical caution and guarded hope for art's role in today's discouraging political and social climate.

In 2008, the year the first Igor Zabel Award was presented, the Igor Zabel Association and the ERSTE Foundation co-published their first book, *Continuing Dialogues: A Tribute to Igor Zabel*. Here many of Zabel's colleagues, both curators and artists, reflected on his theories and approaches to art, including his deep commitment to strengthening and balancing the dialogue between the "East" and the "West". We have given the present book the title *Extending the Dialogue*, not only because, in some senses, it is a follow-up to that first publication, but also because these texts, in the variety of their perspectives, examine issues and offer views that go far beyond local and regional concerns. And indeed, the effort to extend the dialogue lies at the very heart of the mission of the Igor Zabel Award.

Urška Jurman, Christiane Erharter, and Rawley Grau

Piotr Piotrowski

Peripheries of the World, Unite!

The distinguished Polish art historian Piotr Piotrowski (1952–2015) made it his life's work to develop a *horizontal* and *comparative* methodology that would deconstruct the vertical West-centred "universal" art history, which both integrates and subordinates non-Western art histories. Piotrowski's methodology looks not at oppositions and hierarchies but at the interrelations between the centres and the peripheries, and among the peripheries, while at the same time questioning the (historical) notion of the centre. In this essay – a translation of his introduction to his last book, *Globalizing the Art of East-Central Europe* (*Globalizowanie sztuki Europy Środkowo-Wschodniej*) – Piotrowski again emphasizes the need for horizontal comparative studies of "the geo-historical margins and marginalized cultures of the East and Global South, the Far North, and every other part of the globe located outside the centre-based understanding of culture", as well as for efforts that undermine the dominant narrative and expose artistic and art-historical "practices of exclusion".

This text will be published in Polish in 2016 by the Rebis Publishing House in Poznań.

In 2013, the annual Congress of the International Association of Art Critics (AICA) took place in Košice, Slovakia. The location of the meeting reminded me of the artist Gyula Kosice, who was born in the city in 1924 and who, a few years later, emigrated with his parents to Argentina. In the mid 1940s, he became one of the founders of the group MADI in Buenos Aires. The group's members created groundbreaking paintings that engaged in radical experiments with the shaped frame. Later, this "discovery" would be attributed to the North American painter, Frank Stella. While Stella's and other US-based artists' experiments with shaped canvases have been highly regarded by mainstream art historians, those of Kosice and other artists associated with MADI have remained largely unknown. It is only recently that their works have entered the awareness of a wider art public and mainstream art history. When the group's members exhibited their radical works in Paris in 1948 at the Salon de Réalités Nouvelles, French art critics also completely ignored them. Of course, Kosice is not the only victim of the ignorance of mainstream art history. Many artists from the peripheries have shared a similar fate, regardless of whether they came from Latin America, Africa, Southern or Eastern Asia, or Southern or Northern Europe. Such pervasive exclusions pose an interesting challenge for us art historians interested in the art of the peripheries who seek methods for reversing and overturning the dominant art-historical narrative. They reveal that we cannot examine particular artistic peripheries individually but must also consider them collectively, as a phenomenon.

This type of analysis requires the simultaneous adoption of two different methodological approaches: *deconstructive* and *constructive*. Borrowing a metaphor used by Dipesh Chakrabarty in the title of his famous book, I will call the first *provincializing the West*.[1] This approach requires one to deal with the culture of the West in the same way one would deal with the cultures of many global provinces or peripheries. Of course, I do not propose to negate the historical role of the West in the creation and dissemination of modern art. However, I intend to eliminate its privileged hierarchical position in the art-historical narration and to consider it as one would any other place in the world. For example, if one subjects surrealism to a careful analysis, it becomes apparent that Paris was not necessarily its only centre, especially when one considers visual art. Derek Sayer has argued that Prague could be seen as an equivalent centre, if not a de facto co-capital of the movement.[2] While no one is questioning André Breton's historic role in the creation of surrealism, one must acknowledge the contribution of Jindřich Štyrský, both as an artist and the movement's co-creator, and the importance of Prague as a city comparable to Paris in its significance for surrealism. In an aside, we should also note that not only the historic significance of Prague, but the whole history of

---

[1] Dipesh Chakrabarty, *Provincializing Europe: Postcolonial Thought and Historic Difference*, Princeton University Press, Princeton, NJ, and Oxford, UK, 2000.
[2] Derek Sayer, *Prague, Capital of the Twentieth Century: A Surrealist History*, Princeton University Press, Princeton, NJ, and Oxford, UK, 2013.

art in Czechoslovakia fell victim to the communist regime imposed on the country in 1948. Were it not for the communist coup of that year, Czechoslovakia would not be discussed today as an Eastern European country. As it was before 1938, it would still be considered part of the West, and so would its art and culture. Although the history of Prague and Czech artists certainly points to political mechanisms of exclusion, it is not necessary to focus solely on such vivid examples. Let us note that just as with Štyrský or Kosice, one could make a very similar claim about Tadeusz Kantor, a Polish artist working in Krakow (not very far from Košice), if one compared his happenings with those organized by the American artist Allan Kaprow. There are many other examples one could cite here.

The second approach, which I will call *constructive*, does not function as an alternative to the first, but rather as a supplement. It is much more complex than the *deconstructive* approach. The question of how it could be developed further is the main subject of this text.

In order to engage in a non-hierarchical art-historical analysis on a global scale, an analysis to which I have previously referred as *horizontal*,[3] one has to select several key dates and examine artworks that were created during those times in different parts of the world. In particular, one must focus on artworks that were created in the context of important events or even helped bring them about. Because I opened this text with a mention of the Argentinian group MADI, founded in the mid 1940s, I will begin by considering the artistic culture that arose in the wake of World War II. Although the year 1945, which marked the end of the global war, is highly significant for world history, I will focus on a slightly later moment, the years 1947–1948, during which the Argentinian artists were presenting their radical experiments in Paris and the Czech communists were taking over in Prague, thereby depriving the city of its status as a European art capital.

In Eastern Europe, but also to a certain extent in Western Europe (if one considers the culture associated with the leftist movements in countries such as France and Italy, where communist parties held dominant positions), the years 1947–1948 saw the beginning of Stalinization in the cultural policies of the ruling communist parties. They also witnessed the famous debate over realism in Italy, as well as the exit of Yugoslavia from the Soviet sphere of influence (though by no means the end of state socialism or the one-party system there). In other words, the years 1947–1948 marked the beginning of the Cold War. While in the countries that fell under Stalin's direct control one could see the introduction of socialist realism, one saw in Yugoslavia, as early as 1951, the beginning of a phenomenon that would later be labelled socialist modernism. This period also witnessed the emergence of the post- and neo-colonial world, marked by the rise of India and Pakistan as independent countries in 1947. The

---

3   Piotr Piotrowski, "On the Spatial Turn, or Horizontal Art History", *Umění / Art*, no. 5, 2008, pp. 378–383.

political context of the nascent Indian independence and the modernization strategies pursued by the government and personally by the country's first prime minister, Jawarharlal Nehru, was the background for the founding (at the headquarters of the Friends of the Soviet Union) of the Progressive Artists' Group, which combined the tradition of the Bengali School with the Hindu modernism that had developed in the 1920s. This was also the period when apartheid was introduced in South Africa (in 1947), with all its consequences, including cultural ones, and when two new countries were established – Israel, in Palestine in 1948, and the People's Republic of China, in Asia in 1949. Communist China embraced an extreme version of the ideologically based cultural policy that guided the broad-based adoption of socialist realism under the supervision of such Soviet artists as Aleksandr Gerasimov and Konstantin Maksimov. It is worth noting that Cuba, which fell within the global sphere of the Soviet Union's influence ten years later, did not pursue a similar path. Instead of embracing the doctrine of socialist realism, it adapted its own modernist tradition to the new political needs. However, this does not mean that Cuba had no cultural engagement with the Eastern bloc. On the contrary, it frequently drew on the experience and expertise of artists from the region, for example those affiliated with the Polish Poster School.

On the other side of the Iron Curtain, one sees during the years 1947–1948 a consolidation of the political-cultural strategy aimed at establishing the global hegemony of the United States through the international promotion of abstract expressionism. In Western Europe, that strategy was part and parcel of the Marshall Plan, which included an extensive cultural and commercial programme that, among other things, promoted the American film industry. The Marshall Plan was supposed to protect the western part of Europe from the pernicious influence of its own communist parties, which were enjoying enormous popularity among the electorate, especially in Italy and France. Serge Guilbaut described this strategy as "the theft of modern art by New York".[4] Therefore, if we consider the years 1947–1948 in terms of art-historical categories, they represent the beginning of a confrontation between two rival universalizing art doctrines, socialist realism and abstract expressionism, introduced under two competing slogans: respectively, "peace" and "freedom". It is worth noting in this context that, in 1948, Wrocław hosted the World Congress of Intellectuals in Defence of Peace, which was attended by Pablo Picasso, a modernist who was famously a member of the French Communist Party, as well as Aleksandr Fadeyev, a socialist realist writer and an infamous member of the Communist Party of the Soviet Union, who made a rather belligerent speech during the meeting. We should also remember that not only Europe, both West and East, served as a battlefield for "peace" and "freedom"; the combat in the name of those values had a global character.

---

[4] Serge Guilbaut, *How New York Stole the Idea of Modern Art: Abstract Expressionism, Freedom, and the Cold War*, University of Chicago Press, Chicago and London, 1983.

Perhaps for the first time in the history of art, there was an emergence of art doctrines, or strategies, that had global ambitions in their fundamental assumptions and relied on an arsenal of political (and occasionally even military) means. The Egyptian art scene after 1952 provides an interesting example of the complexity of the situation. Gamal Abdel Nasser, who led the 1952 revolution, paid a great deal of attention to his country's modernization and its cultural policies. Although in the political arena he welcomed the support of the Soviet Union in his "anti-imperialist" campaign to nationalize the Suez Canal, which brought him into conflict with the West, he did not welcome Socialist Realism in the cultural sphere. On the contrary, the art that developed in the context of his political policies was both modern and deeply rooted in the local tradition. Based on evidence of the Egyptian artists' participation in the Venice Biennale in the 1950s, it appears that the Egyptian government actively promoted this type of art internationally.[5]

Let's focus for a moment on the tension between those two global art doctrines, in particular, on the perspective of those promoting modernism. According to the Western, or rather North American, account of art history, abstract expressionism, or more broadly non-geometric abstraction, was viewed as the main factor shaping global modernism after World War II. For instance, Eva Cockcroft writes:

> During the post-Stalin era in 1956, when the Polish government under Gomulka became more liberal, Tadeusz Kantor, an artist from Cracow, impressed by the work of Pollock and other abstractionists which he had seen during an earlier trip to Paris, began to lead the movement away from socialist realism in Poland. ... In 1961, Kantor and 14 other nonobjective Polish painters were given an exhibition at MOMA. Examples like this one reflect the success of the political aims of the international programs of MOMA.[6]

Although Cockcroft and Guilbaut examine the global cultural policies of the United States from a critical perspective, revealing their imperialistic and hegemonic character, their and others' emphasis on the leading role of American abstract expressionism in universal art history, and its potential influence on peripheral countries such as Poland, is rather misleading. For instance, in the case of Kantor, whom Cockcroft mentions, it must be noted that the Polish artist, like many others who came from Eastern Europe, Asia, and Latin America, continued to perceive Paris as the centre and source of modern art. The city continued to function for them as the mythic capital of modernism, and they would not have acknowledged "the theft" of modernity and the relocation of its centre across

---

5   Nancy Jachec, *Politics and Painting at the Venice Biennale, 1948-1964: Italy and the Idea of Europe*, Manchester University Press, Manchester, 2007, pp. 169-173.
6   Eva Cockcroft, "Abstract Expressionism, Weapon of the Cold War", in *Pollock and After: The Critical Debate*, ed. Francis Frascina, Harper and Row, New York, 1985, p. 132.

the Atlantic. The quote demonstrates that even such a critical analysis of American cultural policies is based on an ahistoric assumption of the New York School's world domination, an assumption that has little to do with the historical reality. This can be seen most clearly in Czechoslovakia, where artists did not even have to look to Paris to reactivate modernism in the late 1950s, since they had access to the local modernist tradition rooted in Surrealism. It should also be noted that, according to Andrea Giunta, this American cultural strategy and the art historiography that followed also attempted to appropriate Argentinian modernist art.[7] The situation resembles to a certain extent the controversy that surrounded the exhibition of the Japanese group Gutai at the Martha Jackson Gallery in New York in 1958. The Japanese artists were subjected to a double marginalization. On the one hand, American critics saw their works (as they did the work of artists from Eastern Europe) as a sign of the global impact of abstract expressionist painting; on the other hand, Michel Tapié, a leading French critic and one of the main theorists of Art Informel, perceived in their art – which appeared to refer to the Japanese tradition of calligraphy – a universal drive toward abstraction, understood as the fundamental factor of human expression. However, neither position ever acknowledged the role of Japanese modernity and its unique contribution to the development of contemporary art. Both critiques functioned as forms of exclusion, denying Japanese art's formative participation in the processes of modernity's development. Ming Tiampo, referring to Adam Smith's famous work *The Wealth of Nations* (1776), sees this as a symptom of cultural mercantilism (which the 18th-century author criticized on moral grounds, because it is not fair, and economic, because it is not efficient). According to Tiampo's analysis, the West, understood as the metropolis, imports raw materials from the colonies, to which it then exports consumer goods. In turn, the peripheries produce their own imitations of those imports.[8] But the local, unique, and extra-metropolitan contributions to modernity are ignored. This holds equally true for Kantor, the Czech artists, and the Japanese members of the group Gutai. The West shows interest in their art only as a form of imitation of its own culture. While this supposedly serves as evidence of the vitality of Western culture, in reality it only reveals the magnitude of its expansion and hegemony. Paradoxically, the hegemony of the centre is even inscribed into critiques of the centre. As we can see from the statements by Guilbaut and Cockcroft, despite the critical intentions of a given critique, if it is produced by those located in close proximity to the centre, especially if they are not well informed about the culture of the peripheries, it merely reproduces metropolitan interpretive schemes.

[7] Andrea Giunta, *Avant-Garde, Internationalism, and Politics: Argentine Art in the Sixties*, Duke University Press, Durham, NC, 2007, p. 11.
[8] Ming Tiampo, "Cultural Mercantilism: Modernism's Means of Production: The Gutai Group as Case Study", in *Globalization and Contemporary Art*, ed. Jonathan Harris, Wiley-Blackwell, Chichester, UK, 2011, pp. 212–224.

Since I began with Argentina, let's take a closer look at the events that took place in the artistic culture of this country in the 1950s. One can find here very interesting processes that are horizontally comparable with those occurring in post-Stalinist Poland. In the 1950s, both Argentina and Poland faced the challenge of cultural modernization, which naturally occurred under quite different geopolitical conditions, but which shared a common geo-artistic vector, namely the orientation toward France. The historical moment of the mid-1950s can be seen as having a similar character in both countries, as long as one keeps in mind the differences in magnitude. In both instances, it marks the fall or at least the neutralization of authoritarian control over culture: Peronism ends in Argentina, Stalinism (though unfortunately not communism) in Poland. Both systems were opposed in their cultural policies to a modernism identified with abstract art.[9] The modernization and internationalization of Argentinian art, which took place after Juan Domingo Perón's fall from power, led to the reopening in 1957 of the Museo Nacional de Bellas Artes (MNBA) in Buenos Aires under the leadership of the famous Jorge Romero Brest (he was nominated for the directorship in 1956). In 1956, a new museum of modern art, the Museo de Arte Moderno (MAM) opened in the capital as did, two years later, the Instituto Torcuato Di Tella (ITDT). According to Giunta, these institutions played an enormous role in bringing Argentinian art into the arena of global modern culture.[10] Although no new museums were created in Poland, attempts to institutionalize modernism can also be observed there. One need only mention the *Second Exhibition of Modern Art*, which took place in 1957 in the most prestigious Polish art venue at the time, the Zachęta Gallery in Warsaw, and the 1958 presentation of Polish art in Moscow as part of the highest-level official exhibition of art from communist countries. The Polish selection was the only one of the twelve national presentations in Moscow to feature modern art instead of Socialist Realism.[11]

Of course, Peronism was not the same as Stalinism. However, it is interesting to note the shared interest in modernism that appeared in both countries in the context of their emergence out of authoritarian political systems promoting conservative cultural policies. One could even say that this interest in modernism was a response to those policies. I must again emphasize that both reactions were characterized by an orientation toward France. This means, of course, that New York's Museum of Modern Art, with its strategy of "the theft of modern art", did not function as a point of reference for either Argentinian or Polish artists, as has been sug-

9   This issue is well known in Poland and in the whole of Eastern Europe. Andrea Giunta writes about it in the Argentinian context (ibid., pp. 41, 45–48).
10 Ibid.
11 Susan E. Reid, "The Exhibition *Art of Socialist Countries*, Moscow 1958-9; and the Contemporary Style of Painting", in *Style and Socialism: Modernity and Material Culture in Post-War Eastern Europe*, ed. Susan E. Reid and David Crowley, Berg, Oxford, UK, and New York, 2000, pp. 101–132.

gested by Cockcroft. The same also holds true for the Czechoslovak exhibition *Confrontations*, which took place in Prague and Bratislava at the end of 1950s and which, in the Czech art historiography, signals the end of socialist realism and the opening to modernity. All these examples reveal that Cockcroft is fundamentally mistaken.

The year 1968 and everything that occurred around this date provides us with the next horizontal slice through world history, and therefore with another perspective on the global peripheries. We do not have to investigate the historic events of that year in great detail. It is widely accepted that phenomena such as the May demonstrations in Paris, young Germans questioning their fathers about what they did during the war, the rebellion of American youth against the Vietnam War, and the massive wave of counterculture that washed over the world, were historically momentous and their impact on subsequent decades is difficult to overstate. Of course Poles, as well as Czechs and Slovaks, had their own 1968, though the events of that year in Eastern Europe had very different sources, courses, and consequences. For the whole region, the Prague Spring and the invasion of Czechoslovakia by the military forces of the Warsaw Pact were, certainly, of paramount importance. This was also true from an art-historical perspective, in particular if we consider Eastern European art in its political context. Although the reactions were very different in the different countries of the Eastern Bloc, what happened in Prague was nevertheless perceived as more significant than what was happening in Paris, Germany, or on American university campuses. In Czechoslovakia itself, the upheaval of 1968 ended in the so-called *normalization*, a period associated with stagnation, repression, emigration for many artists and intellectuals, and a fundamental lack of freedom in public life (a freedom that in 1968 could be observed, even if in a diminished form, in Poland). Despite the dire situation, some nonetheless retained a sense of humour. For instance, Hugo Demartini mused: "It's a good thing that the Russians came; if they didn't, we would become professors and official artists."[12] Of course, this was a joke. However, it is important to ask how artists were reacting to the restrictions imposed on them under normalization. The most striking response was a general diminishing of art activities and the (of course, forced) withdrawal of artists from official art institutions. One of my favourite art actions of those years is *Beer in Art*, which was performed, or rather organized, by the group Křižovnická Škola. It consisted simply of meetings in bars or restaurants to drink beer. Jiří Kovanda performed other, equally minimal actions in busy public places, such as entrances to the subway or on sidewalks during rush hour. He would stand still with his arms spread wide and impede the normal movement of pedestrian traffic. Many similar actions took place during the 1970s in both the Czech and Slovak parts of the country, in cities and in the countryside,

---

12   Jiří Šetlík, "Umelecká a občanská odpovědnost poválečné generace", *Výtvarné umění*, nos. 3–4 (special issue *Zakázané umění I*), 1995, p. 9.

in forests, in fields, etc. Of course, this raises the question: to what extent and how precisely were these actions political in character? It is difficult to answer this unequivocally. One can only say that they were not explicitly, but rather implicitly, political. They functioned as a response to political conditions in which virtually everything was prohibited. While Hungarian artists, in particular Tamás Szentjóby and László Lakner, made art that responded directly and explicitly to the suppression of the Prague Spring, in Czechoslovakia artists chose a different strategy. Instead of open critique or protest, they engaged in "silent speech" carried out through minimal gestures and actions, which "spoke" about the fact that under the new "normalized" regime practically everything was forbidden.

In Latin America, if we remain with the example of Argentina, the artistic processes responding to politics at the end of the 1960s look quite different. However, here too it is not the Paris May, the German reckoning with Nazism, the revolt against the Vietnam War, or even the Prague Spring that constitutes a point of reference for Argentinian art around 1968. Here, it was the rise of the military dictatorship in 1966. In order to understand the artistic responses during this period, it is worth reminding ourselves about the tragic history of this country in the late 1960s and 1970s and the bloody reign of the military. The year 1968 was not yet the pinnacle of terror – that would take place in the second half of the following decade – nevertheless, police repression was an everyday occurrence. It was in such a climate that, in 1968, the exhibition *Tucumán arde* (*Tucumán Is Burning*) was organized first in Rosario, at the headquarters of a trade union, then in Buenos Aires, in rooms occupied by an association of printmakers. The first show lasted several weeks; the second was closed the same day it opened due to the intervention of the secret police. Tucumán was one of the poorer Argentinian provinces. In the late 1960s, it suffered from severe economic recession caused by the collapse of small-scale private enterprises, involved mainly in sugar production, which could not compete with the powerful, mainly North American, multinational corporations. This resulted in an unprecedented wave of unemployment and poverty in the region. The exhibition, which consisted of materials documenting and analysing the social and political situation of the working class in Tucumán, was more a political than an artistic statement. As a matter of fact, artistic references were discarded in favour of direct political engagement. The exhibition not only embraced a very different strategy from that adopted by artists in Czechoslovakia, but also a very different philosophy of the artist's engagement with the public sphere. It was based on the disavowal of traditional art-making in favour of political or social activism.

The very different status of modernism in the two countries formed the background for these attitudes. In Eastern Europe, including Czechoslovakia, modernism was defined in terms of artistic autonomy, self-referentiality, avoidance of direct social engagement, etc. It was perceived as an alternative to socialist realism, the official style under Stalinism (and in a number of countries even later), which aligned art with politics, if not outright propaganda. As an alternative to the politically engaged socialist realism, apolitical modernism did in fact have a political character in these countries. In Latin America at the end of the 1960s, however, there was the exact opposite situation. Modernism, with its programmatic commitment to autonomy, was associated with the artist's withdrawal from politics. By taking up the struggle with the regime, artists had to choose a different strategy from the one pursued by artists in Eastern Europe. They opted for direct social engagement, abandoning art as such in favour of overt political action.

Let's now approach the final historical comparative moment I would like to examine, namely, the year 1989, which marked the end of the Cold War and the beginning of a globalization that also encompassed the art world and, undeniably, provoked art history into a revision of its gaze on the past. Let's remember several important exhibitions that took place during this fateful year: *Les Magiciens de la Terre* (*Magicians of the Earth*) at the Centre Pompidou in Paris, *The Other Stories: Afro-Asian Artists in Post-War Britain* at the Hayward Gallery in London, and the 3rd Havana Biennial. It is also worth mentioning an exhibition that, strictly speaking, did not have a global character, but its consequences did have a global impact. I am referring to *China/Avant-Garde*, at the National Art Museum of China in Beijing in 1989, an exhibition that was several times closed and reopened by the authorities. In Eastern Europe, there were no major exhibitions that year. The first show to provide a significant overview of art from this part of the continent was *Europa, Europa: Das Jahrhundert der Avantgarde in Mittel- und Osteuropa* (*Europe, Europe: The Century of the Avant-Garde in Central and Eastern Europe*), curated by Ryszard Stanisławski in 1994 for the Kunst- und Ausstellungshalle in Bonn. In my opinion, these exhibitions collectively challenged art history in a meaningful way and led, among other things, to subsequent discussions of global art history.

I will not examine those discussions in detail here, since I have done so elsewhere.[13] However, I will recall one of the critiques aimed at disrupting the art-historical hegemony based in a typical Western understanding of art, namely the critique provided by the work of Hans Belting. His contribution predates the current wave of deliberations on global art history and can be traced to his announcement of the "end of art history" in the 1980s.[14] This "end" signalled the collapse of the paradigm based on a Renaissance understanding of the artwork, Kantian aesthetics, and later, the practice of art historians who defended the sovereignty of their discipline and the autonomy of its research subjects. Belting was not interested in proclaiming the end of art history as such but rather in its reconstruction through an interaction with disciplines such as cultural an-

13   Piotr Piotrowski, "Od globalnej do alterglobalistycznej historii sztuki", *Teksty Drugie*, nos. 1–2, 2013, pp. 272–281.
14   Hans Belting, *Das Ende der Kunstgeschichte: Eine Revision nach zehn Jahren*, C. H. Beck, Munich, 1994. Belting first formulated his idea in 1983.

thropology and media studies in order to allow for a consideration of past and present phenomena that exceeded the current art-historical paradigm. Although Belting was not the first German art historian to reflect on non-European art, including art that was not based on Renaissance or Kantian paradigms,[15] he was the first to draw radical methodological conclusions from those reflections and systematically implement them in his work. Even in the 1980s, his work was already pointing to the sources and practical consequences of those concepts.[16] Developing this idea while observing the art scene, especially after 1989, Belting argued that global art is, in equal measure, both "post-historic", because it renders traditional Western art-historical approaches useless, and "post-ethnic", because it does the same in relation to classical European ethnology. In other words, global art is not concerned with art values as understood from a European perspective, which are associated mainly with the form of expression. Instead, what is stressed is the artist's attitude toward the world, and along with this, not so much the expression of his or her ethnic identity, as the performance of identity (including ethnic identity), which becomes the goal of the work.[17]

In the course of his participation in the extensive research project "Global Art and the Museum" at ZKM – The Centre for Art and Media in Karlsruhe, which resulted in a number of publications and culminated in the 2011 exhibition *The Global Contemporary: Art Worlds after 1989*,[18] Belting developed the thesis that the art we are currently observing, namely, global art, is fundamentally different from our earlier understanding of contemporary art. According to Belting, the strongest impulse to contest the modernist (as well as postmodern) conception of art, and to develop a completely new understanding of art, comes from the peripheries – the countries of the former Third World, now referred to as the Global

---

15 See Ulrich Pfisterer, "Origins and Principles of World Art History: 1900 (and 2000)", in *World Art Studies: Exploring Concepts and Approaches*, ed. Kitty Zijlmans and Wilfried van Damme, Valiz, Amsterdam, 2008, pp. 69–89; and Marlite Halbertsma, "The Many Beginnings and the One End of World Art History in Germany, 1900–1933", ibid., pp. 91–105.

16 See Hans Belting, *Bild und Kult: Eine Geschichte des Bildes vor dem Zeitalter der Kunst*, C. H. Beck, Munich, 1990; and Hans Belting, *Bild-Anthropologie: Entwürfe für eine Bildwissenschaft*, Wilhelm Fink, Munich, 2001.

17 Hans Belting, "Contemporary Art and the Museum in the Global Age", in *Contemporary Art and the Museum: A Global Perspective*, ed. Peter Weibel and Andrea Buddensieg, Hatje Cantz, Ostfildern, Germany, 2007, pp. 16–38; and Hans Belting, "Contemporary Art as Global Art: A Critical Estimate," in *The Global Art World: Audiences, Markets, and Museums*, ed. Hans Belting and Andrea Buddensieg, Hatje Cantz, Ostfildern, Germany, 2009, pp. 38–73.

18 See the studies in *Contemporary Art and the Museum* and *The Global Art World*, cited above, as well as *Global Studies: Mapping Contemporary Art and Culture*, ed. Hans Belting, Jacob Birken, and Andrea Buddensieg, Hatje Cantz, Ostfildern, Germany, 2011; *The Global Contemporary and the Rise of New Art Worlds*, ed. Hans Belting, Andrea Buddensieg, and Peter Weibel, ZKM Centre for Art and Media, Karlsruhe, Germany, and MIT Press, Cambridge, Mass., and London, 2013.

South. In addition to questioning the classical understanding of art history, as well as that of ethnology, Belting also sees the need for a deeper revision of art history's orientation toward non-European art. He distinguishes "world art" (mainly historical) from "global art" (contemporary) and systematically differentiates "world art studies" from "global art history". While the former discipline focuses on the analysis of the world's cultural heritage and is, to a significant degree, burdened by the modernist understanding of universalism, the latter attempts to reckon with the features of global art mentioned above: its post-historic and post-ethnic character, the tendency to be collective rather than individual in nature, its glocal (i.e. simultaneously local and global) orientation, its critical impulse and alter-globalist concerns, and its media-based character, which is grounded in electronic and virtual means of communication.

What, precisely, is such a global art history supposed to look like? Belting does not provide us with an answer to that question; he only argues that it should not assimilate the global newcomers into the sphere of the Western conception of the artwork. In particular, the understanding of global art history cannot be based in a colonial or neo-colonial tradition, nor should it function as an extension of a neo-liberal offer to "generously" admit the Others among Ourselves. He adds that it will take time to develop a new methodology, since the phenomenon is so new. However, as is often true with his work, the answer emerges through his practice. Moreover, in this instance, it comes from a rather surprising direction, namely his study of the origins of the European perspective.[19] In his book *Florence and Baghdad: Renaissance Art and Arab Science*, Belting reveals how the European perspective, this paradigmatically Western construction of an image, incorporates within its sphere of influence knowledge developed within Arab culture. Studies such as this fundamentally undermine Western egocentrism and cultural hegemony, provide an alternative to the anti-Islamic or anti-Arab hysteria of the Western political and ideological conservatives, and simultaneously point to an intercultural exchange free of domination and xenophobia. They create a completely different model of understanding of the world from the one described in Samuel Huntington's infamous book, *The Clash of Civilizations*.[20] This really is a genuinely alter-globalist approach to art history, one that, moreover, provides a perspective on mainstream art (and art history) from the position of the cultural peripheries, or at least from that of non-European culture.

To conclude this short text, I will outline a political perspective that forms part of its background. To do this, I will quote Krzysztof Wodiczko, who has written about New York as a city of refuge. This status, biblical in its

19 Hans Belting, *Florenz und Bagdad: Eine westöstliche Geschichte des Blicks*, C. H. Beck, Munich, 2008 (English translation: *Florence and Baghdad: Renaissance Art and Arab Science*, Belknap Press, Cambridge, Mass., 2011).
20 Samuel P. Huntington, *The Clash of Civilizations and the Remaking of World Order*, Simon and Schuster, New York, 1996.

genesis, would function as the best monument to the victims of 9/11, were the city's administration to adopt it. Wodiczko writes:

> After post-structuralism, it is now time for self-reconstruction, towards new visions and constructions, political, social and cultural. Envisaging and designing new, engaging, inclusive, agonistic, memorial projects must become part of this emancipatory agenda.[21]

This is a call for the creation of a utopia. And it is not an isolated one. Another comes from Immanuel Wallerstein, who suggests that instead of talking about utopia we should talk about *utopistics*.[22] Briefly, this means that while utopia conveys a general idea, utopistics is based on the scientific analysis of the social, political, economic, and cultural situation and therefore allows for the development of the instruments of change as well as for a conception of the character of the future. In other words, whereas utopia provides an idealized vision, utopistics offers a realistic possibility based on the scientific rationale of a hypothesis developed by Wallerstein from his analysis of what he calls the world-system. Moreover, he emphasizes that we ourselves, as participants in the social life, and not the metaphysics or inevitability of history, are responsible for effecting change. What the future will bring we cannot know, but the shape of that future depends to a significant extent on us.

Although, to me, the difference between utopia (idealism) and utopistics (rationalism) sounds somewhat speculative, I am certain that we can do something to change the world, or at least to understand it better. This broadly defined project could include studies of the artistic peripheries of the world and art history that are based on a comparative and horizontal methodology, studies of the geo-historical margins and marginalized cultures of the East and Global South, the Far North, and every other part of the globe located outside the centre-based understanding of culture, as well as all efforts to undermine the mainstream narration and reveal artistic as well as art-historical practices of exclusion. That is why we need a Peripheries International, whose slogan should be: "Peripheries of the world, unite!"

© Piotr Piotrowski, 2013–2014.
Translated from Polish by Anna Brzyski.

---

21   Krzysztof Wodiczko, *City of Refuge: A 9/11 Memorial*, ed. Mark Jarzombek and Mechtild Widrich, Black Dog Publishing, London, 2009, p. 43.
22   Immanuel Wallerstein, *Utopistics: Or Historical Choices of the 21st Century*, The New Press, New York, 1998.

Jelena Vesić

The Annual Summit of Non-Aligned Art Historians

How does "art from Eastern Europe" become *Eastern European Art*? And how does this seemingly neutral branding acquire an ideological function in the administration of global contemporaneity? These are just two of the questions debated by a diverse group of "non-aligned art historians" at Jelena Vesić's imaginary symposium. Employing the ancient literary device of the dialogue, the Belgrade-based curator and theorist has her characters explore such issues as the meaning of *regional art* and the ideological role of *Eastern European Art* in the "New Europe" after the fall of the Berlin Wall. Tensions arise when the affirmative notions of *horizontality* and *contextuality* in the new art histories are confronted with theories about the post-communist discourse as ideology.

TOPIC 2016:
Eastern European Art and Its Discontents: The Politics of the Distribution of Global Contemporaneity

(Notes from discussion)

Hello, everyone, and welcome to our Annual Summit of Non-Aligned Art Historians. As many of you already know, our discussion format is not limited by the formal disposition of speakers–audience or any internal hierarchies among the speakers. Everyone is invited to speak and contribute to the topic, which in line with our usual practice was formulated collectively during last year's summit: *Eastern European Art and Its Discontents: The Politics of the Distribution of Global Contemporaneity*. I will offer a few introductory remarks for those of you who were not with us during last year's sessions.

Today's discussion is intended to investigate the geopolitical paradigm of *regional art* as one of the dominant epistemological tools for situating the notion of contemporaneity in actual spaces and socio-cultural situations. We will focus on reading the notion *Eastern European Art* in the context of the creation of "the politics of New Europe" after the fall of the Berlin Wall, as this was also the end of communism on the horizon of "real politics". How does "art made in Eastern Europe" become part of the hybrid ideological notion *Eastern European Art*? How does this seemingly neutral branding of regional art developments obtain, or attain, an ideological function in the administration of global contemporaneity within institutions and the culture industry?

The focus of this summit, as we have framed it, is both abstract and concrete. We are interested in the connections between the various institutional, political, and ideological structures that mediated the creation and canonization of the notion *Eastern European Art*. We are also interested in the particular theoretical concepts and discourses that frame this practice. I hope that all of us together will reflect on the relevant curatorial and exhibition practices and presentations of art as well as the concept *new art histories* and its accompanying theoretical assumptions. One of the hypotheses from last year's discussion was that the theoretical concepts and discourses connected to the notion *Eastern European Art* are polarized around pragmatic affirmation and critical negation, so the notion itself is laden with this dialectic.

On one hand, we will investigate the paradigms of *horizontality* and *contextuality* in the writing of new art histories that figure as pro-active (affirmative) epistemological proposals for scholarly research on *Eastern European Art*. On the other, we will analyse the set of discourses dealing with the *antinomies* of the binary construction *East–West* in the distribution of global contemporaneity. I assume we will also address some ideological critique of the so-called *post-communist condition* that frames this contemporaneity.

———————

Vladimir: Let's start with the "naive" question of *what it is* before passing to the more complex discussion about *what it does*. In the manner of cultural theorists dealing with geopolitical representations, I will briefly outline some of the contradictions behind the perception and classification of the notion *Eastern European Art*. I think that such an analysis will immediately reveal the different paradoxes behind the notion and open a door for thinking about its concrete ideological uses.

So what is *Eastern European Art*? Is it the art that comprises the activity of artists residing in the countries that used to belong to the former Eastern bloc? Is it the artistic practices developed in the context of existing state socialism? Perhaps it is the art of the countries in which the Soros Centres for Contemporary Art (SCCAs) were active during the 1990s? Or art that thematizes the socialist or communist heritage, with a special interest in the destiny of the individual within the totalitarian regime? As we can see, such questions of definition reveal the hybridity and epistemological wobbliness of the term, which, of course, opens the door to its imaginary and ideological operationality.

Now, let me present some arguments to support this assertion, looking at each question in turn.

First, the linkage between the cultural and political histories of the Eastern bloc is usually taken as one of the central characteristics of *Eastern European Art*, but the notion itself goes beyond the framework of such a definition. For example, today the artistic practice of the former Yugoslavia falls in the category of *Eastern European Art* even though Yugoslavia was not part of the Eastern bloc and, moreover, its break with Soviet Union in 1948 was crucial for the subsequent development of the distinct Yugoslav political and artistic space.

Second, it is often considered that *Eastern European Art* signifies the cluster of cultural and political practices associated with the (ideological) apparatuses of the countries of actually existing socialism. However, exhibitions and theoretical projects dealing with *Eastern European Art* are often grouped around countries that escape this designation – for example, Austria, which, despite its nominally neutral position after World War II and the particularities of its parliamentary politics from the 1970s on, assumed a specific historical connotation in this geopolitical setting, figuring as the former (imperial) centre of Central European (Habsburg) culture.

Third, the notion of *Eastern European Art* is rather a contemporary invention; although the term originates in the vocabulary of the Cold War period, its contemporary re-use is linked to the formation of the Eastern European network of SCCAs in the 1990s. It was precisely through the networking of the SCCAs that the "missing" connections were created and instituted. This was the context in which firm connections between the countries of the former Yugoslavia and the countries of the former Eastern Europe were established for the first time, both in the sense of sharing a common experience (of transition) but also in the sense of introducing a new "cultural bloc" within the global arena of contemporary art vis-à-vis the art of the West and other geopolitical formations. The SCCAs established the first articulations of the term throughout their projects and practices. These new cultural institutions and their mutual networking were crucial in the formative work of the designation *Eastern European Art*, a designation that in itself internalizes the Western gaze – the gaze *towards* the East.[1]

And fourth, the most common feature, explicit or implicit, of *Eastern European Art* as a discursive formation and exhibition practice mobilizes its connections with narratives about the socialist past as provided by the ideologies of the winners of the Cold War, namely, narratives based on the distinction between authoritarian and democratic regimes. The protagonists of *Eastern European Art* are often (self-)represented as lone individuals acting within and against a totalitarian system, on the margins of society and outside the official institutional spaces of culture.

All these problems of definition, as well as the ambivalence created by the lack of a proper historiographical classification, point towards the hybridity of the term *Eastern European Art* and its origin within contemporary cultural practices. That is to say, this term is connected to contemporaneity rather then inherited from the history or from the past.

Marketa: I would like to continue with this focus on "the contemporary" and argue that the term *Eastern European Art* appears as a kind of reflection or imprint of the cultural policies and principles of globalization and multiculturalism, which found their ideological inscription in the blockbuster exhibitions that were organized to mark the fall of the Berlin Wall and other significant dates of the New Europe. We are examining a term that, in its geographical and ideological senses, is both imaginary and real at the same time.

I think the genesis of the term *Eastern European Art* should be examined with regard to its application and contextualization in contemporary

---

1   For more detailed research on the Western "authorship" of the designation *Eastern European Art*, see Zdenka Badovinac, "Histories and Their Different Narrators", in *L'Internationale: Post-War Avant-Gardes Between 1957 and 1986*, ed. Christian Höller, JRP–Ringier, Zurich, 2013, pp. 42–51.

exhibitions that are thematically tied to the interpretation of the socialist past and conceived as sites of exposure and discovery of vibrant and less-known artistic practices from Eastern Europe, particularly the exhibitions held in important cultural institutions in Western Europe. A few examples of such macro-exhibitionary projects would be: *Europe Europe: The Century of the Avant-garde in Central and Eastern Europe*, at Kunsthalle Bonn (1994); *After The Wall: Art and Culture in Post-communist Europe*, at Moderna Museet in Stockholm (1999); *Aspects/Positions: 50 Years of Art in Central Europe 1949–1999*, at Museum Moderner Kunst Stiftung Ludwig (MUMOK) in Vienna (1999); and *Who if not we …? 7 episodes on (ex)changing Europe: Cordially Invited*, at BAK: basis voor actuele kunst in Utrecht (2004). Many other smaller-scale exhibitions, as well as numerous conferences, publications, and individual artworks, have contributed to the capillary dissemination of the term *Eastern European Art*, which was originally established within the big shows.

Together with the administrative concepts of *civil society* and *democratic culture* (expressed as the key terms *transition* and *normalization* and often discussed in curatorial statements and exhibition catalogues), those shows promoted numerous post-socialist stereotypes – from "socialist aesthetics" and "socialist nostalgia" to the "dissident emotions" of solitude and vulnerability. In the contemporary appropriation of the avant-garde communist art legacy, its original social meaning was often neglected, which laid the groundwork for its safe integration in the global industry of political iconography, postmodern pastiche, and different versions of nostalgic-hipsterish, depoliticized retro-formalisms.

In various overviews of art in Europe before the fall of the Berlin Wall, we find the epistemological division reflected in two binomials or binary oppositions that constantly appear in studies on Eastern Europe and in the new art history in the countries of the former "socialist bloc". The first consists of the concept *authoritarian* or *totalitarian art*, which groups together socialist realism, Nazi-Kunst and Fascist art without any real ideological differentiation, as opposed to the concept *free art*, which encompasses various avant-gardes and modernisms, as well as, of course, contemporary art. The second binomial opposes the concept *official art*, which evolves in accordance with the dictates of the authoritarian state, to that of *alternative art*, which stands in formal opposition to the state, "hiding" on the margins of public life in the "dark" spaces of the alternative scene, the (semi-)privacy of artists' apartments, or somewhere in the remote wilderness of nature.

In my view, this approach neglects the common ideological assumption that certain realist practices were shared by the historical avant-gardes and modernism. This problem was analysed more consistently in the Brecht–Lukács debate on questions of realism[2] and in the long-stand-

---

2 See the relevant chapters in *Aesthetics and Politics: Theodor Adorno, Walter Benjamin, Ernst Bloch, Bertolt Brecht, Georg Lukács*, afterword by Frederick Jameson, Verso, London

ing disputes on the cultural left regarding the Congress of Proletarian and Revolutionary Writers held in 1930 in Kharkov.³ However, it seems that within the discourse of contemporary *Eastern European Art*, the historical and neo-avant-gardes serve the purpose of confirming the genuine "creative" identity of Eastern Europe in the newly established post-socialist context. This, of course, is an ideological argument, as it underlines the endurance of a specifically Eastern European contribution to universal artistic freedoms, as well as a discontinuity with the totalitarian demands of "the Soviets", who allegedly had no "feel" for contemporary art. In the reframed context of "cultural regionalization" the avant-garde becomes an *art of identity* – the identity of Eastern Europeanness – and its universal political substance fades away.

Sarka: I would just add an extended footnote to the previous comment on how exhibition practices produce epistemological frameworks for art-historical analysis. I think it is important to mention that this process should not be observed merely as a precedent of contemporary times, witnessing the birth of the curatorial paradigm and, consequently, "the pioneering" role of the exhibition in producing meaning and framing the interpretation of artworks. Quite the contrary, exhibitions have frequently represented a point of departure for the writing of art history; they established discursive outlines that made it possible to understand the individual artworks and created a logic of inclusion and exclusion – according to which certain concepts became part of History or were left outside it.

For example, the history of modern art based on the concept of *-isms* (expressionism, cubism, Fauvism, surrealism, futurism, etc.) was enthroned with the blockbuster exhibition *Cubism and Abstract Art* at the Museum of Modern Art in New York in 1936. It was, indeed, the exhibition curator, Alfred H. Barr, Jr., who canonized the logic of reading and interpreting 20th-century artworks as a linear progression of *-isms* and set

---

and New York, 1980: Georg Lukács, "Realism in the Balance", pp. 28–59; and Bertolt Brecht, "Against Georg Lukács", pp. 68–85.

3   This second conference of revolutionary writers, held in the Ukrainian city of Kharkov, led to the founding of the International Union of Revolutionary Writers, which in the following years published the journal *Literature of the World Revolution* in Russian, German, French, and English. The work of the IURW was conducted through national sections and groups, and its more prominent members included Louis Aragon, Johannes R. Becher, Theodore Dreiser, Henri Barbusse, and Bertolt Brecht. The conference precipitated a number of disputes within the intellectual left: some argued that proletarian literature must be defined by the subject matter, which should be working-class life, and the class origins of the author. Others held that proletarian literature could be defined by ideology, rather than subject matter, and that art should portray not only work in factories but "the whole life of human society, the life of all classes", which should be reflected "from the standpoint of the proletariat" (James Francis Murphy, *The Proletarian Moment: The Controversy Over Leftism in Literature*, University of Illinois Press, Urbana and Chicago, 1991, p. 41). The conference also resulted in long-lasting disputes within the surrealist movement, notably, the clashes between André Breton and Aragon and the split between Breton and Pierre Naville.

certain artworks as key points for understanding this history.[4] The same logic went on to be consecrated in the academic discourse of art history and through such popular books as Herbert Read's *Concise History of Modern Painting* (1959) and *Modern Sculpture: A Concise History* (1964). Today it seems there is a consensus that the politics of exclusion and inclusion in an art history conceptualized along these lines is based on the dominance of the Western logocentric subject as represented by the white male creative genius. Eastern Europe, Asia, Africa, and Latin America appeared in the modernist picture of the world largely as an "ethnographic reference", as a domain of positive primitivism from which modernist Europe and North America drew inspiration.

What actually started to challenge this perfect, totalizing picture of art history were the identity politics and critical culture of the 1960s and 1970s, which raised the question of political freedom for marginalized groups within the dominant order of representation. Nevertheless, it seems to me that writing particularist histories of art with the aim to establish new and distinctive social and artistic contexts outside the given Western-modernist pattern becomes widespread only in the 1990s. This new art history writing usually unfolds in parallel with the production of spectacular exhibitions of art from China, Japan, South Asia, Latin America, Africa, Russia, Eastern Europe, and so on, in major museums and art institutions in Western Europe and North America.

Now, while the actualization of particularist art histories in the context of academia appears together with the paradigm of postmodernism, contemporary exhibition practice has developed on the background of social and economic globalization and is frequently conditioned by the zones of interest of global capitalism and its multiculturalist logic. The exhibition that stands at the beginning of these processes is *Magiciens de la Terre* (*Magicians of the Earth*), held at the Centre Georges Pompidou in 1989; as the curator, Jean-Hubert Martin, famously said: "One hundred per cent of exhibitions are ignoring eighty per cent of the Earth." My point is that the emergence of particularist histories of art – and with them, the history of the art of Eastern Europe – reaches the horizon of symbolic emancipation through a critical relativization of hegemonic historical truths and values stemming from the modernist West-centrism, but their effects remain constrained and conditioned by the flow of economic and cultural power.

Magda: Let me continue by reflecting further on the writing of geopolitical or regional art histories, which are also called *particularist* or *new art histories*.[5] Certainly, on one level we can say that *Eastern European Art* is a

---

4   See Astrit Schmidt-Burkhardt, "The Barr Effect: New Visualization of Old Facts", in *International Exhibition of Modern Art 2013*, Museum of Contemporary Art, Belgrade, 2003, pp. 49–61.
5   The term *new art history*, which implies a methodological and ideological questioning of the politics of historicization, is discussed comprehensively in Jonathan Harris, *The New Art History: A Critical Introduction*, Routledge, London and New York, 2001.

product of the fall of the modernist paradigm and the grand narratives of the history of art. In this sense, the term originally appears as a critique of the hegemony of the West in the universal-modernist reading of so-called *world art history*. On another level, and in an institutional sense, *Eastern European Art* appears in similar cultural and political configurations as we see with contemporary art from Africa, China, the Middle East, or Latin America – as has already been mentioned in this discussion – and is treated the same way as those other regions, which were similarly discovered, or rediscovered, in the light of some economic or political interest, to become new global colonies of expanding capital – and expanding capitalism.

So, how is the notion of *Eastern European Art* discussed in the context of writing particularist art histories?

An example that may be interesting here is the paradigm of *horizontality*, which was introduced by the Polish art historian Piotr Piotrowski in his thoughts on methodological approaches to a possible historicization of art from Central and Eastern Europe.[6] Perhaps I should add that Piotrowski's examination remains on the scholarly terrain of the new art history – it does not so much rely on any ideological and epistemological questioning of the term *Eastern European Art* but rather views the term as already "incubated" and normalized within the exhibitionary practices of 1990s and early 2000s. In his essay "How to Write a History of Central-East European Art", which addresses some of the neuralgic questions of Eastern European art history, Piotrowski uses the paradigm of horizontality to transcend the simplistic dichotomies and binarisms of the East–West divide, where difference is constituted as one-dimensional and self-evident.

He abandoned embedded claims that differentiate the art of the East and the West on the basis of the generalized ideological context – for example, the idea that the liberal-democratic ideology of the West produces a "pluralist and heterogeneous" art while the art of the East develops within or against a "uniform ideological background". This skilful rejection of the generalized ideological context enabled him to avoid the pitfalls of a vampiristic preservation of Cold War configurations in the cultural discourse – the ideological reading that some of my colleagues here underlined when they spoke about *totalitarian* vs. *free* and *official* vs. *alternative* art. Piotrowski, in fact, proposes abandoning the concept of ideology in the classic Marxist-Leninist sense, which, in his view, did not play a crucial role in the local cultural politics of states under actually existing socialism. Instead, he remobilizes the Althusserian concept of ideological state apparatuses,[7] placing emphasis on *apparatuses* in the plural. In

---

6   Piotr Piotrowski, "How to Write a History of Central-East European Art", *Third Text: Socialist Eastern Europe*, special issue, ed. Reuben Fowkes, vol. 23, no. 96, January 2009, pp. 5–14.

7   According to Louis Althusser, ideological state apparatuses are served by a variety of institutions: churches (religious ideological state apparatuses), schools (educational ideological state apparatuses), the media (ideological state apparatuses of communication),

other words, "while the ideology was the same in every Eastern European country, the ideological state apparatuses were different – they implemented different state cultural politics and produced different meanings of the similar artistic movements in the parallel historical moments".[8] Piotrowski in a way introduces an internal Other within the space of Eastern Europe, the nation-state Other not in the sense of *ethnicity*, but in the sense of *apparatuses*. He proposes a comparative study of the regional art histories in order to create different meanings of the local art (*locality* is, perhaps, another important term in this approach) in relation to a certain focal historical moment, a moment that is, from his point of view, *always already* cosmopolitan and international-global.

Piotrowski therefore directs his thesis of *horizontality* against the *vertical* Western art-historical canon, confronting it with another form of plurality and heterogeneity, one based on differentiations within the Eastern European space itself. And he asserts that the specificities of Central-East European art should be sought precisely in the tension between the local art experience and the canon of world art histories, which is primarily a Western canon. Of course, in regard to the operational strength of the art-historical canons, the West here is not yet the Former West.

Sasha: Piotrowski is not alone in such observations. If the goal of geopolitical, regional, or particularist art histories is to maintain a pluralistic and non-hierarchical approach towards spatio-temporal historical categories, as he argues, then such an interpretation is in line with numerous other readings of so-called global art. Contemporary art, as many art historians would put it today, is the art of the Global South, or non-Western art. Or as the Korean-American art historian and curator Miwon Kwon puts it, "Contemporary art history marks a temporal bracketing *and* a spatial encompassing".[9] As a "category", contemporaneity is so pluralistic, wide open, and permissive of change that its effect appears all-encompassing, which raises the question of how, if at all, we can set the frames and parameters of our subject of analysis. And numerous art theoreticians who intervene in the modernist-Western canon speak about these horizontal pluralities of global art, of world art, on a quite *abstract-humanist level*, if I may phrase the current state of things in this "old socialist language". For example, the famous discussion on contemporary art by the journal *October* – and here I should note that it is mostly the English-speaking world that has the opportunity to speak about global (art) world affairs – attempted

---

museums, cinemas, and theatres (ideological state apparatuses of culture), etc. See Louis Althusser, "Ideology and Ideological State Apparatuses" (1969), in *Lenin and Philosophy and Other Essays*, trans. Ben Brewster, Monthly Review Press, New York, 1971, pp. 127-186; available online at http://my.ilstu.edu/~jkshapi/AlthusserISAs.pdf (accessed June 29, 2016).

8 Piotrowski, "How to Write a History of Central-East European Art", p. 5.
9 Miwon Kwon, response to "Questionnaire on 'The Contemporary'", *October*, no. 130, fall 2009, p. 13 (italics in the original).

to specify some of the principal causes and features of contemporary art beyond general references (such as the market, globalization, or the crisis of the neoliberal economy).[10] It is important to emphasize the comprehensiveness of the category of "the contemporary", its all-embracing and ungraspable character, its mobility and elusiveness, its breadth and inclusivity. On the other hand, what is symptomatic of the distribution of contemporaneity and what we can see as its *material existence* is that contemporary art has become an institutionalized practice and regular subject of study in various educational contexts.

Having in mind precisely the paradox of the institutional expansion of the object of contemporary art despite the lack of any firm epistemological ground, the writers in *October* correlated this paradigm with the phrase "the lightness of being",[11] from the novel *The Unbearable Lightness of Being* (1984) by the Czech writer Milan Kundera.

As used by these writers, the phrase "the lightness of being" joins two words that resonate with the question of contemporaneity: *lightness* signifies the free-floating status of contemporary art in relation to the appropriated knowledge and methods of the history of art, while *being* signifies the "premature birth"[12] of the object of contemporary art in relation to the existing apparatuses of articulation within the context of academia.

Participants in the *October* discussion also ponder the question of which door in the academic world contemporary art should knock on in order to receive theoretical and academic recognition: the door of departments of postcolonial studies? Art history? Visual culture and media theory? Or all of them at once?

The discourse on contemporaneity usually implies a *world art history* or *global art history* – an association that has become common and normalized. And many authors writing about the topic use different geopolitical and regional qualifications to portray this global contemporaneity.

Boris: May I jump in here to briefly mention Hans Belting's differentiation between the notions of *world art* and *global art*. For Belting, *world art* is an old idea that is complementary to modernism. It names the art of "the others". The expression *global art*, on the other hand, did not attract much attention until the late 1980s. "By its own definition," Belting says, "global art is contemporary and in spirit postcolonial; thus it is guided by the intention to replace the center and periphery scheme of a hegemonic modernity, and also claims freedom from the privilege of history."[13]

---

10   Hal Foster, introduction, ibid., p. 3.
11   For more on this, see Rachel Haidu's response, ibid., p. 97.
12   Pamela M. Lee, for example, considers how the history of contemporary art appears to be a "premature object" that produces academic anxiety in regard to the present moment. See her response, ibid., p. 25.
13   Hans Belting, "From World Art to Global Art: View on a New Panorama", in *The Global Contemporary and the Rise of New Art Worlds*, ed. Hans Belting, Andrea Buddensieg, and Peter Weibel, ZKM Centre for Art and Media, Karlsruhe, 2013, p. 178.

Sasha: Yes and no. But let me just finish my comment about the free-floating paradigm of *horizontality* that we find in Piotrowski's writings, and more broadly as well. As I said, it is a common epistemological paradigm of many mainstream critical art historians. That is, the term *altermodernism,* which was proposed by Nicolas Bourriaud and is today widely accepted, assumes a modernism of "the others" (*alter* means "other" in Latin) but also evokes ideas of alternatives and change; it is, as Bourriaud puts it, "a leap towards the synthesis of modernism and post-colonialism".[14] Therefore, the concept of altermodernity assumes the development of the global art scene against cultural standardization (or against the Western-modernist canon), against nationalisms and cultural revisionisms. Where I find a direct parallel with Piotrowski is in Bourriaud's suggestion that we understand time as a multiplicity, rather than as a linear progress, or as he puts it, "to navigate through history as through planetary time zones".[15] Both Piotrowski and Bourriaud share a certain optimism in regard to the heterochronic substance of contemporaneity, which enables a retroactive view to past times in terms of "multiple temporalities" and "a positive vision of chaos and complexity".[16] In a similar way, the Nigerian-American curator and cultural theorist Okwui Enwezor underlines the contemporary shift from the Western art canon; he proclaims the 21st century as "the century of Asia" or "the century of China" and views this new time-space categorization in the light of the total change of the previous institutionalized knowledge and the decentralization of the previous modernist and Western paradigm. Borrowing from Dipesh Chakrabarty's writings,[17] he suggests *provincializing modernism*, that is, *spatializing* it as a series of local modernisms, rather than as one big modernism. "For example, to look for an Andy Warhol in Mao's China would be blind to the fact that the China of the Pop art era had neither a consumer society nor a capitalist structure, the two conditions that were instrumental to Pop's usage of images of consumer capitalism."[18] Similar to Piotrowski and his notion of *locality*, Enwezor advocates abandoning the totalizing and universalizing principle of one modernity and thinking instead of "the simultaneity of multiple centres" – for him, such an approach leads towards the breakdown of all cultural hierarchies and especially the hierarchy of one, unique, singular (canonical) place.[19]

Lidia: For me, using the terms *horizontality*, *local*, *pluralistic,* and *non-hierarchical* within the episteme of new art history is nothing but an abstract,

---

14   Nicolas Bourriaud, "Altermodern", in *Altermodern: Tate Triennial*, ed. Nicolas Bourriaud, Tate Publishing, London, 2009 [unpaginated].
15   Ibid.
16   Ibid., pp. 12–13.
17   Dipesh Chakrabarty, *Provincializing Europe: Postcolonial Thought and Historical Difference*, Princeton University Press, Princeton, NJ, 2007.
18   Okwui Enwezor, response to "Questionnaire on "The Contemporary'", *October*, p. 36.
19   Ibid., pp. 33–40.

radically individualist and libertarian optimism, which has a lot in common with the so-called Californian ideology that Richard Barbrook wrote about in the early 1990s,[20] or with the early network enthusiasm of the mid-2000s à la Yochai Benkler.[21] It is an optimism in regard to representation and participation as well as to the alternative, entrepreneurial, and P2P forms of life of individuals, groups, and geographies. It is the belief in the alleged *just world* created by global networking and by abolishing the idea of the centre, of central power – the world that is finally opening the possibility of participation and visibility to everyone. The same optimism we can find with Piotrowski and his explanation of horizontality – the idea that *Eastern European Art* will be presented in the global arena – is, in Piotrowski's view, almost enough in itself to solve the problem, as if the relations of power and the various hierarchies that mediate such representation are dissolved on the backdrop of democratic multiculturalism.

By coincidence, I attended the 2010 presentation of the Igor Zabel Award for Culture and Theory, at MACBA in Barcelona, where Piotrowski was a keynote speaker along with Georges Didi-Huberman. Piotrowski began his talk with an argument about the *provincialization of Europe* – the concept by Chakrabarty that bypasses forms of "postcolonial revenge" (or the shift of power from the centre to the periphery), in which he spoke of a "renewal" of European thought from the marginal position through certain processes of "translation". However, the part of Piotrowski's thesis that I strongly disagree with – I guess partly because I belong to a different generation of art historian – is its equalization of the postcolonial condition with the post-1989 era. According to Piotrowski, the condition of the postcolonial coincides with the post-dictatorial and post-military governments in the South American context, the post-apartheid and post-authoritarian conditions in South Africa, and the post-communist/post-totalitarian conditions in Eastern Europe – all chronologically parallel processes that ended around 1989. In this sense, the victory of Western parliamentary democracy in these regions, or, as he put it, "the final releasing of culture from the authoritarian straitjacket",[22] immediately introduced all kinds of postcolonial freedoms. For Piotrowski these freedoms are embedded in the cosmopolitanism of migration, cultural transnationalization, and the decentralization of the biennial culture towards the, finally, metropolitan cities of "the East". In my view, such claims only confirm the cultural-political canons of global contemporaneity.

20 See Richard Barbrook and Andy Cameron, "The Californian Ideology", http://www.imaginaryfutures.net/2007/04/17/the-californian-ideology-2 (accessed June, 29, 2016).
21 See Yochai Benkler, *The Wealth of Networks: How Social Production Transforms Markets and Freedom*, Yale University Press, New Haven and London, 2006; the book is available online at http://cyber.law.harvard.edu/wealth_of_networks/Main_Page (accessed June 29, 2016).
22 Piotr Piotrowski, "Writing on Art after 1989", talk at the presentation of the Igor Zabel Award for Culture and Theory, Barcelona Museum of Contemporary Art, Barcelona, 2010.

Urška: I have a lot of immediate comments to all that has been said so far, but maybe this is also a good moment for a short "theoretical break". I would like to share with you some details from my research on the operational materiality of the canon, since the term is frequently used in the field of the new art histories and has also been mentioned several times in our discussion. I'm interested in the paradoxical expression *the canons of contemporaneity*. So what I'm actually trying to think together are two seemingly disconnected and opposite (almost contradictory) words: *canon*, which etymologically denotes patristic theology, order, rules, and established values, and *the contemporary*, which in its general understanding denotes a vibrant global society, novelty, and a progressive move in the direction of the New.

On the one hand, the idea of the canon appears to be something we have left behind, something our liberal contemporaneity has broken with. On the other hand, if we accept the basic implications of this notion – the establishment of a certain set of rules, rights, and privileges – we cannot negate the continued existence of power relations and the system of values that lies beneath the "surface visibility" of the freedoms that have been won.

From the 1960s onwards (which is also the time frame of contemporary art according to various art-historical writings), the classic interpretation of art based on the concepts *a great artist and his work* and *a great museum and its historical truth* has been exposed to rigorous criticism, from gender-related, sexual, racial, and other minority positions through forms of institutional critique or the classic Marxist analysis of the production, consumption, and circulation of art. Now, what is perhaps important for the framework of our discussion is precisely the operational structure of the canon. Since in the modern sense the canon represents a "tacit authority" – that is, a truth that is presented as natural, logical, and naturalized in the discourses of art and culture – that means that the canon is pronounced, named, recognized, and announced only through the process of its critique. So my thesis is based on the retroactivity of naming the canon through a counter-canonical operation – breaking the canon overlaps with showing or saying, "This is the canon." More precisely, the moment of the critical act sheds light on what the canon *is*, revealing it and making it visible.

Now, it is a fact that the critical attitude has become an integral part of contemporaneity, but we can ask whether these micro-spaces of transgression, or the negation of dominant realities and established artistic values – the micro-spaces of disobedience, rebellion, shock, refusal, and questioning – have today become a kind of etiquette of contemporary artistic practices and, more generally, the custom of liberal societies. Could it be that the critique of the canon is itself being "canonized" in contemporary art? We are living at a time when shifting away from the canon in the direction of the New has become an established and strategic way of building a successful career, whether you're an artist, curator, or art historian.

How do we cope, then, with the dynamics of canonization today? Does the canon survive in a fixed given form, as a universal historical constant – a set of rules that can easily be called upon, enumerated, and clearly named? Or is it something that involves a constant relationship between the dynamic establishment of authority and rules, on the one hand, and the critical violation of these rules, on the other.

Clearly, the issue of the canon is not a question of stable, fixed positions of power, aesthetic regimes, ethical norms, and the political status quo; rather, it is a dynamic, changeable form that requires an active and mobile attitude towards concrete analyses of concrete situations. In other words, we can speak of canonization as a reactive and dynamic process more than a stable set of values established by some kind of "written law". It is no longer enough to merely repeat critical gestures against the canon, as was once done with success; quite the contrary, one must seek out, find, and relate to new spheres of emerging authority, power, and values. And this can easily be put in the context of our discussion, when we talk about the repetition of critical gestures towards the modernist-Western canon in the work of various contemporary art historians, curators, and critics, but perhaps the biggest challenge, and the greatest need, is to actually assume a position from which you can critique both the modernist-Western canon and the contemporary-globalist canon.

Alexandra: I've also researched the art-historical canon and I agree with your proposals. It is definitely important to think through the ideological narratives that are projective in relation to contemporary art, that is, to think through the narratives that frame the "historical reality" in relation to which our contemporaneity should be produced and into which it must fit.

So in a broader socio-political sense, the concepts of the new art historicization we have been discussing are not in fact truly (that is, conceptually) de-colonial and counter-canonical. In my view, they serve to strengthen the dominant ideology of the anti-communist consensus by uniting seemingly opposed political options such as pro-European democratism and ethno-nationalism.

Any critique of the canon that stems from particularist struggles remains incomplete if it dismisses the relations between the particular and universal. So in that sense I would rather side with Marxist-feminist art historians like Griselda Pollock. When Pollock speaks about the critique of the art-historical canon, she formulates it through the concept of *intervention*, or a "lateral approach" to something we might call an institutional reproduction of the authority and the truth of art history.[23] In her interpretation, intervention is an act that "comes from the inside", from one

---

23   See Griselda Pollock, *Differencing the Canon: Feminist Desire and the Writing of Art's Histories*, Routledge, Abingdon, UK, and New York, 1999; and her *Vision and Difference: Feminism, Femininity and the Histories of Art*, Routledge, London and New York, 2003.

part of the whole, but points to the structural, universal problems of academic disciplines or exhibition politics, indicating their connections with the material and social practices that surround us. Even when it speaks the language of a minority, of the local or the particular, the effects of intervention are always universal. Unlike other historians who have been mentioned, who speak about "horizontality", "democratic participation in the Global Cosmopolis", "positive visions of chaos and complexity", or "the simultaneity of multiple centres", Pollock stresses that intervention is not characterized by "filling in empty spaces" or "supplementing history" with something that has been left out or is less known. It does not mean adding what was "missing", rather, it is characterized by questioning, by pointing to and naming the canon, that is, something that is omnipresent in the narration, evaluation, and categorization of artistic (and social) activities. And it is only through a positioning towards a certain totality that the intervention opens up new spaces for understanding the role of cultural activities in the production of meaning, and more importantly, in the production of social subjects.

Martin: I agree with what you said. If the "negative" canonical horizon for this new, geopolitical, regional art history writing (including the paradigm *Eastern European Art)* is a Western-modernist "exclusivist universality", then the "positive" canonical horizon of the art-historical examples discussed here is marked with the ideological frameworks and material practices of what we refer to as the global society or multiculturalism. Multiculturalism is, in my opinion, closer to the ideological horizon of 19th-century national cultures – nowadays *national-cultures-networked* – than to the ideological horizon of 20th-century internationalism. On the other hand, it is clear that the concept of multiculturalism is based not on the ideas of equality and universality but on a *folklorism of difference*, and discourses on *Eastern European Art* play an important, if not the crucial, role in this *trans-* or *multi*-national folklore. In that sense, *Eastern European Art* operates in the global art world and, on one *éclatant* level, confirms the eternal values of the global capitalist society, such as "the legacy of democratic culture" and the principles of "representation and participation".

Slavoj Žižek has written about European multiculturalism – a topic ever more urgent today with refugees arriving in Europe in huge numbers – through the prism of the cultural logic of multinational capitalism.[24] For him, multiculturalism operates as a self-referential form of racism – racism from a distance; while the identity of the Other is respected (of course, multiculturalism is not directly racist), the Other is observed through multicultural eyeglasses as a self-enclosed authentic community. Here, the very distance, the "culturalized respect", is possible only because the priv-

---

24 See Slavoj Žižek, "Multiculturalism, or, The Cultural Logic of Multinational Capitalism", *New Left Review*, no. 225, September–October 1997, pp. 28–51.

ileged "universal" position is maintained; it is possible only from a position of superiority. So I think that all these new geopolitical categories of art are established trough a twofold relation towards the idea of the West: on the one hand, it is about a critique of the West-centric method – about epistemology and political-economic-cultural hegemonies – a critique that also includes the notion of multiple centres, while on the other hand this critique must still be preceded by the recognition that the relation of the West towards the "Second" and the "Third" worlds is the relation of the centre towards the periphery.

Pavel: Maybe what we are dealing with here also has to do with the epistemological confinements of the paradigm of the contextual. Today, art is perceived as truly contemporary and authentic only if it is able to capture and express the presence of the present; it is understood as something uniquely anchored in its own circumstances (which have to do with reality). The whole big turn with the contemporary is this constructed feeling that artworks can no longer speak for themselves but are instead perceived as signs or symptoms or forms of information that point the observer towards a reading of their context. For example, Terry Smith, in his book *What Is Contemporary Art?*, highlights three main features of contemporary art, features that are also at stake in the construction of the *Eastern European* in the arena of global contemporaneity, namely, *place making*, *world picturing* and *connectivity*. All three have to do with the networking of different contexts. Boris Groys has also written about how our knowledge about the social context in which art originates is no longer an external characteristic of the art piece; rather, artists today can and must expect the observer to *read the context* in which their work is produced and to understand it as an intrinsic aspect of the contemporary artwork.[25]

If the art of previous epochs was surveyed in terms of national schools and formal characteristics (modernist movements), it is today observed in its context, or rather, it "inter-reacts" with various cultural and political contexts. My question is: is it the contextual paradigm itself that produces the representation of art as a horizontal chain of distinctions and particularities?

In contemporary globalized societies the issue of the geopolitical context appears crucial. As Groys points out, global art is primarily structured around the notion of difference – "the art world is constantly in search of the Other, of what is distinctive or alternative, what is New". In this never-ending process of "otherization", the place making and world picturing of *Eastern European Art* is reconnected with the narrative about the period of actually existing communism and its aftermath. This identitary feature of the regional art corresponds with the feeling that the disappearance of communism has undoubtedly made the world a place with fewer alternatives and (seemingly) fewer differences. And *Eastern European Art*

---

25   Boris Groys, "Back From the Future", *Third Text*, vol. 17, no. 4, December 2003, pp. 323–331.

is assigned the task of "liturgically" re-performing this loss from a safe distance, whether this is about bearing witness to the trauma that artists and critics experienced under the communist regime or about a "reflexive nostalgia" for a better past[26] – bearing witness is something that makes *Eastern European Art* stereotypically recognizable in the global cultural arena. Although many artists and critics reject this pre-given position or framework of representation, claiming that they don't want to be *Eastern European Artists* but *simply artists* (as if it is possible to be "simply an artist" – an artist "as such"), or they say they are bored with the perpetuation of one and the same story of *Eastern European Art* and would prefer the universalist aesthetic approach – nevertheless, the reproduction of the same contextual baggage continues mercilessly, the story of *La condition post-communiste* ...

Adela: Right, regarding this last point, the post-communist condition (as an ideological discourse, I must add) is precisely what keeps the particularities and differences together. But we should also think about the material conditions of this relation, this linking. We should ask the question: are the relations East–West in this global, multicultural picture of the world (or the reflection of [post-]communism as the identifying aspect of the contextuality of *Eastern European Art*) truly based on horizontal positions of peaceful coexistence and on the specificity of a multitude of local colours?

Immanuel Wallerstein has offered an understanding of history as a time-space category. For him, the space of the East is burdened by time (the time of communism, the history of the Soviets from 1917 to 1989), while relationally, the "timeless" West is established as a non-space, as a really existing ahistorical category.[27] In his famous text "East!", the Slovene theorist Rastko Močnik takes as his starting point these antinomic relations, claiming that the heterogeneous "Rest" becomes the East only if observed from the West, and this view assumes not so much a distinction as a hierarchy. The contextual paradigm imposes the following operation: when we speak about a certain artist, artwork, practice, or trend from the East, we cannot speak about them in the usual terms of art (such as *conceptualism*, *neo-avant-garde*, *media art* and the like); they must by modified by the qualifier *Eastern*, which in itself establishes a certain taxonomic hierarchy. But, as Močnik writes, "What is prefixed in this way will always remain specific, over-determined, locally defined and local as opposed to what is thus promoted to the status of the general, the canonic, the over-determining – although it is, in fact, only 'Western'."[28] He points out that Eastern means *still Eastern* – "It is specific, localised, because it

---

26   See Svetlana Boym, *The Future of Nostalgia*, Basic Books, New York, 2001, pp. 49–75.
27   Immanuel Wallerstein, "The Inventions of TimeSpace Realities: Towards an Understanding of Our Historical Systems", in *Unthinking Social Science: The Limits of Nineteenth-Century Paradigms*, Polity Press, Cambridge, 1995.
28   Rastko Močnik, "East!", *New Moment: East Art Map*, special issue, ed. Irwin, no. 20, 2002, p. 8.

is enmeshed within its own past, not emancipated from its history: while what parades as general, canonic, as the measure against which the peripheral, the provincial is to be measured – is what long ago was emancipated from its own history, from any history."[29] And, of course this is a strong invitation to amnesia and to the falsification of history (especially anything that makes us feel uncomfortable).

The rejection or "othering" of communism by the West, but also more globally through the discourses of *Eastern European Art*, almost denies the fact that the communist idea was originally the modernist invention of the West, which later moved to the East and anchored itself there. According to Močnik, these discourses, which are repeated time and again in different material practices, serve to portray communism as a phenomenon at odds with Western modernity and, in fact, closer to some remote Eastern European particularity.

Bojana: I would also like to return to the post-communist discourse as ideology. Paradoxically, while we spoke before about *Eastern European Art* being a consequence of the fall of the modernist paradigm, and while we talked about the great art-historical narratives when we were discussing the issue of the particular–universal relation, we haven't said much about how the post-communist discourse became one of these great narratives, which mediate in various epistemes of social theory, as well as those of art theory and practice. Although a feature of the postmodern discourse is the absence of historical narratives, of master-narratives, the Croatian theorist Boris Buden argues that the post-communist discourse in its hegemonic version

> operates, in fact, as a sort of historical master narrative: the well-known story about the collapse of communism in 1989 and the final victory of capitalism and liberal democracy. According to this narrative, after having overthrown totalitarian rule the societies of former Eastern Europe don't enter directly into the world of developed capitalism and Western democracy, but rather must undergo first the process of transition to this final condition, which poses as normality, that is as the universal norm of historical development in general.[30]

The process of transition is understood, accordingly, as a process of *normalization*, as a kind of discipline-based process. And quite often it is precisely the role of the signifier, of the qualifier *Eastern* ("still Eastern"), to point to the dynamics of accepting or delegating these disciplinary processes.

---

29 Ibid.
30 Boris Buden, "The post-Yugoslavian Condition of Institutional Critique: An Introduction: On Critique as Countercultural Translation", http://transform.eipcp.net/transversal/0208/buden/en (accessed June 19, 2016).

The construct *Eastern European Art* is therefore always already hybridized with the colonial discourses of "insufficient development", with the tendency of fulfilling Western norms, and with the concept of *belatedness*. The notion of the postcolonial in *Eastern European Art* is equalized with the processes of post-Soviet decolonization, but it rarely speaks about the new forms of colonization implied by this new transitory state, these disciplinary processes of transition. Similar to what you've been examining with Močnik's theories, here we face an identitary difference – the difference between "those who are embedding the historical standard and those who are behind and so should undergo the processes of transition and normalization (after coming out of the allegedly 'abnormal' real-socialist societies with a one-party system and suspended public)".[31] For example, the rhetoric of normality and normal life in the post-Yugoslav space resulted in a mantra-like repetition of key words and phrases – the blame for the post-Yugoslav wars should be borne not by actual nationalists, but by the *totalitarian communists* who held the country's constituent nations in a coercive state of togetherness, in *the prison of brotherhood and unity*; the post-Yugoslav wars are nothing but a fall into a state of *abnormality* and this is why transition is necessary after the wars, the transition towards *normality* as the new ideal of life.

Buden sees this post-communist transition as the process which makes it possible for the winners of the Cold War to control the inclusion and exclusion of the Eastern European losers. For that reason he suggests that we experience the "nature" of the post-communist discourse by analysing artefacts in the Museum of Communism in Prague. The artefact that narrates all that we "knew" and "believed in" even before visiting the museum is labelled symbolically: "a pair of left shoes: a bonus that each worker of the 'Warszawa' Steelworks was given in the mid 50s"[32] – a description that deeply evokes and mobilizes the visitor's post-communist relation towards the communist past.

In my view, as a framework of representation *Eastern European Art* actually operates as a "museum of communism" by other means: it museologizes communism as belonging to a bygone era and confirms the actual truth of capitalist democracy in the global arena of the contemporary.

Vjera: So, in fact the only emancipatory choice is to abolish *Eastern European Art* together with other identitary denominators of multiculturalism and capitalist democracy. …

I see we are approaching the end of the first session of the conference, so I would like to briefly draw your attention to two examples of refusal to participate in the ideological discourse and context of *Eastern European Art*, both of which are connected with a concrete analysis of concrete situations.

---

31 Boris Buden, "U cipelama komunizma: nekoliko napomena o mehanizmu postkomunističke normalizacije", *Up & Underground*, nos. 7–8, 2004.
32 Ibid.

The examples are connected with two Yugoslav avant-garde artists in different, but historically paradigmatic moments: the actions of Marko Ristić in the 1950s and the work of Goran Đorđević in the 1970s. In 1952, Ristić, the famous Belgrade surrealist who had served as Socialist Yugoslavia's official cultural attaché and ambassador in Paris in the late 1940s, refused to participate in the dubious operations of the CIA-established Congress for Cultural Freedom. He explained the reasons for his decision in a letter to the influential French intellectual Roger Caillois. In the letter, he problematized the framework of the Congress, which in his words juxtaposed *a priori* totalitarianism and the West, drawing an equation, also *a priori*, between the West and the notion of artistic freedom. Ristić wrote: "There is no doubt that Stalinism is a form of totalitarianism, and of the worst kind; and there can be no mention, whatever [Louis] Aragon thinks, of any significant artistic endeavor or creative freedom under the dictatorship of a bureaucratic caste. But also, as I see it, it would be wrong to juxtapose the West as some metaphysical essence (*entité*), as an incarnation of freedom, against that totalitarianism, which would in such simplistic antinomy inevitably encompass, together with Stalin's totalitarianism, everything that is not the West. The implications I leave to your own imagination."[33] He reminded Caillois that while it is true that individual artistic creation is free in the West, this does not mean equating the West with creative freedom as such (since the West also includes such phenomena as Francoist Spain and colonialism, as well as other forms of totalitarianism). Ristić continues by commenting on something that we too tried to tackle at the beginning of our discussion – the paradigm of totalitarianism. He argued: "Totalitarianism is not a single doctrine, but a single political reality, a single state politics over all. ... Marxism is not totalitarian, but totalitarianism is a caricature of Marxism. ... I cannot imagine the future of creative freedom nor any freedom of culture outside a social development towards what today it would be unreasonable not to call Socialism."[34] So, what I find interesting in Ristić's analysis is his rejection of the hegemonic and canonical meaning of the concept of artistic freedom and his de-linking the paradigm of totalitarianism from socialist politics and Marxism.

My second example comes from the late 1970s. It concerns the reaction of a group of young Yugoslav artists connected with the alternative Student Cultural Centre (SKC) in Belgrade towards an exhibition of *Eastern European Art* at the De Appel Foundation in Amsterdam in 1979.[35]

The Yugoslav artists intervened in the planned conceptual framework of exhibition even before it opened. Initially, the show was conceived as a canonical presentation of *Eastern European Art,* in the way that was usual when exhibiting art from behind the Iron Curtain, which was rarely

---

33   The letter to Caillois appears in Marko Ristić, *Politička književnost (za ovu Jugoslaviju) 1944-1958*, Oslobođenje, Sarajevo, 1977, pp. 146-147.
34   Ibid.
35   *Works and Words*, curated by Frank Gribling and Josine van Droselaar at the De Appel Foundation, Amsterdam, September 20-30, 1979.

viewed in the West. The aim was to group the more or less unconnected artworks under the uniform banner of *dissident art*, thus obscuring the reality of the individual artworks by what we have already discussed under the notion of *context*. The Yugoslav participants perceived such an exhibition concept as an act of "confining particular works by individual artists in a uniform ghetto".[36] They requested more equality with the Western art context, while at the same time they problematized the "exclusive" right of the Western art context to recognize individual artistic positions.

The artist Goran Đorđević replied to the invitation to participate in the De Appel exhibition by proposing to exhibit a statement of dissent that would summarize some of the arguments made by the invited Yugoslav artists. He explained to the exhibition organizers that this kind of international exhibition context, which mimics the geopolitical agenda of the Cold War, had in fact become the only context of presentation "on offer" to artists from Eastern Europe:

> [Artists from Eastern Europe] are practically forced to accept any offer, since these are rare occasions when their work has a recognized artistic status, and on the other hand, this exhibition [is intended to] explicitly or implicitly reaffirm the "unlimited" freedom of artistic activities and "universality" of [the] cultural/artistic practise of the West. In that way the significance of such [a] "ghetto" exhibition is mainly reduced to its political dimension (dissident exotic) and the nature of the works themselves, their character and significance, are pushed into background.[37]

However, after receiving Đorđević's letter, the exhibition's curators changed their initial plan; they decided to avoid framing the exhibition within the expected geopolitical agenda and added a previously separate group of artists from the Netherlands to the general selection of artists from socialist countries (Czechoslovakia, East Germany, Hungary, Poland, and Yugoslavia). They also ended up choosing the more "universal" exhibition title *Works and Words* and dropping the term *Eastern European*, which had been prominent in earlier proposed versions of the title.

The story behind the exhibition *Works and Words* is an interesting example of, and comment on, contemporary forms of representation of *Eastern European Art* in the (former) West. In a way, this story heralded the critique of the kind of discourse of *Eastern European Art* that was widely produced by exhibitions and theoretical and art-historical overviews emerging after 1989. As for the artists gathered around the SKC Gallery in the 1970s, this exhibition can be seen as an indicator of some of their positions towards the "outside", towards the context of international

---

36   From a conversation with Yugoslav participants in the exhibition *Works and Words*.
37   Goran Đorđević, letter to the exhibition organizers, available at http://tranzit.org/exhibitionarchive/?attachment_id=4620 (accessed July 3, 2016).

presentation and participation in the politics of exhibiting and framing the New Art in the European and global context.

   (**Lunch break**)

Edit András

What Does East-Central European Art History Want?

Reflections on the Art History Discourse in the Region since 1989

Art historian and critic Edit András re-examines the thought of the late Piotr Piotrowski, particularly his call for regionally specific art histories, in the light of recent political developments in Europe. Seeing as problematic, and perhaps even dangerous, attempts to assert a distinct regional perspective at a time when nationalism is all-pervasive, she points to recent shifts in the academic discourse toward arguments in favour of a reinvented universalism. She goes on to reflect on the present situation in Hungary, where the Viktor Orbán's ruling nationalist government has been shaping the cultural and academic landscape to its own ends, and examines some of pitfalls in the critical response to such encroachments.

If, as is frequently claimed, art history in general is today in crisis, then East-Central European art history[1] has its own, recurring, crisis, as it is unable to settle and secure its position vis-à-vis the rest of the world and so is constantly forced to reposition itself. Here I am not concerned with the post-1989 need to rewrite local art histories without ideological and political constraints; rather, I am interested in an art history discourse that can address the international community in a way that facilitates communication rather than reinforces separation. Nor am I concerned here with the involvement of Western scholars who contribute to the art history of the region – despite the tangible change in their attitude in the the post–Cold War period, where there has been a shift from the earlier "neo-colonialist" attitude that established academic careers on the "invasion" of the region without any knowledge of the local languages and contexts – but with considerable financial support – to the younger generation of scholars who conduct local research in the local languages and take a less partial approach than the natives, since they are less susceptible to local blind spots and taboos. Instead, I am interested in changes in the region's self-image and self-definition and its constant urge to redefine its position within the discourse of global art history; I conceive this urge as a reflection on the haunting dilemma of belonging. This study looks for the reasons and factors behind this compulsive need and seeks to detect the methods and goals of the repositioning. The effort to register the diverse and sometimes opposing positions of art history discourse in the region has been triggered by the recent shift in arguments in favour of greater cosmopolitanism and a reinvented universalism, which I believe is the counter-effect of the nationalisms and populisms that are currently on the rise, from which the discourse of art history certainly wishes to detach itself.

The Identity Crisis of Art History

For quite a while now, art history's traditional position has been heavily criticized, ignored, or challenged in the crossfire of such new critical disciplines as visual culture studies, cultural studies, gender studies, etc., for being reluctant to leave behind certain obsolete tenets inherited from the period in which it was born and enjoyed its heyday. The 19th-century origins of the discipline provided both the transnational connectedness of

---

[1] The terminology used for naming the region that was known during the Cold War as the Eastern or Soviet bloc has had a diverse trajectory since the collapse of the socialist satellite system. Lately the term "East-Central Europe" has been widely adopted by scholars, including Piotr Piotrowski, and since the arguments in this essay are largely based on his writings, I also use this term.

the art scenes of Europe, in the spirit of Enlightenment universalism, as well as the potential for writing national art histories by focusing on local configurations and mutations. Since art history's birth coincided with the emergence of nation states in Europe, the two notions intermingled and art history and its institutions became effective tools in nation building. In the blossoming of the 20th-century modernist paradigm, two competing but nevertheless parallel inner streams (the national and the transnational) were placed in a strictly vertical, hierarchical order. In this construction, the centres, where new ideas and concepts were born, gained a crucial, defining, and normative position, while the peripheries slid into an inferior position that labelled them as clumsy, impure, belated followers.

Maverick Cold War Modernism

The political division during the Cold War was replicated in the divided construction of the art discourse. The split between the Western and Eastern European paradigms of art and their different directions during the Cold War have been extensively discussed, as well as the reason why the art scenes of Eastern Europe, even if to differing degrees, insisted on the basic tenets of modernism well until the end of 1980s, without foregrounding the gradual deconstruction of the modernist paradigm, which started in the West in the 1960s. There is scholarly agreement that modernism represented an umbilical cord to the European culture "behind the wall" and provided as well a distinction from the official culture. As the official culture appropriated realism and socio-political issues, at least in its rhetoric, the underground and countercultural art scenes were resistant to micro-political sensitivity, and the rise of critical theories and identity politics was overlooked. In order to maintain a certain unity among those in opposition, any subculture or distinct identity (such as gender, Jewishness, ethnicity, etc.) represented the threat of dissolution and so was suppressed. With the consolidation of existing socialism, modernism fossilized behind the Iron Curtain even as, on the other side, the paradigm shift was coming into full swing.

These divergent trajectories of the two parts of Europe were supported by a kind of silent, unspoken agreement. The East's "laggard" condition, in contrast to the mainstream discourse of the West, which was regarded as relevant, satisfied the liberal intelligence of the trendsetting centres. The socialist East provided a projection field for imagining art as a powerful political weapon in society, one that was lost in capitalist conditions, where the importance of art rarely exceeded that of a mere commodity.[2]

2   See Edit András, "A Painful Farewell to Modernism: Difficulties in the Period of Transition" (1997), in *Gender Check: A Reader: Art and Theory in Eastern Europe*, ed. Bojana

After the political changes of 1989, the carefully maintained status quo was thrown off and the illusion of an art with a strong politically oppositional content dissolved; the East was accused of being stuck in an obsolete paradigm, namely modernism, while the West was accused of letting down its Eastern fellow travellers, who hoped to be treated equally and were puzzled by the turnaround. The exotic character of the socialist East in the eyes of the beholder simply disappeared overnight, while the East's maverick modernism lost its validity at a single blow. The changing social, political, and discursive conditions inevitably triggered an urgent need for repositioning the interpretative frame of art in the region, which was accompanied by the fervent desire of art historians and others to initiate dialogue with the trendsetting centres and to carve out a space for themselves.

The discursive attempt to abandon the notion of a homogeneous region and disengage from the concept of the Eastern bloc by constructing subregions (e.g. the Balkans, the Baltic States, Central Europe, etc.) was fuelled by the impulse to add colour to the zone behind the wall, which in the Cold War era had been perceived as grey. The geopolitical scope of the last regionally encompassing exhibition and conference, *After the Wall*,[3] in 1999, was criticized even at the time of its presentation. The identity-building process coincided with and was supported by a similar political process of disintegration and realignment – the dissolution of Yugoslavia and the Soviet Union and the formation of the Visegrád Group of countries. The post-socialist countries' efforts to underscore their specific characters and local features was further motivated by a competition to gain access to the now-available identity market.[4] In line with the intense media coverage of the bloody collapse of Yugoslavia, the Balkans received the lion's share of attention in the Western art world, as was evidenced by a string of exhibitions that hyped their Balkan content.[5]

The newly regained democracy in the region was accompanied by new self-awareness. Different cultural agents now felt entitled to claim emancipation in their own fields by criticizing and decentring the canon, that is, retrospectively deconstructing its hierarchical and unequal historical construction, as well as by detecting traces of hidden surviving elements of biased interpretations of contemporary art in both the centres and the

---

Pejić, Erste Foundation, and the Museum Moderner Kunst Stiftung Ludwig, Vienna, Verlag der Buchhandlung Walther König, Cologne, 2010, pp. 115–125.

3   See *After the Wall: Art and Culture in Post-Communist Europe*, ed. David Elliott and Bojana Pejić, Moderna Museet, Stockholm, 1999.

4   See Boris Groys, "Beyond Diversity: Cultural Studies and Its Post-Communist Other", *Art Power*, MIT Press, Cambridge, Mass., and London, 2008, pp. 149–164.

5   Notably, *In Search of Balkania* (curated by Roger Conover, Eda Čufer, and Peter Weibel), Neue Galerie, Graz, Austria, 2002; *In the Gorges of the Balkans: A Report* (curated by René Block), Kunsthalle Fridericianum, Kassel, Germany, 2003; *Balkan Consulate: Contemporary Art in Southeastern Europe* (curated by Margarethe Makovec, Anton Lederer, and Lejla Hodžić), ‹rotor›, Graz, Austria, 2003; and *Blood & Honey: The Future's in the Balkans* (curated by Harald Szeemann), Essl Museum, Klosterneuburg, Austria, 2003.

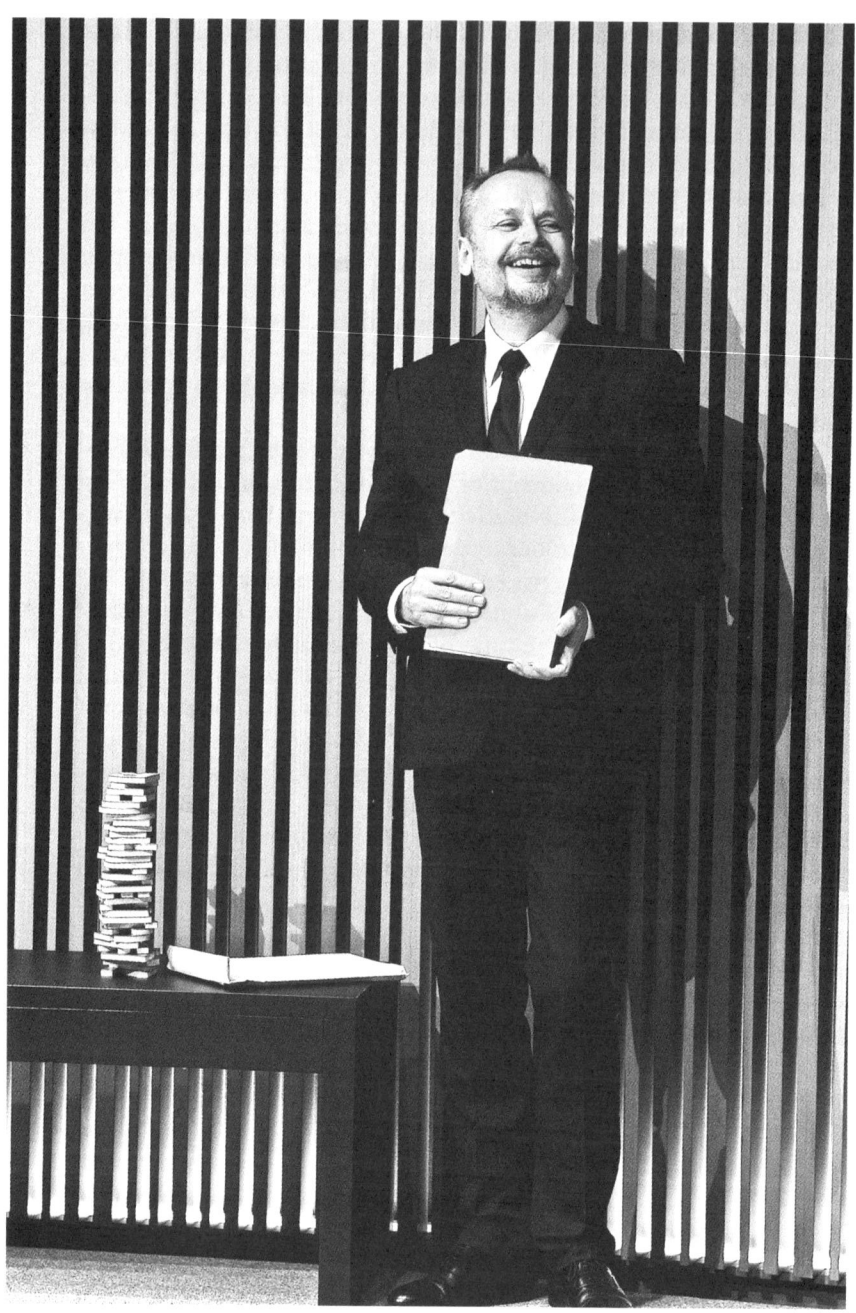

fig. 1

Piotr Piotrowski at the Igor Zabel Award for Culture and Theory ceremony, MACBA, Barcelona, 2010.

Photo by David Campos. Courtesy of ERSTE Foundation.

margins. The post-socialist countries' cultural vacuum, caused by modernism's lost relevance on the global art scene, could successfully be filled with means of a postcolonial discourse, which provided conceptual tools for deconstructing the position imposed on the peripheries, in which Eastern Europe could easily imagine itself. The now-awakened "subaltern" of "the universal art history" could make great use of the term and notion of the "Other", as borrowed from postcolonial discourse, and adapt this theoretical concept to its "semi-other" condition, which was similar to, if not quite the same as (but nor was it the direct opposite), the situation in countries that had been subject to actual colonization. Numerous scholars contributed to the discourse, nuancing the in-between position of the region.[6] The postcolonial discourse was so influential in Eastern Europe – despite a lack of colonial experience in the literal sense – that it was applied even to Russia's position within the Soviet Union, provoking a heated debate over whether the applicability of the theory and concept could be extended in this way.[7] To explain the peripheries' "gladly accepted" position of submission, a very popular but immensely problematic local enterprise developed, namely, the elaboration of the concept of "self-colonization".[8]

6 See, for example, Igor Zabel, "Intimacy and Society: Post-communist or Eastern Art?", *Contemporary Art Theory*, ed. Igor Španjol, JRP–Ringier and Les presses du réel, Zurich and Dijon, 2012, pp. 80-109; Bojana Pejić, "The Dialectics of Normality", in *After the Wall*, pp. 16-28 (see n. 3); Piotr Piotrowski, "The Grey Zone of Europe", in *After the Wall*, pp. 35-41; Marina Gržinić, *Fiction Reconstructed: Eastern Europe, Post-Socialism and the Retro-Avantgarde*, edition selene and Springerin, Vienna, 2000.
7 See Ekaterina Degot, "How to Qualify for Postcolonial Discourse?", *ArtMargins Online*, November 2, 2001, http://www.artmargins.com/index.php/2-articles/325-how-to-qualify-for-postcolonial-discourse; Ekaterina Degot, "How to Obtain the Right to Post-Colonial Discourse?", *Moscow Art Magazine*, http://xz.gif.ru/numbers/moscow-art-magazine/how-to-obtain-the-right/view_print/; Margaret Dikovitskaya, "A Response to Ekaterina Degot's Article: Does Russia Qualify for Postcolonial Discourse?", *ArtMargins Online*, January 31, 2002, http://www.artmargins.com/index.php/2-articles/324-a-response-to-ekaterina-dyogots-article-does-russia-qualify-for-postcolonial-discourse (all accessed April 21, 2016).
8 See, for example, Alexander Kiossev, "Notes on Self-colonising Cultures", in *After the Wall*, pp. 114-118; and Edit András, "Blind Spot of the New Critical Theory: Notes on the Theory of Self-colonization", in *The Art and Media of Accession: Trans-European Picnic*, ed. kuda.org, Nat Muller, and Stephen Kovats, Futura publikacije, Novi Sad, Serbia, 2004, pp. 38-47.

Regional Pride, the Post-Cold War Empowerment of the Margins

Confrontation with post-Cold War conditions, and their rearranged but still unequal power relations, generated diverse feelings among scholars in the post-socialist countries. These included not only disappointment, anger, and criticism over unequal treatment,[9] but also the fear of losing the attention associated with the privileged position of the "Cold War Other".[10] Piotr Piotrowski's theory of horizontal art history changed the orientation of the positioning, literally inverting the loci of the region's art history and challenging the centric position of the canon (fig. 1). He offered a positive solution for how overcoming the limitations of the binary opposition. He juxtaposed the diverse art histories of the centres and the margins and put them on the same level, removing any hierarchical or subordinate relations between them. According to this theory, the necessary act of levelling should be twofold; the manoeuvre of "localizing" the centre should go hand-in-hand with an analogue process on the other side, namely: "The Other must also take a fresh look at itself, define its position and the place from which it speaks."[11] Anger and frustration are channelled into empowerment, for "one can see much more from the margins" than from the centre – a notion that lies at the core of Piotrowski's thought.[12] The position on the margins is much more privileged, Piotrowski postulates, as the centre "quite often unconsciously, due to the ideology of [the] universalization of modern art, ignores the significance of place. ... If art is universal, the place from which it speaks does not matter."[13] He believed that even the centre can benefit from the marginal perspective as "the history of the art of the centre, and the global history of modern art that developed out of it, has a chance to revise its self-perception in light of the studies focused on the periphery, horizontal art history or art histories".[14] However, he was well aware that the newly proposed position was not at all self-evident and required intellectual

---

9   See Edit András, "Dog Eat Dog: Who is in Charge of Controlling Art in Post-socialist Condition?", *Third Text: Socialist Eastern Europe*, special issue, ed. Reuben Fowkes, vol. 23, no. 96, January 2009, pp. 65–78; and Igor Zabel, "Dialogue", in *Primary Documents: A Sourcebook for Eastern and Central European Art since the 1950s*, ed. Laura Hoptman and Tomáš Pospyszil, Museum of Modern Art, New York, 2002, pp. 355–356.
10   Groys, "Beyond Diversity", pp. 149–164.
11   Piotr Piotrowski, "On the Spatial Turn, or Horizontal Art History", *Umění / Art*, no. 5, 2008, p. 380.
12   Ibid.
13   Ibid., p. 381.
14   Ibid.

and psychological efforts from both sides. Piotrowski promoted the perspective provided by critical theory in order to gain access to the global discourse, but in the same measure, he vigorously advocated the need for self-empowerment, namely, that those on the margins should value their own marginal position, its peculiarity, its diverse historical experiences, and its constant alertness. He relentlessly opposed identification with the submissive position and the consequent inferiority complex.

Piotrowski initiated the seminar series "Unfolding Narratives: Art Histories in East-Central Europe after 1989" in order to discuss the urgent questions of art history writing in the region.[15] The seminars, which were held in different parts of the region in 2010 and 2011, had a favourable impact on the local self-image and may have positively influenced the attitude of certain leading institutions as well. For example, a new initiative at the Museum of Modern Art in New York, "Global Research at MoMA: Contemporary and Modern Art Perspectives" (C-MAP),[16] was now able to rely on this professional self-awareness. Sanja Iveković's solo exhibition *Sweet Violence*, held at MoMA in 2011–2012, also demonstrated a changed attitude towards the peripheries, one that was less elitist and controlling and more inclusive and attentive.[17] However, old habits die hard. The exhibition *Ostalgia*, at the New Museum in New York in 2011, can be viewed as a backlash. It showed how difficult it is to give up the privileged dominant position and accept a shared terrain based on equal and mutual recognition.[18] Another MoMA show, *Transmissions: Art in Eastern Europe and Latin America, 1960–1980*, in 2015, revealed the inner dynamic of the changing discourse in its careful attempt to avoid the pitfalls of the *Ostalgia* exhibition; instead, it went to the other extreme. While *Transmissions* did not exoticize the displayed works, as the New Museum had done, it sterilized them by completely eliminating the different political contexts and by avoiding anything that recalled the dissimilar historical and sociopolitical conditions in which the artworks originated. It clearly manifested the kind of museological operation that puts artefacts through a "purification" process in which they, and the ideas associated with them, are

---

15 The series of three travelling seminars was organized by the Research and Academic Programme of the Clark Art Institute, in collaboration with regional partners. See more at http://www.clarkart.edu/rap/about (accessed April 21, 2016).
16 C-MAP is a research and exchange initiative at MoMA that looks at art in a global context. It is divided into three groups, each focusing on a geographic region with a strong history of modernism. The current focus areas are Asia, Central and Eastern Europe, and Latin America. For more information see http://www.moma.org/learn/intnlprograms/globalresearch (accessed April 21, 2016).
17 See Edit András, "The Ex-Eastern Bloc's Position in the New Critical Theories and in the Recent Curatorial Practice", *IDEA*, no. 40, 2011, pp. 79–96.
18 See Edit András, "Whose Nostalgia is Ostalgia? An Eastern Europe and Former Soviet Republics Survey Exhibition in the New Museum, New York", in *Curating 'Eastern Europe' and Beyond: Art Histories through the Exhibition*, ed. Mária Orišková, Veda, SAS Publishing House, Slovak Academy of Sciences, Bratislava, and Peter Lang International Academic Publishers, Frankfurt am Main, 2013, pp. 165–171.

cleansed of political and ideological "dirt", regardless of changes in the art-historical paradigm. Artworks from the socialist countries of the Cold War era became polished artefacts, art treasures of the museum, in the very same way that works from the revolutionary Russian avant-garde, with its radical social ideas, are domesticated in neutral displays for mass entertainment in various leading museums.

Piotrowski was conscious of the paradox that equality might come at the price of losing local, and especially national, specificities, peculiarities, and subtle distinctions. While the concept of horizontal art history has mostly been praised, his dilemma with regard to national art history is largely overlooked and unrecognized. As he argues, the key problem of horizontal art history is the problem of localization: "We have the 'history of modern art' with no local specification, while on the other hand [outside the centre] we have all kinds [of] adjectives specifying the regional."[19] Reflecting on the "global turn" in the humanities, he observed in 2008 that the type of locality related to the structure of nation states and the modernist form of nationalism "is now changing on account of the process of globalization," specifically with "the transformation of nation-states into more cosmopolitan organizations".[20] However, despite the enthusiasm of the time, he was still hesitant to accept that locality had disappeared as an identity marker:

> The "nation" seen from a postmodern perspective is deprived of its essential features. Post-colonial scholarly practice, however, relies on the essence of the nation to define its critical strategy and resistance to the centre. On the one hand, in international horizontal art history, operating with the "notion" of the "nation", there must be a defence [of] the (national) subject. It is thus closer to the post-colonial interpretation than to the postmodern.[21]

Piotrowski tried to syncretize the two streams in his vision, stating that "horizontal art history written from a micro perspective, by contrast, has to make a critique of the essence of the national subject, has to deconstruct it, in order to defend the culture of the 'Other' against the national mainstream". He came up with the solution of transnational, regional art history narratives, which negotiate values and concepts along lines other than the opposition between national and international.

---

19   Piotrowski, "On the Spatial Turn, or Horizontal Art History", p. 381.
20   Ibid.
21   Ibid., p. 382.

National Art History Fights Back

This ideal solution, however, seemed to fade or become immersed in wishful thinking as the ghost of nationalism and isolationist and parochial national art histories came to the forefront in the everyday reality of post-socialist countries. One of topics addressed in the "Unfolding Narratives" seminars was the notion of time, in which connection the issue of nascent nationalism popped up in 2011, at the seminar in Bucharest.[22] What excited me then were the inbuilt flaws that – despite the premise of multiple and non-hierarchical temporalities advocated by the critical theories of contemporaneity – still haunted those who had had a "secondary time" in the long period of modernity, with its hierarchical arrangement of places and imposed time-measuring system. I was interested in the leftovers of the concept of the universal flow of time, in which those in the centre, in canon-setting positions, hold possession of the time of the present. In the paradigm of modernism, the time of the "East European Other" was considered the past, the prehistory and memory of the "relevant present", which was associated with Western Europe. However, despite the change in paradigm, substantial discrepancies could be detected between the conceptions of the synchronicity of the present time in the advanced theory of contemporaneity, and between the hidden implications of hierarchies with regard to the different pasts. In other words, while we gladly acknowledge that the dominance of the privileged present of the centres has evaporated in our postcolonial time, when it comes to remembering or dealing with the past, the discourse falls short and the past needs to be adjusted by the "old-time others". When and what is remembered still needs to be synchronized to the disguised yet powerful "prime time".

While the remembrance of socialism was flawlessly channelled into a Western way of understanding, the unresolved and still disturbing legacies of nation building in the eastern part of Europe,[23] along with imagined or real wounds and unfulfilled desires, were regarded as untimely issues for the trendsetting Western discourse. Charles King, an American political scientist, accused the region of being obsessed with "cliophilia" – *the obsessive concern with finding explanations for contemporary political troubles in the distant troubled past*, which "has sometimes been a brake to comprehending real world politics".[24] His claim, indeed, echoes the deep-

---

22   The Bucharest seminar, the third in the series, took place May 20–21, 2011. For more about the programme, see http://www.clarkart.edu/rap/RAP-Events/Event-58 (accessed April 21, 2016).
23   See Edit András, "An Agent Still at Work: The Trauma of Collective Memory of the Socialist Past", *Springerin*, no. 3, 2008, http://www.springerin.at/dyn/heft.php?id=56&pos=1&textid=2103&lang=en (accessed April 21, 2016).
24   Charles King, *Extreme Politics: Nationalism, Violence, and the End of Eastern Europe*, Oxford University Press, Oxford and New York, 2010, p. 181.

seated desire of Western academia to describe its Eastern counterpart as being absorbed in its own past and in its own history.

The climate of re-awakening nationalisms and their memories reveals a further twist, specifically, with regard to the genealogy of nation states, where we find even East–East differences, with the notion of time diverging between the different states. For example, Hungarians tend to view the Trianon Peace Treaty[25] as a punitive dismemberment and the end of an era, while non-Hungarians see it as part of the process of decolonization and the birth of their new nation states, and as such, the beginning of a new era. During the Cold War, Trianon was a taboo issue for socialist countries, but this boomerang came back with a vengeance when the satellite countries of the Soviet Union regained their sovereignty. Right-wing political forces on both sides of the Hungarian border have played the national card, and there is a heated rivalry over whose conception of time should be accepted by the international community. Thus, despite the tolerance for the synchronicity of different time settings that is promoted by recent critical theories, when the issue is remembering the recent past of socialism, and even more, the origins of nation building by the East-European Other, the position of control is activated by the "prime-timers", who impose their own time frame for memory. However, on the margins, notions of time differ greatly from those that have dominated scholarly debates and trends, both before and after the Cold War era, and that tend to push aside certain issues, considering them irrelevant and untimely.

At the "Unfolding Narratives" seminar in Bucharest, in a country that had directly benefited from Trianon, mention of the 1920 treaty caused a certain discomfort, to judge by the anxious reactions of the audience. On the one hand, the topic triggered unconscious and inherent national feelings and created tensions, leading to complaints about hurting people's feelings. On the other hand, it appeared obvious that the time was not yet ripe for elaborating these sensitive issues, even within the scholarly community. Applying a psychological metaphor, we can say that the suppressed unconscious of art history, namely, the national art histories, was interfering with the idea of a horizontal art history. At the time, for the Western participants at the seminar, the question of nation building and nationalism seemed distant and obsolete, an outdated and inconvenient topic, given that the violent formation of the West European nation states is generally regarded as a settled issue, one that was long ago normalized and integrated into history; for people from the East, however, the issue was still an embarrassing topic that hit close to home.

Five years ago, of course, none of us could have been aware of how far we would go from the "innocent" symbolic politics of Hungary, which was addressed in Bucharest, to today's scenery, or, as Boris Buden has formulated

---

25   The Trianon Peace Treaty, signed on June 4, 1920, was imposed by the victors of World War I; it deprived Hungary of two-thirds of its territory and placed millions of ethnic Hungarians under the rule of neighbouring countries, including Austria and the newly founded nation states of Czechoslovakia, Romania, and Yugoslavia.

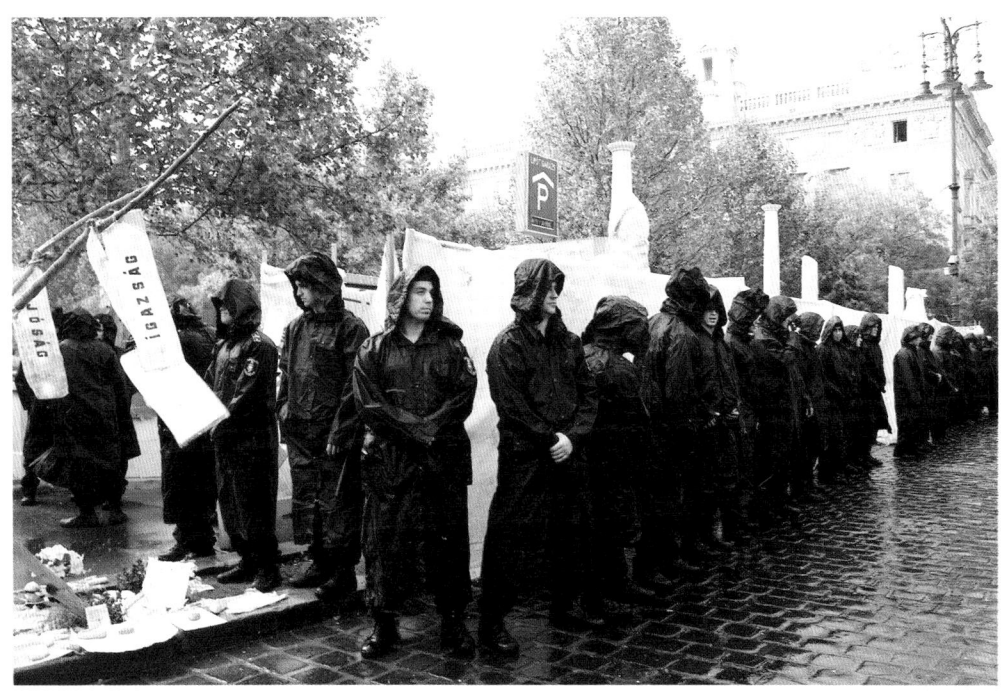

fig. 2

Police protecting the *Nazi Occupation Monument*
on Freedom Square, Budapest, March 2014.

Photo by Gabriella Csoszó / FreeDoc.

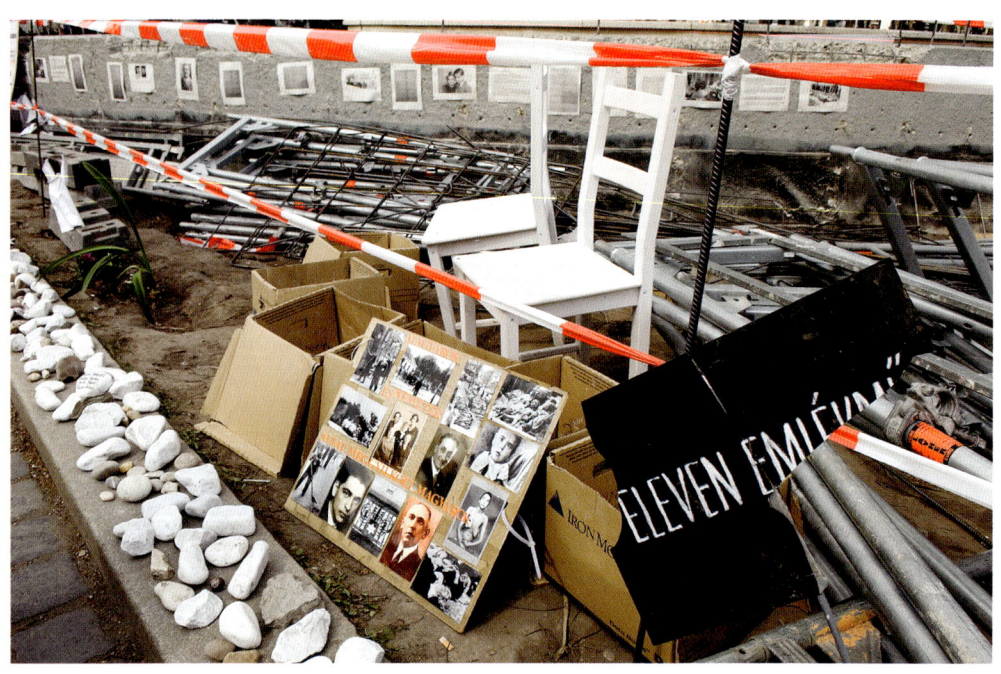

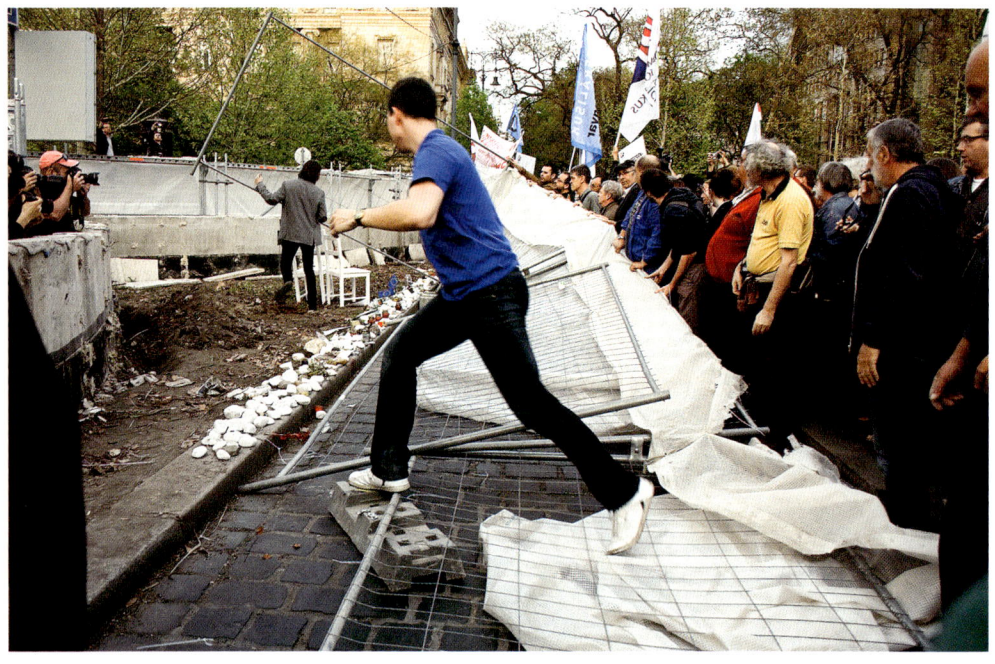

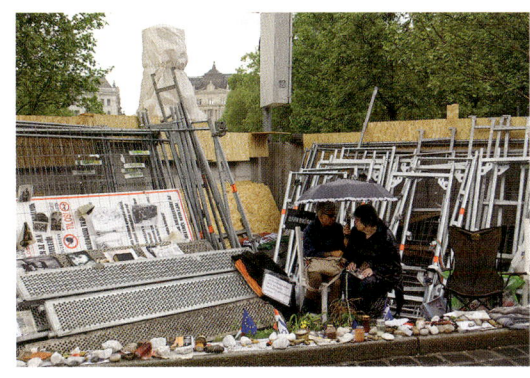

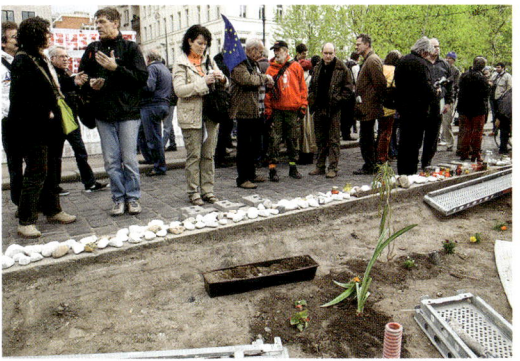

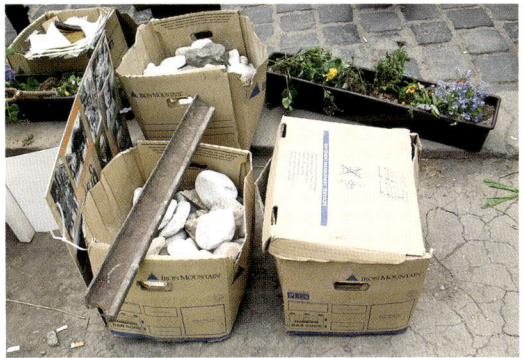

fig. 3

Photographs showing *Living Memorial* (across the street from the *Nazi Occupation Monument*), Budapest, ongoing project initiated by Free Artists, March 23, 2014–present.

Photos by Gabriella Csoszó / FreeDoc.

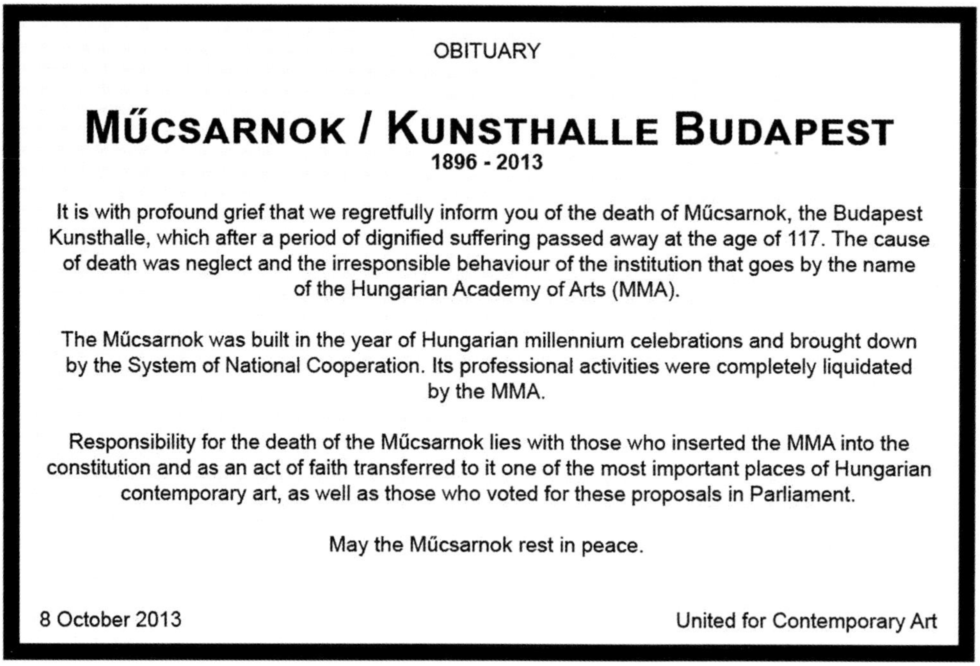

OBITUARY

MŰCSARNOK / KUNSTHALLE BUDAPEST
1896 - 2013

It is with profound grief that we regretfully inform you of the death of Műcsarnok, the Budapest Kunsthalle, which after a period of dignified suffering passed away at the age of 117. The cause of death was neglect and the irresponsible behaviour of the institution that goes by the name of the Hungarian Academy of Arts (MMA).

The Műcsarnok was built in the year of Hungarian millennium celebrations and brought down by the System of National Cooperation. Its professional activities were completely liquidated by the MMA.

Responsibility for the death of the Műcsarnok lies with those who inserted the MMA into the constitution and as an act of faith transferred to it one of the most important places of Hungarian contemporary art, as well as those who voted for these proposals in Parliament.

May the Műcsarnok rest in peace.

8 October 2013 United for Contemporary Art

fig. 4

Obituary – Műcsarnok / Kunsthalle, 1896-2013,
Budapest, October 8, 2013.

Photo by Gabriella Csoszó / FreeDoc.

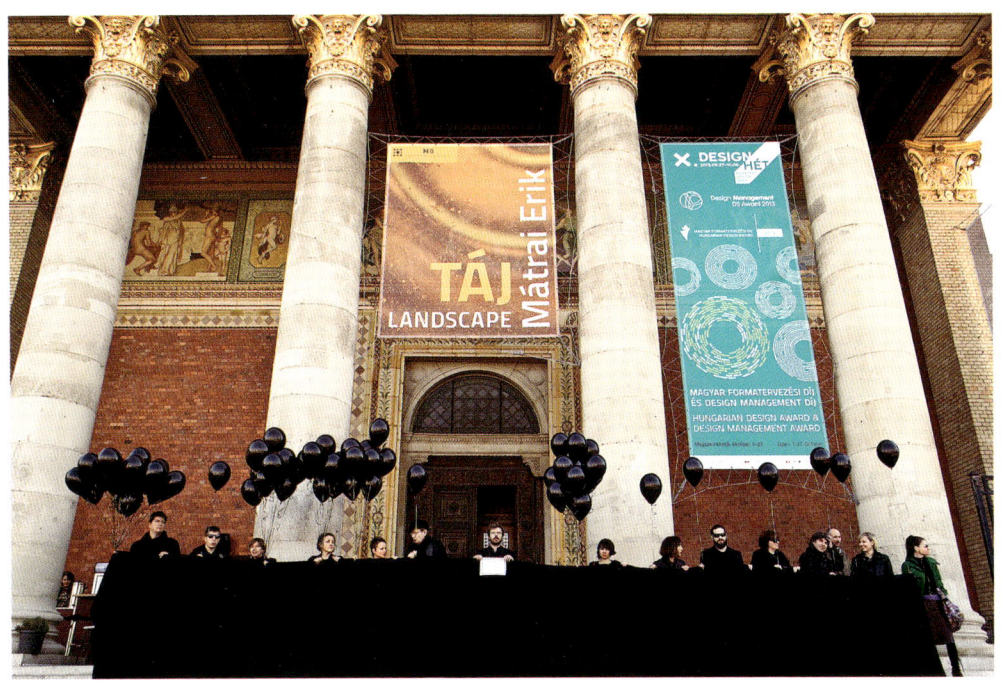

fig. 5

Mourning ceremony in front of Műcsarnok / Kunsthalle, Budapest, October 8, 2013.

Photo by Gabriella Csoszó / FreeDoc.

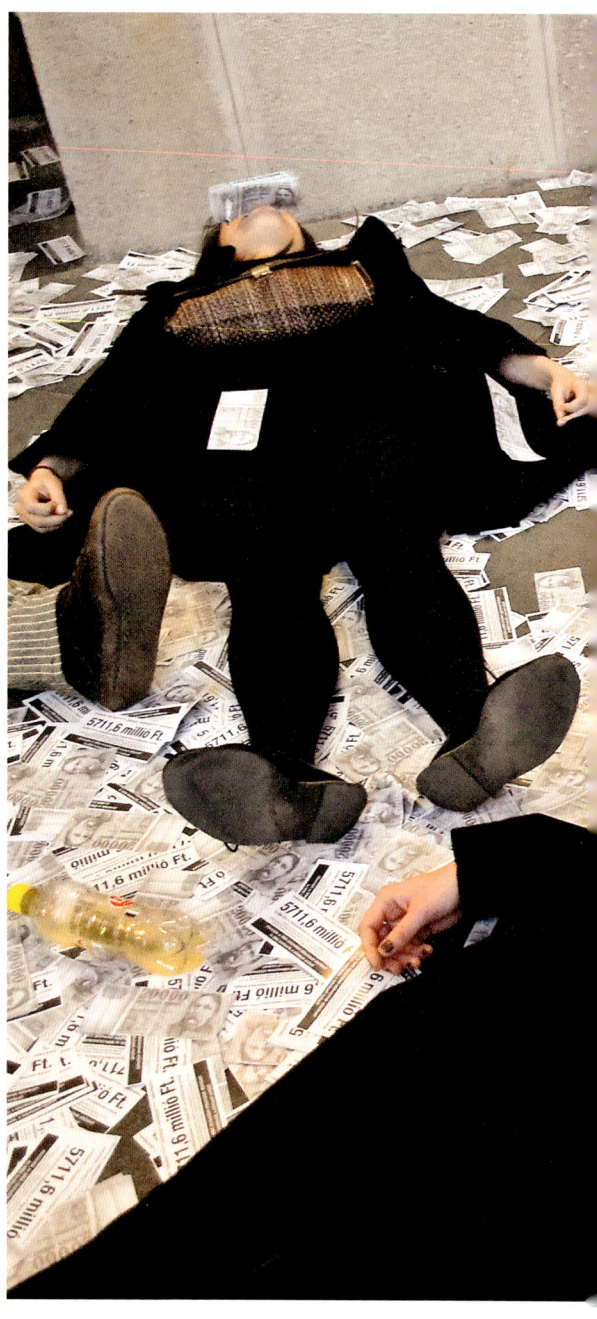

fig. 6

"Raining money" action at the Vigadó Concert Hall, Budapest. The demonstration was co-organized by the Tranzit Action Group and Free Artists, March 14, 2014.

Photo by Gabriella Csoszó / FreeDoc.

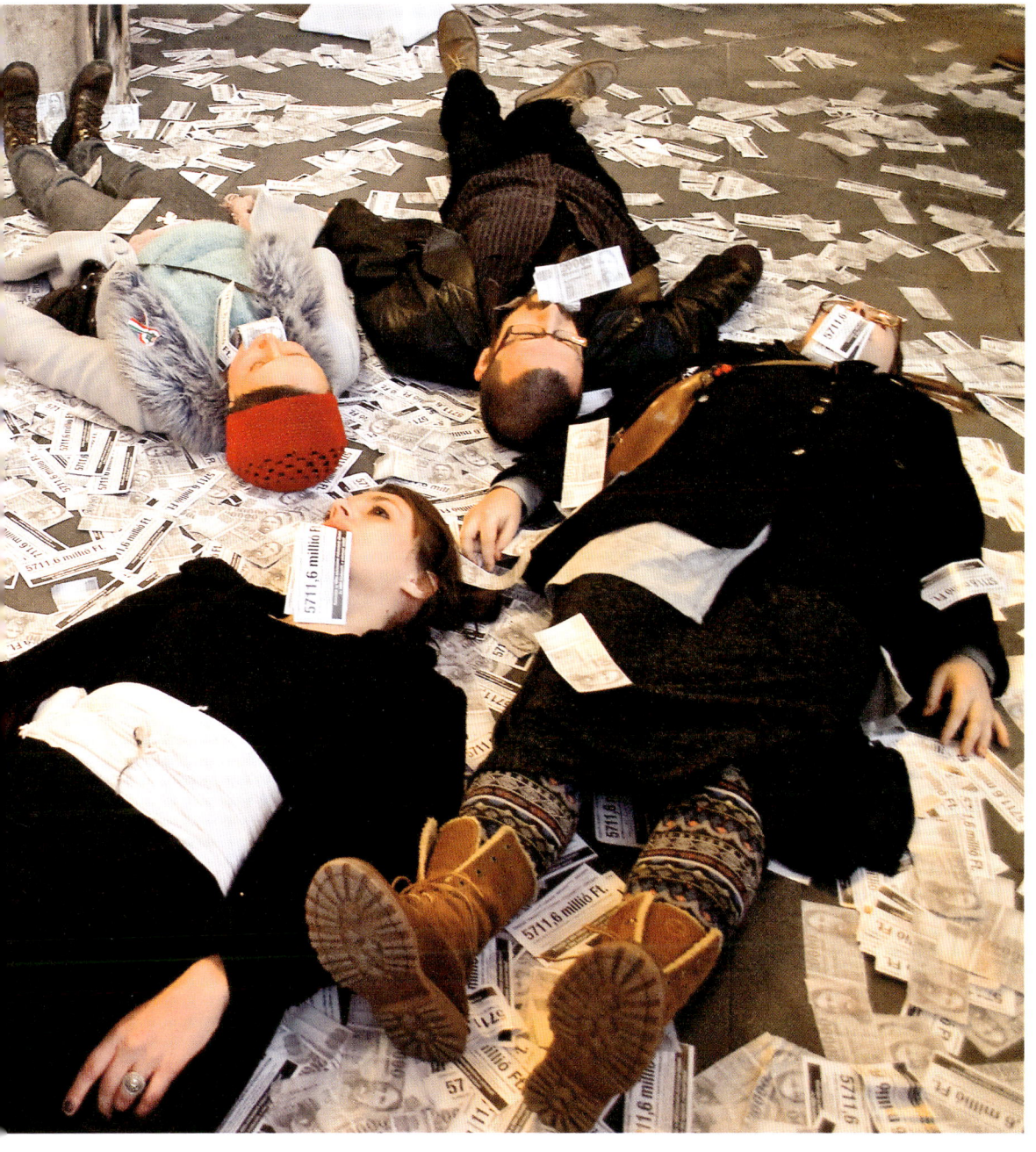

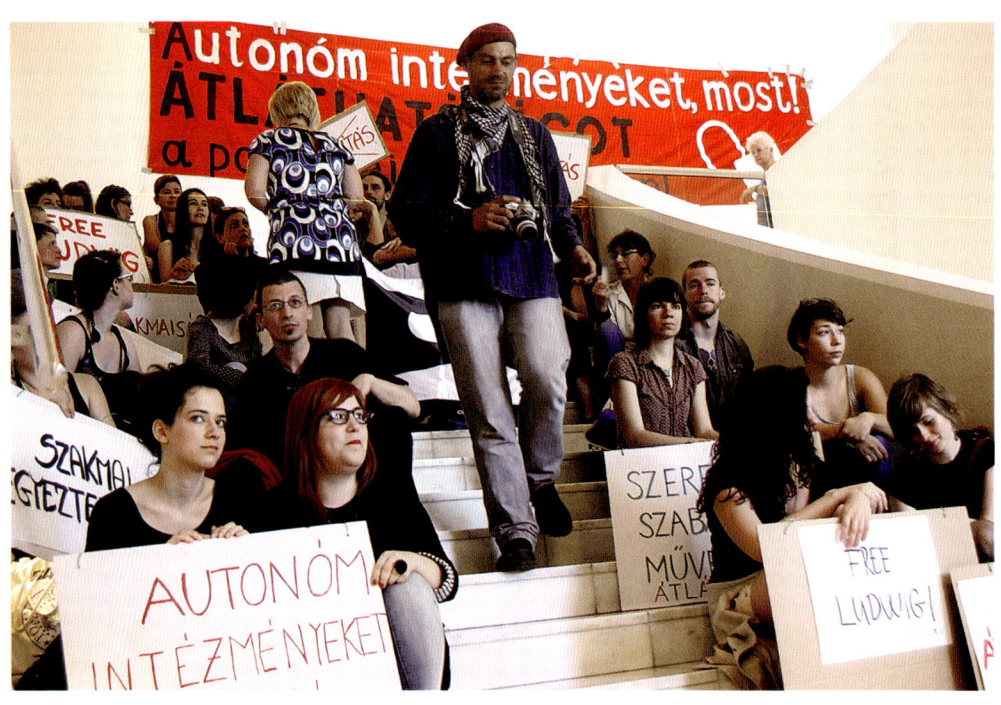

fig. 7

"Occupy Ludwig" action, Budapest, May 2013. Organized by United for Contemporary Art and Free Artists.

Photo by Gabriella Csoszó / FreeDoc.

it from today's perspective, that the Hungarian case would be "so exemplary for the production of national pasts generally".[26] In Buden's view, Hungarian nationalism is, in political terms, simply a single, albeit striking, example of how nations construct their past. From this perspective, what generates interest nowadays is "not dealing with a traumatic past but rather, Hungary's traumatic dealing with the past".[27]

The Hungarian Patient

Almost two decades after the fall of Communism, the main concern and obsession of Hungary's re-elected right-wing government is to recreate a strong national state while claiming that the process of political change was not completed by the previous liberal-leftist-socialist regimes. The process of renationalization and centralization, which comes with the territory, is ambitious and all-encompassing, ranging from history writing to memory politics, from public monuments and cultural heritage management to state subsidies of culture, from cultural institutions and media policy to education, along with the complete change of elites. No institution has been able to elude state control. Disciplines and ideas outside the state-supported culture are condemned to starvation, lacking the necessary institutional and financial support and without access to most media outlets, which are owned or controlled by the regime. So state control and centralization, as well as the drive for renationalization, goes deep in today's Hungary.

The rightist rhetoric is that Hungarian sovereignty was lost during two consecutive occupations, first by the Nazis then by the Soviets. A recently erected monument dedicated to "all victims of Nazi occupation"[28] has stirred a heated public debate, with opponents to the monument accusing the regime of falsifying history by rejecting any Hungarian responsibility in the Holocaust (figs. 2–3). A second site heavily loaded with symbolic politics is Kossuth Square, in front of the Parliament, which offers visitors a way to travel back in time to the mid-20th century, as its 1944 display has been meticulously reconstructed with newly commissioned, reconstructed replicas of the statues that once decorated the square during the interwar, irredentist period.

At this point we should note that the post-socialist condition does not mean that socialist conditions have disappeared or that we have got past them. Rather, the term signifies an inherent, easy transformability, a

---

26   From my correspondence with Boris Buden in 2015.
27   Ibid.
28   See Edit András, "Vigorous Flagging in the Heart of Europe: The Hungarian Homeland under the Right-Wing Regime", *e-flux journal*, no. 57, 2014, http://www.e-flux.com/journal/vigorous-flagging-in-the-heart-of-europe-the-hungarian-homeland-under-the-right-wing-regime/ (accessed April 21, 2016).

smooth shift from one type of authoritarianism (socialist) to another (nationalist and populist) with an equally normative understanding of art and culture. As the interpretation of the past always serves the political interest of the present, the regime of Prime Minister Viktor Orbán has devoted itself to bringing the present in line with an imagined past. Accordingly, art and culture, along with their institutions, have been in every aspect transformed so as to favour the regime and its cultural policy.

The regime's goal has been to support "national culture within the culture of the nation",[29] an idea that Piotrowski vehemently opposed in his definition of national art history. In order to achieve the dominance of a national culture, the bastions of the profession have gradually been occupied by loyal commissars of the official culture. The Hungarian Art Academy (MMA), a kind of shadow ministry that evolved from a private organization into a public body enshrined in the constitution, assumed leadership of the officially supported culture and eventually came to dominate the entire art scene while enjoying enormous state support. Today it has control over state subsidies, in that its delegates, together with the representatives of the cultural ministry (now called the Ministry of Human Resources), make up two thirds of the membership of the National Cultural Foundation.[30] After taking over the Műcsarnok, Budapest's main contemporary art venue, and installing its loyal supporters in leadership positions in other institutions as well – despite large demonstrations in protest[31] (figs. 4–7) – the MMA claimed a professional legitimacy that went beyond even its own inner circles. It then changed its strategy, and instead of an open attack, started to further divide what remained of the sporadic resistance, specifically, by courting those who faced serious financial problems and were willing to collaborate with it.

The consolidation of the reinvented nation state and the institutional dominance of a conservative cultural politics influences the operation of all segments of the art scene, from curatorial practice to art criticism. OFF-Biennale Budapest,[32] which took place in 2015, managed to operate outside the state-sponsored, state-dictated culture by relying on private and foreign support, but in a climate of total state control it was difficult even for this independent initiative to maintain any radical positions. OFF-Biennale was declaratively not against the official culture but rather offered an alternative parallel structure. Its core programme was not about questioning the non-democratic conditions of the art scene under

29 Ibid.
30 More about MMA can be found at https://nemma.noblogs.org/2012/12/07/a-short-history-of-mma/ (accessed April 12, 2016).
31 The NEMMA blog (its Hungarian name means "No to the Hungarian Art Academy") contains important information about these protests. The blog was established and is maintained by the artist Szabolcs KissPál, one of the founders of Free Artists, a group of radical opponents to the cultural politics of the ruling regime. See https://nemma.noblogs.org/category/english/ (accessed April 21, 2016).
32 See the OFF-Biennale's website, http://offbiennale.hu/what-is-off/ (accessed April 21, 2016).

nationalism, but rather sought to establish an alternative terrain in which contemporary art could survive. As Dóra Hegyi succinctly put it, OFF-Biennale did not try to directly reflect on the current political situation since the concept of democracy appeared to be a secondary principle for the organizers. They did not begin with the idea that a cultural scene based on a critical conception was a precondition for democracy.[33] Indeed, they found themselves in the same dilemma as the theoreticians: either to explain to the international art world why they were neglecting the local situation or to address local concerns and apply a local perspective. Because they were trying to achieve both national and international professional recognition by involving well-known "star" artists and curators, both foreign and Hungarian, the initiative bore a certain unavoidable duality and was caught between the globalized art world and the localized, nationalized reality.[34] These two sides proved irreconcilable.

Artists, critics, and art historians are all facing their own dilemmas in this period of the consolidation and normalization of Hungarian nationalism, or, as others have put it, the total establishment of a mafia state.[35] The moral and professional dilemma is whether it is justified to criticize the flaws and minor mistakes of alternative efforts in a context where artists with democratic or critical ideas are being systematically excluded from the art scene and communities are being dismantled. As a theatre critic bluntly put it last year during a radio broadcast about art criticism in Hungary: at a time of dictatorship, a negative review reads like denunciation and persecution. As an art critic on the radio show accurately summarized: it is very difficult to handle criticism if the social model is that criticism is non-existent in the society and not part of daily life. The attitude that politicians and public figures cannot be questioned or criticized permeates all layers of society. But as Boris Buden observed, the example of Hungary, while striking, is not untypical of the region, and other countries, such as Poland and Croatia, may soon follow it.[36]

---

33   Dóra Hegyi, quoted in Gábor Andrási, "A Survey after the First OFF-Biennale from Budapest: Alternative, Hope and Chances for Survival", *IDEA*, no. 47, 2015, p. 51.

34   The organizers faced a number of dilemmas: 1. Should the biennial define itself as part of the global "entertainment industry" of art biennials? 2. Should it try to draw attention to Hungarian contemporary artists? 3. Should it try to bring these artists into the "grand competition" and include them in the international art market? 4. Or, conversely, should it try to bring famous foreign artists and curators to Hungary? 5. Should it present artistic practices and discourses that reflect on the current situation in Hungary?

35   See Bálint Magyar, *Post-Communist Mafia State: The Case of Hungary*, Central European University Press and Noran Libro, Budapest.

36   In private correspondence with me in 2015.

What Is to Be Done with Regional Art History?

Although it may seem more virulent in the post-socialist countries, methods of governance in which nationalism is closely entwined with populism can no longer be consigned exclusively to territories that lie on the other side of the former Iron Curtain or in its still-existing shadow. Similarly, the academic discourse of nationalism can no longer be regarded as something that does not concern the West or that is merely a historical issue, a past that is now over. Borders are being crossed, and closed, throughout the continent. The genie of xenophobia, hatred, and racism has been let out of the bottle and looms even over affluent countries where the foundations of wealth and well-being appear to be at stake. The Enlightenment values of universal humanism, world citizenship, and emancipation, which for a long time Europe seemed to take for granted, are now being shaken and seem to fade in the midst of people in motion.

The changing political landscape of Europe has slowly altered the rhetoric, urgencies, alliances, and agencies of academic discourse as well. The attempt to apply a regional perspective at a time of pervasive nationalism – that is, Piotrowski's project of subverting the hierarchical position of different art histories by positioning them in a horizontal relation, instead of integration and subordination – seems to be blown away and has lost its relevance, or rather, lost its reality, as universal values must nowadays be defended and argued for. In my view, the underlying concept of the conference entitled "East European Art Seen from Global Perspectives: Past and Present", which Piotrowski initiated in 2014,[37] was the clearly perceived need to shift positions in today's changed world: from defining a specific space for the region to placing it in a global perspective.

Even in the time since the conference, the landscape of Europe has drastically changed, with the massive influx of refugees, asylum seekers, and migrants and many newly fortified borders and fences, with extreme right-wing parties winning seats in the elected parliaments of Poland and Slovakia, and with frequent terrorist attacks, which are being used to justify moves toward centralization, authoritarianism, and the expanding control of state power all over Europe. Along with the political and social changes, the rhetoric of distinct features in the region's art has also changed its meaning for the wider community. One can no longer argue for the specificities of art and culture of the East-Central European region as a consequence of the different trajectory of its history, since this argument, even if only on its surface, resembles and partly overlaps with the rhetoric of the nationalist discourses and so could be mistakenly identi-

---

37 Held at Galeria Labirynt in Lublin, Poland, October 24–27, 2014; see http://labirynt.com/en/east-european-art-seen-from-global-perspective-past-and-present/ (accessed April 21, 2016).

fied with them. The momentum for arguing for a regionalism with its specificities is simply gone. This approach is being squeezed out of scholarly debate, losing priority, in the recent turmoil of history, which pushes this commitment aside and renders it, yet again, ill-timed and irrelevant. East-Central European art history again finds itself at a crossroads with regard to its position, trapped between the forces of the global and local perspectives.

Tímea Junghaus

Our Beloved Margins

The Imaginings of the Roma Transformative Subject and Art History Scholarship in Central Europe

As an art historian and curator, Tímea Junghaus is interested in the conjunctions of modern and contemporary art with critical theory, with particular reference to questions about cultural difference, colonialism, and minority representation. She is the founding director of the European Roma Cultural Foundation, a Budapest-based NGO that created Gallery8 – Roma Contemporary Art Space; the gallery provides a frame for her writing on postcolonial critical strategies in Roma art practice, art history, and theory. In her essay, Junghaus explores models for imagining a radical vision of the Roma identity, one shaped by both feminist insights and recent explorations of the forgotten and unwritten history of the Roma, in which Roma resistance replaces a history of oppression.

Like the late Polish art historian and theorist Piotr Piotrowski, I too was "trained in an art history in which we were told that the centre, especially French art, was universal".[1] This approach to art history was liberating in its deterritorialized, unsituated, and universal form, but it was also, at times, superficial, overly theoretical, abstract, and completely oblivious to my Central European and Roma reality. Examining the marginal phenomena of Roma artistic production and Roma representation in more than five decades of art history,[2] we can perhaps ask whether it is possible to draw any conclusions about how our beloved margins – in this essay, specifically Roma margins – have shed light on this scholarship?

Paul Gilroy, in his essay "Race Ends Here", published in 1998, claims that the usefulness of race as an analytical category has come to an end because of the profound transformations of the last few decades in how the body is understood, largely as a result of the emergence of molecular biology, digital processing, and other technologies.[3] While I would like to nurture this fantasy, today it seems that for the Roma of Central and Eastern Europe – where states still retain control over access to political rights and economic opportunities, where under the banner of free speech hate speech has become the public norm, and where anti-Gypsyism is still considered a moderate attitude – the reconstruction and reconceptualization of race and the connection of Roma emancipatory efforts with global and transnational networks offer a potential outlet for the expansion of suppressed hopes. They also provide an opportunity to implicitly question the primacy of the national.

Reconstructing the "Roma race" is a double-edged sword. Still, it is an important "weapon" at a time when Roma face a wide spectrum of anti-Gypsyism, ranging from fascist violence to sophisticated and subtle academic racism. In this strategy, Roma scholars argue, exhaustively, that the Roma community should be considered Europe's largest colony. The postcolonial discourse framing the Roma has been disputed in academic circles that argue that the countries of Southern, Central, and Eastern Europe (where Roma populations are the largest) are historically and structurally different from those of Western Europe.[4] Roma theorists argue that

---

1   Piotr Piotrowski, in an interview by Richard Kosinsky, Jan Elantkowski, and Barbara Dudás, "A Way to Follow: Interview with Piotr Piotrowski", *ArtMargins Online*, January 29, 2015, http://www.artmargins.com/index.php/interviews-sp-837925570/758-a-way-to-follow-interview-with-piotr-piotrowski (accessed April 1, 2016).
2   Exploration of Roma artistic production in Central European art history scholarship began in the late 1960s with the first exhibitions of Roma art – in Hungary, Romania, and Czechoslovakia – and the associated publications and critical responses.
3   Paul Gilroy, "Race Ends Here", *Ethnic and Racial Studies*, vol. 21, no. 5, 1998, pp. 838–847.
4   This battle within the knowledge-production system has led to many researchers arguing passionately and exhaustively for the legitimacy of postcolonial discourse in the Central European Roma context. Debating something that should have been recognized long ago seems bewildering and perplexing, even more so because the arguments often meet with paternalistic reactions or contemptuous marginalization from the

Central Europe cannot be excised from the rest of the world and that postcolonial theories about whiteness and race offer a new understanding of the complexities of Roma oppression in this region as well. The most comprehensive and convincing argument in this regard was offered by Angéla Kóczé and Nidhi Trehan in their article "Racism, (Neo)colonialism and Social Justice: The Struggle for the Soul of the Romani Movement in Post-socialist Europe". Kóczé and Trehan point out that colonialism, in relation to the Roma, should be understood as the "majorities' strategy for maintaining asymmetrical relations of economic and political power (just as Edward Said talks about 'orientalism' as deploying a variety of strategies which common factor is the resultant position of superiority for Westerners vis-à-vis the 'Orient')".[5] Kóczé, a social anthropologist who is herself of Roma origin, concludes that if we fail to apply the postcolonial theoretical framework when describing the situation of European Roma, we merely preserve the idea of the "Gypsy problem", which she defines as "the discourse that tends to construct the problems that Roma experience (unemployment, poverty, and other manifestations of social exclusion) as essentialized by-products of the Gypsies' own culture (e.g., Roma are inherently 'socially inadaptable' and 'intellectually deficient')".[6] But when we situate the Roma in the domain of the postcolonial, we challenge the "Gypsy problem" characterization by "identifying European institutional and individual racism and discrimination as being at the root of the problems Roma people face".[7]

The idea that the "Gypsy" is "black" is present in literary sources and contemporary discourses alike. At Hungarian flea markets we can see an entire trade based on "gypsy girl" paintings, and on just a single trip to Budapest's Ecseri flea market I counted over thirty such home decor objects. And as one vendor told me, "The sellers confess that the darker they [the girls in the pictures] are the better they sell."[8] As Ian Hancock, a professor of Roma studies, notes, Roma have long depended on a system of black/white imagery. He also describes how the Romani term for South-eastern Europe (Hungary, Romania, Bulgaria, etc.), where the highest number of Roma live, is "Kali Oropa" (Black Europe).[9]

As early as the 15th and 16th centuries, Western art history unveils a set of images that reduce Roma people to an iconography of the stranger,

---

academic world. Bringing this struggle to light, however, is already a great achievement.

5 Angéla Kóczé and Nidhi Trehan, "Racism, (Neo)colonialism and Social Justice: The Struggle for the Soul of the Romani Movement in Post-socialist Europe", in *Racism, Postcolonialism, Europe*, ed. Graham Huggan and Ian Law, Liverpool University Press, Liverpool, 2009, p. 53.
6 Ibid., p. 54.
7 Angéla Kóczé, "Sites of Visibility", presentation at the international conference "Context, Visibility, Representation", April 17, 2010, Trafó House of Contemporary Arts, in collaboration with the Hungarian Roma Parliament, Budapest.
8 From an interview with a vendor at the Ecseri Flea Market, Budapest, in 2013.
9 Ian Hancock, "The Struggle for the Control of Identity", *Transitions: Changes in Post-Communist Societies*, vol. 4, no. 4, 1998, pp. 36–59.

the pagan, the alien, the thief, showing them as evil and ugly. Further art-historical research[10] is needed to explore the formation of the iconographic types by which Roma have been depicted so we can deconstruct these images and offer other examples where the analyses of these visual products contribute to our knowledge about the Roma and the Romani past. We already have several studies that demonstrate how the Roma body has been denigrated, sexualized and feminized in Western Art.[11]

In the panoptic regime of Central European modernity, when Central European artists set out to "find" their own primitives and their own "blacks", they turned to the colonies closest to them in which they could locate the wild and untamed – the Roma settlements of Central Europe.[12] As the sociologist Éva Judit Kovács concludes in her essay "Black Bodies, White Bodies": "Gypsies became the pendants of Western Europe's African and Asian primitives."[13] It is also a strategy of Roma art history writing to reclaim images that have been (mis)appropriated or (mis)interpreted as representations of other minorities (e.g. Blacks, Jews, Arabs, etc.) in order, ultimately, to bring Roma into the complex postcolonial power games of our contemporary reality. Perhaps in a few decades this segment of art history scholarship will develop sensitivity and practice in scrutinizing the dominant regimes of visual gazes so as to relate them to the intentions in the Roma's own mode of looking.

There is constant tension between epistemology and chronology as we attempt the construction of the long-suppressed and hidden genealogy of Roma cultural history. Through its use of methodological devices consid-

10. Studies about the image of the Roma in Western art and Roma iconography in art history include: Alena Volrábová, *Die deutsche Zeichnung des 15. und 16. Jahrhunderts: Zeichnungen von Autoren aus deutschsprachigen Ländern in den Museumssammlungen der Tschechischen Republik,* Národní Galerie, Prague, 2003; Charles D. Cuttler, "Exotics in 15th Century Netherlandish Art: Comments on Oriental and Gypsy Costume", in Herman Liebaers, *Liber Amicorum Herman Liebaers,* ed. Frans Vanwijngaerden et al., Les Amis de la Bibliothèque royale Albert Ier, Brussels, 1984; Erwin Pokorny, "The Gypsies and Their Impact on Fifteenth-Century Western European Iconography", in *Crossing Cultures: Conflict, Migration and Convergence: The Proceedings of the 32nd International Congress in the History of Art,* ed. Jaynie Anderson, Miegunyah Press, Carlton, Australia, 2009, pp. 597–601.
11. See for example, Ian Hancock, "The 'Gypsy' Stereotype and the Sexualization of Romani Women", *Danger! Educated Gypsy: Selected Essays,* ed. Dileep Karanth, University of Hertfordshire Press, Hatfield, Herts., UK, 2010, pp. 212–222; and Éva Judit Kovács, "Fekete testek, fehér testek" ("Black Bodies, White Bodies"), *Beszélő,* vol. 14, no. 1, January 2009 (in Hungarian), http://beszelo.c3.hu/cikkek/fekete-testek-feher-testek (accessed April 1, 2016).
12. This strategy was examined in the 2007 exhibition *Roma und Sinti: "Zigeuner-Darstellungen" der Moderne,* curated by Gerhard Baumgartner, László Beke, Tayfun Belgin, Tanja Pirsig-Marschall, Péter Szuhay, and Éva Judit Kovács, at the Kunsthalle in Krems, Austria. See Gerhard Baumgartner and Eva Kovács, "Roma und Sinti im Blickfeld der Aufklärung und der bürgerlichen Gesellschaft", in *Roma und Sinti: "Zigeuner-Darstellungen" der Moderne,* ed. Gerhard Baumgartner and Tayfun Belgin, exh. cat., Kunsthalle Krems, Krems, Austria, 2007, pp. 15–23.
13. See Éva Judit Kovács, "Fekete testek, fehér testek" (referenced in n. 11).

ered radical in the field of Roma studies – such as the notion of decoloniality, postcolonial theory, trauma studies, feminist scholarship, and cultural studies – such research, including the examination of Roma artistic production, demonstrates (self-)awareness of the "postcolonial constellation" in which it is embedded.[14] And while any critical interest that takes contemporary art as its focus necessarily refers to the foundational base of modern art history and its roots in imperial discourse, and should also point to the pressures that the postcolonial discourse exerts on art-historical narratives today, situating Roma in the postcolonial discourse, even today, is considered a kind of playful and experimental endeavour, a practice preferred primarily by the Roma intelligentsia. But as literary critic Édouard Glissant writes: "All subjectivities that emerge directly from the convergences and proximities wrought by imperialism … direct us to the postcolonial."[15]

In this strategy of inhabiting the colony and identifying with the racialized coloured subaltern Roma, artists take up the strategies of critical whiteness. A great deal of artistic practice and curatorial work focuses on the analysis or description of the non-Roma, in other words, whiteness and its racism, nationalism, and Roma-hatred. These efforts resituate "whiteness" from its unspoken status in order to shed light precisely on the perpetuation of the asymmetry that has marred critical analyses of racial/ethnic formation and cultural practice, in which the majority (white) position remained unexamined, unqualified, essential, homogeneous, seemingly self-fashioned, and unmarked by history or practice.

Researching photographic archives in the Roma collections of Central European public museums,[16] we can find an outrageous number of pictures of Roma that either serve the rather prurient desires of the collectors or are simply indecent and offensive. At the exhibition *Archive of Desires*, which I curated at Gallery8 – Roma Contemporary Art Space in Budapest in April 2015, photos from these collections were displayed in miniaturized form: visitors could view them only under magnification (fig. 1). This subversive curatorial strategy was a gesture that emphasized the surveillance and voyeurism. The magnifiers not only enlarged the images, but also stressed the significance and nature of the gaze. The images themselves trigger a flood of questions, and many arouse a deep sense of outrage, including, for example, an amateur ethnographer's picture of half-naked Roma girls standing in line, which verges on pornography; a Roma

14   See Okwui Enwezor, "The Postcolonial Constellation: Contemporary Art in a State of Permanent Transition", *Research in African Literatures*, vol. 34, no. 4, winter 2003, pp. 57–82.
15   Édouard Glissant, *Caribbean Discourse: Selected Essays*, ed. A. James Arnold, University of Virginia Press, Charlottesville, 1992, p. 72.
16   State museums with extensive Roma photographic collections include, in Hungary, the Museum of Ethnography (Budapest), the Nógrád Historical Museum (Salgótarján), and the Museum of Hungarian Naive Artists (Kecskemét), as well as the National Museum of Romanian Peasant in Bucharest, the Ethnographic Museum of the National Museum in Prague, and the Weltmuseum in Vienna.

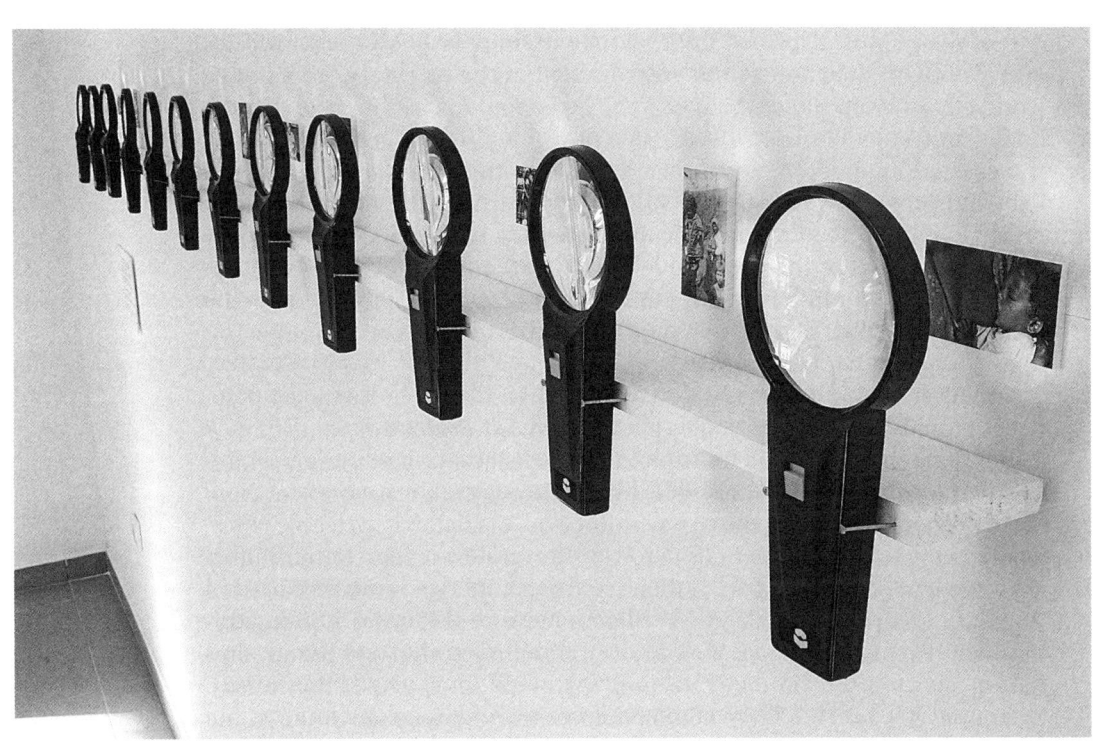

fig. 1

Archive of Desires, detail from the installation,
Gallery8, Budapest, April 2015.

Courtesy of Gallery8.

family whose dog, too, is able to pose for the ethnographer's camera; and photographs that show strange grinning figures with exposed breasts, who, according to the non-Roma ethnographer, are mothers breastfeeding their over-aged children.

From the captions that are attached to these archival materials, it is clear that the Roma cultural heritage, the Roma past, and pictures of our Roma ancestors are lying in archives that register only the names of the collectors and ethnographers, not the people in the photographs. In the same exhibition, the triptych *Museum of Ethnology* (figs. 2-4), by contemporary artist Tamara Moyzes, worked with the image from the 1944 photograph *Line of Roma Girls* by an amateur Austrian ethnographer, one of the photos displayed under a magnifying glass. Moyzes imagines and plays with the context and environment of the original photographic work. Her artwork stages the specifically white nudist tradition next to the line of half-naked Roma girls: the line of white girls remains surprisingly transparent, unmarked, and "normal" next to the dark-skinned, coquettish, and provocatively exposed Roma girls. Perhaps the Roma girls had been violently forced to pose for the camera, a suggestion presented by the second panel of the triptych. Meanwhile, the third section, using humour to make its point, calls attention to the normalcy of the culture of the naked white female body, and how it is fetishized, in the context of the tradition of beauty competitions.

Another example of postcolonial critical strategies in Roma art practice is provided by Tibor Balogh's photograph *Self-Portrait as Sándor Petőfi* (2015). Balogh grew up as an orphan in Hungary's largest state orphanage, in the village of Tiszadob, where many Roma children were sent from other orphanages during the 1970s and 1980s. Tiszadob is an iconic place, where many Roma intellectuals in today's Central European Roma cultural movement once spent part of their childhood. Balogh is the first artist of Roma origin to receive a degree in fine art in Central Europe. The engravings he presented in *Whose Nation?*, an exhibition at Gallery8 in the summer of 2015,[17] pay tribute to Tiszadob, the place he considers home. *Self-Portrait as Sándor Petőfi* (fig. 5) is a complex work: the image of the Roma artist, posing as Petőfi, the "most famous" Hungarian poet, suggests a revision of Hungary's essentialist nation-concept that questions the patriotism of minorities. Balogh's work demonstrates both his loyalty and his longing for a new nation-concept in which the desire to belong can be fulfilled.

Exposing the Western universality of art as a historical legend has always been the objective of Gallery8, which opened in 2013. As Piotr Piotrowski once noted, when we explore the "local", we find that "art that is located

---

[17] The exhibition *Whose Nation? Reimagined National Identities* was curated by cultural theorist Árpád Bak, June 23-July 30, 2015. See http://gallery8.org/en/news/2/67/whose-nation-reimagined-national-identities (accessed April 1, 2016).

in a particular historical and cultural context would lose its universality".[18] He further suggested that "the way to provincialize the center is to locate it".[19] Gallery8's chosen critical-theoretical framework and its focus on the topography of Hungary's cultural scene follow this strategy of "provincializing the centre" and questioning the "universality" of art. The space, established and run by European Roma Cultural Foundation, is strategically located on Mátyás Square, at the heart of Budapest's 8th District, which is densely populated by Roma. Despite the gallery's modest size, it is ideal for both a progressive intervention in Europe's contemporary art scene and a long-term, sustainable cultural initiative in the Hungarian Roma community. The gallery envisions a future of artistic and cultural diversity in which Roma art, culture, history, and language are valued and respected as equal to other traditions; it believes that the power of artistic creation and education, especially by and for young people, is essential in changing negative stereotypes toward people of Roma origin. The gallery serves the Roma community, facilitating and supporting the production, presentation, and interpretation of Roma artworks. It is an intercultural space, a "contact zone", in the sense put forth by cultural theorist Mary Louise Pratt in her inspirational essay "Arts of the Contact Zone":[20] here Roma and non-Roma can engage in experimentation, creation, collaboration and discussion, resulting in new works and solutions for a future of peaceful coexistence.

To find models for imagining a radical vision for the Roma transformative subject, the Roma movement turns to other transnational networks and cultures. If we acknowledge that the idea of decoloniality in the Roma context suggests, among other things, that the Roma movement is in search of a "new humanity"[21] or that it seeks "social liberation from all power organized as inequality, discrimination, exploitation, and domination",[22] then as the Indian literary critic and theorist Gayatri Chakravorty Spivak has proposed, we should rightly turn to the feminists, who have long known how to use state mechanisms so that neither nationalism nor fascism shall gain ground.[23] The art of Roma woman artists – such as Omara, Selma Selman, Kiba Lumberg, and Delaine Le Bas – is organized around the question of visibility and how the Roma artist can rewrite or modify the mainstream discourse once she arrives at a position

---

18   Piotr Piotrowski, in an interview by Richard Kosinsky, Jan Elantkowski, and Barbara Dudás, "A Way to Follow".
19   Ibid.
20   Mary Louise Pratt, "Arts of the Contact Zone", *Profession*, 1991, pp. 33–40.
21   See Walter D. Mignolo, *The Darker Side of Western Modernity: Global Futures, Decolonial Options*, Duke University Press, Durham and London, 2011.
22   Aníbal Quijano, "Coloniality and Modernity/Rationality", *Cultural Studies*, vol. 21, nos. 2–3, 2007, p. 178.
23   Gayatri Chakravorty Spivak, in conversation with Suzana Milevska, "Resistance that Cannot Be Recognized as Such: A Conversation between Gayatri Chakravorty Spivak and Suzana Milevska", in *New Feminism: Worlds of Feminism, Queer and Networking Conditions*, ed. Marina Gržinić and Rosa Reitsamer, Löcker, Vienna, 2008, p. 278.

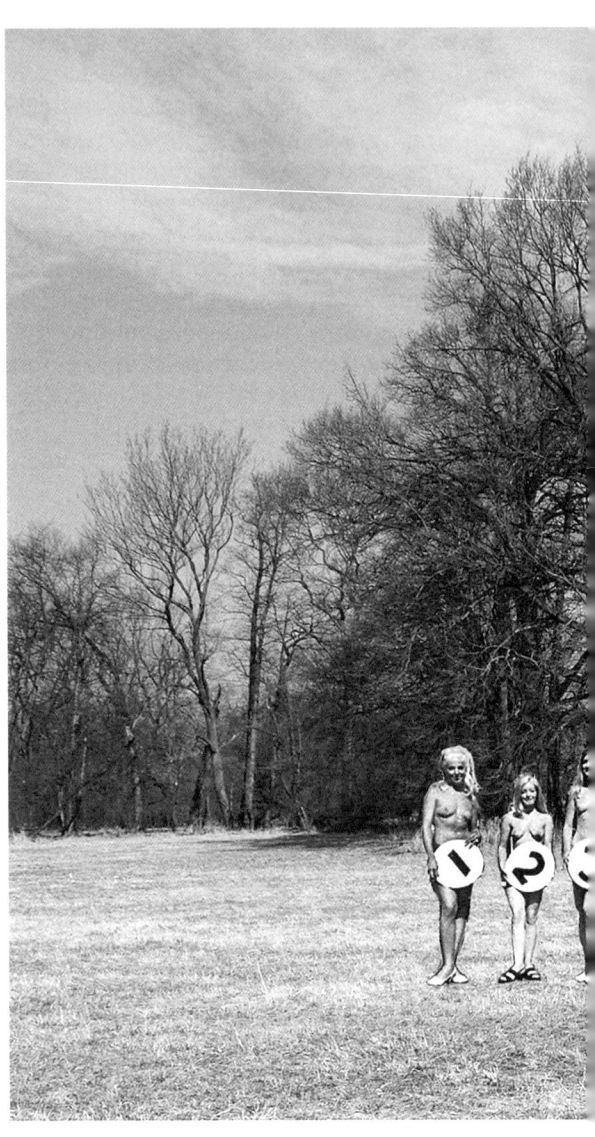

figs. 2–4

Tamara Moyzes, *Museum of Ethnology I–III*, 2015, photomontage. Photo by Árpád Bak.

Courtesy of Gallery8, Budapest.

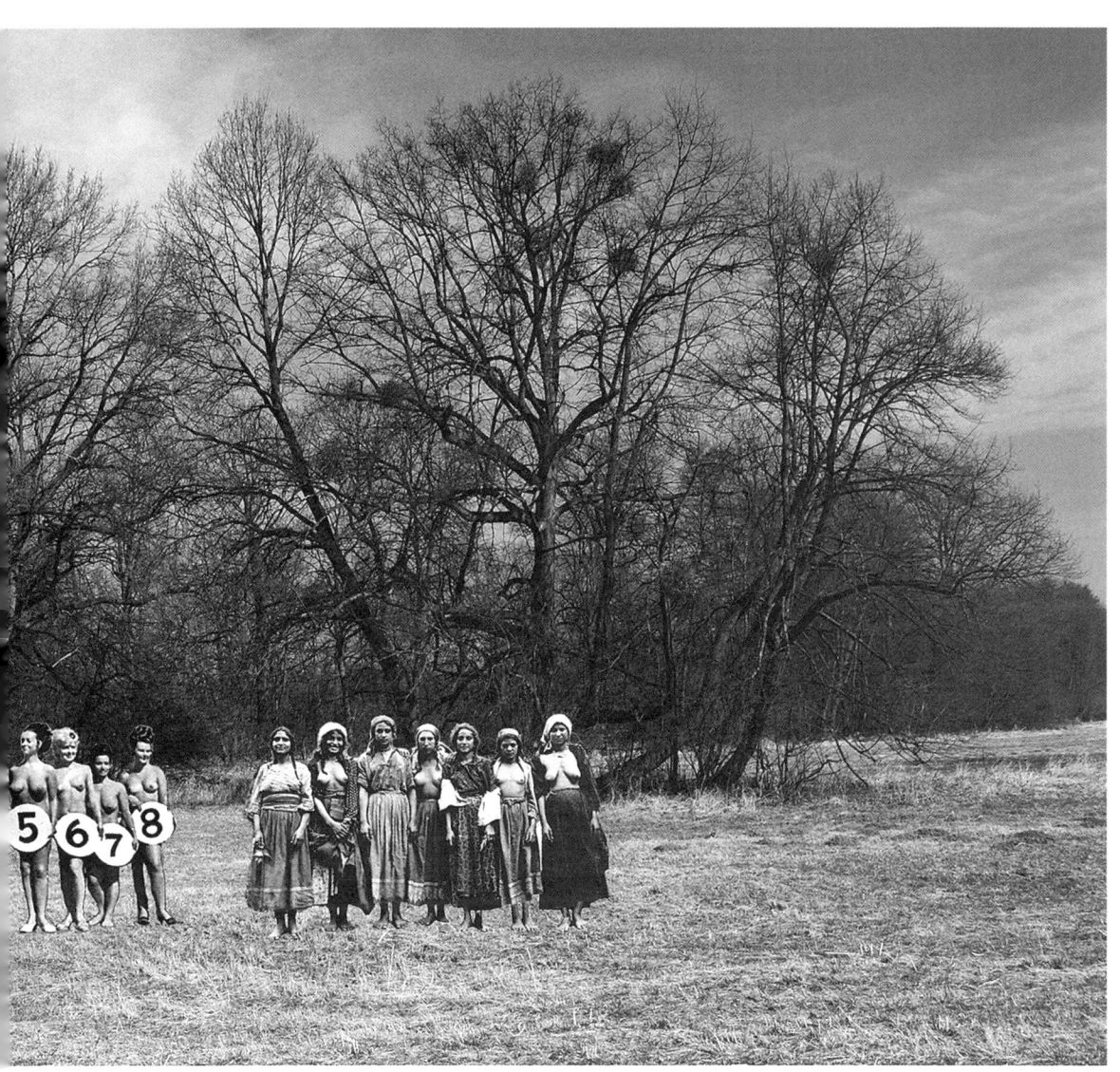

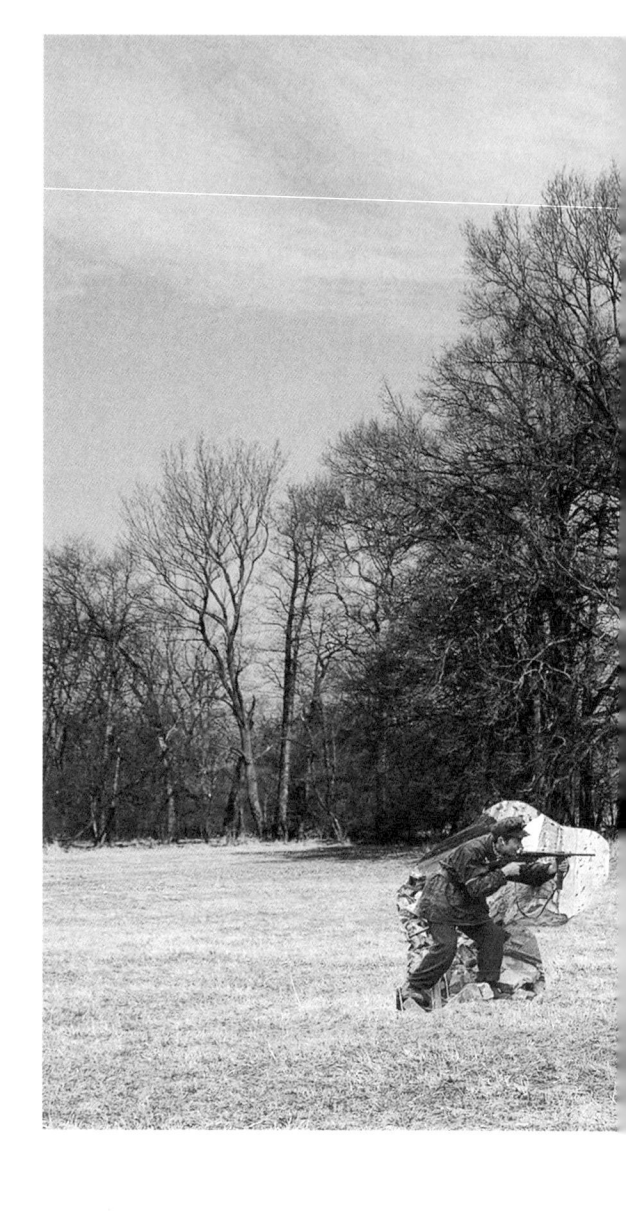

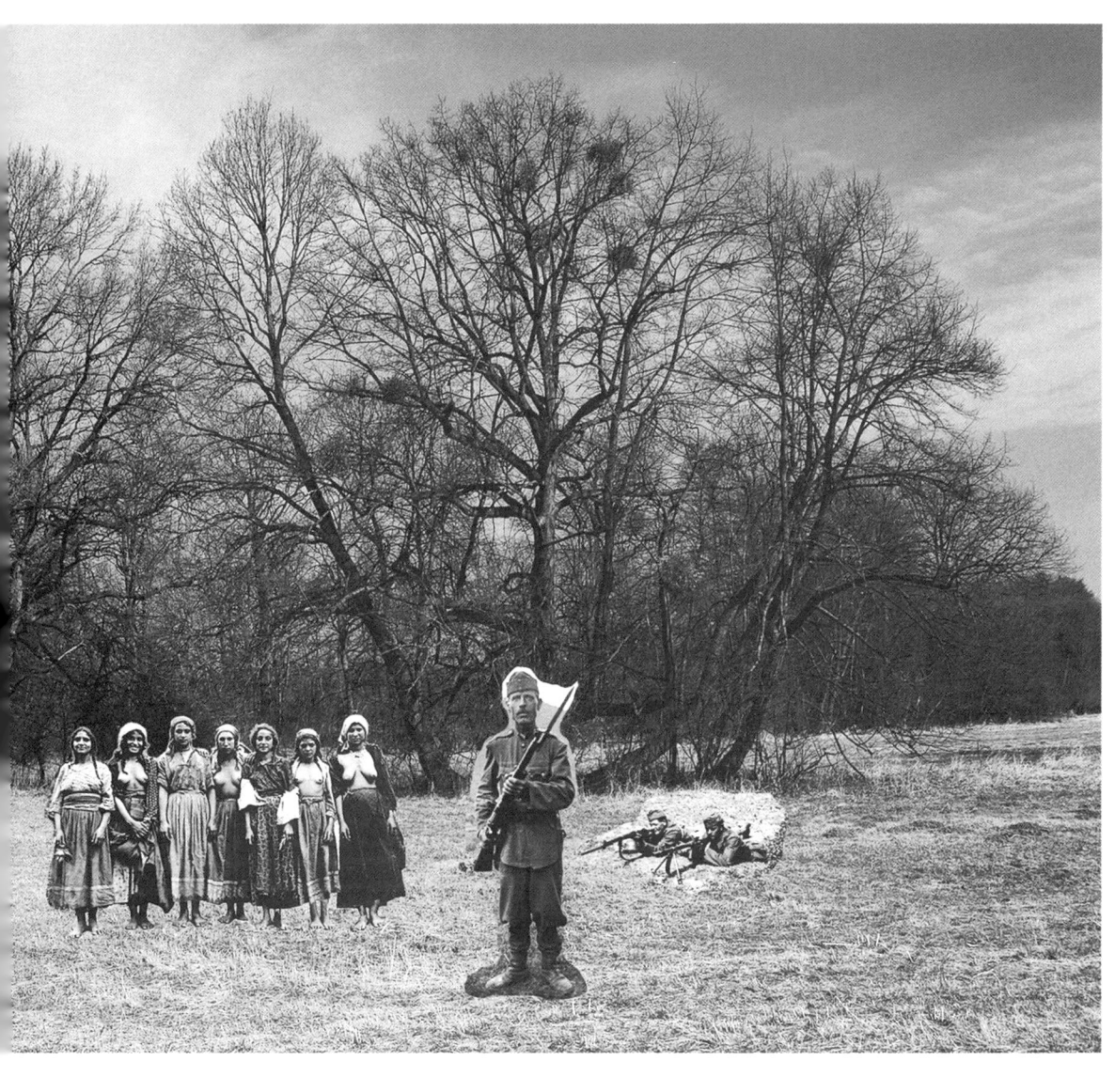

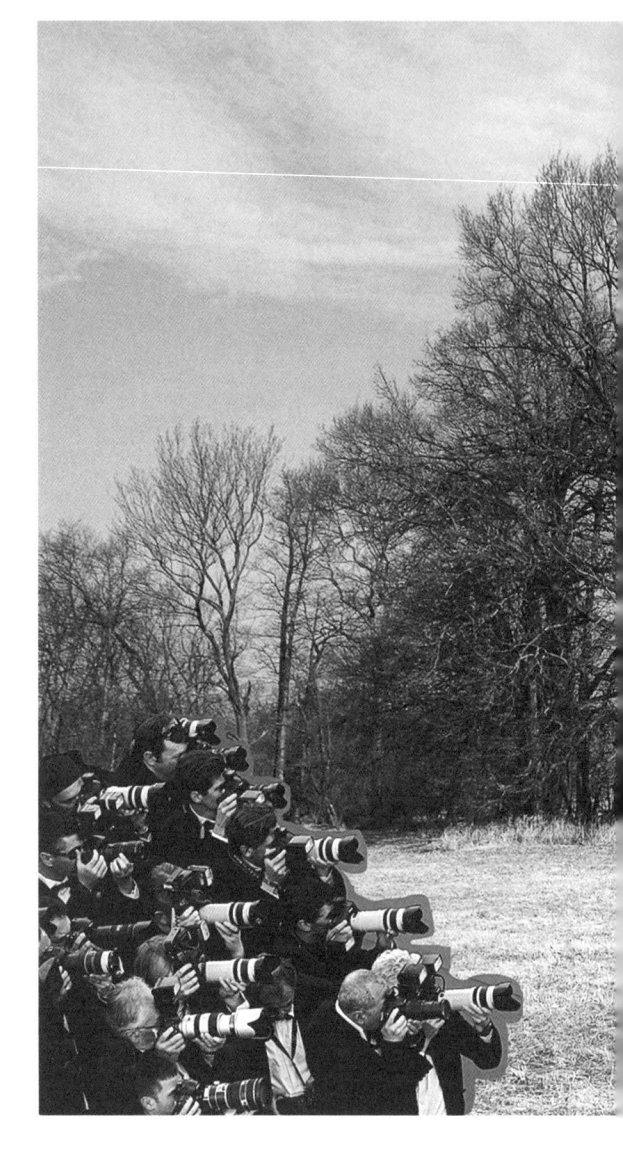

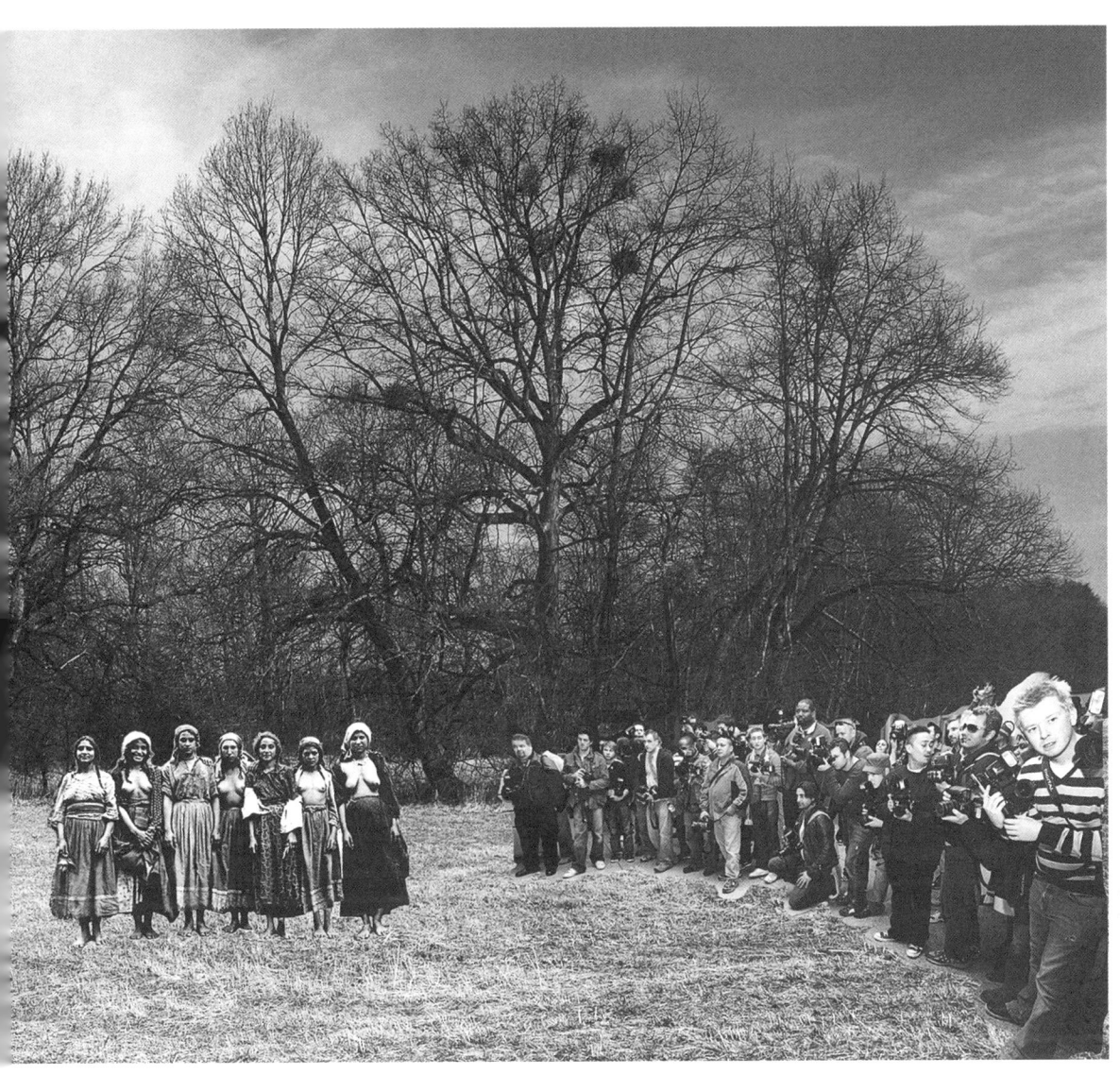

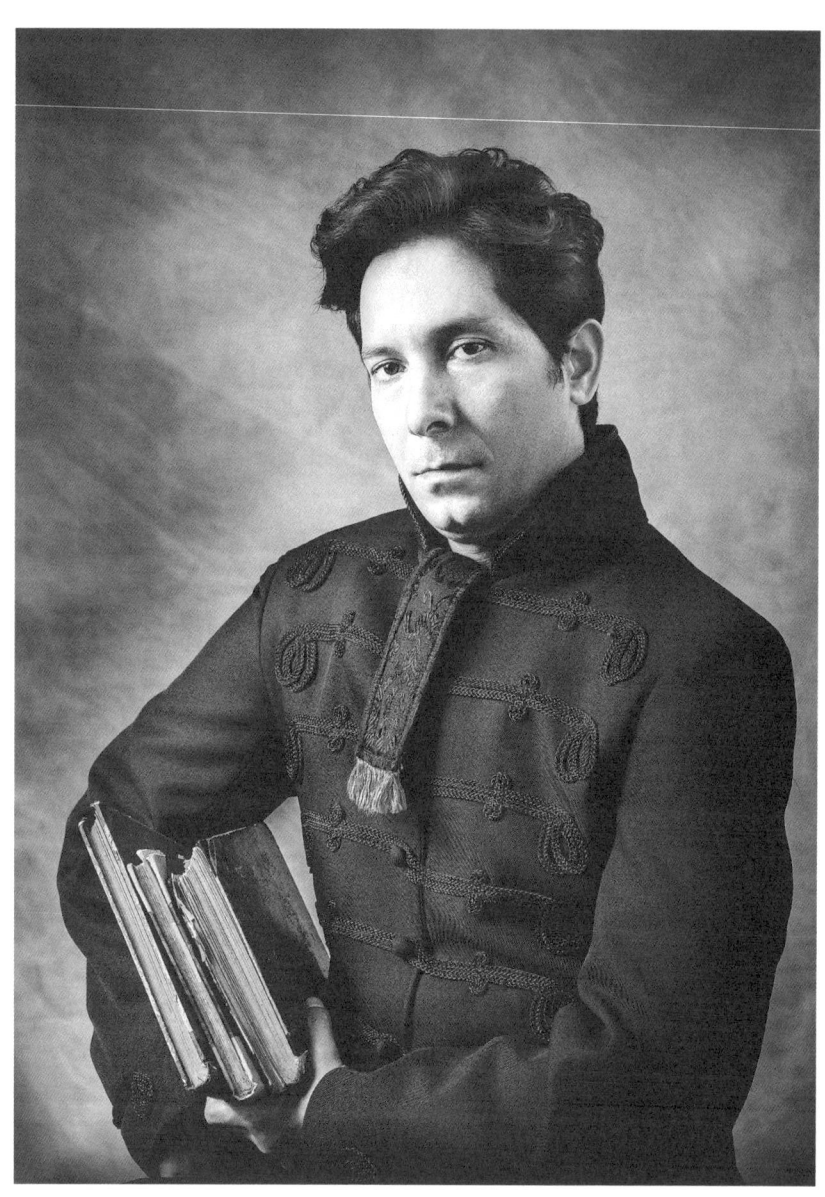

fig. 5

Tibor Balogh, *Self Portrait as Sándor Petőfi*, 2015, photography.

Photo by Miklós Déri. Courtesy of Gallery8, Budapest.

of visibility. In this sense these artists apply feminist strategies: when it comes to defending the interests of the Roma minority they do not rely exclusively on visual art but operate also through actions, scandals, demonstrations and political statements, using the media (print, broadcast, or electronic) to disseminate their views.

The radical discourse of the Roma diasporic identity can already be identified in the common policies developed at the First World Romani Congress in 1971 in Orpington, a suburb of London, including the ratification of a politically correct name (Roma), the establishment of a national anthem, and an agreement on the Roma flag. These policies manifest a transgressive extraterritorial political identity; identification with an imagined commonality based on a non-territorial "us", scattered in diasporic spaces. This new discourse employs narratives, images, events, and objects – in other words, culture. It is aware of other transnational movements, and has so far been inspired by the transnational feminist movement, the movements of other subaltern groups, and the liberating notions of contemporary identity theory, such as creolization, border gnosis, third space, decoloniality, etc.

When searching for radical visions for the Roma identity, Roma make a conscious effort to de-link from existing bodies of knowledge and unlearn what has been taught about the Roma in Europe. The recent reexploration of the forgotten and unwritten history of the Roma shows us that Roma have had the strength to oppose oppression and participate in various forms of resistance, and so have the capacity to inhabit roles other than that of victim. In this immersive unlearning and rewriting of Roma history, the history of Roma resistance replaces a history of oppression. The exhibition *(Re-)Conceptualizing Roma Resistance*, which I curated at the Hellerau European Centre for the Arts in Dresden in April 2016, approaches the concept of resistance as enacted by Roma people across the diaspora by focusing specifically on the emerging body of literature and current narratives, embodiments, and expressions.

The new research on Roma resistance during the Holocaust and afterwards[24] – which is being conducted as a collaborative project between Roma scholars, artists, organizations, and activists – testifies to Roma taking an active and conscious role in shaping their lives and defining their own fate. It reveals new sources that demonstrate how Roma stood out in their conduct, as compared to other inmates in the camps, and developed survival strategies to preserve and maintain their dignity even in the most daunting circumstances. The research compiles a history of escapes from the camps as well as uprisings in the Zigeunerlager at Auschwitz on May 16 and August 2, 1944; it explores the memory of Roma heroes and

---

24 The ongoing research project "The Roma and Resistance during the Holocaust and in Its Aftermath", begun in 2010, was initiated by the non-profit organization La Voix des Rroms, in collaboration with the TernYpe International Roma Youth Network and the Tom Lantos Institute and supported by the International Holocaust Remembrance Alliance.

the non-Roma supporters of the Roma resistance movement, as well as the active and heroic participation of Roma people in anti-fascist partisan movements throughout Europe under the National Socialist regime. In this process of relearning, Roma resistance emerges as an inspiring model for Roma knowledge, agency, and consciousness. Roma contemporary artists also play an important role in emphasizing manifestations and narratives of Roma resistance as central to the Roma experience. And Roma art itself is seen as a well-thought-out and creative method of Roma resistance, a well-established form of cultural survival and a demonstration of ethical and political commitment to the future of the Roma community.

In preparation for International Roma Day and the forty-fifth anniversary of the First International Roma Congress on April 8, 2016, Europe celebrates the aspirations of the Roma transformative subject, the prospect of a new historical and political tectonics, the power of assembly and the alliances we are building for Roma self-determination (fig. 6).

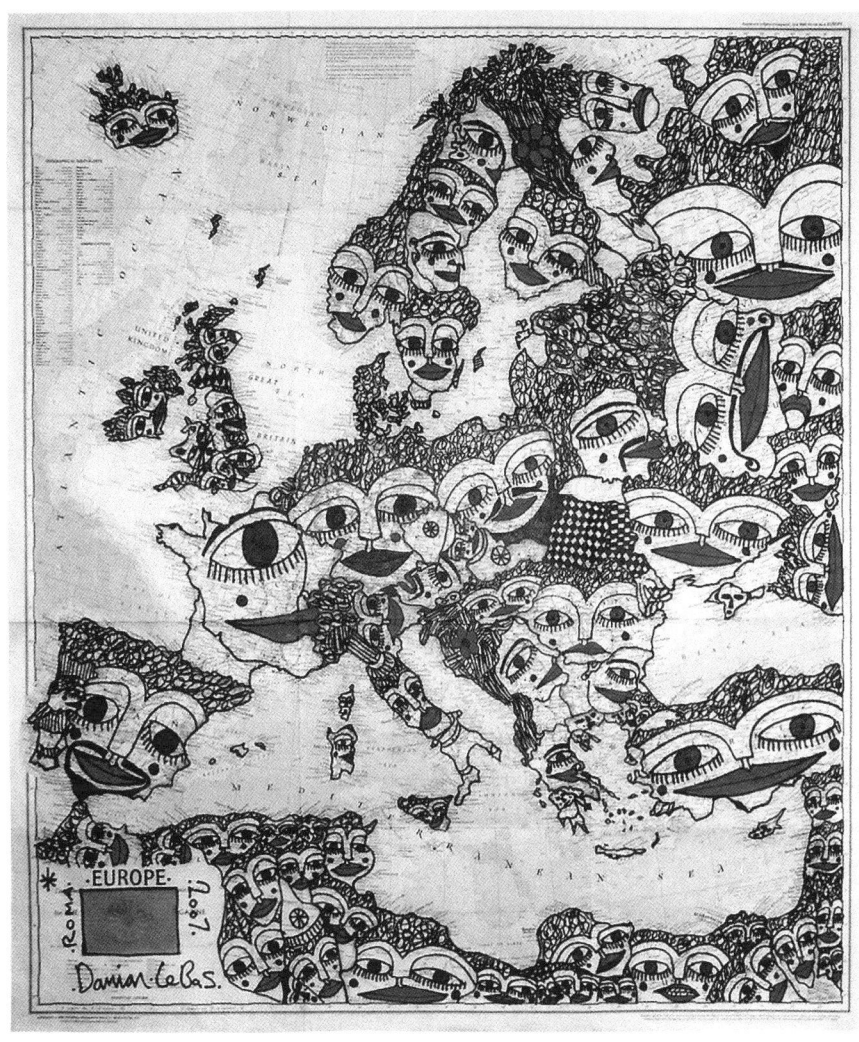

fig. 6

Damian Le Bas, *Roma Europe*, 2007, mixed media on printed map.

Courtesy of Kai Dikhas Gallery, Berlin.

Fouad Asfour

A Letter

Writer and editor Fouad Asfour divides his time between South Africa and Europe; in his work, he reflects critically on the colonial matrix of power in art writing, art history, and art education. His contribution here takes the form of a letter in which we learn about several significant artworks and exhibitions in South Africa that address the complex task of decolonizing art history and criticism. But the letter itself also plays its part in Asfour's effort to unlearn and undo the received practices of art writing.

Grahamstown, South Africa, March 2016

Dear Editors,

Over the last few years, I have been trying to find ways of doing things differently, ways of collaborating, writing, and publishing (see figs. 1 and 6). Appreciating slippages and allowing for ambiguities, following where misreading takes me. Working in the field of art and writing about contemporary art, I feel caught up in a tension between discourse and its conditions, which Pablo Lafuente, in "Notes on Art Criticism as a Practice", frames as "practical questions with ethical and political implications", underlining the idea that "one of the key features of art ... is that it constitutes a privileged place for showing how things can be different". Art criticism, he argues, should be a "productive contribution that constructs the subject of its discourse and aims to produce change", which stands in contrast to the framing of "theory" in the contemporary art discourse I usually experience, namely, in a way that involves the backgrounding of lived realities. It seems to me that the performativity of "knowledge" in critical reflection needs to be reviewed, furthering reflections about its role and how it is activated in contemporary art. Working with artists and writing about their work, I started to understand that this constant interrogation can enable a more fluent and poetic approach towards "theory", which at the same time can constitute the basis to reframe it beyond the written text – to look at it, rather, as a continuous practice, as bell hooks writes in "Theory as Liberatory Practice", in her book *Teaching to Transgress: Education as the Practice of Freedom* (1994): "Theory is not inherently healing, liberatory, or revolutionary. It fulfils this function only when we ask that it do so and direct our theorizing towards this end."

Here as well, thinking about theory means to engage with the fluent space of what "liberatory" or "healing" means, which I think demands a constant refocusing on the shifting relation between the private and the political. Also, asking how art writing can become a space of contemplation and dreaming, I find that Paulo Freire's reflections on "The Act of Study" lead to further ideas when he says that the reader needs not only to understand and research the "sociological-historical conditioning of knowledge" and the content of a text, but also to develop an "ingenuity in relation to the text". By assuming the "role of subject of the act", studying becomes a form of "reinventing, re-creating, rewriting". Reflecting on processes of reading art works as texts, then, it's a small step to art writing as a creative process which resists its smooth incorporation into "art history" and "art theory". Moving away from colonially schooled art practices (and gazes) has brought about a long history of disruptive practices, channelled in an invisible knowledge transfer undermining Western/European epistemology.

That theorizing hinges on ways of performing knowledge is framed in more detail by Antonio Gramsci in his text "The Study of Philosophy". Opening with the statement that it is essential to "destroy the widespread prejudice that philosophy is a strange and difficult thing just because it is the specific intellectual activity of a particular category of specialists or of professional and systematic philosophers", he continues that "everyone is a philosopher" because of their use of language in reasoning and applying concepts in forming opinions. A useful comment on this text comes from Renate Holub in the book entitled *Antonio Gramsci: Beyond Marxism and Postmodernism*, which rejects the thought that Gramsci intended to flatten distinctions between different forms of intellectuals; Holub points out that this passage aims rather to change the framing of ideology, meaning, and hegemony: "It is by addressing the political content of conceptions of the world, by making people aware of the non-neutrality of their ways of thinking, by raising their consciousness, that all people can potentially become critical thinkers." Both Freire's and Gramsci's texts point towards the potential of a critical awareness when using language in creating new thought.

Correspondingly, Michel Foucault also imagines criticism differently in an interview which was originally published in *Le Monde*, then reprinted in *Entretiens avec Le Monde, vol. I: Philosophies* (1984), and later published in English translation as "The Masked Philosopher": "I can't help but dream about a kind of criticism that would not try to judge, but bring an oeuvre, a book, a sentence, an idea to life; it would light fires, watch the grass grow, listen to the wind, and catch the sea-foam in the breeze and scatter it. It would multiply, not judgments, but signs of existence; it would summon them, drag them from their sleep. Perhaps it would invent them sometimes – all the better. All the better. Criticism that hands down sentences sends me to sleep; I'd like a criticism of scintillating leaps of the imagination. It would not be a sovereign or dressed in red. It would bear the lightning of possible storms."

But does dreaming the critical up into the poetic realm suffice when new ways must be found to think the possibility of un-writing art history and unsettling and disturbing art writing? Not only questions about the market or who decides what is being published are relevant here, but crucially, what is the basis of writing about art, of assessing, estimating, and judging art? Much has been written about the condition of art writing and art criticism, discussing its relation to the precarious conditions of self-employment, market forces, and the discourse of contemporary art. Again I would refer to Lafuente who maintains that art writing is and should remain a largely unregulated practice, shaped by the practices of art critics, artists, curators, and other writers, as well as the market and publishing companies, and not dependent on a taught and formalized curriculum.

However, art writing and knowledge production in art theory and history outside of the Western/European discourse has been mostly disavowed as "lacking". And while decolonial practices have been discussed and theorized, a critical reflection on decolonizing art history, which necessarily implies the need for art education to critically reflect the colonial matrix of power, was recently elaborated by Madina

Tlostanova and Walter Mignolo in "Global Coloniality and the Decolonial Option" (*Kult 6, Special Issue: Epistemologies of Transformation*, fall 2006): "The control of knowledge and subjectivity through education and colonizing the existing knowledges ... is the key and fundamental sphere of control that makes domination possible."

In this context, South African curator and writer Khwezi Gule points out (in an email conversation) that there is "something to be said about the way art history and various ways of resuscitating it in the present also has to do with, not necessarily shifting its basis in the enlightenment project but merely dressing it up in the contemporary and that is because the project of 'knowing the Other' has taken other dimensions in the neo-liberal context and in the context of the knowledge economy which is about reproducing privilege rather than multiplying subjectivity and forms of agency". Furthermore, he points out that the relative insularity of "art history" is beneficial for maintaining its exclusionary attitude, separate from popular art and forms of writing.

Art writing, it seems, has to consciously labour in the tension of the need to remain an "unregulated practice" while both (ab)using an academic disciplinary language and confronting the conditions of art writing which have been naturalized in gallery education, museum practices, and the Western/European curriculum, which weaves this habitual and implicit thread of knowledge all the way through primary, secondary, and tertiary education.

Therefore, when it comes to decolonizing art history and art writing, the basis of art appreciation, judgement, and criticism in art education has to be confronted. This is underlined in an interview by Rubén Gaztambide-Fernández with Walter Mignolo, "Decolonial Options and Artistic/AestheSic Entanglements" (2014), which differentiates between "aestheSis" – "related to popular culture and popular arts, and 'everyday aesthetic practices and the senses'" – and Western art education based on the European "modern aestheTics", which "emerged from European

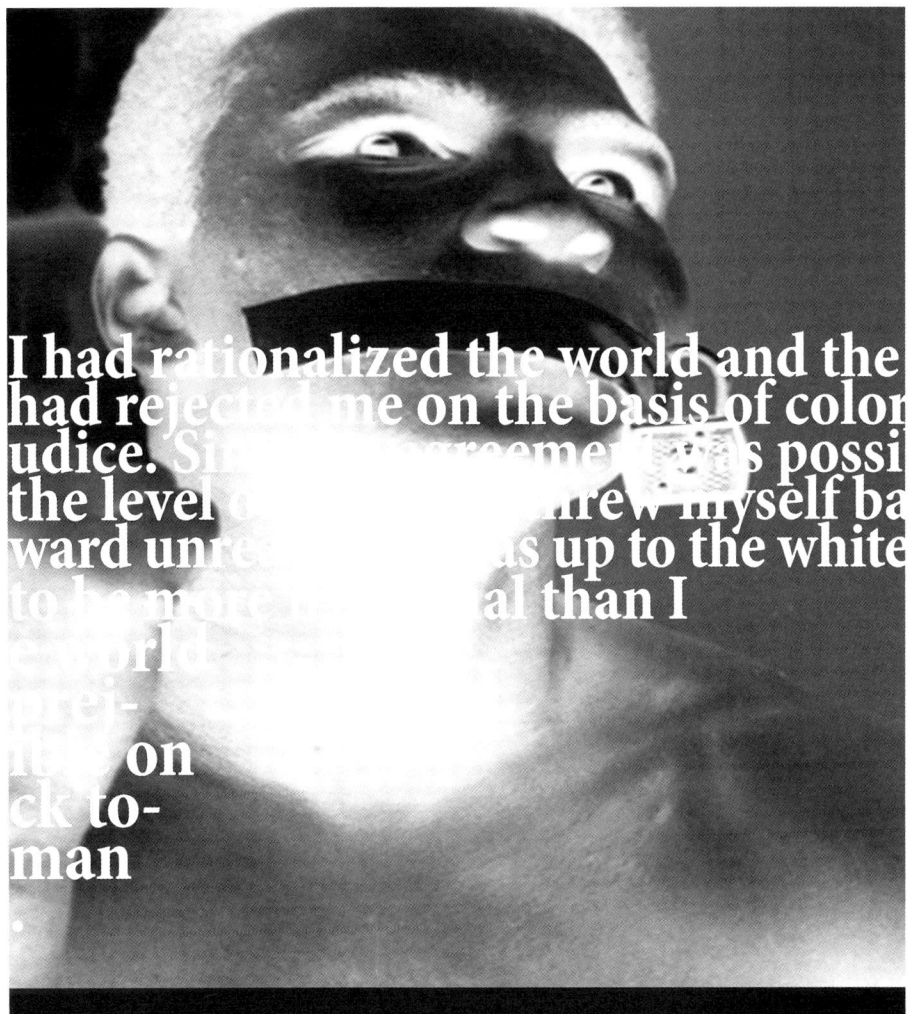

fig. 1

Reason and Its Discontents, poster for the exhibition performance by the AvP art collective, 2016, Grahamstown, South Africa.

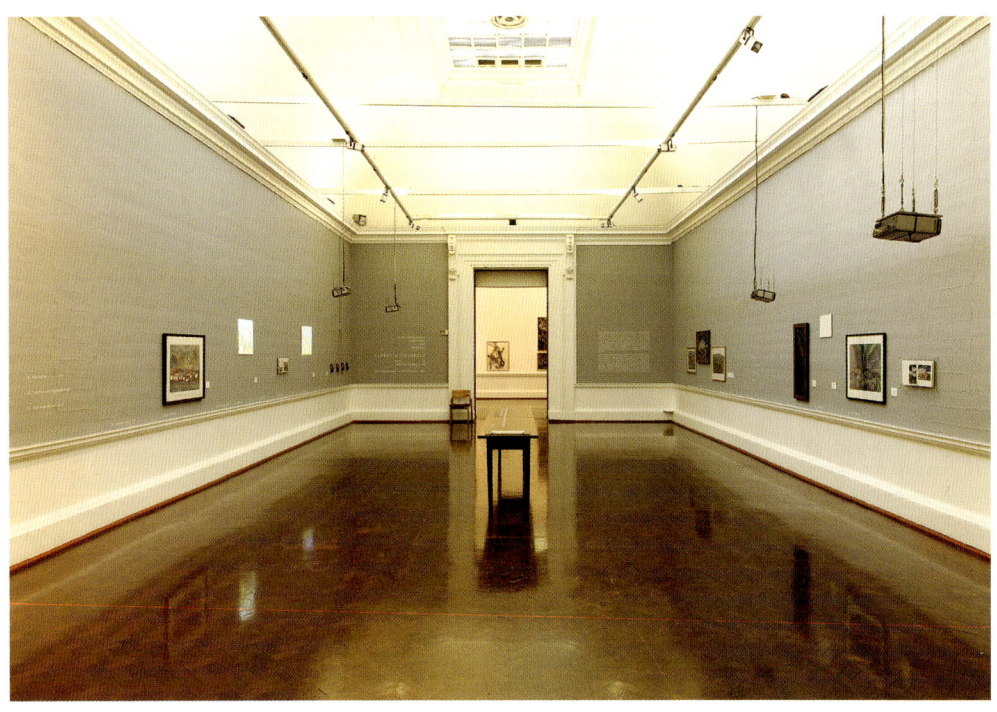

fig. 2

Nontobeko Ntombela, *A Fragile Archive*, exhibition view, Johannesburg Art Gallery, 2012.

Photo by Russell Scott.

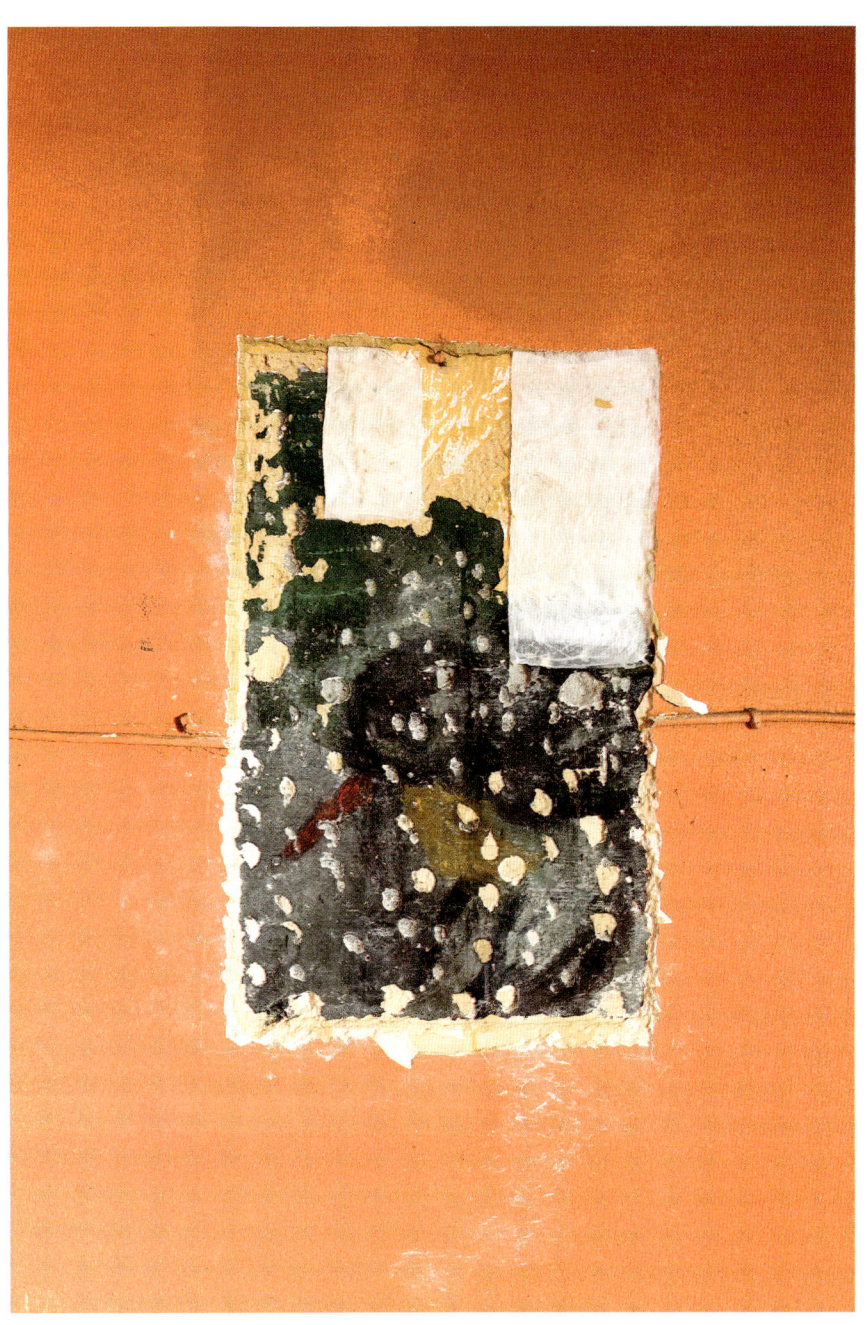

fig. 3

Kemang Wa Lehulere, *The Bird Lady in 9 Layers of Paint*, 2015.

Courtesy of the artist.

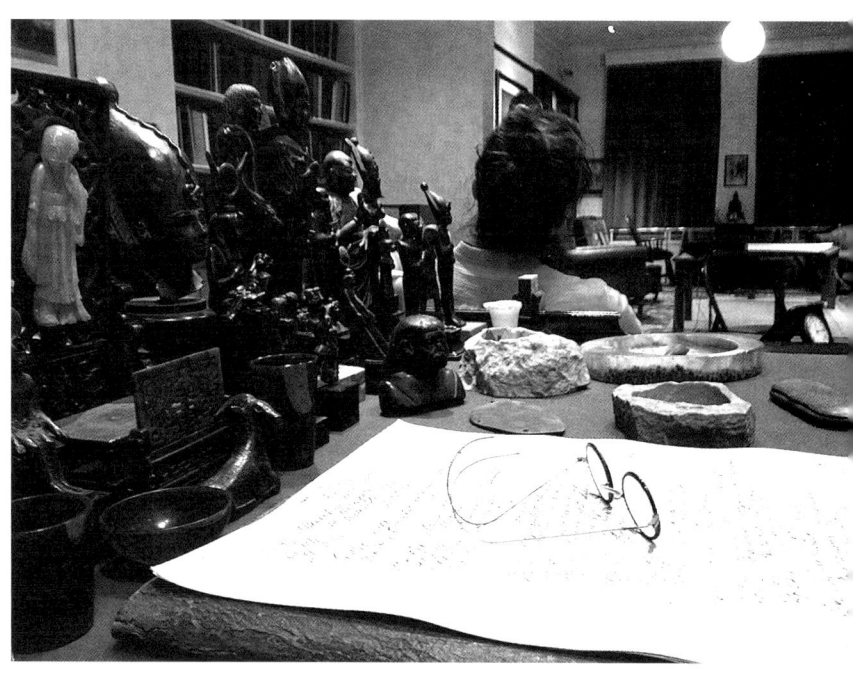

fig. 4

Sharlene Khan, *Nervous Conditions*, 2015, video stills.

Courtesy of the artist.

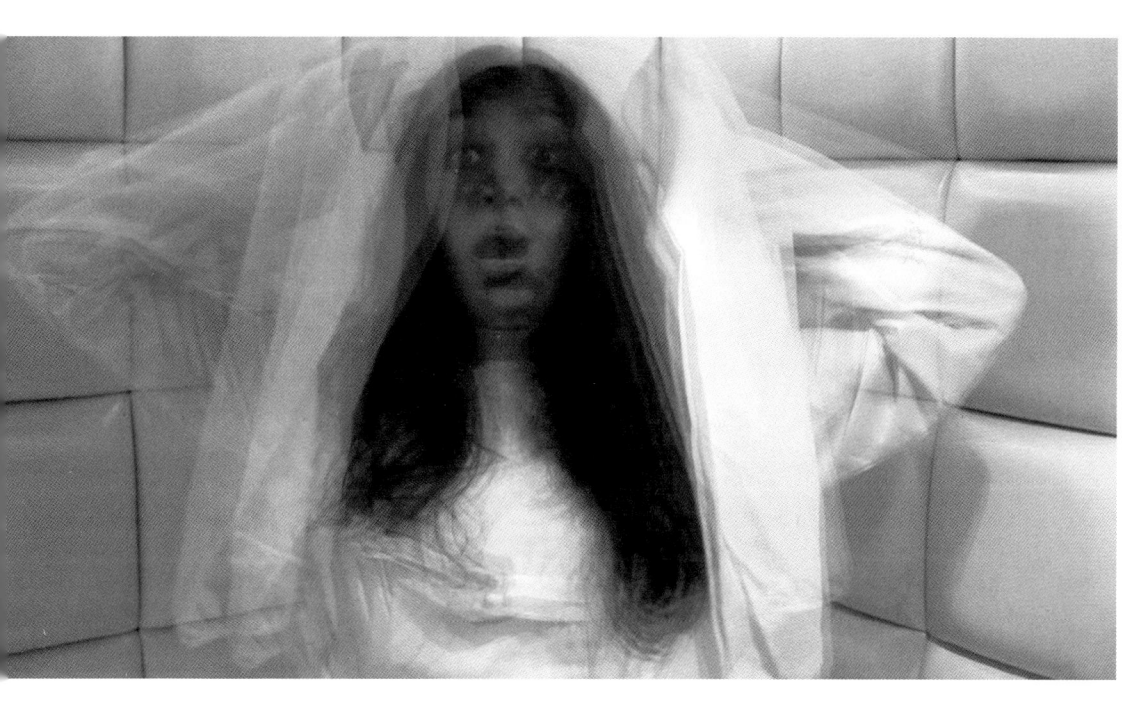

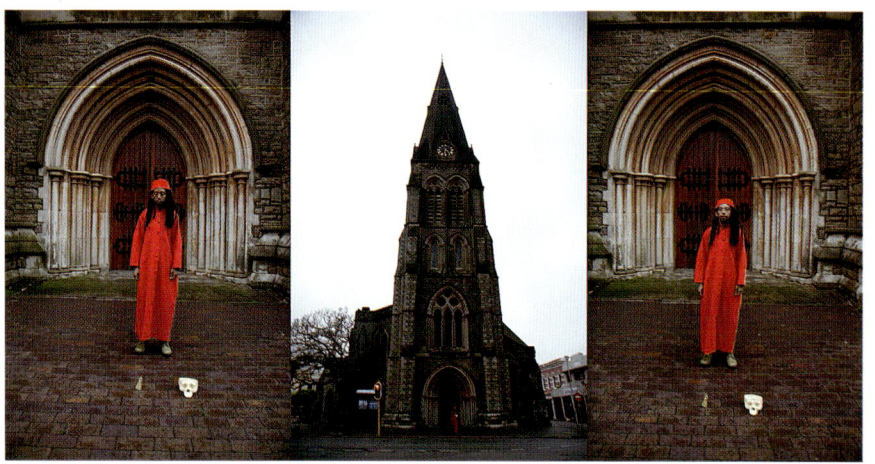

fig. 5

Sikhumbuzo Makandula, *Mission; Imagination in a Troubled Space; Part of the History*, 2016, video stills.

Photo by Shalom Mushwana.

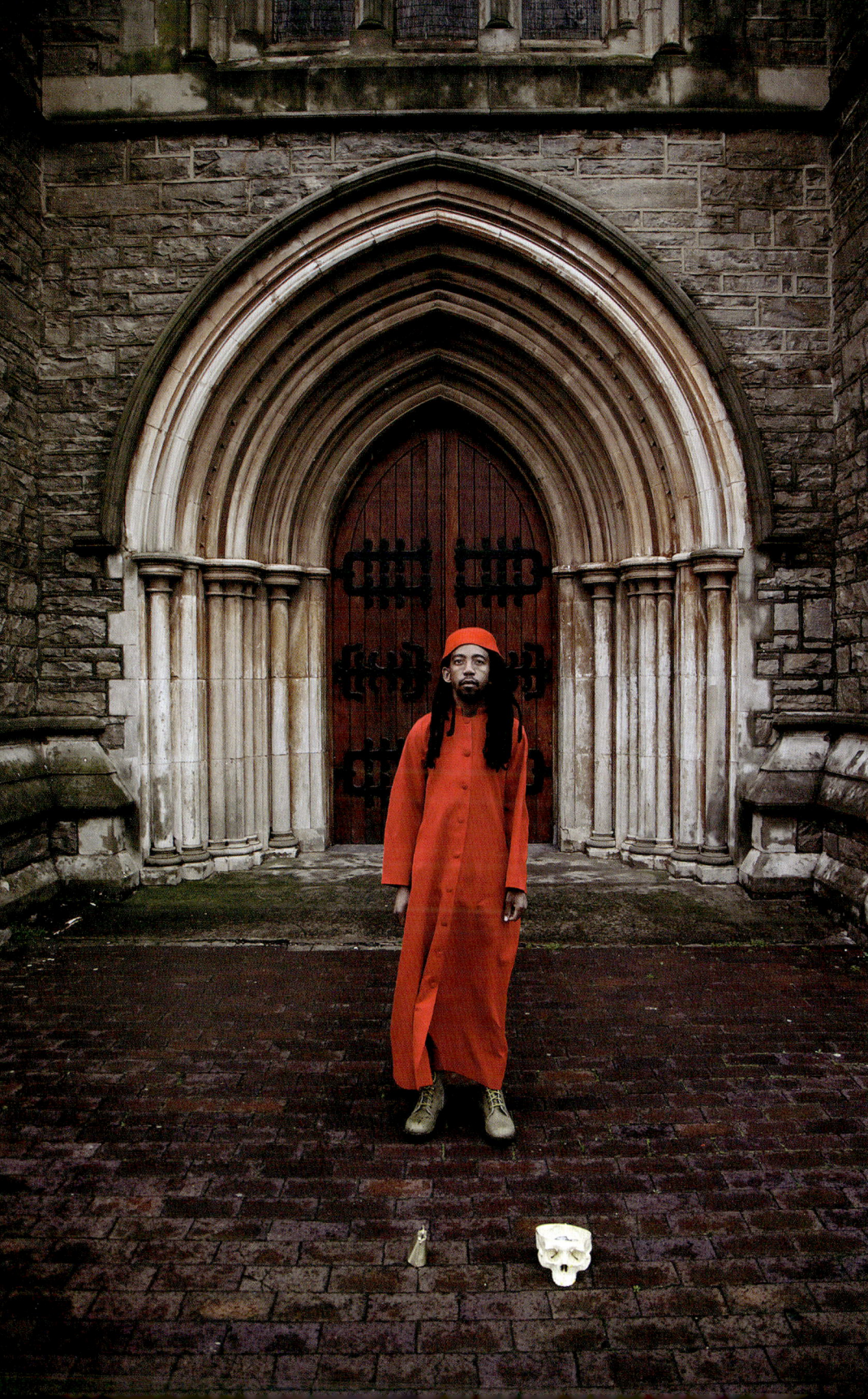

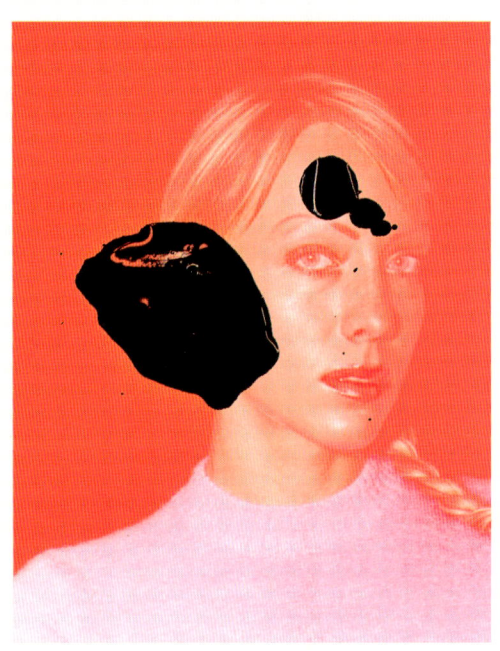

fig. 6

SHAHRZAD collective (aka MEDIUM), *Providence*, 2007,
10 page booklet (pp. 4-5); exhibited in wall newspaper format at
the exhibition *Reason and Its Discontents*, 2016, Grahamstown, South Africa.

Courtesy of the SHAHRZAD collective.

experience and local history, and that became, even already in Kant's work, the regulator of the global capability to 'sense' the beautiful and the sublime" – as Mignolo and Rolando Vázquez discuss in detail in their text "Decolonial AestheSis: Colonial Wounds/Decolonial Healings)". I want to use this as a perspective for interrogating the practice of art writing and the concepts art writing uses as it looks more closely at the colonial roots of differentiations such as "art" and "craft" – elaborated, for example, by Hamid Irbouh in his 2005 book, *Art in the Service of Colonialism: French Art Education in Morocco, 1912-1956* – showing in particular how it plays out in the current art writing discourse in South Africa. Here it might be important to point out that according to Mignolo, the decolonial programme is based not on a "decolonial mission" but on outlining a "decolonial option" which is "open to all who would like to embrace it"; this, he says, is "an option ready to work together with other decolonial projects, whether they consider decoloniality an option or not". Furthermore, turning towards "options" allows for an open practice with multiple perspectives.

In South Africa, there have been inspiring works and exhibitions in recent years which address the complex task of finding a decolonial framing for discussing art history. In 2010, the first Black curator of the Iziko South African National Gallery, Riason Naidoo, curated the exhibition *1910-2010: From Pierneef to Gugulective* which explicitly aimed to politicize art, as Nomusa Makhubu elaborates in her article "Open Debate: Ephemeral Democracies: Interrogating Commonality in South Africa" (2013), in response to which the South African White conservative tabloid *Art Times* opened its May 2010 issue with an article by Lloyd Pollak declaring, "SANG's reputation trashed for 2010 show" (discussed by Sharlene Khan in "But What's All Dis Here Talkin' 'Bout?" [2011]). In 2012, the South African curator Nontobeko Ntombela curated the exhibition *A Fragile Archive*, which restaged South African artist Gladys Mgudlandlu's commercial exhibition at the *Contact* magazine boardroom in Cape Town in 1961 (fig. 2). The artist was acclaimed as the "first" Black woman artist to enter the art market (critically discussed in Ntombela's MA thesis, *A Fragile Archive: Refiguring | Rethinking | Reimagining | Re-presenting Gladys Mgudlandlu*, Wits School of Arts, 2013). Acknowledging artists and disciplines that have been written out of art history is one of the first moves in liberating and inspiring an art writing that draws on local practices of aestheSis. The exhibition *History Will Break Your Heart* (2015), by artist Kemang Wa Lehulere, presented paintings by Gladys Mgudlandlu and Ernest Mancoba, as well as recorded interviews with Wa Lehulere's aunt, who remembers seeing these murals as a child when visiting Mgudlandlu's house in Gugulethu in 1971; she was asked by Wa Lehulere to recreate Mgudlandlu's drawings from memory and a video documented the excavation of these murals (fig. 3).

Another example would be the text, sound installation, and performance series *1000 Ways of Being* (2010) by Donna Kukama, who rereads Joseph Conrad's novel *Heart of Darkness*, unearthing the sexual desire for the "other" as a subtext of colonial oppression; or Sharlene Khan's *Nervous Conditions* (2015), which enacts the uncontainable anger of women of colour between paranoia in overdrive and overdramatization, leaving the viewer feeling something between perplexity and guilt (fig. 4); or Sikhumbuzo Makandula's performance series *Mission; Imagination in a Troubled Space; Part of the History* (2016), which stages rituals for exorcizing the violent history of the colonial settlers of Grahamstown (fig. 5), which is named after the British commander John Graham, who is said to have used "a proper degree of terror" to fight the indigenous amaXhosa during the colonial expropriation of South Africa.

In this context, it is important to point out that art writing in South Africa continues to be dominated by White writers and academics who still take issue with the need to re-write art history. The need for "deschooling" in their eyes is, similarly to Europe, framed mostly in the context of art school and artistic practices. What I am interested in here, however, is thinking in terms of *decolonial options* which aim at undoing the foundationalism of Western art education and interrogating how it informs the production of criticism, judgement, assessment, and dissemination of art in the former colonies, which have also brought about the hegemony of the Europeanized canon. The forms taught in art education are implicitly present as a "hidden curriculum" and are rooted in the European conventions of teaching art appreciation and looking at art. Art writing is evaluated as "acceptable" according to a hegemonic globalized discourse shaped by the Western/European history of teaching and disseminating knowledge about aesthetics, art history, and art education.

This discussion is also about staking claims in discourse – which keeps coming up in South Africa, where the conservative reliance on European art teaching is upheld by White academics. The issue is being tackled by the collective Black Mark: Collective Critical Thought (BMCCT), whose members – Khwezi Gule, Same Mdluli, Nontobeko Ntombela, Londiwe Langa, and Tiffany Mentoor – last year organized the "Visual Arts Symposium eMonti" at Walter Sisulu University, where curators, artists, and lecturers discussed these questions. In June of this year, in an article published in the newspaper *The City Press*, Lwandile Fikeni questioned the curatorial practices of Prof. Anitra Nettleton, a White academic who has been considered an "expert" on South African art for many decades but who keeps Black academics from doing curatorial work – until the recent exhibition *Black Modernisms in South Africa (1940-1990)*, which Nettleton curated at the Wits Arts Museum (April 2016). Black curators and academics, with degrees from established universities, had been asked to complete minor tasks such as writing up biographies; then at the last minute they were added to the exhibition credits. To discuss this example of the tokenist use of curators of colour, the BMCCT convened the public panel discussion "Black Artists | White Labels" at The Point of Order gallery in Johannesburg. The public had kept silent about these issues, although they have been raised since the early 2000s, reaching a peak with Sharlene Khan's article "Doing it for Daddy" in *Art South Africa* (August 2006). Being in opposition means not only that avenues of discourse are blocked, but also that little notice is taken when Black academics refuse to contribute to publications because they do not wish to be used as tokens – as when Khwezi Gule and Sharlene Khan refused to contribute to the four-volume work *The Visual Century: South African Art in Context 1907–2007* (2011), which continued the tradition of a largely White art history writing in South Africa.

It seems necessary to keep voicing disagreement and to find ways to confront what appears to have become a normalized, pacified discourse. Moreover, art writing needs to be disturbed and new approaches must be found, for both criticism and other forms of writing, that are concerned with unearthing invisible contributions made by counter-hegemonic discourses to global art movements.

When it comes to the question of *how* to raise these issues, I found two further readings helpful. In her latest book, *Willful Subjects*, Sara Ahmed develops the practice of "not-philosophy": "To be doing *not philosophy* is a way of framing one's relation to philosophy albeit in apparently negative terms. *Not philosophy* is practiced by those who are not philosophers and aims to create room within philosophy for others who are not philosophers." It's a wilful practice of reading and writing, not only as not-philosophers practice it. More crucially, it is about "making the 'not' an object of thought"; as Ahmed goes on to point out, the wilfulness of saying "no" to the opinion and judgement of others is what people do who are judged as being "not", implied as being "not human": "not being white, not being male, not being straight, not being able-bodied". I think it is important to point out, too, that wilfulness here is *not* a reaction but rather is a potential for other ways of understanding and performing what it means to be able to act. I became aware of this concept from Sharlene Khan's PhD thesis on "Postcolonial Masquerading" (Goldsmiths College, University of London, 2014), where she discusses it as an "important critical aesthetic tool in black feminist and decolonialising discourses in postcolonial societies". The other source I'd like to thread in here, together with the "not" in wilful thinking and reading, the study of texts, and the reflective use of language as a philosophic activity, is a short passage from Igor Zabel's text "The Soil In Which Art Grows": "Sometimes, observing all the commotion and discord of the art world, which seems at times to hover somewhere in its own illusory reality, remote from ordinary real life, I ask myself if it makes any sense at all to be part of it. And I always tell myself that it does. This entire jumble is the soil from which art sprouts up. Everything in it that is bad or unpalatable is, perhaps, the price that must be paid for everything extraordinary and brilliant this world is able to give and produce."

Without settling the question of whether "it makes any sense at all to be part of it", Zabel speaks in the paragraph before this about the obvious imbalance of power, exclusion, and restricted access: the whole circus of the international art scene where you "physically feel the dividing lines and hierarchies that crisscross this world; you can see how, besides that which is public and open to everyone, there is also something hidden and closed; you can feel the centres of power and the conflicts between them, but also the peripheral regions and their petty scheming". Which, however, is interrupted by the short moments when someone "stops before an artwork" and suggests that these "moments of revelation and sudden captivation" could maybe eclipse all that.

But is it, then, a choice of being part of "it" or not? It is not only about the way one decides to contribute, to write, to discuss, to debate, or to engage in any of these forums – framing the "how" in "being part of it"? Which brings me to the last bit I want to share with you.

Over the past few years, I have found myself in a cyclicity of thought, which I hope to think of as a different sort of "study" or as another possible aspect of a practice of "not". I kept consciously engaging in recurring processes, in cyclical ways of engaging with text and writing, note-taking and elaborating. At times, I would be surprised by the notes I had written, realizing how suddenly something I thought was important was forgotten. Then I'd go back to read more. Other times, I'd take up texts which I had read and annotated, underlined and worked through. Sometimes, when these texts crossed my way in other contexts and I read them again, something different resonated. I would read a passage and understand it one way, and another time understand it differently.

This kind of repetition in my own process of writing brought me to look at the way fiction conveys theory, and I found books such as *Critical Fictions: The Politics of Imaginative Writing*, edited by Philomena Mariani. Following from this, I decided this year to attend a programme in creative writing at UCKAR (University Currently Known As Rhodes) in South Africa.

Engaging in creative writing and discussing the work with others, I was surprised to learn things about my own writing, desires in writing which I was not aware of, and at the same time stuff came up which had been silent. I was surprised to see how much I tried to seem knowledgeable and informed in my writing. I realized that I had tried to distance myself from the "imperfect" German my Palestinian father speaks and that becoming an editor and writer to craft well-versed sentences was part of this. My writing reveals how I have tried to get rid of an imagined "lack" which comes with my "mixed" cultural identity, while the Arab language is virtually absent in my voice. Also, I found that I had been exerting a lot of control, instead of opening up to intuitive and emotive processes and allowing for a voice in my writing.

This brings me to the chapter "Towards a New Consciousness" in Gloria Anzaldúa's book *Borderlands / La Frontera: The New Mestiza*, which spoke to me as it opens up towards a fluid identity, encouraging incoherence and abandoning the strict control over the form of how the self enters a text: "The ambivalence from the clash of voices results in mental and emotional states of perplexity. Internal strife results in insecurity and indecisiveness. The *mestiza's* dual or multiple personality is plagued by psychic restlessness."

Conflicting emotions come through the backdoor of language and settle on the text. I can't read what I have written so far without reading the same conflict – not that it is unresolved, there is no way to resolve anything here, but it remains silent, not addressed. For me this process is moving away from a controlled use of language towards a defective one which is closer to my life. Even if it doesn't sound right, or if it sounds like it lacks something, if it is repetitive, meandering, unclear and full of ambiguities. In Anzaldúa's chapter "A Tolerance For Ambiguity" I found a new sense of both ambiguity and being undecided, and I am going to quote the text here at length:

"These numerous possibilities leave *la mestiza* floundering in uncharted seas. In perceiving conflicting information and points of view, she is subjected to a swamping of her psychological borders. She has discovered that she can't hold concepts or ideas in rigid boundaries. The borders and walls that are supposed to keep the undesirable ideas out are entrenched habits and patterns of behavior; these habits and patterns are the enemy within. Rigidity means death. Only by remaining flexible is she able to stretch the psyche horizontally and vertically. *La mestiza* constantly has to shift out of habitual formations; from convergent thinking, characterized by movement away from set patterns and goals and toward a more whole perspective, one that includes rather than excludes.

"The new *mestiza* copes by developing a tolerance for contradictions, a tolerance for ambiguity. … She learns to juggle cultures. She has a plural personality, she operates in a pluralistic mode – nothing is thrust out, the good the bad and the ugly, nothing rejected, nothing abandoned. Not only does she sustain contradictions, she turns the ambivalence into something else."

This passage resonates with me as it points towards what needs to be unlearned, away from habits of thinking, of reasoning, of trying to relate to established thought, abandoning the need to reference or the urge to measure up to imagined standards. To realize that there's a voice in theory writing which represents something other than what's written – a desire that co-creates. And instead, learning to allow for a form of writing which happens when urgent issues are addressed, learning to listen to one's voices and focusing on them, and to elaborate this mode of writing. For me, this is a decolonial option.

Let me close with a poem by the Serbian writer Vasko Popa titled "A Wise Triangle", which speaks about this issue in a different way:

Once upon a time there was a triangle
It had three sides
The fourth it kept hidden
In its burning center

By day it climbed its three peaks
And admired its center
At night it rested
In one of its three angles

Each dawn it watched its three sides
Turn into three fiery wheels
And vanish in the blue of never return

It took its fourth side
Embraced it and broke it three times
To hide it again in its old place

And again it had only three sides

And again it climbed each day
To its three peaks
And admired its center
While at night it rested
In one of its angles

Being currently in the process of learning to write in a new way, I read this poem as the recurring work of the writer: building a frame and knocking it down, flinging bones at empty rooms and listening to its echo.

This letter, too, is an attempt to establish communication with its readers and an invitation to engage in different readings and possibilities of engagement.

Greetings,
Fouad Asfour

Raluca Voinea

The Tranzitory Garden

Curator and art writer Raluca Voinea is the director of the tranzit.ro/ București art space. In her work she seeks to build and explore relationships between contemporary art and wider political and social concepts. Her essay looks at the ongoing urban gardening project *Tranzit Garden*, which she started as a way for the Bucharest art space to connect to the various communities in the area, and to the city itself, while engaging in current discussions about ecology. In her reflections on the garden as a place for learning about such values as patience and resilience, Voinea weaves subtle threads between *Tranzit Garden* and a number of environmentally focused works by Romanian artists and local initiatives; at the same time she places the project in the wider context of the recent political situation in Romania.

A mature tortoise (*Testudo graeca ibera*) recently arrived in *Tranzit Garden* (fig. 1), joining the stray cats and dogs, blackbirds, snails, pigeons, bees, and insects, which make up the fauna on the site. The tortoise moves slowly under leaves of greater celandine, eating the freshly planted lovage and hiding beneath a pile of straw. Staring at us, familiar bipeds, without curiosity, it is probably a pet someone dropped in our garden thinking it would have enough food and freedom here to survive. Its presence in the middle of Bucharest is not unusual, especially when we consider the way animals adapt to urban life at a time when humans are rapidly destroying their natural habitats.

Besides, it has become quite encouraging to see how quickly nature takes over urban ruins – which may be even more surprising in a city famous for its concrete deserts, pollution, and congested car traffic. A few years ago, naturalists and photographers started to observe a stretch of land that is becoming the Văcărești Nature Park,[1] a nature reserve of 183 hectares four kilometres south of central Bucharest (and just a ten-minute drive from the art space operated by tranzit.ro/ București). Located in a wetland on the site of a never-finished hydro-technical project initiated by the former socialist regime in 1986, Văcărești Park today hosts a diverse ecosystem – which has developed only in the past two decades – with over ninety bird species (mostly waterbirds), small mammals, some interesting reptiles, amphibians, and invertebrates, as well as several species such as otters, which are protected at the European level.

In 2014, in connection with the exhibition *Like a Bird*,[2] organized by the Budapest-based curators Maja and Reuben Fowkes at our Tranzit space, we took the Fowkeses and another thirty people (Bucharestians who don't dare be adventurous on their own in the city) on a field trip to the Văcărești Delta, as the area is popularly called (fig. 2). There, a local family – people who have lived there for many years in an improvised shelter – gave us a tour of the place and a ride in their makeshift boats on the Delta lakes. The gawky high-rises on the edge of the area, built during the real-estate boom of mid-2000s, now suddenly disappeared, as did the noise of the metropolis, with mobile phones the only indicators left to tell us what century we were in. The boys who had been raised in this little paradise, and were familiar with every inch of it, quietly paddled the boats, interrupting the unearthly silence only to point to some bird they had noticed. Surrounded by reeds, water, and sky, we didn't even feel like intruders; we realized and accepted our limits as urban colonizers and for a few long minutes lost our sense of time and place, guilt and responsi-

---

1 See the park's website, http://parcnaturalvacaresti.ro/english/ (accessed July 1, 2016).
2 *Like a Bird: Avian Ecologies in Contemporary Art*, May 9–June 4, 2014; see http://ro.tranzit.org/en/exhibition/bucuresti/2014-05-09/like-a-bird. In connection with the exhibition, the curators organized the *River School Bucharest*, which included a trip to the Bucharest Delta, a lecture by artist and ecologist Ursula Biemann, and a trip to the Danube Delta. See http://ro.tranzit.org/en/lecture/0/2014-05-09/river-school-bucharest (both links accessed July 1, 2016).

bility, pressure and urgency, depression and anguish – all the emotional pairs we had got used to from reading the daily news about our planet. The Văcărești Delta itself has made it into the mainstream news in recent years (publicity may be its best chance of survival), but even so, it is a place outside and beyond the news.

In a way, that's what the tranzit.ro/ București art space promised when we first found it: a sanctuary for contemporary art as another – a freer and more positive – way of looking at life (fig. 3). Positioned just off-centre, not far from the House of the People but just below the line where the city was profoundly changed in the 1980s, in an area that escaped socialist systemization, where a lot of the old city can still traced in its organically developed shapes, the space at Gazelei 44 (a street bearing the name of an exotic and agile animal) seemed hidden by a maze of overgrown thorns, derelict but with a lot of potential (something so defining of Bucharest as a whole that it hurts when most of it is not realized). In a city so desperate for profit that most of its vacant spaces go to ruin by staying empty rather than being used temporarily, with contemporary art stranded either in damp basements or fancy villas, the Gazelei space lured us with promises of a temporary autonomous zone where art and artists could, at least for a while, catch their breath.

Almost immediately, *Tranzit Garden* became a buffer zone between the city and the gallery, disrupting the regular rhythm of contemporary art viewers while drawing a new audience that gradually discovered the extremely permeable definitions of an art space. We opened the Tranzit space in 2012, after the end of *documenta 13*, which curator Carolyn Christov-Bakargiev had specifically dedicated to "all the animate and inanimate makers of the world".[3] That exhibition had delved into new animisms, presented scientific and artistic research that blurred the borders between art and life, and showcased, among other works, many artistic projects related to gardens and nature. So there we were, pretty far from Kassel and even further from the mainstream art scene, with one foot in the buzzy zeitgeist and the other in our local emergencies, political crises, historical oblivion, social injustice, and the precariousness of the artistic context. The garden was still hardly more than a plot of soil that had only just been cleared, dug up and planted with a few roses and tulips, a place where people could chill and smoke a cigarette while looking at art and talking politics.

In the autumn of 2013, talking politics took a new turn. For the first time since 1990, the city's wide boulevards were spontaneously occupied by protesters condemning the gold-mining project at Roșia Montană, in north-western Romania, which at the time was close to being approved by the government. For several weeks there was an open space where apathy, unvarnished consumerism, and discouragement left room for discussions

---

3   From the information page of the *documenta 13* website, http://d13.documenta.de (accessed July 1, 2016).

about ecology, the appropriation of the city by its citizens, direct democracy, and desires for the future. Not that it lasted long. The radically opposing agendas that had been put aside by the different groups for the sake of a very particular objective (later partly attained) returned to their previous state of conflict. But at least the positions had become much clearer and more visible: radical leftists and anarchists, moderate leftists, European leftists, nationalists, the Orthodox Church, extreme nationalists, neo Legionnaires,[4] monarchists – all found a platform and a stage in the Roșia Montană protests; they all, for a very short time, marched side by side and gained strength from the protests. Unfortunately, some gained more strength than others and voices linking the gold-extraction project, and other environmental disasters, to neoliberalism grew fainter and were easily dismissed.

Intermezzo 1
In their video *All That Is Solid Melts into Air* (2012–2013), artists Mona Vătămanu and Florin Tudor present footage they took at Roșia Montană and around Roșia Poieni, where copper and gold deposits have been mined since the 1970s (fig. 4). The area became a dead landscape after cyanide waste was discharged into a lake that had engulfed an entire village and threatened to spill over its dam. In Vătămanu and Tudor's film, close-ups of the landscape are accompanied by a monotonous voice reciting verses from the Book of Revelation and the soundtrack of NASA's *Voyager Mission to Jupiter*. We are thus suspended in liquefied time, when the Apocalypse has already happened, leaving behind sterile ground, like the surface of a different planet. The film begins and ends with two anti-corporate and anti-colonial speeches, by Salvador Allende of Chile and Thomas Sankara of Burkina Faso, both of whom were assassinated because of their political positions. In the Capitalocene Age,[5] soil is red from cyanide and blood, voices of dissent are silenced, and the tubby noise of space travel seems to offer the only salvation. Coming in the middle of the activist campaign against the Canadian company that was planning to

4 The Legionnaires were members of the far-right movement and political party known as the Iron Guard, active in Romania in the 1930s. Also called the Legion of the Archangel Michael, the movement strongly supported the Romanian Orthodox Church; today, its post-communist followers include a number of church figures.
5 The term has been proposed by Jason W. Moore, the coordinator of the World-Ecology Research Network, in response to ongoing discussions about the Anthropocene Age, the geological era we are supposedly living in now, which is defined by humanity's impact on the earth and its catastrophic consequences for the planet. See http://www.jasonwmoore.com/uploads/The_Capitalocene__Part_I__June_2014.pdf (accessed July 1, 2016).

extract gold from Roșia Montană, Vătămanu and Tudor's film conveyed the spectre of the mining enterprise that had already existed for decades on the site, which was not much different in its effects, except that it was a national Romanian company that had done the mining. Ever since the industrial revolution, the air has been getting denser and denser from all the solids that have been melted into it, and socialist Romania was no exception. The artists are neither judging nor comparing; instead, they measure the space between present and past by focusing the camera on the empty, visually bleak but memory-laden landscape. It is the same approach they used in an earlier video, *Văcărești* (2006), in which they used string and wooden sticks to mark out the shape of the former Văcărești Monastery, which had been demolished by Ceaușescu, on the same abandoned field in Bucharest that now promises to become a green paradise. In both videos, the land appears to be the paradoxical witness and survivor of regimes that disregard it and abuse it (fig. 5).

The democratic exercise of using popular protest to stop a hugely devastating project seemed fantastically optimistic and created an important precedent. Just two years later, after a toxic fire burned down a Bucharest nightclub and killed almost sixty people, thousands of people took to the streets in October 2015 to protest lax public safety laws and the poor conditions of hospitals; they brought down the government in a single night. The fact that the subsequent technocrat government – put in place to satisfy the people's angry voice demanding that the dragon of corruption be slain, along with the entire political class – then proposed several cabinet ministers who had stored money away in offshore accounts and were the presidents of corporate cartels, well, that's another story. And the fact that the secret service and riot police were given even larger budgets may just be the local reflection of a global trend. Still, no need to let our victory be overshadowed by its aftermath.

Perhaps we should be content with small achievements and the illusion of popular power at times when the situation becomes unbearable – as a sign that the latent collective consciousness can be awaken and mobilized – and in the meantime, we should keep working in a way that gives more people reason for emancipatory mobilization.

So in February 2014, the first in a series of very depressing Februaries, we decided to follow Voltaire's advice and cultivate our garden as therapy against the impotence of art and philosophy when confronted by realpolitik. *Tranzit Garden*, although an enclosed territory and not the free and open space we dreamed of for the entire city, would be a fleeting and contingent Arcadia, a place for learning about time and patience, resilience and adaptation, serenity and commitment.

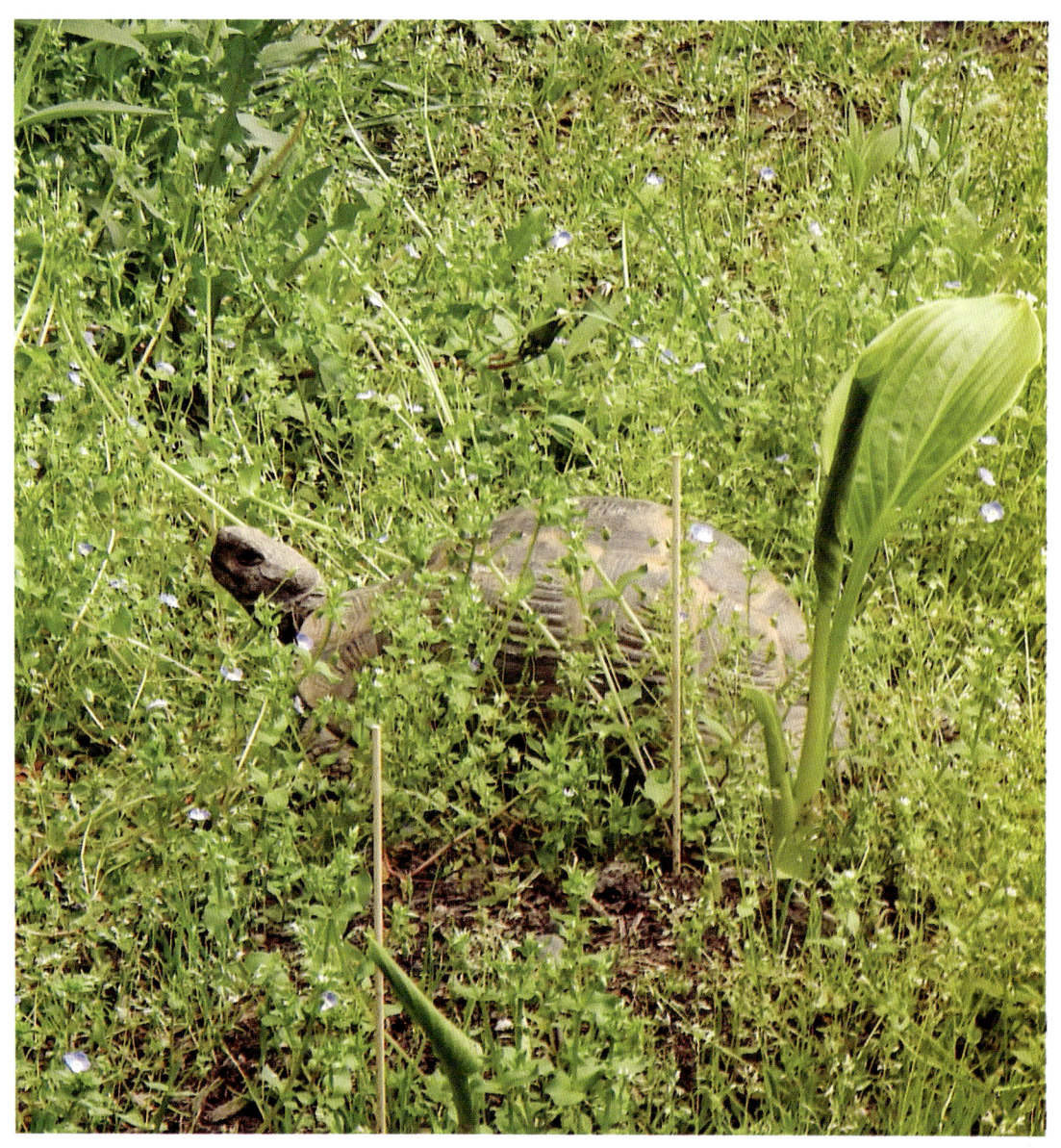

fig. 1

Tortoise in the *Tranzit Garden*, Bucharest, April 2016.

Photo by Raluca Voinea.

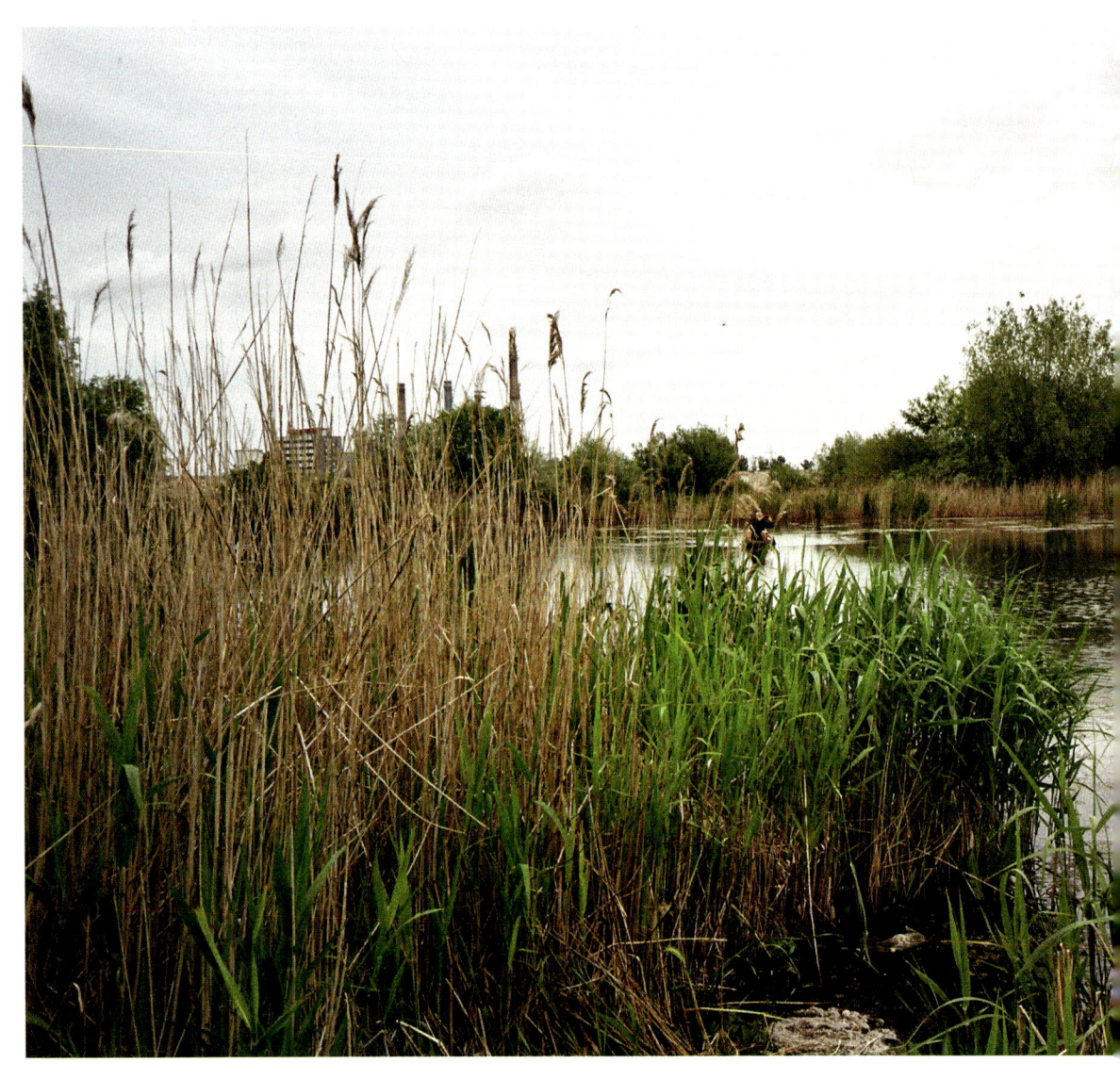

fig. 2

Văcărești Delta, Bucharest, May 2014.

Photo by Sânziana Șerbănescu.

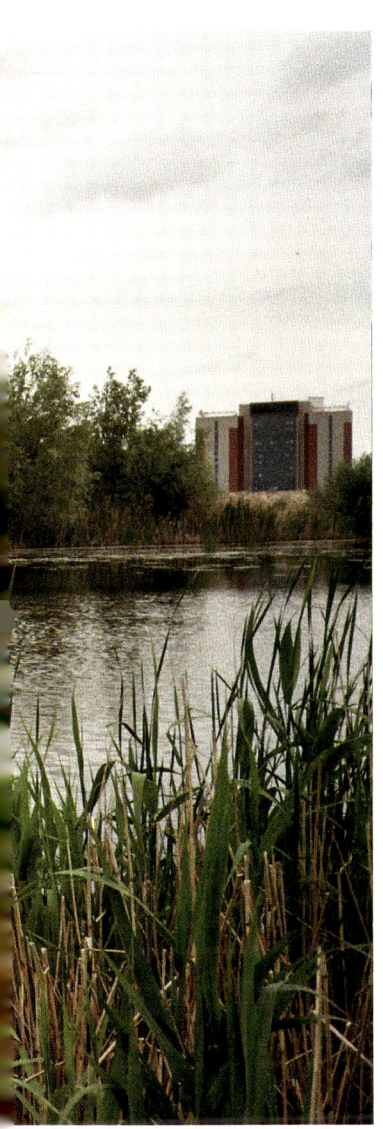
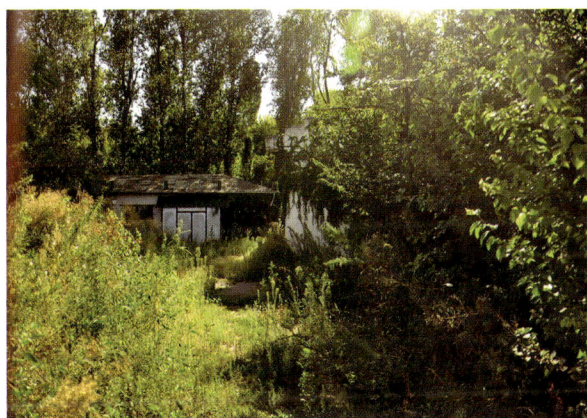

fig. 3

tranzit.ro/ București, first glimpse of the space, September 2012.

Photo by Eduard Constantin.

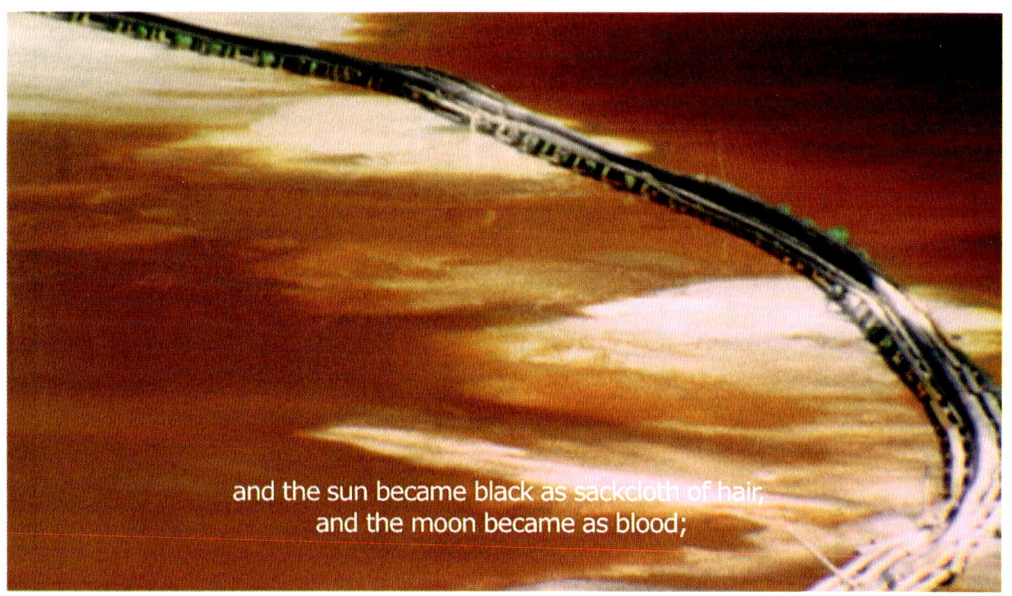

fig. 4

Mona Vătămanu and Florin Tudor, *All That Is Solid Melts into Air*, 2012–2013, video still.

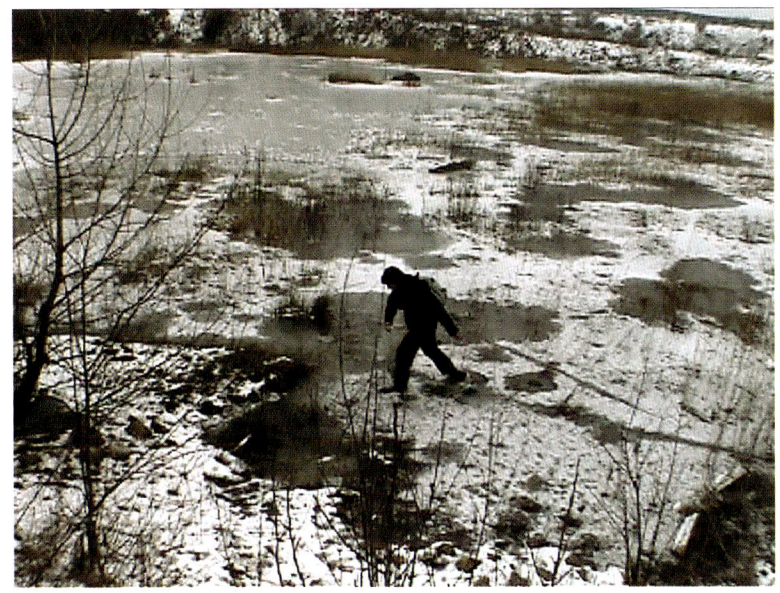

fig. 5

Mona Vătămanu and Florin Tudor, *Văcărești*, 2006, video still.

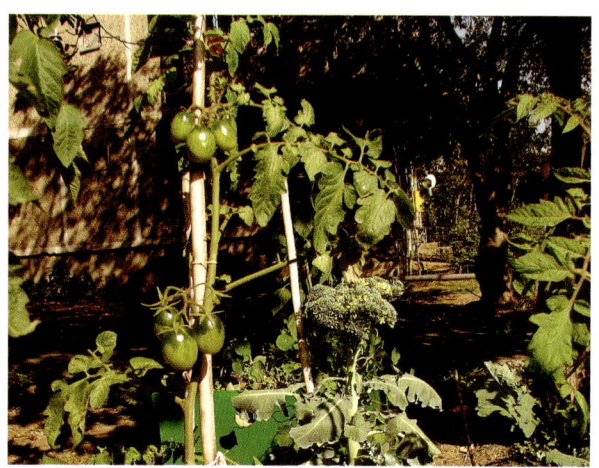
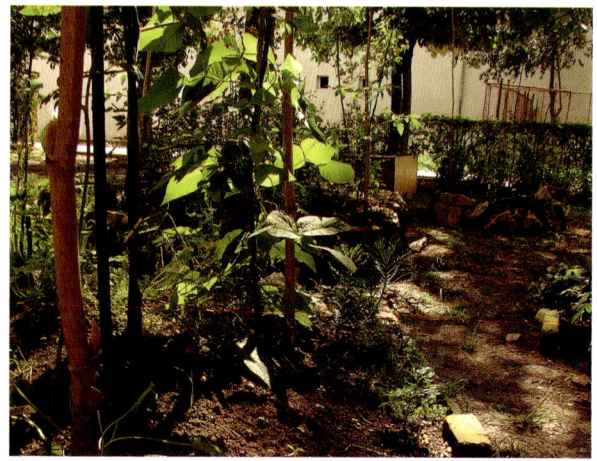
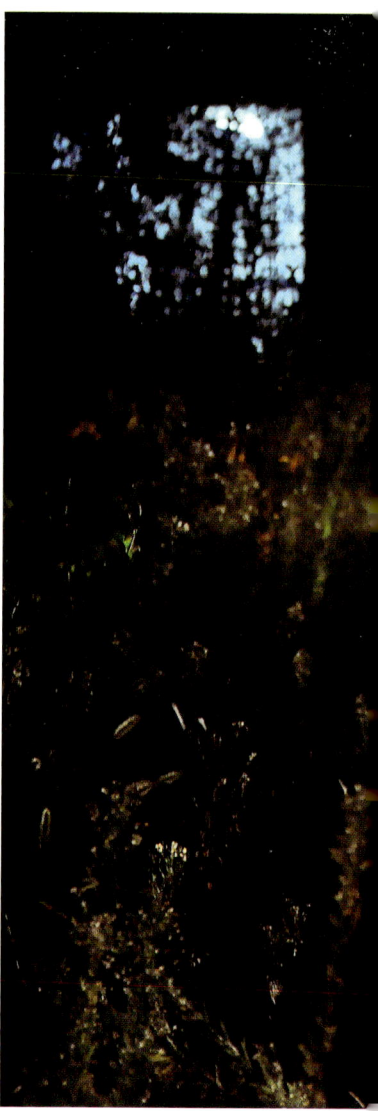

fig. 6

h.arta, *Free Urban Gardens*, Bucharest, 2013–present.

Photos by h.arta.

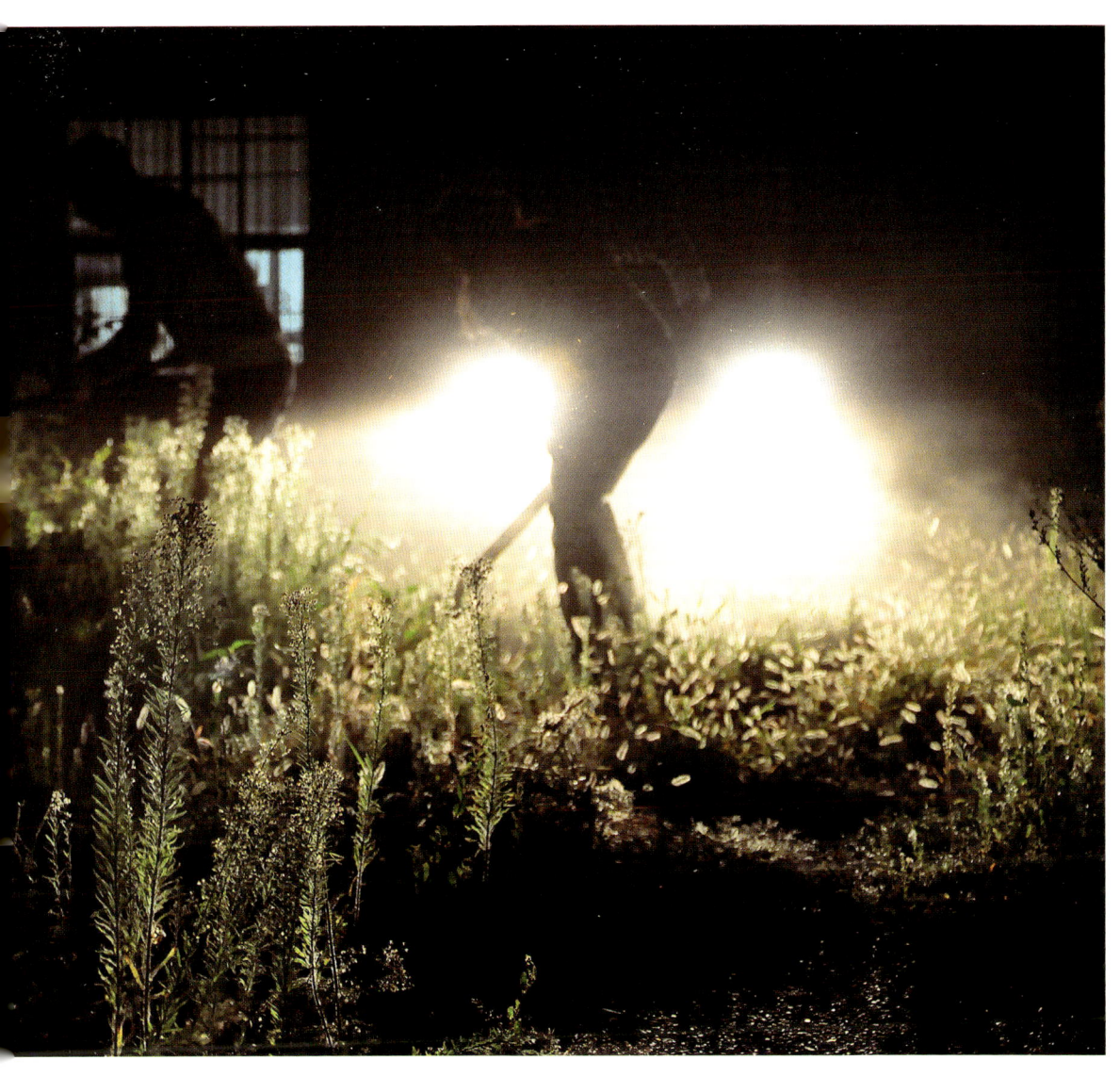

fig. 7

Tranzit Garden at night, Bucharest, September 2012.

Photo by Eduard Constantin.

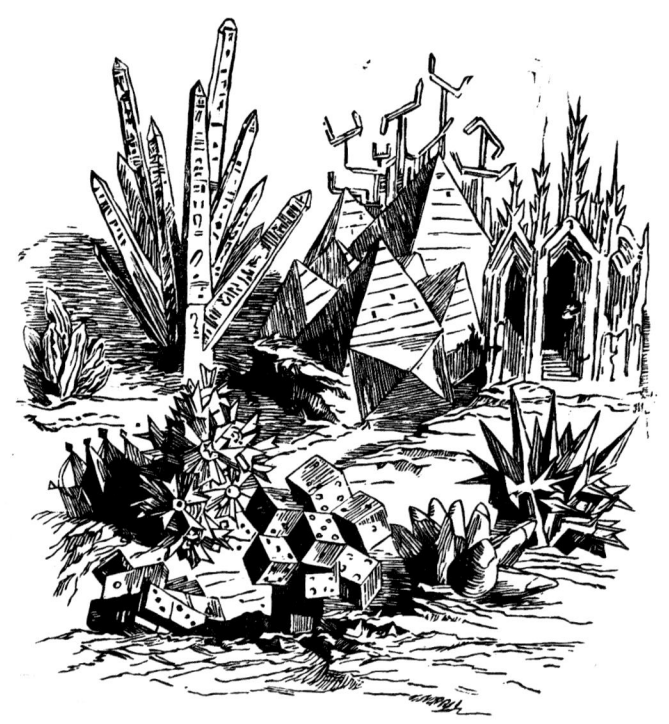

fig 8

Raluca Popa, *Paris Futur*, 2015, linocut,
edition of 12, signed, numbered, 76 cm x 56 cm.

Intermezzo 2

In 2013, the women artists collective h.arta started a permaculture project in Timisoara, *Free Urban Gardens*; they cultivated small plots around their block of flats, in areas of passage or apparent non-use. The ongoing project, while seldom presented as art, is part of their quest for alternative, ecological, and non-capitalistic forms of existence and economy; at the same time, it is a way to imagine independence and freedom in a city (and country) dominated by fences and the hunt for profit. By unconditionally offering the gardens to their neighbours, h.arta were also challenging the idea that the commons is not a viable method for consolidating communities; after three years, the gardens are still there, providing ordinary people, whether neighbours or strangers, with both vegetables and an excuse for socializing (fig. 6).

Tranzit Garden' proximity to the art space and the mix of backgrounds among the people who use it have determined its special character as a hybrid between a community urban garden built on the principles of permaculture[6] and a *locus amoenus*, "a pleasant place", where a person can dream of being outside the city, where the poplars in the back make a different murmur with every breeze, and in the moonlight every plant looks a little mysterious (fig. 7).

Tranzit Garden is not only a food garden and small community project; it is also a site of reflection on time and limits. As we count the years on the concentric lines of the tortoise shell, wait a few seasons until the heavily pruned poplars grow their leaves again, watch the seeds sprouting and transforming, the garden interrupts the accelerated pace of our lives; it requires us to stand still and observe (when we're not bending our backs over the soil, eyes and hands focused on specific tasks). It is also a continuous exercise in linguistics and botanical etymology. "To name is to possess," says writer Jamaica Kincaid, who evokes the ancient, indigenous plant names of Mesoamerica, which were later renamed by the colonizers and transformed into objects of aesthetic ritual; their initial medicinal uses were gradually forgotten, as their European names disconnected them from the soil, rendering them visual trophies.[7]

In Romania, the post-communist economic colonization led to the disappearance of farmers' markets and their replacement by supermarkets, where products from all over the world are found side by side. "The botan-

---

6   The permaculture workshops were held in collaboration with the local association InTranzitie, which launched several similar projects at the same time as *Tranzit Garden*, including gardens on the terrace of a public institution and in a public school. See their website, http://intranzitie.org/ (accessed July 1, 2016).

7   Jamaica Kincaid, "In the Garden: Flowers of Evil", *The New Yorker*, October 5, 1992, pp. 155–159.

The Tranzitory Garden

ical garden reinforced for me how powerful were the people who had conquered me; they could bring to me the botany of the world they owned," Kincaid wrote.[8] The Belgian, French, and Austrian supermarkets in Bucharest are our contemporary botanical gardens, displaying in their equalizing light, at any time of the year, garlic from China and artichokes from Argentina; meanwhile, for a few cents, local peasants selling their *garden patience* (*Rumex patientia*) and parsley on the sidewalks are harassed by police. Working in our garden meant learning again about local species, identifying them with their popular names, following the seasons by their cycles and planting schedules, and remembering the effort that goes into making each plant grow. At the same time, translating the names from Romanian into English has often indicated (temporally and geographically) distant genealogies, connecting us with other margins. The names of the *Jerusalem artichoke* (a root vegetable that can survive the long harsh winter and is harvested in February, when the rest of the garden is still dormant) and the *ghetto palm* (aka the *tree of heaven* or *ailanthus*, a tree that is omnipresent in every wild garden in Bucharest, growing in cracks of asphalt or among the ruins) are indicators not only of the colonial roots of the global economy but also nature's resilience in the face of urban conquest.

> *Intermezzo 3*
> For an exhibition at tranzit.ro/ București in 2015,[9] artist Raluca Popa produced an engraving based on a work by J. J. Grandville, the nineteenth-century French utopian illustrator. Grandville's original engraving, called *Paris Futur*, depicted a city of the future, where nature assumes architectural and mineral shapes, with obelisks and pyramids and Gothic arches. Popa brought Grandville's vision to the exhibition about Bucharest – a vision from a time when technological revolutions were still exciting the imagination – only to reveal an urban future that assembles the relics of antiquity in a desert landscape. "In copying nature, man has become its equal," Grandville wrote – but in anthropomorphising nature and submitting it to his will, man also ends by replacing nature altogether with man-made constructions (fig. 8).

Outside *Tranzit Garden*, the city is choking on the fumes of its own dystopian present, palm trees are exiled even from the ghettos, and the ghosts of high-rises tremble on developers' worktables, waiting to replace the old houses in the city centre. But if the present is grey, the future remains

---

8 Ibid., p. 158.
9 *Une autre cité* (April 16–May 30, 2015), which I curated; besides Popa, the two other participating artists were Carmen Acsinte and Olivia Mihălțianu. See http://ro.tranzit.org/en/exhibition/bucuresti/2015-04-16/une-autre-cite (accessed July 1, 2016).

undefined. From time to time, people go back to the streets and Roşia Montană is again heard in their slogans, a reminder of the only agenda shared by the post-1989 popular movements. A few more community urban gardens have appeared, and more and more people are growing tomatoes on their balconies and rejecting the city's plans to build blocks of flats and commercial pubs and restaurants in their public parks. Eventually, we sent the tortoise south, to its natural habitat in Dobruja, hoping that this vulnerable species would not become extinct.

Maja Fowkes and Reuben Fowkes

Cracks in the Planet

Geo-ecological Matter in Eastern European Art

Art historians and curators Maja Fowkes and Reuben Fowkes run the Budapest-based Translocal Institute for Contemporary Art, a research centre focused on Eastern European art and ecology. Their research explores the history of post-war Eastern European art, environmental art history, and the relationship between contemporary art and ecological thought – all issues that frame the present essay, which looks at how Eastern European artists address the kind of anthropogenic environmental change that today is seen as occurring on a geological scale. The authors examine the potential of contemporary art and the legacy of the Eastern European neo-avant-garde as part of the collective response to global environmental threats.

The art history of Eastern Europe has often been framed in political terms through an overarching emphasis on the way the communist ideology and the socialist experience have affected art practice, and while there have been attempts to reassess art-historical narratives in light of other criteria, such as gender, the environmental dimension in the art history of the region has been regularly overlooked. Nevertheless, environmental concerns have been a significant aspect of Eastern European art since the 1960s and are inseparable from its social and political history, exerting a decisive influence on artistic developments. This chapter considers specifically the engagements of Eastern European artists with anthropogenic environmental changes, which today are perceived to be occurring on a geological scale.

Two sizeable yet rather unremarkable stones were at the centre of an artistic action that took place in the summer of 1971 on the northern outskirts of Prague: the stones were wrapped in netting, hoisted onto the artist's shoulder, and carried along a path through a nondescript green landscape. The neutral and elemental character of the action, in which the mineral fragments of the Earth's crust were simply removed from their current position and transported on the artist's back to another outdoor location, is confirmed by the documentation: six photographs that sombrely depict the stages of the action, supplemented by a city map on which the route is marked (figs. 1–2). Carried out by Czech artist Petr Štembera (b. 1945), *Transposition of Stones* focused on the phenomenological apprehension of the natural landscape through astute bodily experience. Eschewing any hidden human-centred social interpretation, as was typical for much of Štembera's work, the action foregrounds direct physical encounters with the natural matter of the world. In this case the artist, who at the time used to describe his practice as ecological, was simply carrying rocks, feeling their weight on his back as he moved through the landscape. Privileging neither his body nor the stones, he merely acknowledged their coexistence; nevertheless, he was actively removing them from their original site.[1]

The unassuming stones, which the artist picked up in a green area of his home town, actually preserve in their structure the deep history of the place, revealing information about past geological epochs – in which, for instance, Prague's location was flooded by three primeval seas, with rock sediments reaching back 570 million years.[2] In fact, according to geologist Jan Zalasiewicz, stones can be understood as "a microcosm of the Universe" in that some of their atoms were part of the stardust produced by the Big Bang 13.7 billion years ago, while other atoms derived from super-

---

1 See Maja Fowkes, *The Green Bloc: Neo-avant-garde Art and Ecology under Socialism*, Central European University Press, New York and Budapest, 2015, p. 208.
2 See "Geological Conditions", in *Protected Areas of Prague*, ed. Jan Němec, Agency for Nature Conservation and Landscape Protection of the Czech Republic, 1997; available on the City of Prague's environmental information service, ENVIS, http://envis.praha-mesto.cz/rocenky/chruzemi/cr2_antx/chu-geol.htm (accessed January 17, 2016).

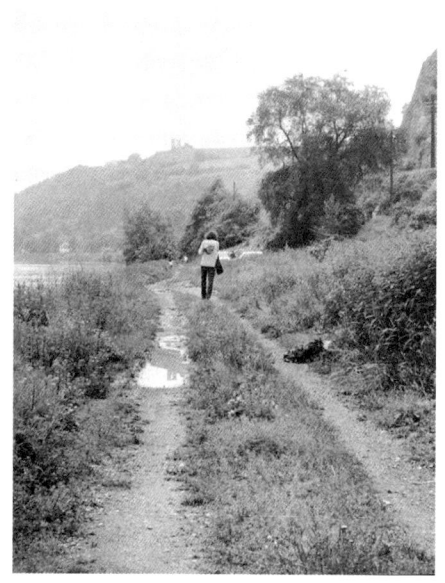

fig. 1

Petr Štembera, *Transposition of Stones*, outskirts of Prague, 1971, detail.

Courtesy of Petr Štembera.

novas and travelled "across the vastness of interstellar space, before they arrived in the cloud of dust and gas that was to become our Solar System".³ Stones have also endured the millions of years it took for the Earth's magma to cool and survived climatic variations, waves of extinction, the formation of continents, and the rise and fall of ocean levels, preserving in their layers the drama of planetary history long before humans stepped onto the stage.

From the time our species appeared on the planet, stones have been extracted, transported, and forcibly rearranged through relentless human activity. Furthermore, in recent decades, these interventions into the physical matter and natural processes of the Earth have accelerated to the extent that anthropogenic changes to the environment are now perceived to be happening on a geological scale. Acknowledging these new circumstances, a recent scientific initiative has proposed naming the current geological epoch the Anthropocene, or the Age of Humans. Significantly, rather than being "a mere global ecological crisis", the onset of the Anthropocene is seen to herald "a new geological regime of existence for the Earth and a new human condition".⁴

Attentiveness toward rocks, earth, mud, and the surface of the planet, with their deep history and immediate materiality, and an appreciation of the transformative perspective provided by the immensity of geological time, belonged to the shared pool of conceptual props that Eastern European neo-avant-garde artists drew from. This became evident around the watershed year of 1968, when worries about the environmental destruction of the planet were crystallizing, marking the beginning of a global ecological concern that has only intensified over the past half-century.

If we were to analyse the geological materials present in such art practices, what hidden sediments of Eastern European art history would they reveal? To what extent did engagement with planetary dimensions and Earthly matter provide artists with a way to sidestep the social and political circumstances of life under late socialism, and how distinctive a residue has it left in the layers of environmental art history? Additionally, how has the "Great Acceleration" of production, consumption, and technology since 1945, "whose impact on the Earth system is unambiguous",⁵ been reflected in the way contemporary artists have referred to geological processes in their work?

The rapid advance of technological achievement, epitomized by the space travel that enthralled the world at the dawn of the 1970s, opened new vistas for contemplating life on the small blue pearl of Planet Earth.

3   Jan Zalasiewicz, *The Planet in a Pebble: A Journey into Earth's Deep History*, Oxford University Press, Oxford, UK, and New York, 2010, p. 15.
4   Clive Hamilton, Christophe Bonneuil, and François Gemenne, "Thinking the Anthropocene", in *The Anthropocene and the Global Environmental Crisis: Rethinking Modernity in a New Epoch*, ed. Clive Hamilton, Christophe Bonneuil, and François Gemenne, Routledge, London and New York, 2015, p. 4.
5   Ibid., p. 1.

Technological optimism, however, was tempered by new anxieties as it became clear that, at present, "human influence on all disciplines of life is tremendous" while at the same time "enormous energy production in almost all areas has led to the destruction of the natural landscape". This is how Polish art critic Jerzy Ludwiński (1930–2000) voiced his concern about the ecological predicament of the time when he spoke to a gathering of neo-avant-garde artists at the Wrocław Symposium in 1970, warning that "in the era of flights to the moon, we should pay particular attention to protecting what remains of the Earth". Interestingly, in his influential paper he also hinted at the link between the newly felt environmental awareness and the spread of dematerialized art practices, emphasizing that in a time of "material and technological giganticism" it is "important to create as little as possible".[6]

Another member of the Wrocław neo-avant-garde circle was the artist Natalia LL (b. 1937), who articulated her own distinctive approach to the natural environment by problematizing the interactions of geographical phenomena with the human body. In her performative work *Points of Support*, from 1978, she extended her enquiries to a cosmic level, using her own body to reflect the constellations of the night sky onto the surface of the Earth (fig. 3). Through a sequence of body poses she reproduced eighteen celestial formations of the Northern Hemisphere, from Andromeda and Cassiopeia to Orion and Ursa Minor, as points impressed on the ground. The work, which was carried out in the natural environment of the Pieniny National Park in Western Poland, was accompanied by a statement in which Natalia LL addressed the role of art, stressing its ability to access subjective realms and thereby uncover the "underlying principles of reality". Entering into a communication between two realms – the macrocosm of the universe and the microcosm of personal experience – while limited by the awareness of her own "physical finitude", the artist explained: "I live on Earth and take in everything from a specific angle which characterizes my presence in the Universe." In this action, composed of "ephemeral touches bestowed on the ground", the artist turns the Earth into a screen on which the boundlessness of the "infinite Cosmos" is projected and made tangible.[7]

Rather than embracing the technological optimism of the period and, for instance, engaging with cybernetics, which was a popular option among Polish artists who were drawn to the idea of "shaping a new, 'neo-technical' reality in close collaboration with scientists",[8] Natalia LL chose a different approach. Her dematerialized work was closer to that of

---

6   Jerzy Ludwiński, "Wrocław '70", in *Notes from the Future of Art: Selected Writings of Jerzy Ludwiński*, ed. Magdalena Ziółkowska, Van Abbemuseum, Eindhoven, 2007, p. 35.

7   Natalia LL, "Points of Support", in *Permafo 1970–1981*, ed. Anna Markowska, Wrocław Contemporary Museum, Wrocław, 2013, pp. 260-261.

8   Joanna Kordjak-Piotrowska, "Art and Cybernetics in the Long Sixties", in *Cosmos Calling! Art and Science in the Long Sixties*, ed. Joanna Kordjak-Piotrowska and Stanisław Welbel, exh. cat., Zachęta National Gallery of Art, Warsaw, 2014, pp. 66-67.

the OHO Group in Slovenia, where Milenko Matanović (b. 1947) arranged candles in the Zarica Valley near Kranj so they reflected actual constellations in the night sky (fig. 4).[9] OHO's more ontological cosmology, however, was rooted in the countercultural drive to achieve unity with the universe through an exchange of cosmic energies, while Natalia LL was primarily concerned with posing epistemological questions about the degree to which the vastness of the universe may be comprehended.

It was not just artists and critics who were enthused by the age of space travel in the 1960s, but also scientists, including those in the field of geology who could now add another stream to their research – astrogeology. By applying the methods of terrestrial stratigraphy, which studies the succession of rock layers to establish a geological timescale, astrogeologists were gaining new insight into the age of celestial bodies. As a consequence of the space programme, geologists were encouraged "to adopt a fully cosmic perspective on Planet Earth", in the light of which the history of the Earth was reconceived "as one specific case in a much wider set of divergent planetary histories".[10] In parallel, artistic practices corresponded to the developments in scientific thinking that made cosmic realms more palpable and increasingly cast doubt on the previously assumed centrality of human beings to planetary history.

The specific conditions of socialist Eastern Europe presented challenges to artists that were as much of an economic and practical character as they were ideological, creating particular institutional settings that also shaped artists' approach to ecological issues. In Poland, artistic engagement with the natural environment was thus framed primarily by the context of regular open-air symposia, which were organized by regional industrial plants in collaboration with local artist associations. These diverse gatherings, which are now acknowledged as having provided "the main form of official art patronage" in Poland during the period of late socialism, covered a wide spectrum of artistic interests.[11] Numerous artworks produced during these events had overtly ecological concerns, which in some cases formed the focus of entire editions, such as the 1974 Osieki Symposium, which took as its theme "Artists and Earth 400 000 km Afar".[12] Under the actual conditions of socialist Poland in the 1970s, and in contrast to many countries in the Eastern Bloc, it was generally possible to broach environmental problems within the institutional structures of the art world as long as the message did not slip into overtly political territory.

[9] See Fowkes, *The Green Bloc*, pp. 94–95.
[10] Martin J. S. Rudwick, *Earth's Deep History: How It Was Discovered and Why It Matters*, University of Chicago Press, Chicago and London, 2014, pp. 289, 291.
[11] Sylwia Serafinowicz, "About the *Concept Art* Exhibition and the Osieki *Plein-Air*", in *The Wild West: A History of Wrocław's Avant-Garde,* ed. Dorota Monkiewicz, exh. cat., Wrocław Contemporary Museum and Zachęta National Gallery of Art, Wrocław and Warsaw, 2015, p. 85.
[12] See *Avant-garde in Plein-Air: Osieki and Łazy 1963–1981*, ed. Ryszard Ziarkiewicz, Museum of Koszalin, Koszalin, 2008, pp. 248–259.

The situation was very different in Czechoslovakia, where the arrival of Soviet tanks in 1968 "brought a definitive end to the blossoming" of culture experienced there in the 1960s; in the wave of "normalization" that followed, "harsh censorship" was reintroduced that overturned civic freedoms.[13] As a result, neo-avant-garde art had to relocate to the "seclusion of the private alternative spaces or nature", with the latter option proving especially attractive "as it was easy to avoid the gaze of secret police agents and informers".[14] Notably, while artists in Poland were officially invited to do their work in the countryside, in Czechoslovakia they were seeking refuge from surveillance by the authorities. Artists who were interested in issues relating to nature and ecology also faced almost insurmountable problems in gaining access to information about the state of the environment; consequently, they had to rely completely on their own inclinations and personal contacts.

In Slovakia, the artist Rudolf Sikora (b. 1946) was instrumental in introducing discussion about environmental concerns to the Bratislava art scene in the 1970s, both through the meetings he initiated, known as "Tuesdays", where he and his colleagues, as well as other "unofficial" intellectuals, would debate these issues,[15] and through his own conceptual art practice, which drew strongly from a wide range of Earth sciences, including geography, geology, astronomy, and ecology. Among the influential sources for the artist's work was also a precious *samizdat* version of a Polish translation of a Club of Rome report on the environment.[16] The study, published under the title *Limits to Growth* in 1972, disconcertingly concluded that if "the present growth trends in world population, industrialization, pollution, food production, and resource depletion continue unchanged, the limits to growth on this planet will be reached sometime within the next one hundred years".[17] Although the study's algorithmically processed scientific data may have been partial and its methods of prediction questionable, its daunting conclusion, that the Earth's capacities were limited, was groundbreaking.

The troubling prospect facing humanity in the new circumstances revealed by science was addressed in a number of Sikora's works from the early 1970s. For instance, in *Time...Space I*, from 1971, he dealt with the

---

13   Pavlína Morganová, *Czech Action Art: Happenings, Actions, Events, Land Art, Body Art and Performance Art behind the Iron Curtain*, Karolinum Press, Charles University, Prague, 2014, pp. 23–24.
14   Ibid.
15   See Jiří Valoch, "Rudolf Sikora: Conceptual Thinking in Changing Times", in *Rudolf Sikora: Against Myself*, ed. Helena Musilová, National Gallery, Prague, 2006, pp. 7–36.
16   The Club of Rome was founded in April 1968 by a small international group of professionals from the fields of diplomacy, academia, and civil society to discuss the prevalence of short-term thinking and concerns regarding the unlimited consumption of resources in an increasingly interdependent world. For more information, see the club's website, www.clubofrome.org (accessed March 18, 2016).
17   *The Limits to Growth: A Report for the Club Of Rome's Project on the Predicament of Mankind*, ed. Donella H. Meadows et al., Earth Island Limited, London, 1972, p. 23.

relation between the temporal and spatial dimensions through six images that, if we follow the white arrows on them, take us on a journey from the universe, to galaxies and the solar system, to Planet Earth and humans. The textual key beneath the images presented scientific facts about the size of universe, the distance between stars, and the age of the Earth, as well as data about the history of life on the planet. With regard to the human element, Sikora noted population numbers in the past and present and predictions for the future. However, there are also entries that elude the usual scientific categories, introducing more experiential notions, such as work, love, and courage, as well as injustice, cruelty, selfishness, war, poverty, fanaticism, and constant conflict among people.[18] These respond to the simultaneous recognition that social justice, economic development, and personal well-being are inseparable from ecological issues and all have a fundamental impact on the environment.

Following this realization, Sikora proclaimed that *Earth Must Not Become a Dead Planet*, a warning that served as the title of a work he made in 1972, in which six elongated graphic sheets were divided into three sections, of which the bottom and top one were the same, while the middle one changed through the succession of the leaves (fig. 5). The bottom sections contained textual elements that read: *sial, sima, crofesima, nifesima*, and *nife* – geological terms that describe the successive layers of the Earth's crust and core. A similar formula is repeated in the upper sections, with the printed words progressing through the layers of the atmosphere, from the lower troposphere to the outer exosphere, which borders space. Thus, Sikora presents a conceptual cross-section of Planet Earth, with its deep history hidden in its geological layers and atmospheric blanket, enabling him to establish the apparently stable temporal–spatial components of the planet's dimensions.

What happens in the middle sections of the prints is of a different order, conveying the story of the development of human civilization as told through the history of architecture. It begins with the megaliths of Stonehenge, after which come the Egyptian pyramids, followed by the ruins of a Greek temple; next in line are Gothic cathedrals, which are succeeded by modern high-rises, some with cranes still attached to them. Tellingly, the final image of the series, rather than continuing the progress of architectural achievements, is a nuclear mushroom cloud. Clearly articulating the danger posed by our own unprecedented development, the work also demonstrates an awareness of the human potential for self-destruction as encapsulated in nuclear technology. A red exclamation mark added to the final print further accentuates the artist's warning about the risky path our civilization is pursuing. On closer inspection, we see that on all the prints the word *sial*, referring to the topmost layer of the Earth's crust, on which human civilization has left its mark, is written in a different shade to the rest, while in the final print the colour variation also applies to the first

---

18   See Fowkes, *The Green Bloc*, pp. 177–179.

layer of the atmosphere. By depicting the human-produced changes to the geological and atmospheric layers of Earth, Sikora gives visual form to the profound idea that humans have usurped natural processes to become geological agents. Some thirty years later, geologists have come to a similar conclusion.

Living and working in Bratislava in the normalization era, Sikora refused to be bound by the very specific social and political circumstances, attuning his thinking instead to the vaster coordinates of time and space. Cosmic escapism, a well-known phenomenon in the Slovak art scene of the 1970s,[19] was of a different nature in Sikora's work, however, since although he pointed to the incongruity between thinking on a cosmic scale and the pettiness of the normalization system, he remained firmly within a scientific frame of reference. Convincingly arguing that "the damage to ecological balance would affect the entire world" because "devastation knows no borders",[20] he implicitly commented on the fact that forcibly keeping the Iron Curtain running across the European continent was not going to change this prospect.

The Slovene artist Marko Pogačnik (b. 1944) also developed his practice in the upswing of conceptual art, political protest, countercultural experiment, and global ecology that shook the world around 1968. As one of the core members of OHO,[21] he participated in many of the group's investigations into natural processes and states of consciousness, and he was also one of the initiators of the Šempas Family commune in the Slovene countryside that was set up in the early 1970s. Still based there, Pogačnik has dealt in his later work primarily with the relationship between "the visible (materialised) and the invisible (vital energy, emotional, and spiritual) dimensions of space".[22]

Using the insights of geomancy, a divining discipline that investigates the complex structure of energy flows that permeate the entire Earth, Pogačnik devised a method to translate the alternative healing technique of acupuncture into an artistic-ecological practice directed toward remedying the troubles of the planet itself. This large-scale procedure, which he refers to as *lithopuncture*, is based on the principle that applying pressure to particular spots on the ground – using stone pillars instead of needles – elicits a change in energy in sites that, for example, have experienced war-

---

19 See Daniel Grúň, "Der Kosmos der slowakischen Neoavantgarde zwischen Utopie, Fiktion und Politik", in *Crossing 68/89: Grenzüberschreitungen und Schnittpunkte zwischen den Umbrüchen*, ed. Jürgen Danyel et al., Metropol, Berlin, 2008, pp. 136–155.
20 Rudolf Sikora, "Biographical Notes", in *Rudolf Sikora: Against Myself*, pp. 274–276 (see n. 15).
21 The other members of the OHO group were David Nez, Milenko Matanović, and Andraž Šalamun. See *OHO: A Retrospective*, exh. cat., 2nd ed., Moderna Galerija, Ljubljana, and Revolver, Frankfurt am Main, 2007; the OHO retrospective, at the Moderna Galerija in Ljubljana in 1994, was curated by Igor Zabel.
22 Marko Pogačnik, "Back to Art – Art Forward", in *Marko Pogačnik: The Art of Life – The Life of Art*, ed. Igor Španjol, exh. cat., Moderna Galerija, Ljubljana, 2012, pp. 565–567.

time trauma or environmental violence.[23] The stones are carved with visual messages that take the form either of kinesiograms, which might be understood as ornamental depictions of the energy recordings of a certain place, or cosmograms, more symbolically coded pictograms that deal with particular issues, such as world peace, bridging the East–West divide, or the treatment of animals. Over the last thirty years, Pogačnik has installed such healing stones at dozens of natural sites across the world (figs. 6–7), including Tamera, Portugal (*Sociogram*, 2004–2006), Fuerteventura in the Canary Islands (*Atlantis*, 2007), and Louisville, Kentucky (*28 Aspects of the Divine Presence on Earth*, 2008).

Comparing his works to Neolithic stone circles, Pogačnik makes a significant distinction between these contemporary alignments and structures like Stonehenge, which were erected at a time "when the coexistence between Gaia consciousness, nature and human culture was not distorted".[24] Gaia, the ancient Greek goddess of the Earth, has also lent her name to the hypothesis proposed by the British scientist James Lovelock, which posits a self-regulating system consisting of the planet's biosphere and physical components that keeps the Earth's climatic and biochemical conditions in a state of balance. In the original version of Lovelock's theory, Gaia appeared as a benevolent living organism, a "vast being who ... has the power to maintain our planet as a fit and comfortable habitat for life".[25] However, as climate change has turned the world into an increasingly unpredictable place, Gaia has revealed a darker side, encapsulated also by the title of Lovelock's more pessimistic follow-up, *The Revenge of Gaia*.[26] Pogačnik's thinking about Gaia consciousness has also evolved in ways corresponding to the changing scientific and theoretical interpretations of Gaia, as the artist has detected "a series of crucial changes in the vital energy and spiritual levels of the space of the Earth" since the late 1990s, in the wake of the rapidly deteriorating global environmental situation.[27]

In Pogačnik's practice, rocks are not just the inanimate matter of the planetary crust but are seen as conductors of the cosmic energies that reverberate through the planet. They serve as conduits for communication with the immaterial phenomena of the Earth – on the one hand, informing the planet "about the reawakening human awareness", the consequence of realizing that we are at a tipping point, and on the other, sending out the message to people that we need to care for the invisible dimensions of

23 Ibid.
24 Marko Pogačnik, "Geopuncture Circles", on the artist's website, http://www.markopogacnik.com/?page_id=888 (accessed January 14, 2016).
25 James Lovelock, *Gaia: A New Look at Life on Earth*, Oxford University Press, Oxford, 1995, p. 1; originally published in 1979.
26 James Lovelock, *The Revenge of Gaia: Why the Earth Is Fighting Back – and How We Can Still Save Humanity*, Allen Lane, London, 2006.
27 Pogačnik, "Back to Art – Art Forward", p. 67.

Earth, not just its material properties.[28] It is this kind of "profound ecology", which takes into account both the spiritual domain of the Earth's body and human consciousness, that constitutes the new "geoculture". In the artist's view, by adopting such a holistic geocultural position we are able to "transform our civilization into a culture of peace and coexistence between nations, and also between humankind and the worlds of nature and the Earth".[29]

Another proposal for a unified world, solidarity among peoples, empathy for other species, and an environmentally sustainable way of life is put forward in the multilayered installation *Pangaea: Visual Aid for Historical Consciousness* (2011), by the Hungarian artist duo Tamás Kaszás (b. 1976) and Anikó Loránt (b. 1977), who work together as the Ex-Artists Collective. Their approach, however, differs from Pogačnik's insistence on the communion of planetary beings, as their motivation lies rather in finding alternatives to the prevailing economic system, which is ultimately responsible for bringing the world to the verge of ecological disaster. As others have pointed out, to challenge the dominance of the "fundamental, growth-based, profit-seeking logic of capitalism" and its effects on the planet means having the "audacity to think differently and conceive of alternative futures".[30] In that sense, instead of proposing general political programmes and attempts to reform the entire system, the artists prefer to explore the potential of small-scale solutions that operate on the level of the individual, family, or collective and offer the possibility of more autonomous and creative ways of living in the shadow of the industrial-technological paradigm.

As the duo's name implies – and not unlike OHO in the early 1970s – the Ex-Artists Collective strive to one day achieve the conditions for "an art practice without institutional mediation" that is based on a self-sustaining life in proximity to nature.[31] Indicative of their environmentally sensitive approach, meanwhile, is the practice of interlinking, rearranging and recycling materials from their previous works in new configurations. This was the case too with their *Pangaea* installation (fig. 8), which consisted of a wooden structure with bulletin boards and shelves on which old and new drawings, objects, and posters were arranged in four thematic sections: *Symbol Rehab*, *Agro-culture*, *Collapsism*, and *As We Live It*.[32] The selected zones reveal the artists' interests in collecting evidence of previous social struggles to improve the world, their special sensitivity toward indigenous communities and folk culture, and, as in the poster "After Oil", their understanding that the global petro-capitalist system is on the verge

---

28   Ibid., p. 71.
29   Ibid., p. 74.
30   Naomi Klein, *This Changes Everything: Capitalism vs. the Climate*, Simon & Schuster, New York, 2014, p. 89.
31   Maja and Reuben Fowkes, "Tamás Kaszás's Art Laboratory: Anticipating Collapse, Practicing Survival", *Ars Hungarica*, no. 3, December 2013, p. 112.
32   See Tamás Kaszás, *Visual Aid*, Kisterem, Budapest, 2013.

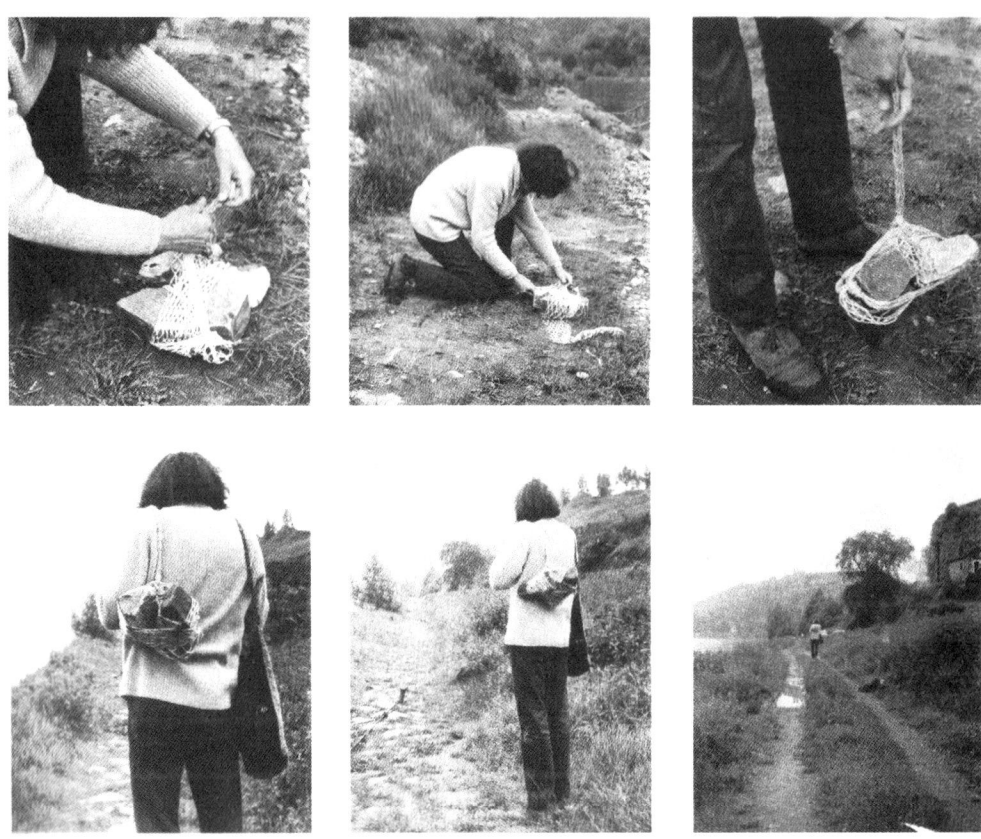

fig. 2

Petr Štembera, *Transposition of Stones*, outskirts of Prague, 1971.

Courtesy of Petr Štembera.

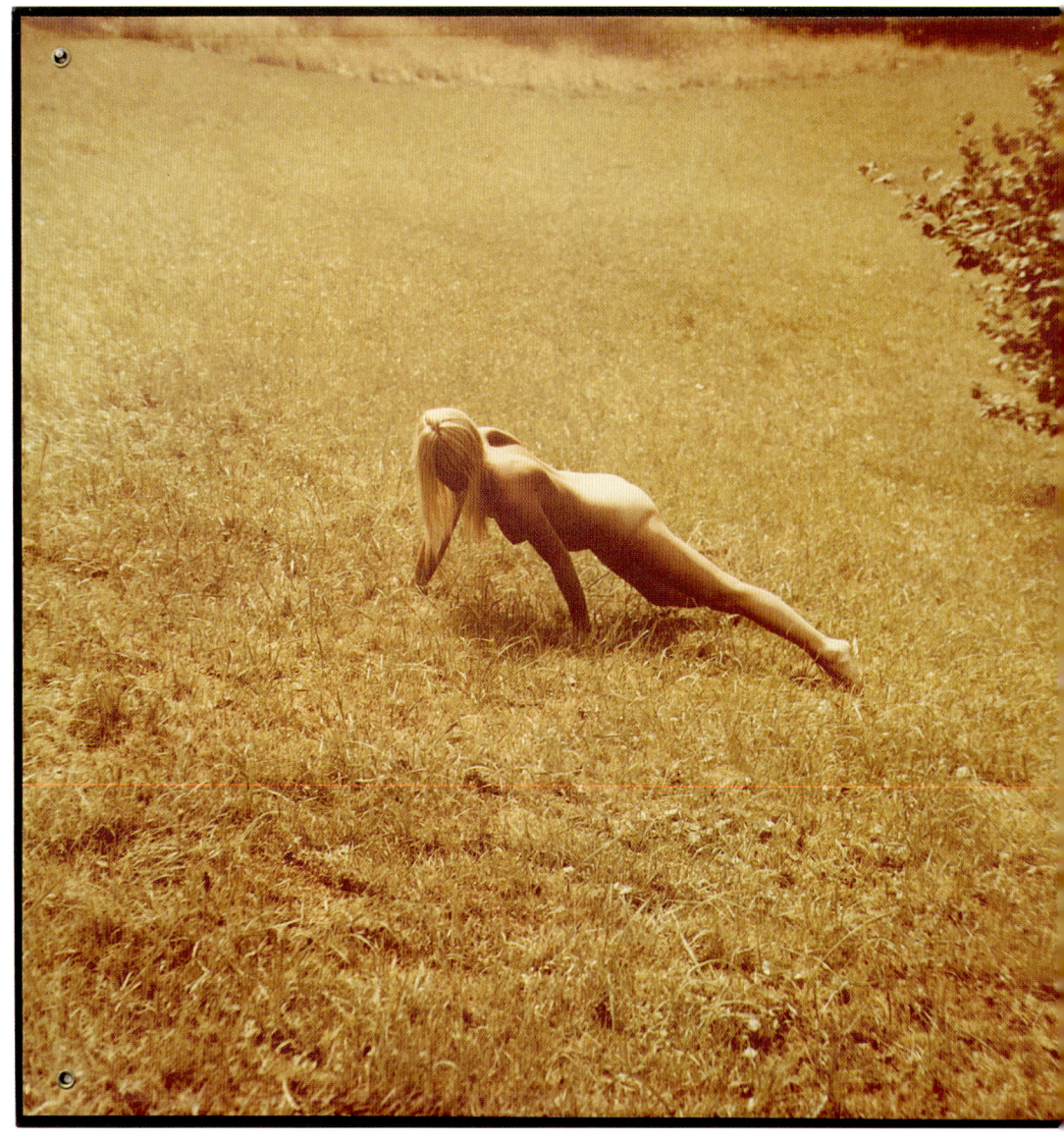

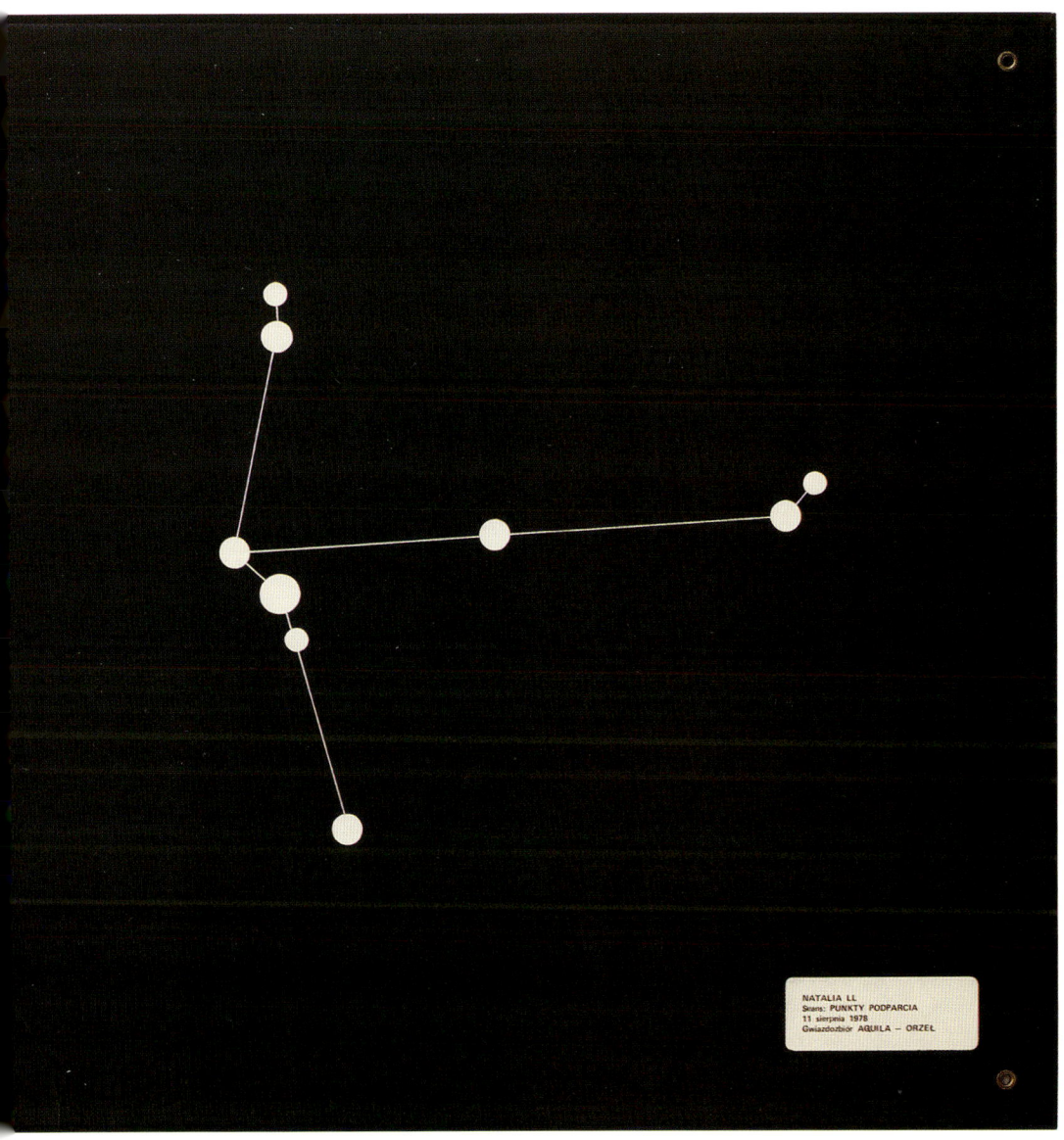

fig. 3

Natalia LL, *Points of Support: Aquila Constellation*, 1978.

Courtesy of Natalia LL and Lokal 30 Gallery, Warsaw.

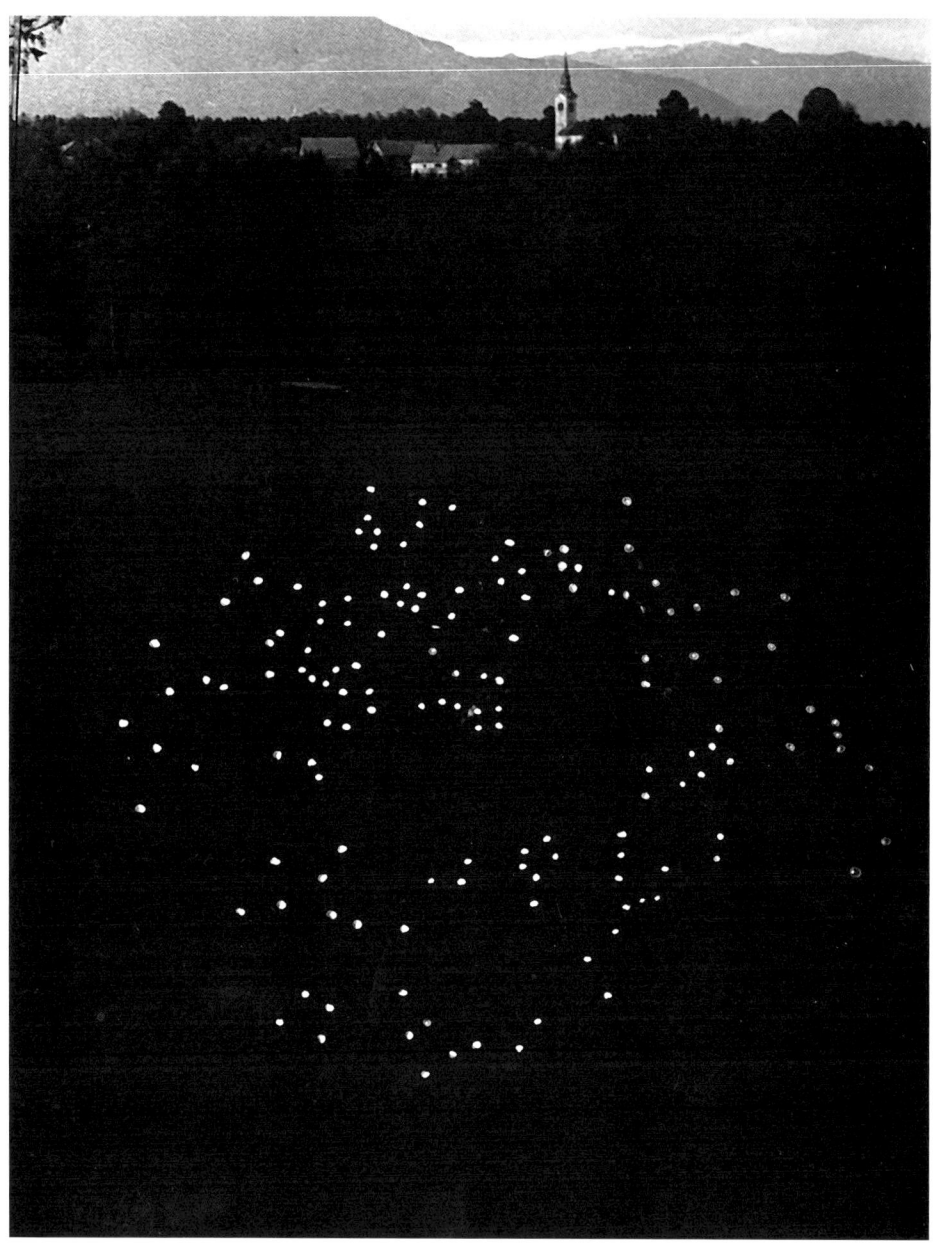

fig. 4

Milenko Matanović / OHO, *The Constellation of Candles in the Field Corresponds to the Constellation of the Stars in the Sky*, Zarica Valley near Kranj, Slovenia, April 30, 1970.

Courtesy of Moderna galerija, Ljubljana.

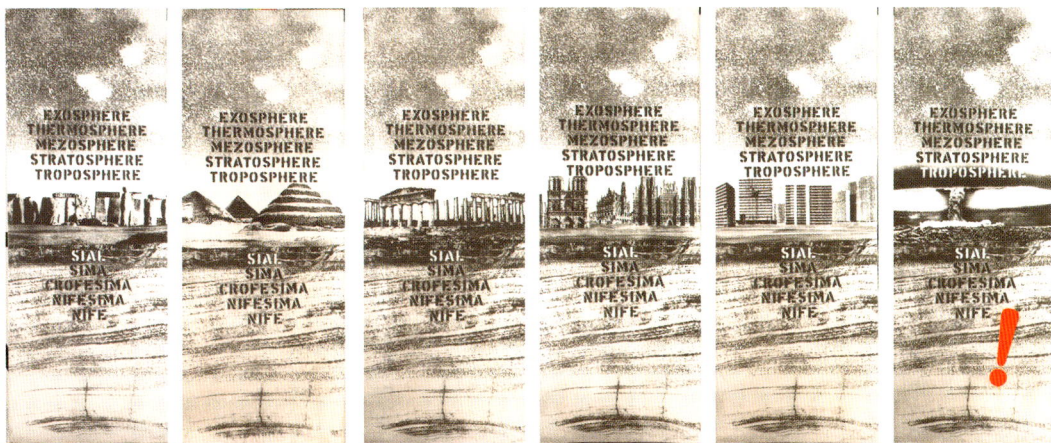

fig. 5

Rudolf Sikora, *The Earth Should Not Become a Dead Planet*, 1972.

Courtesy of Rudolf Sikora.

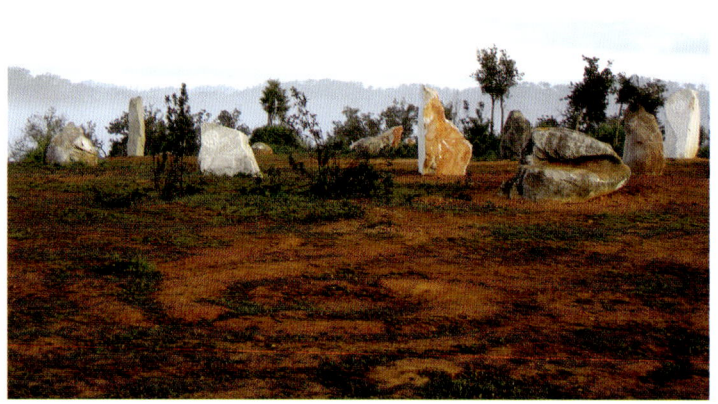

fig. 6

Marko Pogačnik, *Geopuncture Circle*, Tamera, Portugal, 2006.

Courtesy of Marko Pogačnik.

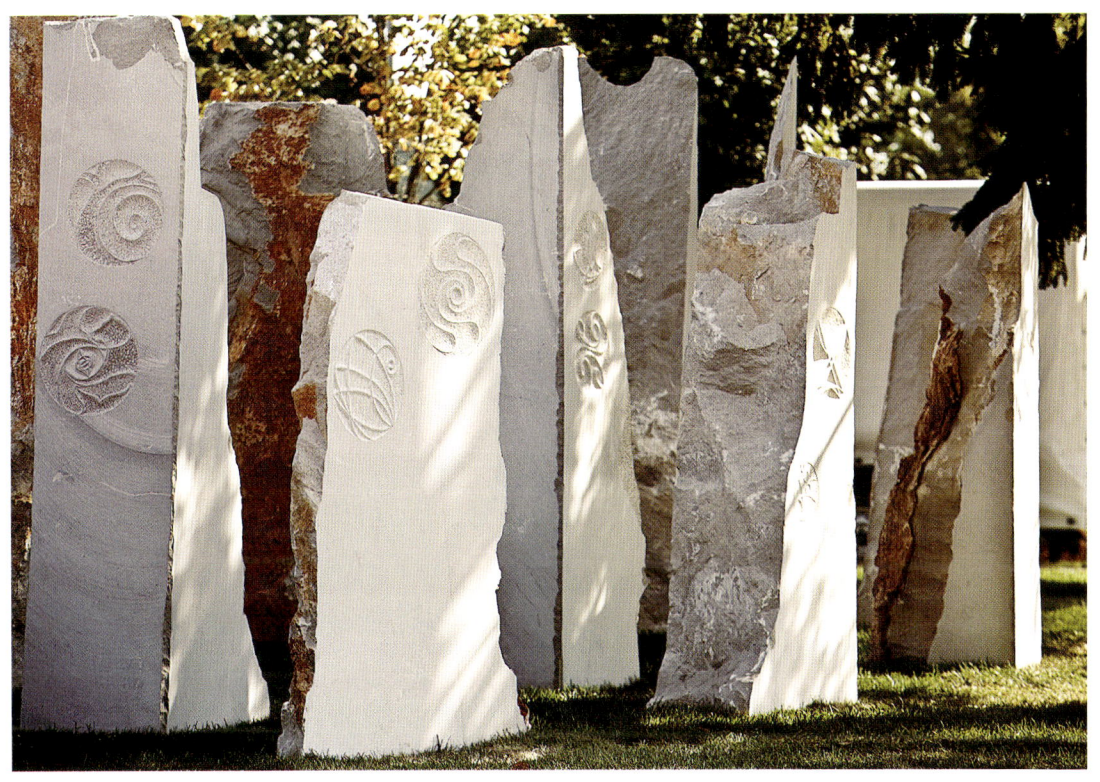

fig. 7

Marko Pogačnik and VITAAA Association, *Peace Point*, geopuncture circle, BTC City, Ljubljana, 2009.

Photo by Bojan Brecelj.

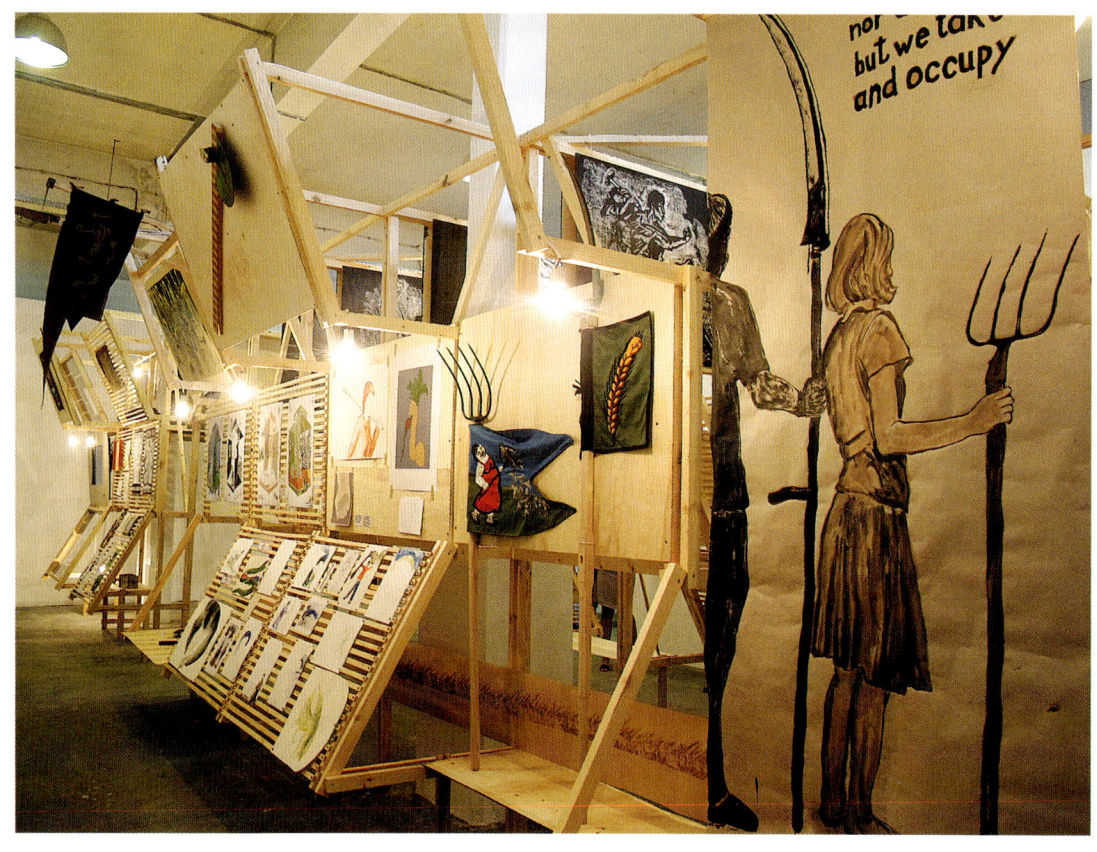

fig. 8

Tamás Kaszás and Anikó Loránt (Ex-Artists Collective),
Pangaea: Visual Aid for Historical Consciousness, 2011.

Courtesy of Tamás Kaszás.

of breakdown; finally, the last section addresses the question of personal responsibility and points to the transformative potential that lies in acquiring practical skills and shared creativity in everyday life.

One of the recurring motifs in Kaszás and Loránt's work is the figure of the peasant, to whom they assign an affirmative role as a revolutionary force by recalling radical peasant uprisings throughout history. Their choice of the peasant over the industrial worker demonstrates a critical attitude to the political utopia of socialism, which was ultimately based on the economic model of industrial growth. By repurposing agro-utopian imagery they additionally comment on the issue of industrial agriculture and unsustainable food production in today's globalized world, in which the trio of genetically modified foods, herbicides, and artificial fertilizers are degrading the topmost layer of the Earth's crust. Indeed, it has been observed that the scale of the "contemporary patterns of soil degradation, expressed through both net nutrient loss and soil erosion, make it one of the defining environmental characteristics of the Anthropocene".[33] Opposing intensive, chemical-based agriculture, the Ex-Artists Collective advocate small-scale gardening based on the principles of permaculture, which also acts as a source of social and ecological empowerment.[34]

The *Pangaea* installation not only makes references that fall within the realm of geology – such as to the Earth's top layer of fertile soil and deeper-lying oil deposits – but the work's very title, accentuated by the banners "Pangaea United" and "We are all from Pangaea", which flank the entrances to the installation, is also borrowed from the discipline. Literally meaning "all-earth", the term Pangaea is used in geology to refer to the last supercontinent, which existed 200 million years ago, when all of today's continents formed one enormous land mass surrounded by a single ocean. Scientific advances enabling the construction of "increasingly plausible global maps of different geological periods", as in the case of Pangaea, reinforce the sense that the "Earth's history has been highly contingent throughout and therefore utterly unpredictable".[35] Conceiving *Pangaea* as a "visual aid", the artists point to the longevity of our planet's geological history and the accelerated processes of today's globalized world and thus put the current dominance of humans into perspective. The transformative power of natural matter that once formed the world without borders also stands as a powerful metaphor for the interdependence of "all-earth", erasing geopolitical rivalries and the cultural and ethnic polarities of a world faced with the planetary consequences of the ecological crisis.

---

33 Mark Whitehead, *Environmental Transformations: A Geography of the Anthropocene*, Routledge, Abingdon, UK, and New York, 2014, p. 70.
34 Tamás Kaszás, "The Artist as Farmer", *Lumen Station: Reap and Sow*, no. 3, special issue, ed. Virág Major, Lumen Photography Foundation, Budapest and Berlin, 2015, p. 47.
35 Rudwick, *Earth's Deep History*, p. 260.

At first glance, the deep history of the Earth allowed Eastern European artists – both those who worked during the long period of late socialism and those caught up in the maelstrom of capitalist globalization – to make a statement about the transitory character of political history. Equally, the cosmological perspective that they regularly brought into play helped illustrate the absurdity and ultimate insignificance of the geopolitical divides on the planet. On closer inspection, the strata of art history reveal the complexity of artistic engagements with the materiality of the planet. No matter how they approached the issue, whether through phenomenological, epistemological, scientific, transcendental, or socially critical lenses, all these artists chose to direct attention to specific aspects of the parallel existence of the human and planetary realms, as manifest both in their physical actuality and in less tangible dimensions.

Geology, however, does not figure in their work simply to indicate the vastness of non-human time and space; it also serves as a marker of the magnitude of the current ecological crisis. Visualizing the proportions of human interventions in the geological matter of the Earth, the artists commented on humanity's unprecedented interference in natural processes and the ominous consequences both for the planet and its inhabitants. In the geologic present of the Anthropocene, it is clear that there is no turning back the clock, but rather, as the artists discussed here have proposed, we should either concentrate on small steps as an antidote to the effects of the merciless economic system or enter into a sincere conversation with the Earth about renewing the cosmic contract on more equitable terms. A debate of cosmo-political proportions about the future of the planet would necessarily have to include the whole of humanity, not just the global elite, and extend as well to non-human actors from animals and plants to rocks, rivers, and the elemental materiality of the Earth. In the rekindling and scaling up of the planetary imagination, the shaping of a collective response to the environmental fracturing of the world and the articulation of an unprecedented global project to challenge the dominant extractivist model, the potential of contemporary art and the legacy of the Eastern European neo-avant-garde are only just beginning to be understood.

Klara Kemp-Welch

Autonomy, Solidarity, and the Antipolitics of NET

Klara Kemp-Welch's main research interests are the cultures, countercultures and experimental art of Eastern Europe and Latin America during the Cold War. Her essay looks at NET, a conceptual proposal that provided a unique framework for an unofficial international artistic exchange. The proposal was developed by the Polish artists Andrzej Kostołowski and Jarosław Kozłowski in 1971 and mailed out the following year to over 350 artists worldwide. The broader issue of artistic networking in the Soviet bloc also forms the subject of her forthcoming book *Networking the Bloc: Experimental Art in Eastern Europe 1968–1981*, which draws on archival research and oral testimony to survey the scope and significance of artistic exchange and dialogue behind and beyond the Iron Curtain in the late Cold War period. Her aim, both here and in her book, is to transcend Cold War narratives of isolation and historically reposition Eastern European art within the global art field.

An earlier version of this essay was published in *NET: The Art of Dialogue / NET: Sztuka Dialogu*, ed. Bożena Czubak, Fundacja Profil, Warsaw, 2013, pp. 34–56, the catalogue for the exhibition *NET: The Art of Dialogue*, at the Profile Foundation in Warsaw in 2012.

By the time Hungarian dissident György Konrád asked, in his landmark essay *Antipolitics* (1984), "How can we strengthen the horizontal human relationships of civil society against the vertical human relationships of military society?",[1] experimental artists had been exploring such questions, in their own way, for well over a decade. Although the "new spiritual order between East and West" that Konrád and others sought to imagine remained as unthinkable as the idea of the collapse of the Soviet bloc, the refusal of a minority to accept the status quo bore witness to the importance of thinking the impossible. Václav Havel called this living in truth.[2] His friend Ivan Martin Jirous cited Marcel Duchamp's prediction that "the artist of the future will go underground" and explained that

> the goal of our underground is to create a second culture, a culture completely independent from all official communication media and the conventional hierarchy of value judgements put out by the establishment. It is to be a culture that does not have as its goal the destruction of the establishment, because by attempting this, it would – in effect – mean that we would fall into the trap of playing their game. The real aim is to overcome the hopeless feeling that it is of no use to try anything.[3]

One hallmark of the "second culture" was its commitment to autonomy – its refusal to compromise with the authorities or to engage in any way with official politics; another was its faith in solidarity. But while Konrád wrote that "autonomy and solidarity are the root values of every democratic ideology", he considered that "democracy and independence, here and now, are not possible for us; the basic framework of political and economic power cannot be reformed".[4] Crucially, though, this did not mean that there was no alternative; there was: "to attempt the near impossible: even if our nation and our institutions have no autonomy, to try to work out our own."[5] Artists, too, were preoccupied with working out ways to act autonomously; connecting with like-minded others around the world was key.

Andrzej Kostołowski and Jarosław Kozłowski's conceptual proposal NET, conceived in 1971 and mailed out to over 350 artists worldwide in

1 György Konrád, *Antipolitics: An Essay*, trans. Richard E. Allen, Harcourt Brace Jovanovich, San Diego, New York, and London, 1984, p. 74. See also Klara Kemp-Welch, *Antipolitics in Action: Art and Theory in Central Europe 1956-1989*, IB Tauris, London and New York, 2014.
2 Václav Havel, *Living in Truth: Twenty-two Essays Published on the Occasion of the Award of the Erasmus Prize to Václav Havel*, ed. Jan Vladislav, Faber and Faber, London and Boston, 1989.
3 Ivan Martin Jirous, "A Report on the Third Czech Musical Revival" (*samizdat* publication, 1975), trans. Eric Dluhosch, in *Primary Documents: A Sourcebook for Eastern and Central European Art since the 1950s*, ed. Laura Hoptman and Tomáš Pospiszyl, Museum of Modern Art, New York, 2002, pp. 56-65.
4 Konrád, *Antipolitics*, pp. 123-126.
5 Ibid., p. 128.

1972, laid out a unique framework for artistic exchange (fig. 1). NET redrew the cultural map, in line with Konrád's observation that "cultural criticism of the most intensive kind" was necessary in order to replace the binary order of the Cold War with what he referred to as "polycentrism".[6] It proposed a topography of connectedness from below. In Kozłowski's words, NET came together

> in semi-shadow, there were other artists at work, artists who were not interested in careers, commercial success, popularity or recognition: artists who devoted more attention to the issue of their own artistic, and therefore ethical, stance than to their position in the rankings, whether the ranking in question was based on the highest listing on the market, or the highest level of approval from the authorities. These artists professed other values, and other goals led them onward, they were focused on art, conceived as the realm of cognitive freedom and creative discourse.[7]

Kostołowski and Kozłowski's project yielded not only one of the most theoretically robust conceptions of the network, but also a vast archive of materials received from those who were invited to participate and, in turn, from their contacts.

NET had "no central point [or] coordination", Kostołowski and Kozłowski announced in the proposition they mailed out; "points of the NET can be anywhere" and "all points of the NET are in contact among themselves and exchange concepts, propositions, projects and other forms of documentation." What mattered was the transmission of an articulated idea to an interested receiver: "propositions are presented to persons interested in them." Although the "points of the NET" could be anywhere, the list notably included "private homes" as well as "studios and any other places, where artistic propositions are articulated".[8] The stress placed on the private home was significant. The first reception of materials received through NET took place at Kozłowski's apartment in 1972 (figs. 2–5), which was raided forty-five minutes later by the security services. Through a series of inversions characteristic of the absurdities of late-socialist life, the private home became a place of last resort – an anti-institution that would later be formalized though initiatives such as the APTart exhibitions of the 1980s in the USSR.[9] Nevertheless, Bojana Pejić

---

6   Ibid., p. 36.
7   Jarosław Kozłowski, "Art between the Red and the Olden Frames", in *Curating with Light Luggage: Reflections, Discussions and Revisions*, ed. Liam Gillick and Maria Lind, Kunstverein München, Munich, and Revolver, Frankfurt am Main, 2005, p. 44.
8   The quoted material comes from the English version of the NET proposal, or manifesto, dated January 1972. It consisted of a series of bullet-points and was typed in two languages, Polish and English. The artistic propositions discussed in the remainder of the article are all drawn from the NET archive and were received by Jarosław Kozłowski in response to his mailing of the NET proposal.
9   For an excellent discussion of the public and private in relation to NET, see Luiza Nader,

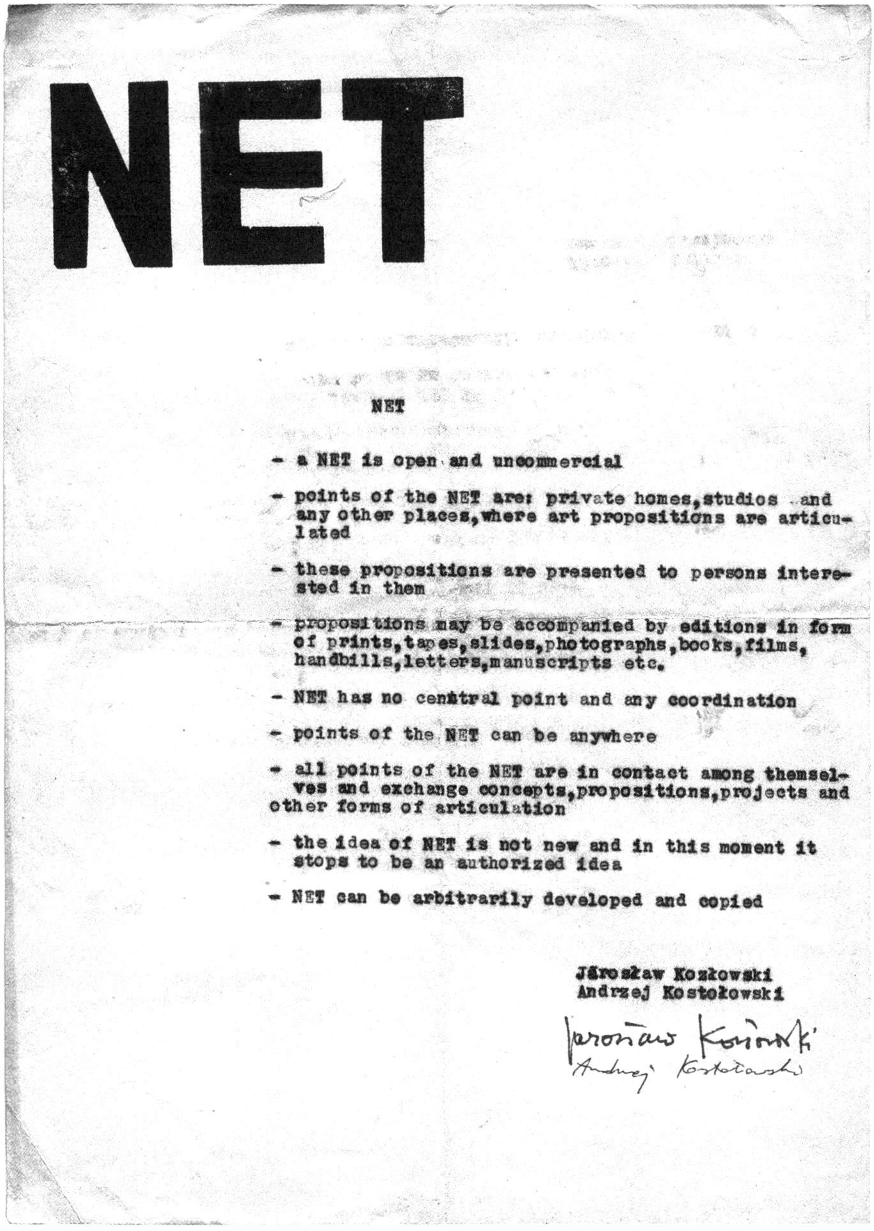

NET

- a NET is open and uncommercial

- points of the NET are: private homes, studios and any other places, where art propositions are articulated

- these propositions are presented to persons interested in them

- propositions may be accompanied by editions in form of prints, tapes, slides, photographs, books, films, handbills, letters, manuscripts etc.

- NET has no central point and any coordination

- points of the NET can be anywhere

- all points of the NET are in contact among themselves and exchange concepts, propositions, projects and other forms of articulation

- the idea of NET is not new and in this moment it stops to be an authorized idea

- NET can be arbitrarily developed and copied

Jarosław Kozłowski
Andrzej Kostołowski

fig. 1

Andrzej Kostołowski and Jarosław Kozłowski, NET, 1971.

Photo by Jarosław Kozłowski.
Courtesy of Jarosław Kozłowski's private archive.

has argued that whenever we "encounter the privileging of the domestic sphere" as "the only secure zone which was outside the reach of the state and thus could 'resist socialism'", we are usually dealing with a Western cliché.[10] The raid on Kozłowski's apartment proved that this space was far from inviolable. Indeed, we might argue that in dissident circles at least, the private itself had evaporated: private space became the main forum for political activities impossible to pursue in public.[11] As Konrád pragmatically put it:

> We have to do without democratic political institutions, and so we do without them. Whether or not we give a name to our friendly get-togethers is unimportant. If they have no name, they can't be banned. We have no Solidarity, but we can still have solidarity, which can't be suspended. Friendship cannot be outlawed. Our organizations are networks of sympathy; we have no headquarters and no leaders, so it is harder to touch us.[12]

The parallels with Kostołowski's and Kozłowski's text are clear. Moreover, to the extent that the primary aim of NET was to be "open and uncommercial", it was potentially as powerful in the West – where, arguably, the market held sway over claims to artistic autonomy – as it was in the East, where the threat to autonomy was posed by the state.[13] Kozłowski saw that autonomy in the West was just as compromised and politically loaded as it was in the East, both ideologically and economically. Arguably, then, it is with a view to a historical equivalence between East and West, rather than from the position of difference, that we should view the exchanges of the period. Our focus should be on identifying shared languages of concern developed by artists in the face of the protracted and stagnant Cold War stand-off.

NET was an important node on an increasingly global artistic map, bringing artists together within the structure of the same proposition, putting them in contact with one another, enabling them to share their

"Heterotopy: The NET and Galeria Akumulatory 2", in *Fluxus East: Fluxus Networks in Central Eastern Europe*, ed. Petra Stegmann, exh. cat., Künstlerhaus Bethanien, Berlin, 2007, pp. 111–125.

10 Bojana Pejić, "Proletarians of All Countries, Who Washes Your Socks? Equality Dominance and Difference in Eastern European Art", in *Gender Check: Femininity and Masculinity in the Art of Eastern Europe*, ed. Bojana Pejić and Museum Moderner Kunst Stiftung Ludwig Wien, exh. cat., MUMOK and Erste Foundation, Vienna, and Verlag der Buchhandlung Walther König, Cologne, 2009, p. 24.

11 Although Pejić introduces this problem in order to foreground the situation of women in the context of the swallowing up of family life by the antipolitical patriarchy, I use it here to discuss the paradoxes of the space itself.

12 Konrád, *Antipolitics*, pp. 132–33. When Konrád speaks of "Solidarity" (capitalized), he is referring to the Polish political movement, after the detention of Polish dissident Adam Michnik.

13 This was a declaration of art's possibility act as a third space – what Luiza Nader has called, after Michel Foucault, a "heterotopia". See Nader, "Heterotopy", pp. 111–125.

work and to initiate new collaborations. This was more than just a matter of getting in contact with others: there were plenty of artists doing this to promote themselves internationally; the aim here was to produce a forum that could also be used by others. NET sought to be multilateral. Kostołowski and Kozłowski produced a framework for a category of activity, launching a platform that could be shared by others independently of its designers (the authors announced that it could be "arbitrarily developed and copied"). As a nominative exercise, a conceptual artwork, the NET manifesto served as a generative principle – a "connector". The authors of this idea, which "ceased being an authorized idea" as soon as they declared it, schematized a phenomenon which was already taking place in fragmented form; the statement declared that all this activity was now connected – that all independent initiatives were significant and that everyone acting autonomously in some way was doing so within the framework of a new solidarity. What mattered was that NET was active, that it was powerful, and that it was unstoppable.

One of the themes we find repeatedly in the NET archive is international communication itself. Artists producing work for international distribution were concerned to explore the conditions of international production, distribution and reception. Jun Mizukami's *Pan Rites Report 95* (1976) is a case in point (fig. 6). Mizukami proposes a conceptualist game of Chinese whispers by changing the second *c* in communication to produce a finite series of permutations. He then goes on to invent a set of words derived from the prefix "commun-", as though posing the loaded question: What else might become a form of communication? The Hungarian mail artist Géza Perneczky's series of white stamps on postcards played a similar game. Each is stamped with the word "secret" in different languages, suggesting the idea of a secret travelling the globe. Bogdanka Poznanović's announcement (in 1976) of "communication in continuo", for its part, contains the word "breath" translated into nine languages and arranged to form a hexagon in the centre of the page, drifting from conceptualism into concrete poetry (fig. 7). We might also mention here Endre Tót's nullified dialogues and his correspondence art full of zeros and erasure. These went a step further by destroying meaning altogether in some cases and by making a virtue of incomprehensibility, so that everything except the desire to communicate itself is lost in translation and swallowed up by zeros. Although English often served as the international language of conceptualism in this period, visual poetry was equally prevalent in the artistic network, to some extent rendering language redundant in favour of more universal visual forms of communication.

Among the most interesting respondents were those who took the NET proposal as a springboard for initiating further proposals for exchange, in this way responding to the challenge posed by NET for "all points of the NET" to be in contact "among themselves". Key Hungarian networker László Beke's reply was designed to explore the functioning of NET itself. His letter of March 19, 1972, addressed to friends through

NET, asked them each to fill out a questionnaire with their name and address and to add a message before forwarding the letter to another member of NET. The game would continue for as long as everyone was willing to show their solidarity. It would end when one person decided they didn't want to add their name, in which case they were asked to return the information gathered so far to Beke, in Budapest. In a later letter to Kozłowski (June 10, 1972), Beke outlined a selection of his own initiatives, inviting his Polish colleague to participate in a "World Archive of Ideas" and an "international exhibition of mails in my and my friends' ownership". He told Kozłowski which of the people on the NET list he already knew and asked him whether he really knew and had met everyone on the list. Of course he hadn't, but it is telling that even such a well-networked Hungarian was impressed by Kozłowski's contact list and might have thought it conceivable for a Polish artist to have met so many international figures in this period. The Polish unofficial art scene was both less evidently politicized and less regulated by the state than its Hungarian counterpart.

Any imputation of artistic autonomy has to be qualified, however. Piotr Piotrowski argued that, by the 1970s, the ideological state apparatus in Poland was "interested in maintaining, not restricting, art's autonomy; they wished to do so in order to delegitimize political critique, which was the legacy of the avant-garde".[14] Policing the boundaries between autonomous and critical art proved far from simple, though. If, following the thaw of 1956, the political boundaries for artists were to some extent unspoken ones, then this was in line with the biopolitical turn of late socialism in general. Although restrictions and censorship were not always openly announced, this did not mean that there weren't any, or that artists did not seek to confront them. There were invisible limits and artists did transgress them – with visible consequences, expanding and exposing these limits in the process.

One of the key networkers of this generation, who was in regular contact with Kozłowski, was the West German mail artist Klaus Groh. Groh's mailings include a series of artists' rubber stamps on paper, among them the bold indigo stamp of NET and the three-letter initialism IAC, referring to Groh's organization the International Artists' Cooperation, founded in 1969 (fig. 8). Dotted around these two nodes, we find a series of postal instructions in German and Polish, a stamp asking "why?", a small hedgehog, arrows, equals signs, and the words "manipulation" and "relativities". The piece represents graphically the collaboration between the pioneers of unofficial exchange in the 1970s. Groh was in possession of an extensive "list" of artists, who in 1972 formed the basis for what he called the Mail Artists' Index. By the following year, with the help of Czech performance artist Petr Štembera and Beke, Groh had collected enough documentation of work by Central and Eastern European artists to publish

---

14   Piotr Piotrowski, *Art and Democracy in Post-Communist Europe*, Reaktion Books, London, 2012, p. 90.

the most important survey of the experimental practitioners of the period: *Aktuelle Kunst in Osteuropa: ČSSR, Jugoslawien, Polen, Rumänien, USSR, Ungarn* (*Current Art in Eastern Europe: Czechoslovakia, Yugoslavia, Poland, Romania, the USSR, Hungary*).[15] This legendary publication allocated two or three pages to each artist and was arranged alphabetically by the artist's surname – a democratic structure that embraced random juxtapositions and was characteristic of exhibition catalogues of this period. The emphasis was on the documentation of propositions rather than on the artists themselves – with biographical information limited to their year of birth and place of residence.

Projects such as NET and Groh's book were pioneering sources of information for artists about what their peers in neighbouring countries were doing. Paradoxically, despite certain restrictions, it was far easier for artists in the Soviet satellite countries (not to mention in Yugoslavia, which was not part of the Soviet bloc after 1948) to access information about recent developments in Western art – which arrived in the form of magazines, exhibition catalogues, and books sent in the mail or delivered in person by colleagues, or via direct contact with artists and occasional trips abroad – than it was for them to make contact with like-minded colleagues from other countries behind the Iron Curtain.[16]

As the 1970s progressed, however, all sorts of photographs, projects for installations and performances, artist's statements, visual poems, assembling magazines, etc. began to circulate through the ever-expanding informal network. People knew people who knew people; they followed each others' work and sent each other documentation of what they were doing. It became habitual, in this improvised community, to send an artist you were interested in information about your activities and to request the same in response. There were many intersecting networks, not just one: the circles of concrete poets, performance artists, conceptualists, and mail artists overlapped. As the Czech concrete poet Jiří Kocman, in Brno, wrote to Kozłowski in 1972, there was a general feeling that "communication between us all is very important now!"[17] Writing to request a copy of the NET list, he mentioned that he already knew Groh, Perneczky, Štembera, and Jiří Valoch. And so the circles grew.

Artists in Poland and other Soviet satellite countries often went to great lengths to escape the provincialism to which history, geopolitics, and economics had consigned them; establishing contacts with like-minded people at home and abroad was an important part of this. This sense of a community beyond borders was condensed by the Brazilian artist Angelo de Aquino into his simple statement "Work in Progress 2" (1972), where

15   Published by DuMont Schauberg, Cologne, 1972.
16   Compared with the USSR and the Soviet satellite countries, where artists were frequently refused permission to travel abroad, even within the bloc itself, their Yugoslav counterparts encountered few political impediments to travel.
17   Letter dated June 17, 1972.

Autonomy, Solidarity, and the Antipolitics of NET   173

he wrote: "all country is my country / all name is my name / all work is my work / I'm you / And I'm me. Milano, October 1971." Solidarity was also conveyed through more complex conceptual propositions; we find a surprising message of hope concealed within a series of handwritten pages by Hanne Darboven, dated June 1975 and sent to Kozłowski. She cites a passage from Byron's journal "Detached Thoughts" (1821-1822): "There is no one instance of a long contest, in which men did not triumph over systems. If tyranny misses her first spring, she is cowardly as the tiger, and retires to be hunted."

The Japanese Fluxus artist Mieko Shiomi's *Spatial Poems* offer a remarkable instance of the power of NET as a mechanism for connecting people and their activities around the world. *Open Event (Spatial Poem no. 5)* (1972), encouraged invitees to do whatever they like within a set performance period and to send a three-hundred-word report on the activity to Shiomi in Osaka. *Sound Event (Spatial Poem no. 7)* (1974), which was designed to produce a "global symphony", listed times in countries around the world across time zones and asked people to listen to the sounds around them at their designated time and send a report back to Shiomi describing them. She then undertook to plot these activities on world maps, producing what became documents of international creative cooperation. Kocman, meanwhile, invited those on the NET mailing list to take part in his *Butterfly-Environment Series* (1973): to "interpret" an environment for a given butterfly, sign it, and return the results to him in Brno (fig. 9). In 1976, Štembera provided a reproduction of Hans Holbein the Younger's painting of Charles de Solier (1534-1535) and requested that people mimic the sitter's gestures, photograph themselves in the performance, and send copies to him in Prague. Such proposals conspire to prove that there is nothing terribly new about what has recently come to be termed "delegated performance". Conceptualist László Lakner invited recipients to eat a slice of paper torte in 1972, providing a circle cut into equal portions with one of the sections scrawled on, noting that this particular piece had crossed over into "reality". He invited participants to either photograph themselves eating the cardboard slice or hang it on the wall, but if they did not wish to do either, they should to give it to "an ex-convict". Lakner's playful exercise demonstrated that there were many ways to take an image and make it real – consumption and display are two possibilities, but sharing represents an important and potentially more altruistic third option. Ben Vautier sent in his 1972 piece "My Statement for Documenta 5 no. 1", which characterized the cynical game of art as one of "finding something that others have not already done so that others talk about you". He proposed that the next step was clearly "to get out of the game". The problem, however, was: "If we want to change art we must change its common denominator Ego – (signing – dating – copyright etc.) in other words to change art one must change Ego – that is to say – Man." Humorously concluding that this had not yet been accomplished, he signed and dated the piece "Ben, 1972". These and other Western proposals clearly chimed with Kostołowski and Kozłowski's renunciation of the authorship of NET and their invitation to others to develop and copy it.

Many of the experimental artistic proposals on the archive express solidarity through play, proposing disinterested collective action as a means to overcome physical distance. But there are also others that issued targeted calls for artists to rally around particular causes and support each other's campaigns against perceived injustices. Attaching a copy of the Flux Mail list of 1975, George Maciunas wrote to Kozłowski requesting a blank Polish postcard to use in what he called his *Flux Combat with New York State Attorney (& Police) (Event in Progress)*. His proposed arsenal of weapons included "humorous, insulting and sneering letters" and "various disguises (gorilla mask, bandaged head, gas mask etc.)". The stamped Polish postcard was intended to persuade the attorney general that Maciunas was travelling all around the world mailing letters to him flagrantly mocking what he viewed as the State Department's attempts to curtail Fluxus activities. Equally unusual in its direct appeal for support was Klaus Groh's 1972 call for solidarity with the Argentine cultural networker Jorge Glusberg, an industrialist who had funded and directed the international project space CAYC – Centro de Arte y Comunicación (The Centre of Art and Communication), founded in Buenos Aires in 1968; he also coordinated the CAYC newsletters that found their way into the archives of experimental artists across Central Europe in the 1970s. Groh's partially typed, partially hand-scrawled letter of appeal on Glusberg's behalf was addressed to friends and members of Groh's IAC and the "International Foreign Contact Centers in Argentina, Australia, Austria, Belgium, Brazil, Cameroon, Canada, Chile, Bulgaria, CSSR [Czechoslovakia], Denmark, the United Kingdom, France, Finland, the German Democratic Republic, Hungary, Iceland, Israel, Italy, Japan, the Netherlands, Poland, Switzerland, Romania, Uruguay, the United States, and Yugoslavia". He noted that the message was being disseminated to thirty-six countries in the world in 250 copies and called on recipients to "HELP!!" Groh reported that Glusberg, who was "wanted by the Argentinian Police", was being persecuted as a result of CAYC's groundbreaking international exhibition *Arte de Sistemas* (1971). Groh mentioned that he had already sent a telegram to Argentina's "President Alessandro Augustin la Nussi" (by which he meant Alejandro Agustín Lanusse), in Buenos Aires, in support of the "cultural work of CAYC conducted by Jorge Glusberg with international repercussion for the Argentines" and requesting that he "review measures". He signed the telegram as "Klaus Groh (President of the International Artists' Cooperation, Oldenburg-Germany-West)".[18] The language and style of the message is typical of the particular parallel bureaucracy developed by alternative artists in this period, notably the authors who used NET. Like NET, the IAC had its own letterhead and operated on a private basis, extending its international reach through Groh's newsletter-

---

18   Klaus Groh, letter dated October 2, 1972.

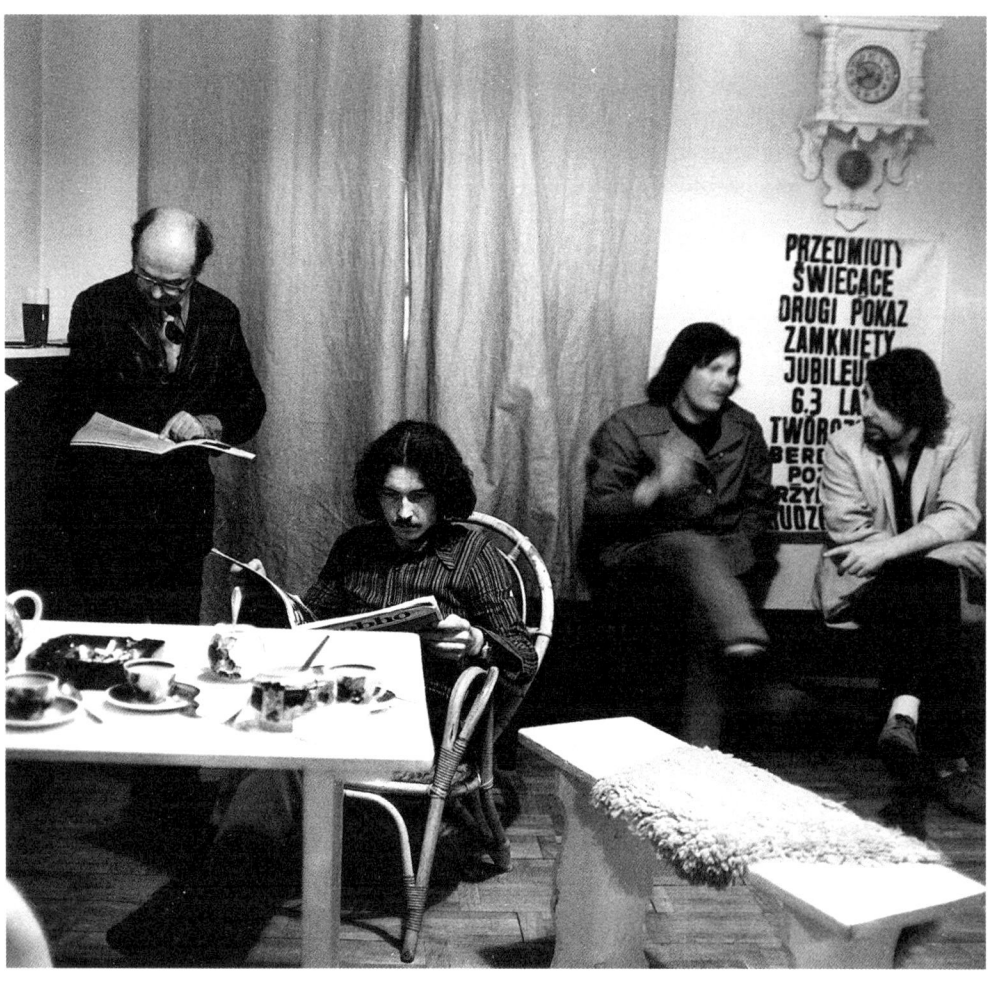

figs. 2–5

Photographs from the first "reception" of NET, Poznań, May 1972.

Photos by Jarosław Kozłowski.
Courtesy of Jarosław Kozłowski's private archive.

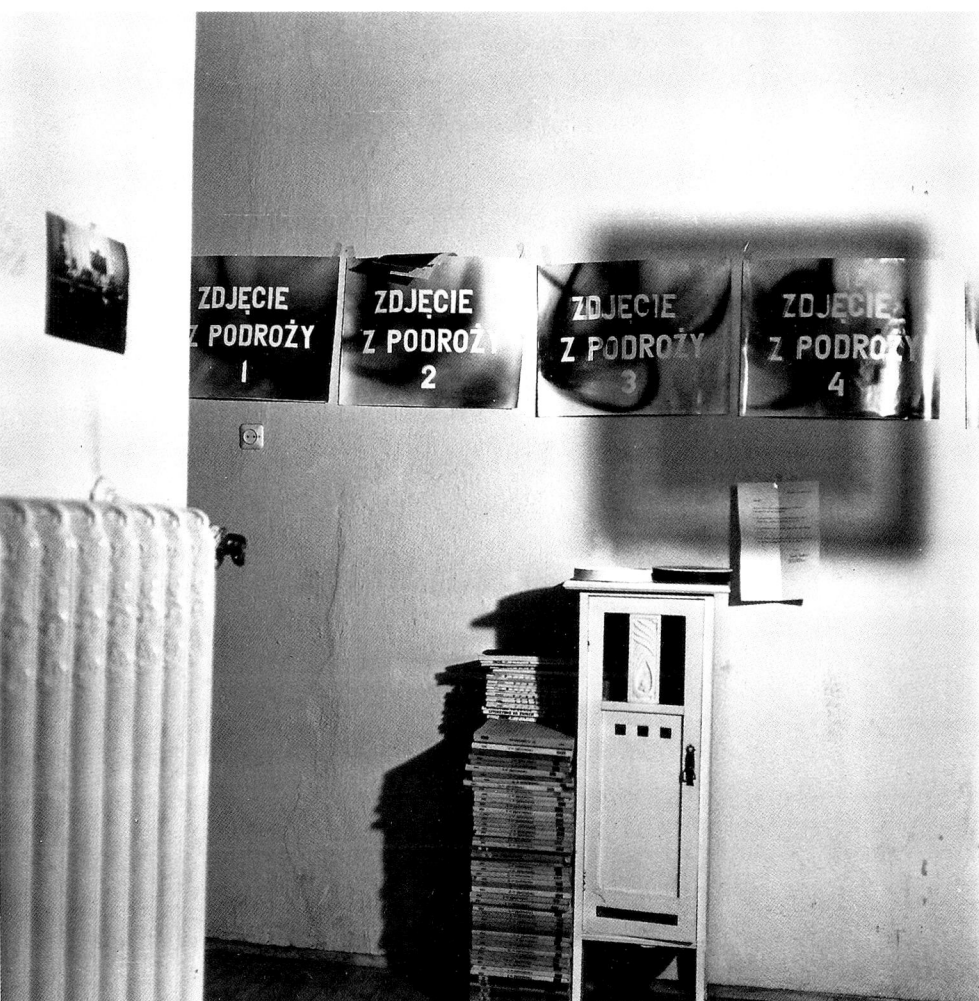

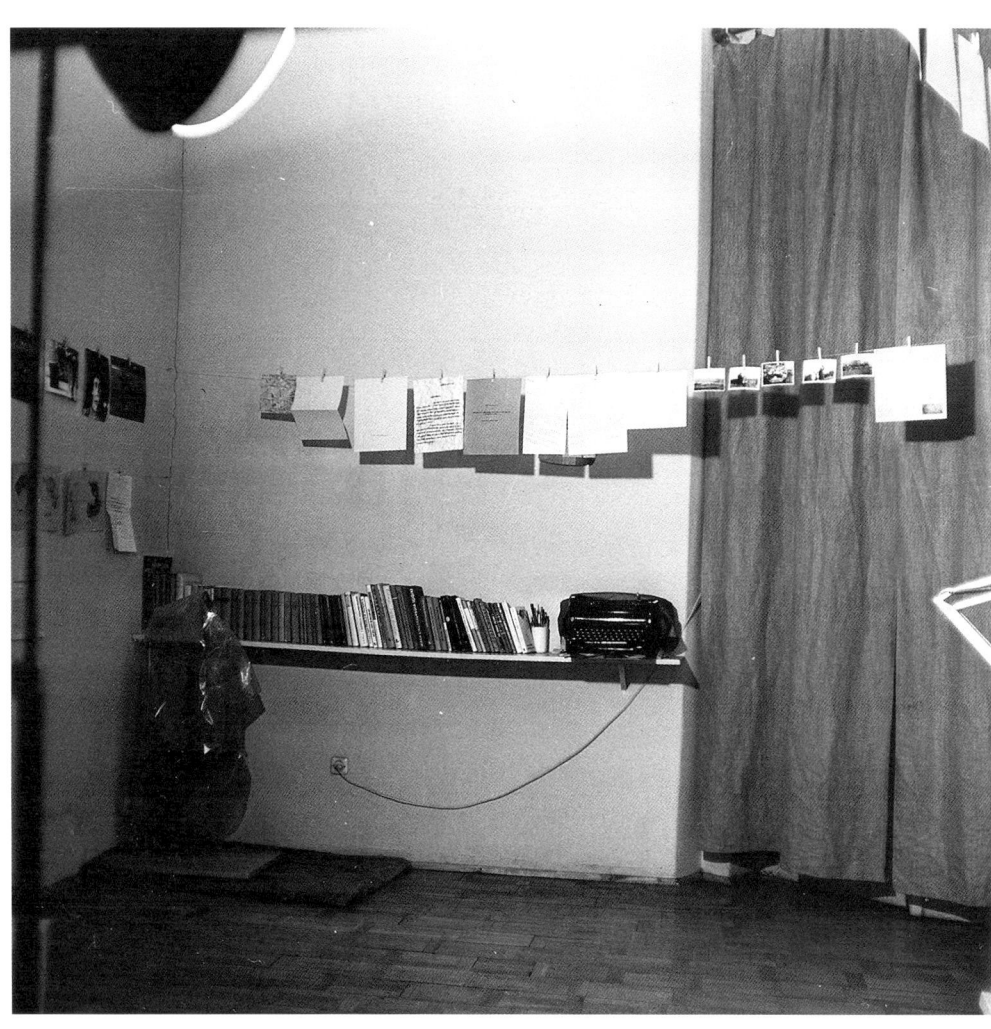

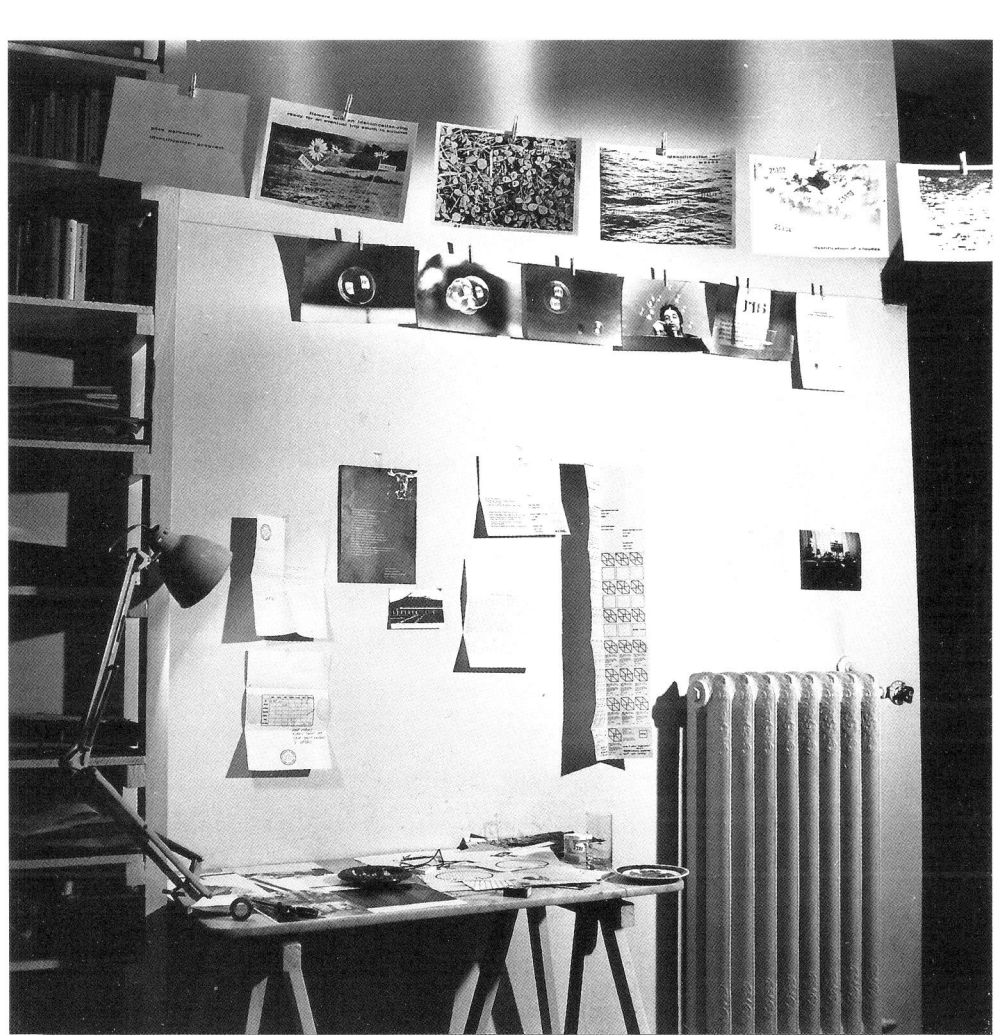

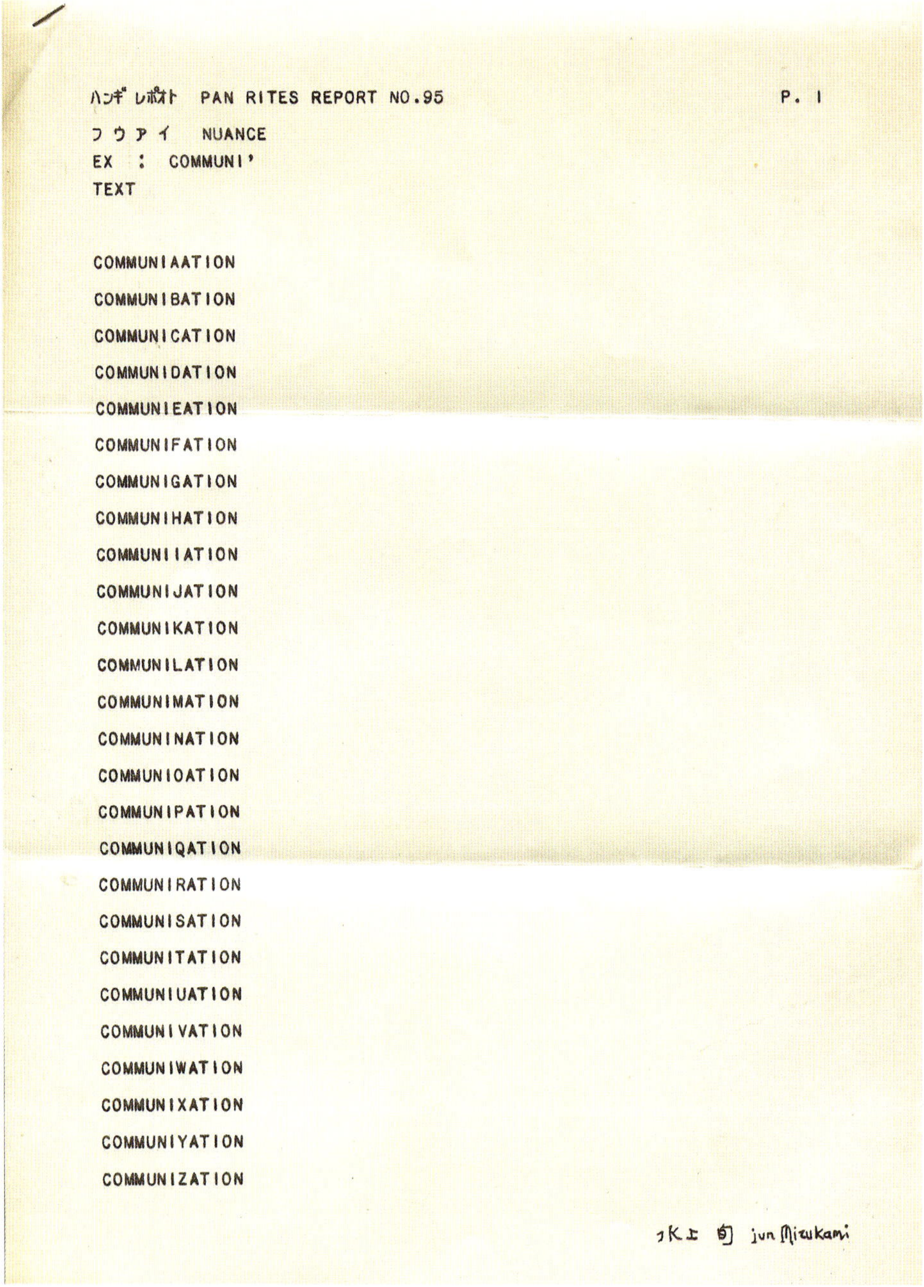

ハンギ レポト　PAN RITES REPORT NO.95　　　　　　　　　　P. 1
フウアイ　NUANCE
EX : COMMUNI'
TEXT

COMMUNIAATION
COMMUNIBATION
COMMUNICATION
COMMUNIDATION
COMMUNIEATION
COMMUNIFATION
COMMUNIGATION
COMMUNIHATION
COMMUNIIATION
COMMUNIJATION
COMMUNIKATION
COMMUNILATION
COMMUNIMATION
COMMUNINATION
COMMUNIOATION
COMMUNIPATION
COMMUNIQATION
COMMUNIRATION
COMMUNISATION
COMMUNITATION
COMMUNIUATION
COMMUNIVATION
COMMUNIWATION
COMMUNIXATION
COMMUNIYATION
COMMUNIZATION

fig. 6

Jun Mizukami, *Pan Rites Report 95*, 1976.

Photo by Natalia Brandt.
Courtesy of Jarosław Kozłowski's private archive.

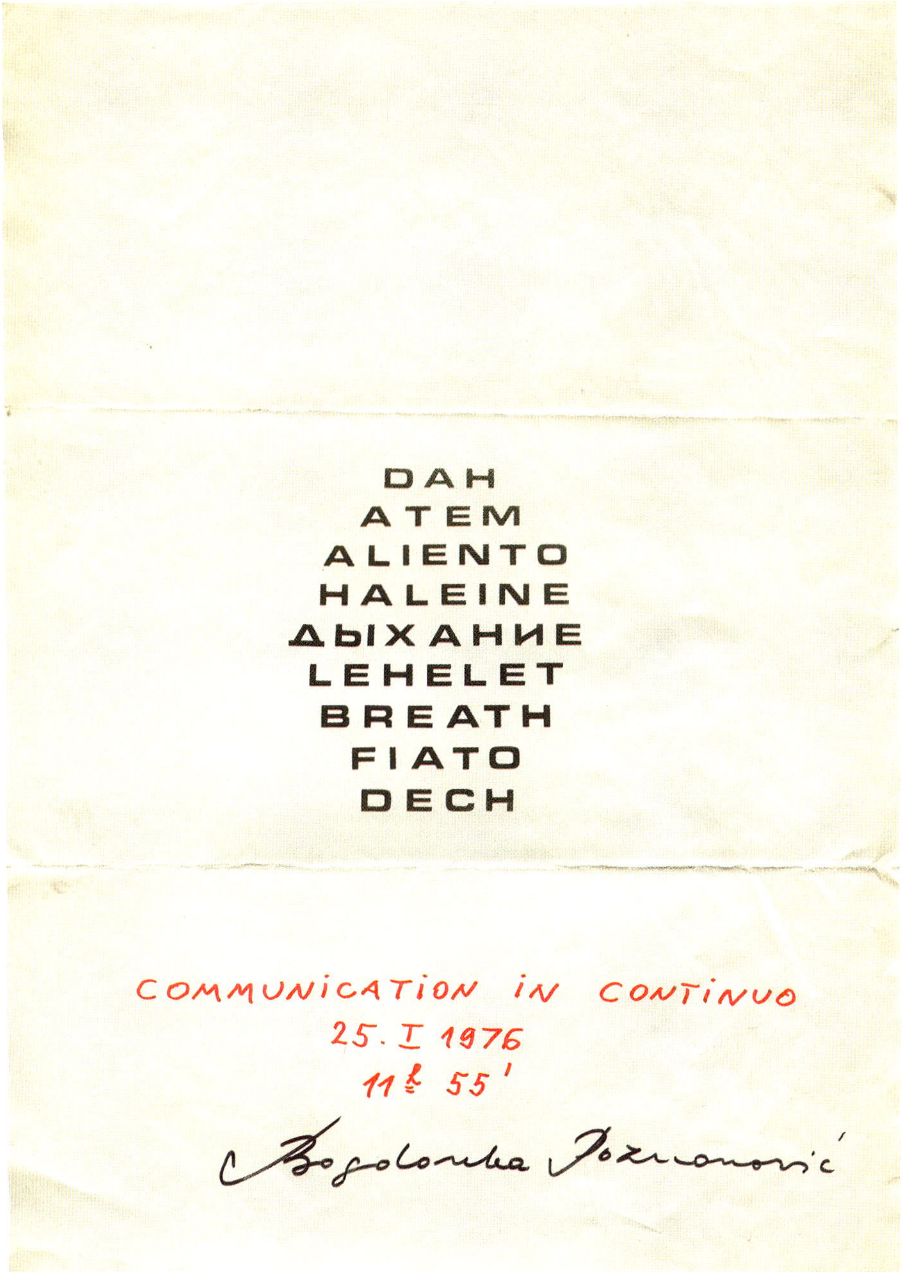

fig. 7

Bogdanka Poznanović, *Communication in Continuo*, 1976.

Photo by Natalia Brandt.
Courtesy of Jarosław Kozłowski's private archive.

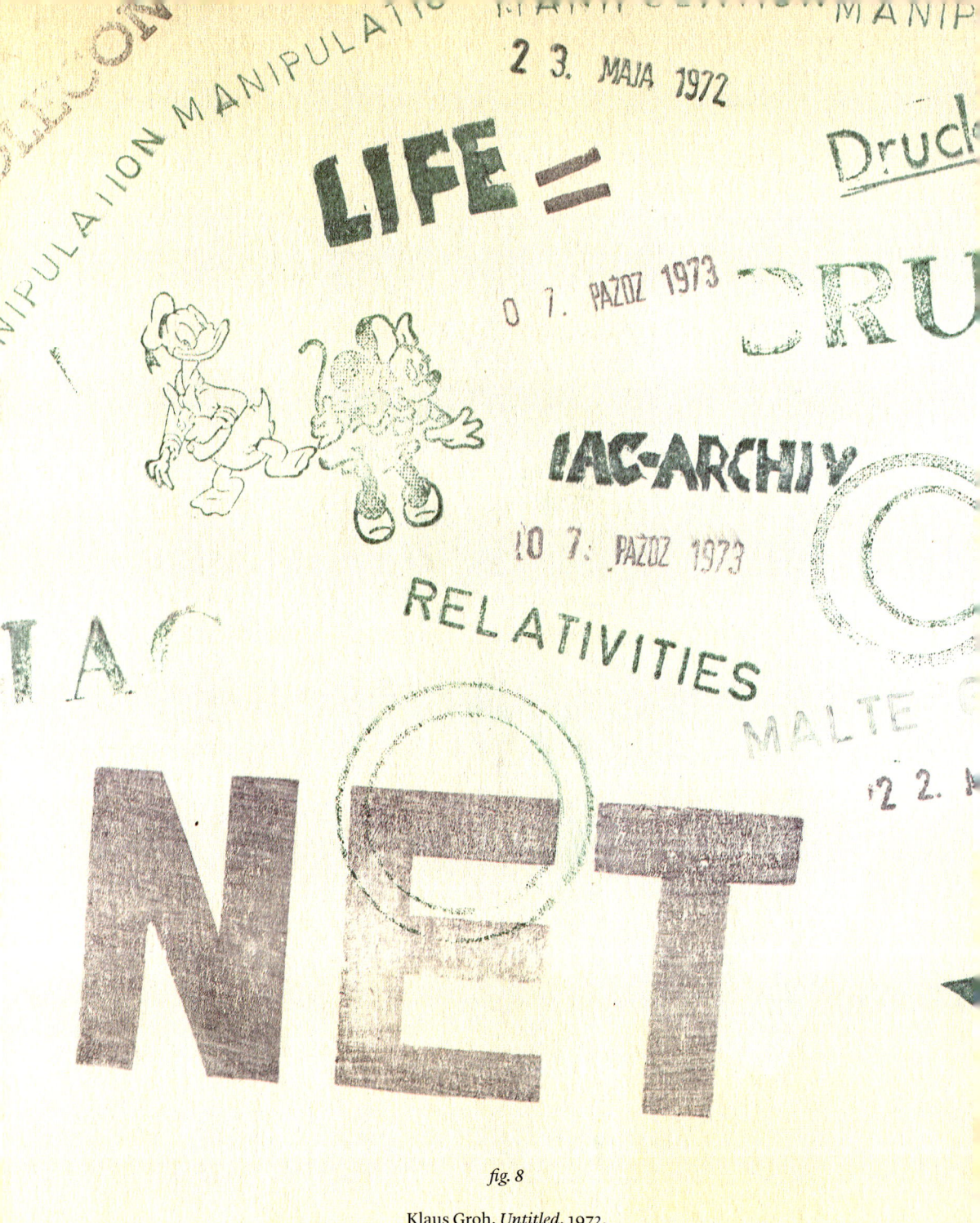

fig. 8

Klaus Groh, *Untitled*, 1972.

Photo by Natalia Brandt.
Courtesy of Jarosław Kozłowski's private archive.

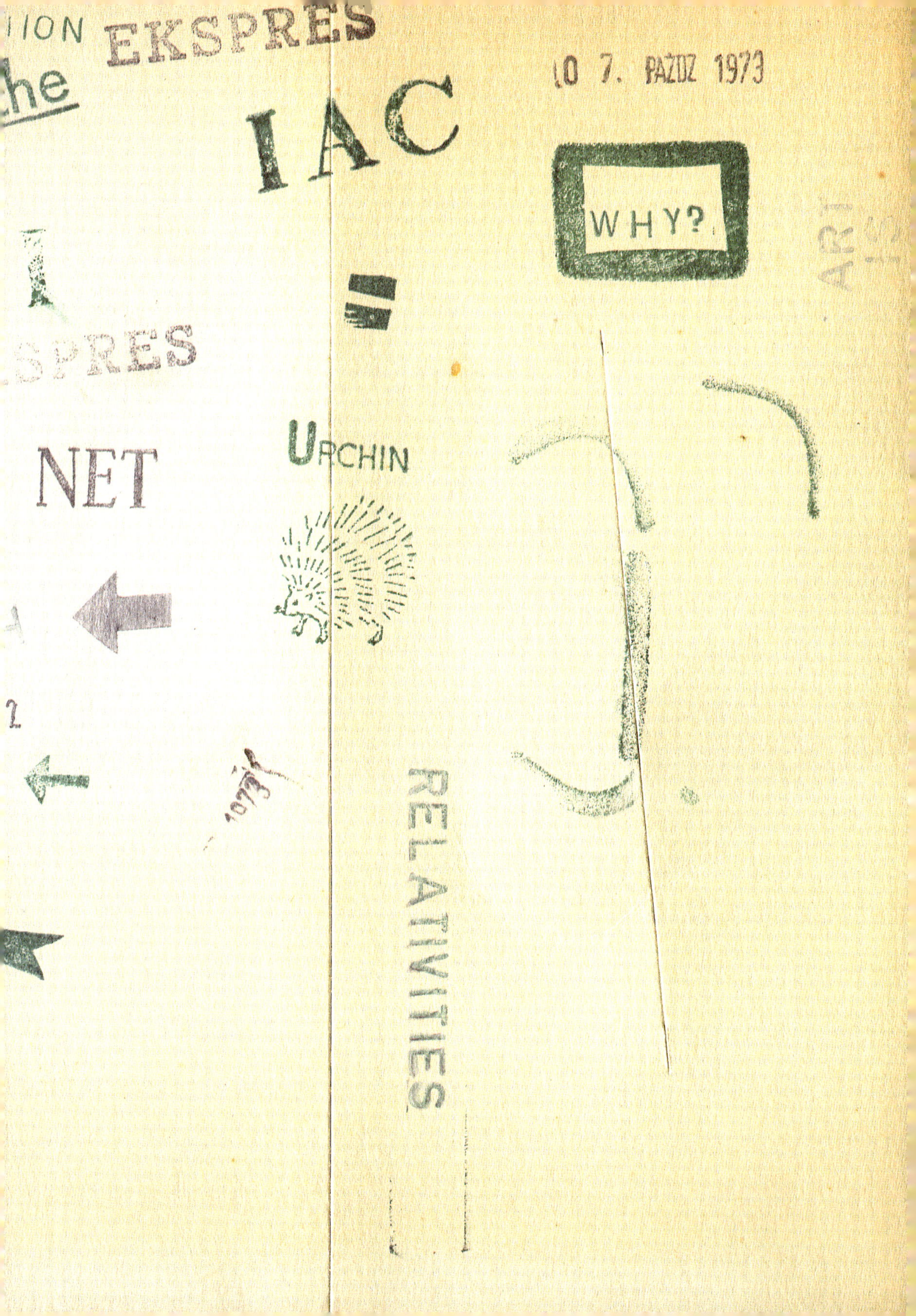

the EKSPRES   IAC   10 7. PAZDZ 1973

                                WHY?

EKSPRES   =   ART IS

NET   URCHIN

←   RELATIVITIES

↑

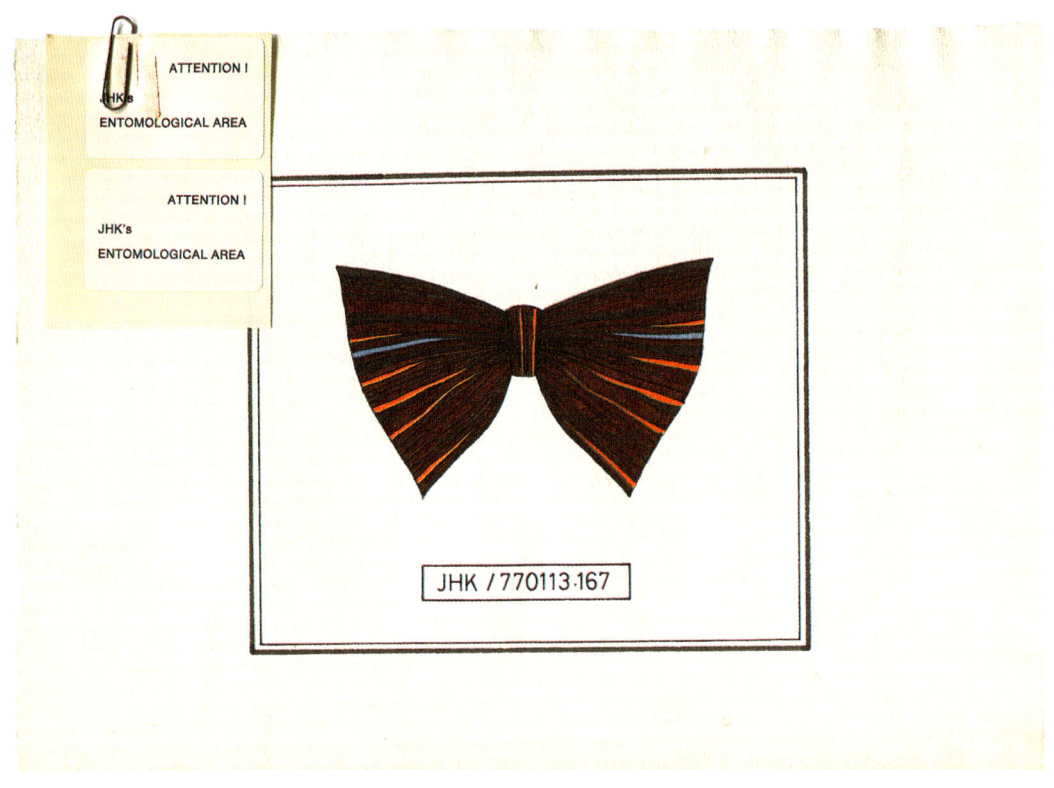

fig. 9

Jiří Kocman, *Butterfly-Environtment Series*, 1973.

Photo by Natalia Brandt.
Courtesy of Jarosław Kozłowski's private archive.

like journal *INFO*, an important vehicle for disseminating artists' calls and proposals worldwide. Artists on both sides of the Iron Curtain were increasingly keen to bypass existing institutions and organizations and create and propagate their own institutions instead. By doing so, they were also contributing to the gradual rebirth of civil society, at least within the artistic community.

The Chilean-born artist Guillermo Deisler's graphic postcards, distributed worldwide by mail to participants in NET, among others, were also rare in the openly agitational stance they assumed. A communist, Deisler found himself imprisoned after the Pinochet takeover of Chile in 1973 and later went into exile, spending twelve years in Bulgaria before being able to move to East Germany, where he worked as a stage designer. He became instrumental in supporting the development of links between his Latin American colleagues and artists in Europe – connecting people through his artists' books, mail art initiatives, and publishing projects, among them the extraordinary mail art magazine *UNI/vers*, which appeared from 1987 until his death in 1995. His pieces in Kozłowski's collection include a range of graphic denunciations of violence and corruption, combining bold text and imagery to draw attention to disappearances under Pinochet or to announce solidarity actions. Especially notable is a work pertaining to the imprisonment of the young Uruguayan poets Clemente Padín and Jorge Caraballo after their participation in the Latin American section of the Paris Biennial in 1977. Deisler's postcard calling for "Freedom for Clemente Padín and Jorge Caraballo, avant-garde artists of UruguAY AY" played with the doubling of the final syllable of "Uruguay" in reference to an earlier piece by Padín, where the final syllable was separated from the body of the word as an expression of pain – "ay!" – specifically, the pain that the military dictatorship was inflicting on the country. Another significant contribution to the campaign was made by the East German graphic and mail artist Robert Rehfeldt, who created an illustration of Rembrandt behind bars with the slogan "Freedom for Artists / C. Padín / Caraballo / Uruguay" (fig. 10). The sustained pressure by the international community over the following years is said to have helped to secure the pair's eventual release in 1983.

As such examples show, the NET community was cemented and nourished by the proposals that circulated through its structure. Things sent and received served both as demonstrations of autonomy from the existing institutional regimes (refusal to act within a market framework / refusal to act within a state-sponsored framework) and as agents of solidarity. In this respect, NET's structure resonates strongly with Bruno Latour's actor-network theory, in which the subject recedes and the object is revealed as a powerful agent. Objects do not just "'express' power relations or 'symbolize' social hierarchies", Latour argues: they act.[19] I want to ar-

---

19 Bruno Latour, *Reassembling the Social: An Introduction to Actor-Network Theory*, Oxford

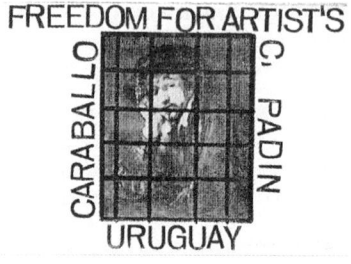

fig. 10

Robert Rehfeldt, *Freedom for Clemente Padín and Jorge Caraballo*, 1974.

Photo by Natalia Brandt.
Courtesy of Jarosław Kozłowski's private archive.

gue that we, too, should beware of consigning objects (in this case works on paper) merely to the status of supporting materials: NET signified both the circulation of documents and the social composition of a community. The materials in the archive – objects, publications, letters, documents – once served as connectors, instrumental in the production of the social field. To borrow Latour's words, they were "connections, the cables, the means of transportation, the vehicles linking places together"; they served as ways of "launching tiny bridges to overcome the gaps created by disparate frames of reference".[20] I therefore want to argue that community was the consequence of object-based associations rather than their cause.

In order to provide a framework within which to "retrace the many different worlds actors were elaborating for each other", Latour replaces the term "actor" with "actor-network", reflecting the extent to which the actor is rather like a "moving target".[21] He describes the actor-network as a "large star-shaped web of mediators flowing in and out of it" and argues that "it is made to exist by its many ties: attachments are first, actors are second".[22] NET, too, might be visualized in the form of a star-shaped structure, with mediators flowing in and out of it as radiating lines. It is only as we track these lines and look closely at the connectors that we begin to "reassemble the social", as Latour puts it. To make sense of larger

University Press, New York, 2005, p. 72.
20   Ibid., pp. 176, 177.
21   Ibid., pp. 49, 46.
22   Ibid., p. 217.

patterns of exchange and transformation, we have to work outwards from the micro level. As Latour remarks: "formats, structures, globalization and totalities circulate inside tiny conduits".[23] The researcher's position is thus that of an ant, he says, whose "knowledge of the social is limited to the termite galleries in which we have been travelling".[24]

An archive such as that produced by NET, accumulated by Jarosław Kozłowski over four decades, clearly represents an extraordinary resource for tracking connections between actor-networks around the world, offering precious snapshots of the complex constellations that contributed, on the ground, to what is too often referred to in shorthand as the zeitgeist of the 1970s. Artist-run initiatives such as NET reveal the impossibility of disentangling local from global developments in the late Cold War context. In the 1970s, experimental artists in North and South America and in Eastern and Western Europe were all, arguably, involved in a common project. As I have discussed, they were seeking, above all, to "strengthen the horizontal human relationships of civil society against the vertical human relationships of military society", as Konrád put it. If the "global turn" in art history is to do more than to further legitimize the globalization of the art market – and it ought to do more – then the history of artistic networks needs to be located carefully in relation to their historical imperatives. Doubtless, there were those who saw networking in professional (albeit inevitably non-market-oriented) terms, but there were also many who showed, as Jirous put it, "that it is possible to do a lot, but only for those who are willing to act and who ask little for themselves, but instead, care a lot for others".[25] As we reconnect past dialogues across archives in different localities and trace historical constellations in which particular objects and archival holdings served as "connectors", we inevitably run the risk of reducing artistic practice to a substitute for activism or social networking. The challenge, I think, is to take autonomous artworks seriously as agents in the production of solidarity without fetishizing the concept of the network.

23   Ibid., p. 252.
24   Ibid., p. 242.
25   Jirous, "A Report on the Third Czech Musical Revival", pp. 64–65.

Daniel Grúň

The Case of Milan Adamčiak

Visual Music between the Acoustic Process, Performance, and the Autonomous Sphere of Writing

Bratislava-based art historian and curator Daniel Grúň researches the legacy of the neo-avant-garde movements of Central Europe. In his essay, he begins by analysing the work *Vodná hudba* (*Water Music*), a now-legendary musical happening created by the Slovak artist Milan Adamčiak and two others in a Bratislava swimming pool in 1970. Grúň goes on to explore the archival material associated with this and other works by Adamčiak, paying particular attention to the modes and strategies of documentation (and their political context) as well as to the interdependence of documentary/notational formats and artistic forms. Among other things, Adamčiak's art provides Grúň with a case study for discussing the complex questions related to the "performativity" of documentation and the reasons for the self-historicization of Central European neo-avant-garde artists.

Every movement is accompanied by a trembling, that is to say, a sound.

We are looking at photographs that capture a musical happening in the covered swimming pool area in a student hostel. The musicians have graphic scores hastily opened in front of them, and are performing the work by playing three string instruments, a xylophone, and cymbals. The arrangement of the performance with musicians seated on the floor in immediate proximity to the public contributes to the disappearance of the traditional division of stage and auditorium (figs. 1–2). A subsequent part of the concert takes place in the swimming pool, the water further uniting the performers and the public. Wearing diving goggles and carrying oxygen cylinders and violins, the musicians dive down to the bottom of the pool and are followed by curious members of the audience, some of whom also use diving gear (fig. 3). The last of the series of documentary photos shows the participants enthusiastically applauding, while in the background we see swimmers looking on from a distance, and a group of students leaving the swimming pool area (fig. 4).

Milan Adamčiak (b. 1946), with Róbert Cyprich (1951–1996) and Jozef Revallo (1944–1993), played this legendary concert entitled *Vodná hudba (Water Music)* in Bratislava in 1970. It is no coincidence that the happening has the identical name of John Cage's *Water Music* (1952). Its manner of presentation, literally under the surface of the water, radicalizes its performative component. What we cannot see in the photographs are the acoustic qualities of the covered swimming pool area: for example, the natural echoes on the water surface and the smooth tiles. Unquestionably, the specific qualities of the chosen space played their part in the happening. It is well known how significantly Cage's work influenced the artists associated with the Fluxus Movement, and, we are reminded in this connection of the so-called event scores such as *Drip Music* (1964) by George Brecht, several works by Yoko Ono included in the book *Grapefruit* (1964), the following work, *Event for the Twilight* (1963), by Mieko (Chieko) Shiomi:

> **Event for the Twilight**
> Steep a piano in the water of a pool
> Play a piece of F. Liszt on the piano
>
> Chieko Shiomi, 1963

In *Water Music*, in contrast to the works mentioned above, Adamčiak does not use a written text as a method of notation, but nonetheless his work is premised, as we can see in the photographs, on the musical composition noted in a graphic score. In other works, such as *Sizyfovské*

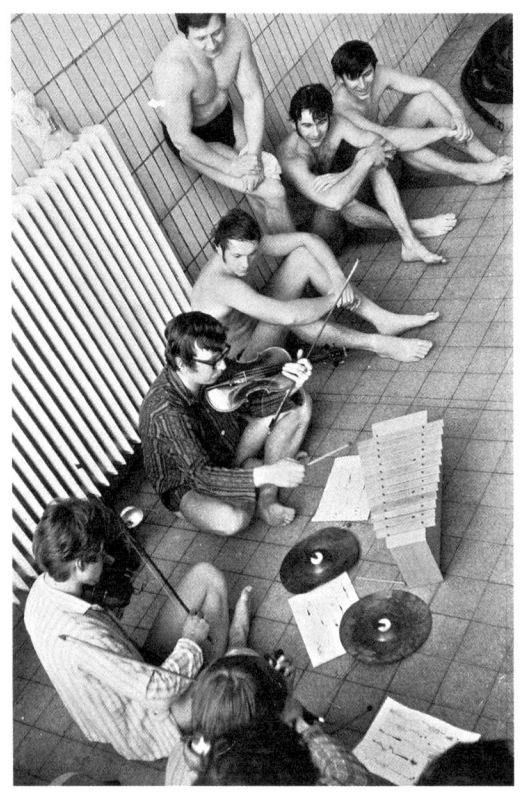 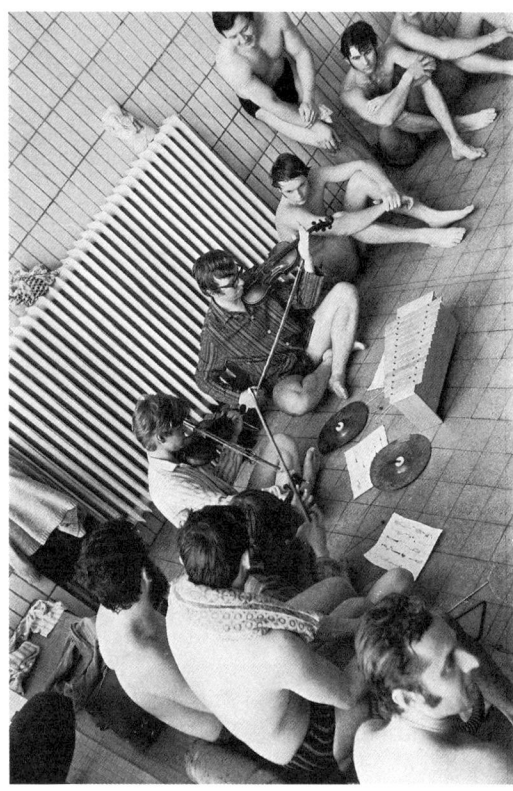

figs. 1–2

Milan Adamčiak and Róbert Cyprich in collaboration with Jozef Revallo, *Water Music*, musical happening in the covered swimming pool area, Juraj Hronec student hostel, Bratislava, 1970.

Photos by Juraj Bartoš. Courtesy of Milan Adamčiak.

roboty (*Labours of Sisyphus*, 1965-1969), we find unambiguous parallels with the event scores produced by Fluxus artists. But, unlike the Fluxus artists, Adamčiak never published his event scores, nor did he realize them as actions in concerts. Rather, he allowed them to circulate in the form of verbal instructions among friends and randomly selected partners. The scores were transcribed in typewritten form on sheets of paper in 1969-1970. One of the recurring motifs is the triangle of performer – instrument – public (fig. 5):

Solo per gran cassa (Labours of Sisyphus)
- someone brings a large drum onto the stage
- he sets it up and goes away
- the public gazes at the large drum

jama 1968[1]

From the mid-1960s onward, the ideas of the international Fluxus movement made their way into Czechoslovakia, and Adamčiak could have found them published in a number magazines or books, or he could have picked them up from other artists in Prague. Jiří Kolář applied similar principles in his cycle of exhortatory poems, *Návod k upotřebení* (*Instruction Manual*, 1969 [1965]), as did Milan Knížák in directions for his actions.[2] What interests us here is not so much finding a solution to the problem of delayed development, dependency, or derivation from Western or other models. Our concern is to show what part writing as an autonomous sphere played in these records, how it invited the author and the recipient into performative unity, and the potential presentation in action of a given piece. What Adamčiak managed to capture in *Labours of Sisyphus* was not merely a disjunction of the classical relationship between performer and public. His situations staged in a minimal number of words, for example, *Monoactions* in 1969, also gave utterance to emotions evoked by the occupation of Czechoslovakia.

Monoactions 3-5
rise!
quickly count all your buttons!!
sit down!!!

jama 1969

---

1   During 1968-1970, Adamčiak used the monogram *jama*, an abbreviation of "*ja, milan adamčiak*" ("I, Milan Adamčiak").
2   See Pavlína Morganová, *Czech Action Art: Happenings, Actions, Events, Land Art, Body Art and Performance Art behind the Iron Curtain*, Karolinum Press, Charles University, Prague, 2014, pp. 42-43, 60-61.

Milan Adamčiak was one of the first Czechoslovak artists who began to systematically research intermedia overlaps. He conducted his research principally in the creative spheres: in the field of experimental poetry, action art, and so-called new music. In the second half of the 1960s, he created cycles of diverse kinds of typographic grids in which graphic and semantic realization overlapped with the acoustic rhythmization of the text. One part of his work has its premise in experimental poetry, taking the form of directions and instructions for various activities. Another part opens the way toward visual music with unconventional notations and graphic scores. A third links the inspirations from the two preceding parts in performative presentation: game-playing experimentation and the non-completion of the compositional process, significantly opening up the possibility of perfecting the work using both classical and non-classical instruments and unusual settings. It was above all Adamčiak's creative participation (together with Róbert Cyprich) in happenings and concerts in 1969–1970 that art historians characterized as being a parallel to the Fluxus Movement.[3] Unlike Milan Knížák, whom George Maciunas appointed director of Fluxus East, Adamčiak had no direct personal contacts during that period.

From 1964 to 1967, Adamčiak acquired some important contacts through translations by the Czech poets, Josef Hiršal and Bohumila Grögerová, who were the editors of the first Czech anthology of programmatic texts of concrete and experimental poetry, action art, happenings, and the Fluxus movement. The anthology was entitled *Slovo, písmo, akce, hlas* (*Word, Letter, Action, Voice*).[4] In 1967, Milan Adamčiak met the Brno author, Jiří Valoch, who ranked his works among the most progressive examples of Czechoslovak graphics and would later publish extracts from them in a book on graphic scores.[5] Adamčiak was in touch by correspondence with artists such as Dick Higgins, Ben Vautier, the Spanish group ZAJ, Marshall McLuhan, Joseph Beuys, Edgardo Antonio Vigo, Clemente Padín, Elena Pelli, Karlheinz Stockhausen, John Cage, and many others. He exchanged his texts for other texts and publications. As late as 1969–1970, with the euphoria of the 1960s expiring, he organized an independent exhibition of graphic scores (*Visual Music*, V-klub, Dom umenia, Bratislava) as well as a number of performances, where he took part in happenings and exhibitions, including the music project *Kánon 5 × ¼*, part of the *1. otvorený ateliér* (*1st Open Studio*) exhibition in the private house

---

3   Zora Rusinová, "Milan Adamčiak a Robert Cyprich", in *Umenie akcie 1965-1989*, ed. Zora Rusinová, Slovenská národná galéria, Bratislava, 2001, pp. 89-93; and Andrea Bátorová, "Alternative Trends in Slovakia during the 1960s and Parallels to Fluxus", in *Fluxus East: Fluxus Networks in Central Eastern Europe*, ed. Petra Stegmann, exh. cat., Künstlerhaus Bethanien, Berlin, 2007, pp. 165-166.

4   Josef Hiršal and Bohumila Grögerová, eds., *Slovo, písmo, akce, hlas*, Československý spisovatel, Prague, 1967.

5   Jiří Valoch, ed., *Partitury: Grafická hudba, fónická poezie, akce, parafráze, interpretace*, Jazzová sekce Svazu hudebníků, Prague, 1980.

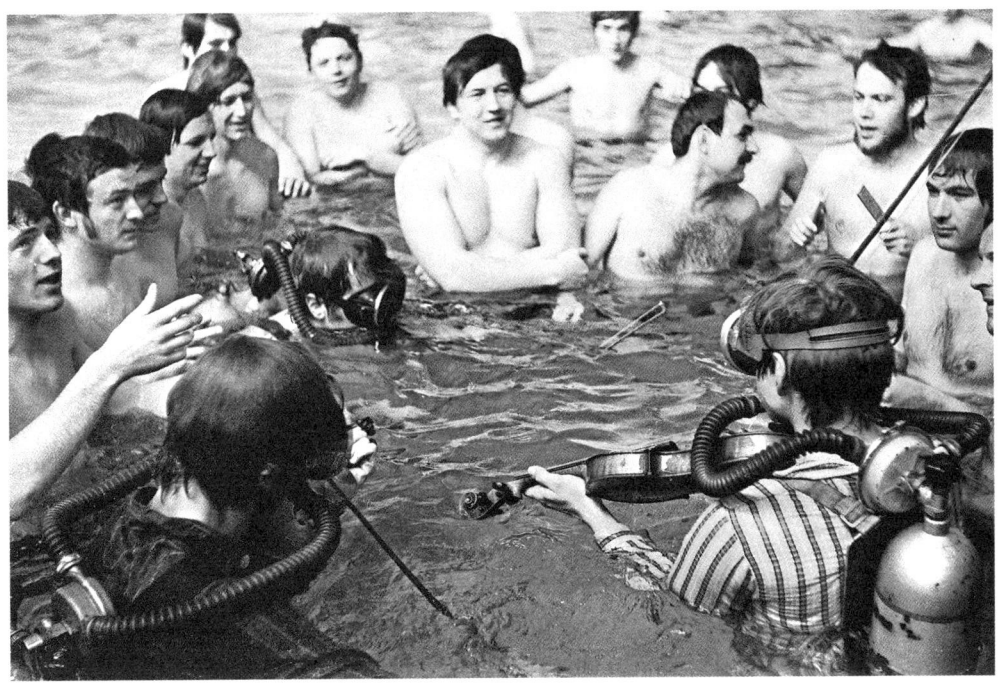

figs. 3-4

Milan Adamčiak and Róbert Cyprich in collaboration with Jozef Revallo, *Water Music*, musical happening in the covered swimming pool area, Juraj Hronec student hostel, Bratislava, 1970.

Photos by Juraj Bartoš. Courtesy of Milan Adamčiak.

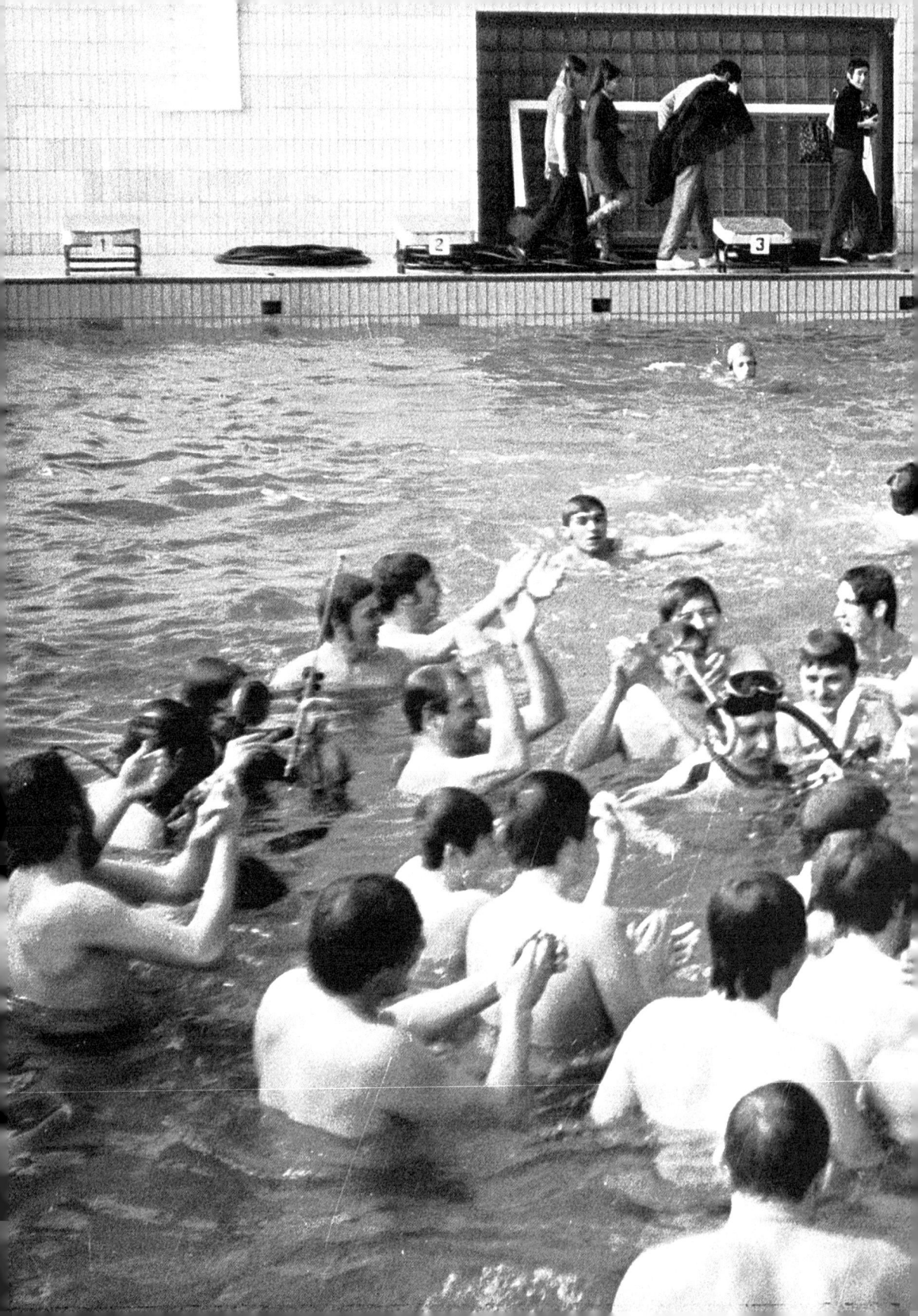

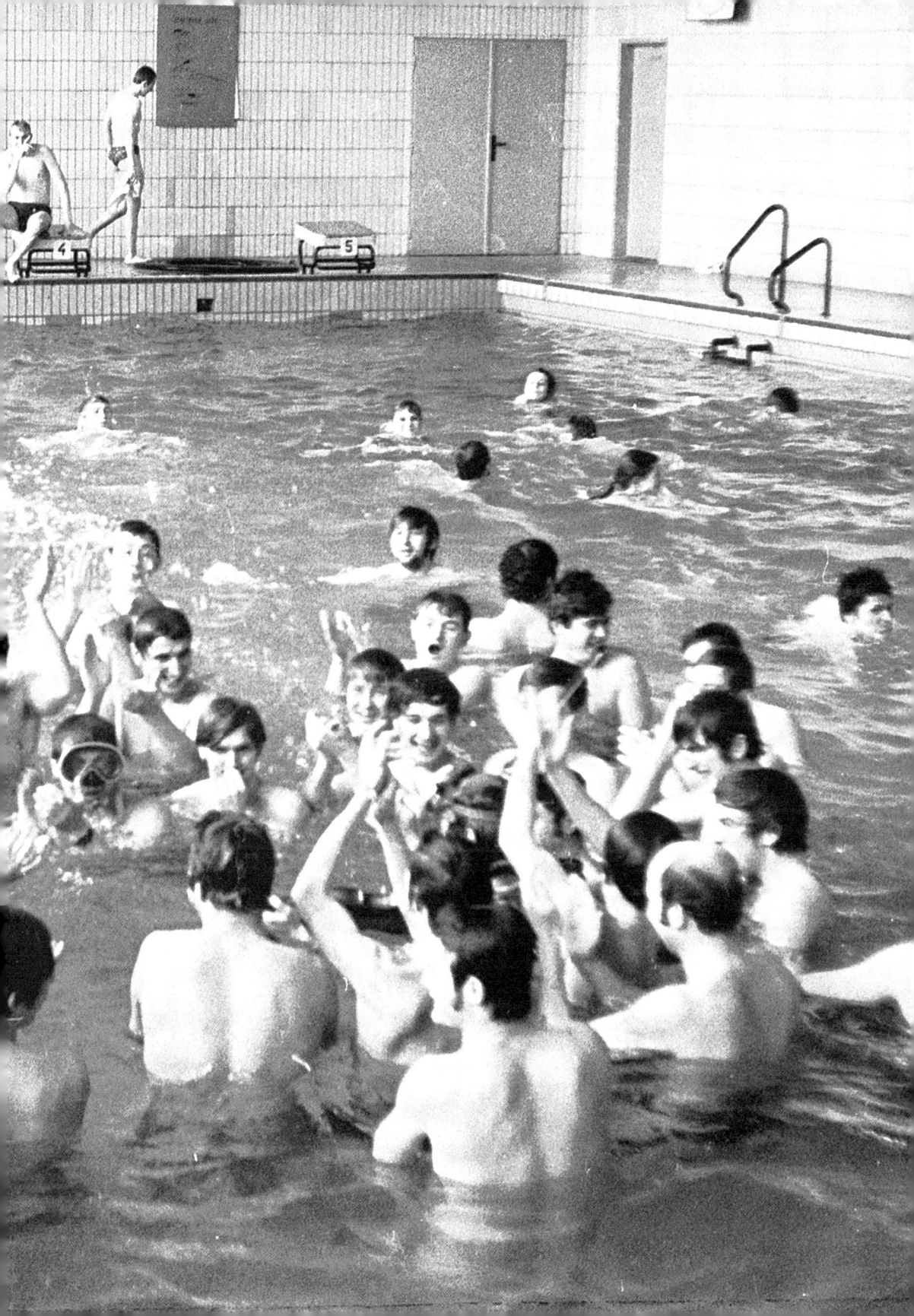

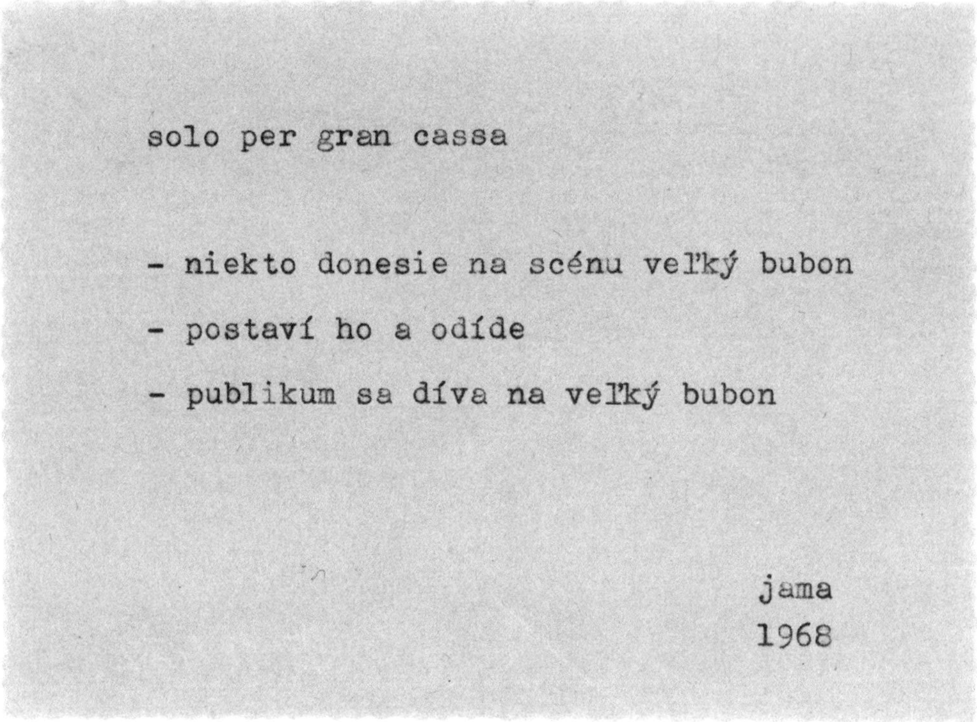

> solo per gran cassa
>
> − niekto donesie na scénu veľký bubon
> − postaví ho a odíde
> − publikum sa díva na veľký bubon
>
> jama
> 1968

fig. 5

Milan Adamčiak, *Solo per gran cassa*
(*Labours of Sisyphus*), 1968, typing on paper, 10 cm x 13.5 cm.

Courtesy of the Slovak National Gallery.

of Rudolf Sikora, *Gaudium et Pax* (action in the nature), the *Festival snehu* (*Festival of Snow*) together with Alex Mlynárčik, Róbert Cyprich and Miloš Urbásek, and *Dislokácie II* (*Dislocations II*), part of the *Smolenice Seminars for New Music*.

Adamčiak was a professional musicologist. He took a job with the Slovak Academy of Sciences and joined the Communist Party at the beginning of the period of normalization (1972–1989). To continue with the activities he had launched earlier would have had unacceptable implications for his career. While he worked publically as a scholar, columnist, and popularizer of so-called contemporary music, in private he created for a narrow circle of recipients.

In 1964, Adamčiak first heard John Cage's works on the radio (in that same year Cage visited Czechoslovakia and together with the Merce Cunningham Dance Company appeared in Prague and Ostrava) and, since then, his work confronted the principles and procedures that the great inspirer brought into music and musical notation on numerous occasions and at numerous levels. Only in 1992 did Adamčiak finally meet Cage personally during a visit to Bratislava when Adamčiak organized an exhibition of his scores in the Slovak National Gallery.[6] One of Adamčiak's favourite and frequently repeated *bon mots* went something like this: "Cage's aim was to have no aim. My aim, on the contrary, is to have as many aims as possible." As Jozef Cseres says, this statement reflects Adamčiak's polemical character: he was never content with the status quo.[7] What's more, there is the multidimensional mode of the artistic distribution of ideas which, under the conditions of marginal existence, proceeds in several, often mutually conflicting, spheres of application. At this point, we might cast doubt on the originality of Adamčiak's work as "art" since he created many of his works as paraphrases or pastiches of the work of world-renowned artists. For Adamčiak, *hommage* was a conscious principle: he appropriated and adapted, polemicized, paraphrased, and recontextualized.[8] He viewed two composers, Bogusław Schaeffer and Mauricio Kagel, as his teachers in graphic notation.[9] It was Shaeffer's scores that gave substance to the idea of polyversional music, the ambition of which was to equalize composer and performer. Shaeffer's compositions are based on the principle of unpredictability and potentiality, leaving open possibilities for the performance of the score. Likewise, Adamčiak's graphic scores also place considerable demands on performance, above

---

6   Milan Adamčiak, "A Few Words about J. C.", in *John Cage*, exh. cat., Slovak National Gallery, Bratislava, 1992.
7   Jozef Cseres, "John Cage in US: On John Cage's Influence among Czecho-Slovakian Artists", in *The Freedom of Sound: John Cage behind the Iron Curtain*, ed. Katalin Székely, exh. cat., Ludwig Museum – Museum of Contemporary Art, Budapest, 2013, pp. 80–81.
8   Ibid., p. 80.
9   Michal Murin, "S Milanom Adamčiakom o grafických partitúrach, hudobných projektoch a muzikologickej tvorbe", in *Milan Adamčiak Archív III (Nôty): Notácie a grafické partitúry*, ed. Michal Murin, Dive Buki, Košice, 2013, p. 66.

all on moments of improvisation. Although most of them can be played and also often contain verbal instructions for the performer, their visual resolution is sufficient for the reader simply to imagine the recorded auditory processes (fig. 6). For Adamčiak, the graphic score was a field of permanent conflicts, movements, and collisions, like batteries charged with dynamic energy. The meeting of graphic signs in the score emits the stimulus that in reading triggers acoustic associations according to the suggested instructions and also sketches spatial relationships (fig. 7). Many of these imitate and paraphrase electrical circuits, mechanical engines, or machines for playing (beginning with chess and ending with the gramophone or hi-fi tower). Hence, they correspond with the principles of invention, playfulness, and improvisation.

As Liz Kotz puts it in her book on language in 1960s art, language is central to the expanded concept of notation. "As already evident in Cage's compositions of the late 1950s, language, graphic inscription, and diagrams all provide a means of defining parameters or indicting a structure, while retaining sufficient ambiguity to permit distinct performances or instantiations."[10] The model of unconventional musical notation was developed above all in the circle of artists close to the Fluxus Movement, for whom words to be read and actions to be performed became inseparable. "In their direct invitation to enactment and performed response, event scores could seem like almost absurd literalizations of 1960s's critical claims for reading as an activity of production."[11] Hence the event scores, using a typewritten or other kind of text, can be categorized simultaneously as poetry, performance art, and musical graphics. That is precisely the intersection point of performativity and writing to which *Labours of Sisyphus* (1965–1969) and *Monoactions* (1969) correspond. Both of them use a minimum of words and are written as directions or instructions for the achievement of an action. The first cycle of texts is divided into twenty-two parts, and in many of them the actors are musical instruments and a performer. In the case of *Monoactions*, the textual form was not as important as the presentation, because most of them served to defamiliarize everyday, ordinary situations and activities.

In Milan Adamčiak's work, the visual poem created on the typewriter is the result of a gesture, and thus may be a written, sonic, and graphic record of an action. The problem of impulse (a point, a stroke on the typewriter key) and the problem of process (a line developed in time) gradually led him to an intention to consider typewritten grids as scores with their own rhythmic and acoustic event. In achieving this purpose he actually found a new expressive field, the result of a unique fusion of the impulses of concrete poetry, auditive poetry, new music, and action art. During the early 1960s, the French poet, translator, and theoretician Pierre

---

10 Liz Kotz, *Words to Be Looked At: Language in 1960s Art*, MIT Press, Cambridge, Mass., and London, 2010, p. 49.
11 Ibid., p. 62.

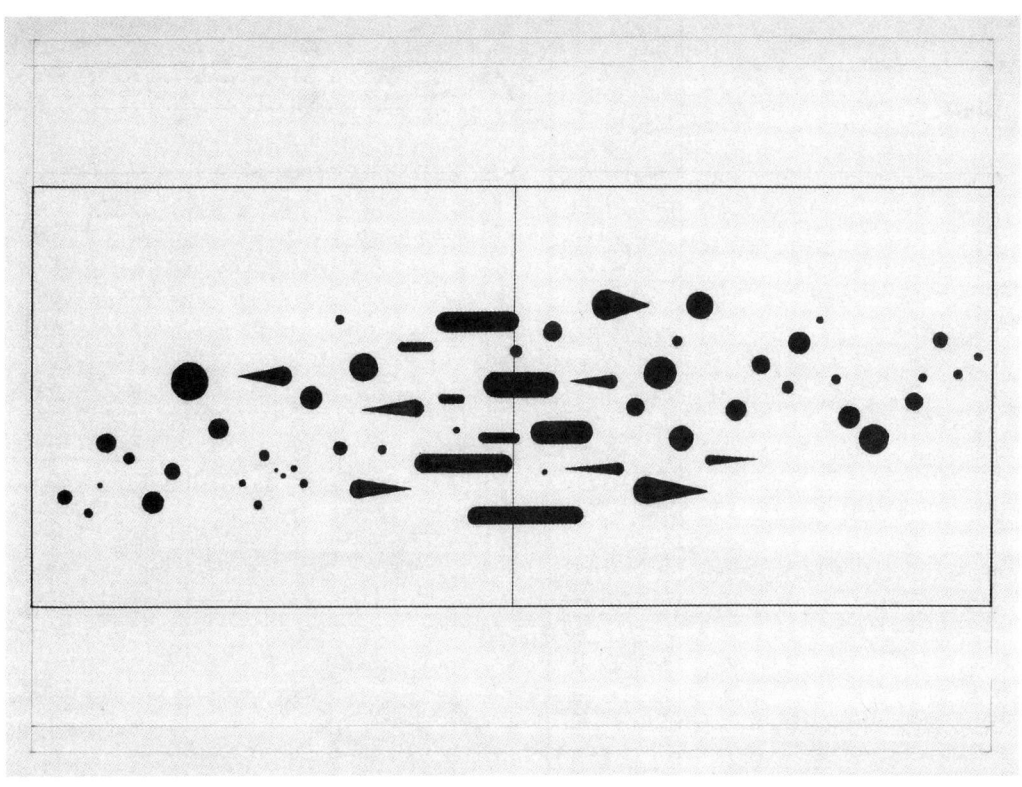

fig. 6

Milan Adamčiak, *Sign'ings*, 1968, ink drawing on paper, 32.5 cm x 45 cm.

Courtesy of the Slovak National Gallery.

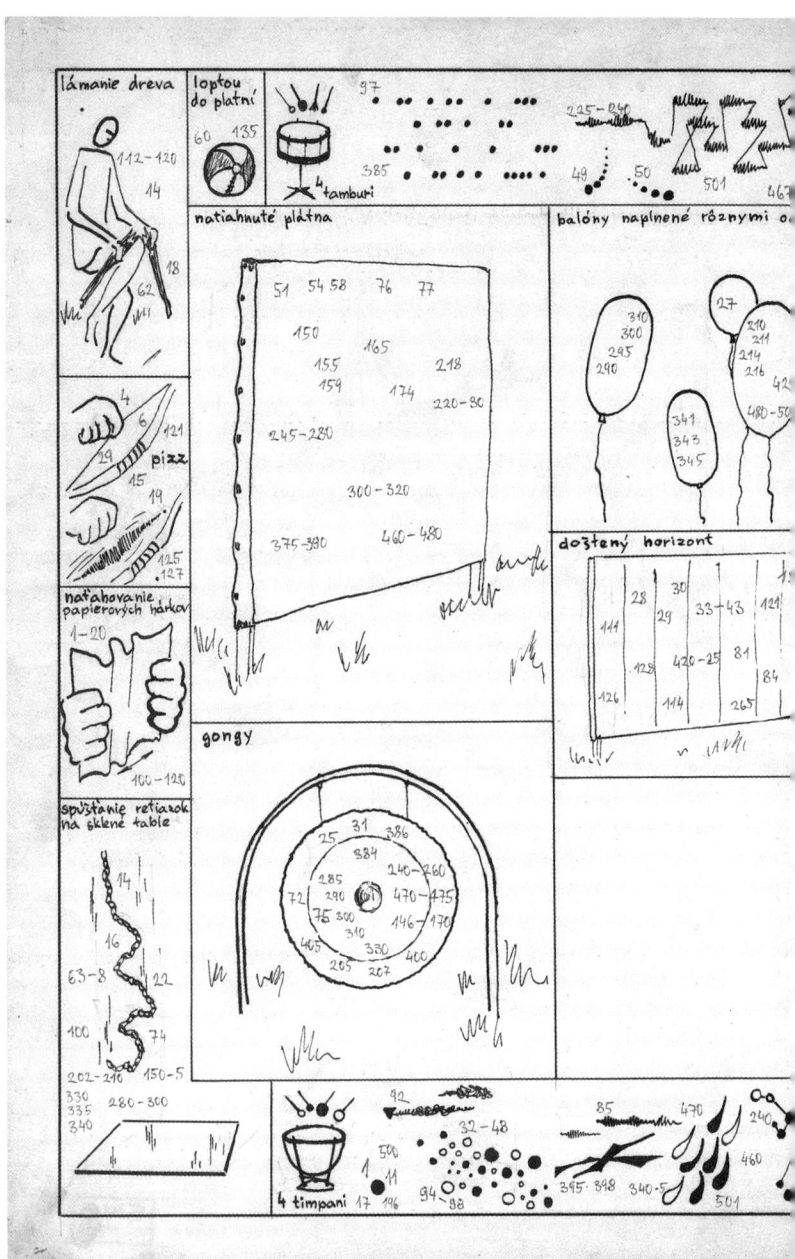

fig. 7

Milan Adamčiak, *Sebastian Poem*, 1969, ball pen and ink drawing on paper, 32.5 cm x 45 cm.

Courtesy of the Slovak National Gallery.

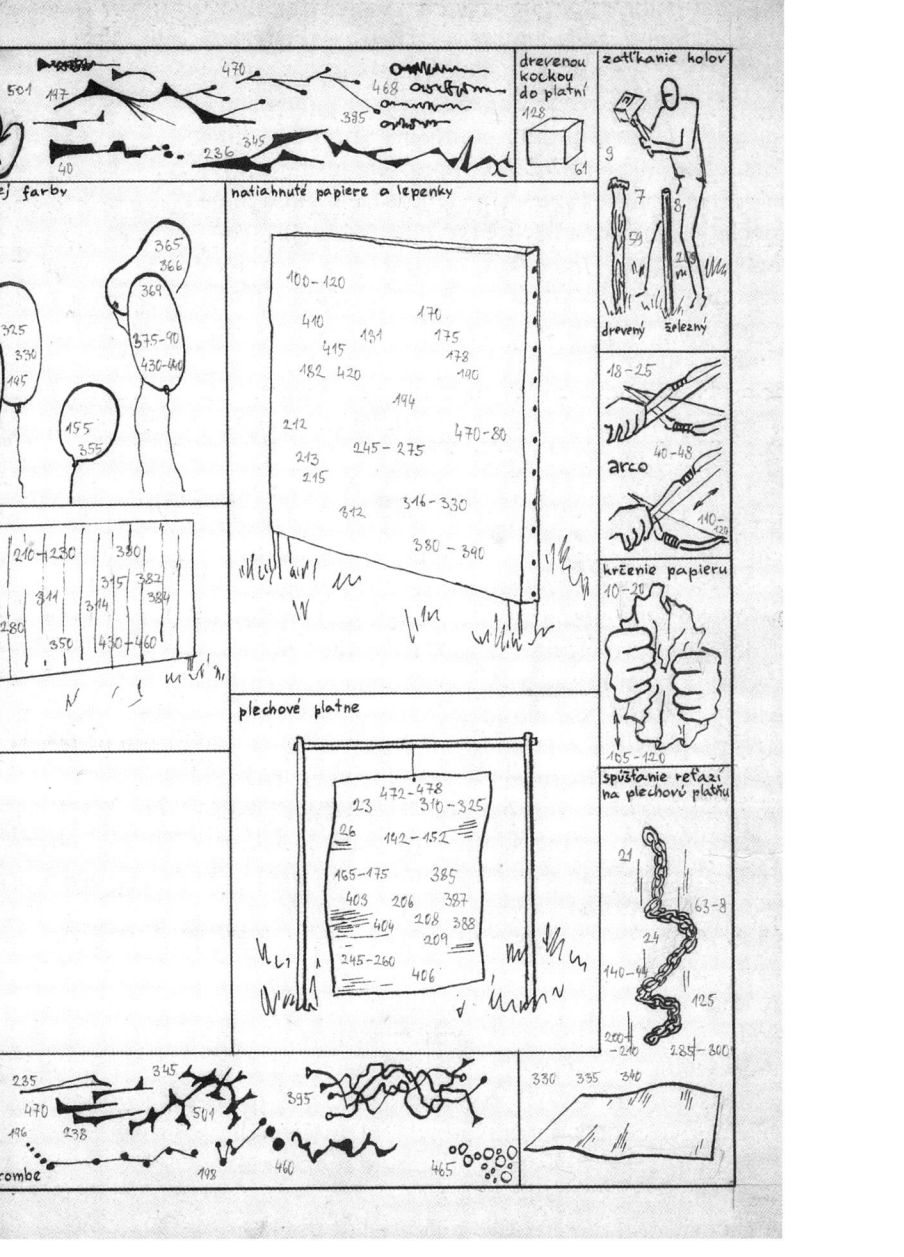

Garnier had proclaimed the challenges of phonetic poetry, which initiated new techniques of working with language as a material. He used the term "force-fields" (*Spannungsfelder*) for audiovisual experiments in concrete poetry where the constelled force of each word, each syllable, and each sound is exploited, and even the non-sounding points are charged with magnetism. Adamčiak's visual poems entitled *Liniengedichte* (original title) was rooted right in the cylinder of the typewriter, where he applied the idea that each line is a process and has its own life on the paper's surface. *Liniengedichte* was preceded by the cycles *Intenciogramy* and *Invenciogramy* (*Intentiograms* and *Inventiograms*, 1969) in which the line represents a kind of ideograph of life energies (e.g. tension–relaxation). To record them, Adamčiak used, in addition to "loose" paper leaves, sheets with a variously pre-inscribed metric grid (millimetre paper, logarithmic paper, etc.). Later, in the 1970s, these evolved into a cycle of cinematic drawings and scores created with recordings of his own constructions from a child's construction set and other models of various kinds. In the series *Pseudogramy* (*Pseudograms*), Adamčiak extended the register to include writing using unconventional instruments (feathers, matchsticks, reeds), which he used as a working inventory for a gestic record in the limited space of the graphic score. Continuing along this path, he later arrived at score "inventories" and spatial installations from various materials (sugar, rice, sand, bones, cores, spices) that applied graphic tracing and gestic manipulation.

In 1969, Milan Adamčiak published his manifesto "Ensemble Comp." in *Mladá tvorba* journal. The manifesto appeared in one issue, along with the libretto of Róbert Cyprich's action *Čas slnka* (*Time of the Sun*). These two artists collaborated intensively during this period. The production of "Ensemble Comp." was preceded by the staging of joint events in Žilina and Ružomberok (1967–1968), the creation of experimental poetry, music production (together they organized the so-called *Evenings of New Music*), and joint creations with Alex Mlynárčik.[12] In their remarkable output, both artists were responding to the topical ideas of experimental poetry, aleatory music, and action art. Adamčiak proclaimed the fusion of the three spheres – poetry, music, and event – and this remained a key aspect of his lifelong work. He presented a whole gamut of examples: bipoetry; patext; numerical texts; selective texts; prepared texts; montage, mix, and permutational text; verbal, substantive, adjectival, adverbial text; intermedia texts (phonic, auditive, etc.); visual texts; objective, topic, and shape texts; mobile, destatic, and spatial poems.

In all spheres of Adamčiak's work, the creative potential of the reader/performer/viewer was emphasized. Poetry represented an active (performative) engagement of the reader in the completion of variations of the

---

[12] The following are the actions documented by Alex Mlynárčik: *Trenie* (*Spawning*), *Festival snehu* (*Festival of Snow*), *Hommage à Courbet*, and *Donácia* (*Donation*). See Alex Mlynárčik and Pierre Restany, *Inde / Ailleurs*, exh. cat., Slovak National Gallery, Bratislava, 1995.

text units. The reader, consumer of linguistic expression, is made equivalent to the author in the text. Adamčiak also used the designations "programmer" and "realizer", for example in the following quote:

> In the finished text ... the programmer pre-codes some kind of word ... to a system of numerically appropriate interpunctual signs .... The consumer/co-creator replaces the code with a word of the given verbal kind that suits him. A new text emerges, syntactically corresponding to the program.[13]

In music, the consequence of this collaboration is the principled engagement of the composition's performer and the public. The musical work should not be precisely determined; rather it becomes directions for the performer's self-realization. The event is understood as a synthesis of the two preceding categories:

> ... the public's engagement in creative activity erases in full measure the distinction between creator and consumer, and levels the differences between artist and public ... it allows the subject to activate his human creative capacities, and permanently to participate and to manifest his true relationship to the action of life and society.[14]

Adamčiak speaks of becoming conscious of "active existence", and his graphic scores and experimental poetry not only represent the achievement of "a liberated language", but also anticipate open play with anyone who is prepared to take part. In 1966–1967, he was concentrating entirely on visual poetry composed on the typewriter. A year later he began using the monogram *jama*, an abbreviation of "*ja, milan adamčiak*" ("I, Milan Adamčiak"). The period at the turn of the 1970s represents the culmination of his poetic work. That was when he produced the cycles *Konštelácie, Selektívne texty, Preparované texty, Montážne a Mixážne texty, Patexty*, and *Bipoemy* (*Constellations, Selective Texts, Prepared Texts, Montage and Mix Texts, Patexts, and Bipoems*) in which he made practical trials of the avant-garde principle of the semantic decomposition of the text. Parallel with this, he was producing, from 1969 on, the associative manuscript *Skripturálne básne* (*Scriptural Poems*) and the rubber-stamped *Typoemy* (*Typoems*), crafted as shape compositions. In the *Typoems*, and throughout one part of the *Typoraster* (*Typogrid*) series from 1966–1969, he concentrated on a graphic record of the musical aspects (serialism, aleatorics, and polyphony) on a given surface. Both series of typographic poems are produced by typewriter on paper. Adamčiak had by then achieved a masterly combination of the initiatives of concrete poetry and graphic music in his visual poetry. The structure of the typographic grid also dominated his

---

13   Milan Adamčiak, "ENSEMBLE-COMP", *Mladá tvorba*, vol. 14, no. 10, 1969, p. 26.
14   Ibid., p. 28.

visual poetry, which was inspired by the ornamentation of folk embroidery, and the texture of carpets, curtains, and fabrics.

What perhaps characterizes Adamčiak's poetry most persuasively is the performative and sonic dimension of machine-written type – the keystroke, the succession of types, their overlapping and blurriness, the coherently composed image field. The visual qualities of the rubber stamp and machine-written type are determined by the rhythm and intensity of the strokes. The deciding factors are a randomly selected alphabetic code, a previously chosen combination of types, and their permutational application in the graphic realization. We can read the surface arrangement, and the density and overlapping of rubber-stamp types as a record of acoustic processes and simultaneously as directions for their interpretation. The graphic traces recording this synesthetic process are analogous to a number of important concepts such as Eugen Gomringer's *constellation* (*Konstellation*) and *randomness* as defined by George Brecht, who was known to Adamčiak from translations in the 1960s.[15]

Adamčiak was also preoccupied with composing the artwork in space. His organization of graphic signs evokes crystalline structures and the architecture of sounds. The non-completion of the compositional process, the principle of "the open acoustic system", became an enduring attribute of his work. Starting in the early 1970s, Adamčiak was creating *Systémové partitúry* (*Systemic Scores*) with the aim of indicating solutions to notational problems in the form of matrices, graphs, tables, and diagrams. Within the space of one page he employed a regular grid in the form of a network, which he called *Lineatúry* (*Lineatures*). *Lineatures* and *Systemic Scores* are aimed at the organization of musical time. The precise written entry of their rhythmic composition represents directions for a subjective interpretation.

In addition to Eugen Gomringer's constellation theory, the principles of Abraham A. Moles's permutational art and Max Bense's statistical aesthetic of the text also resonate in Adamčiak's texts. The work of Josef Hiršal and Bohumila Grögerová brought new criteria originating from statistical aesthetics, manifestos, and literary experiments proclaiming a turn towards the materiality of language and the structure of the text to Czechoslovakia.[16] The above-mentioned artists were proclaiming not only a new type of artwork, but also a new type of poet-creator that would be able to theoretically clarify the principles of composing concrete poetry. Earlier, Walter Benjamin presented the following conundrum in "The Author as Producer": "Before I ask: what is a work's position vis-à-vis the production relations of its time, I should like to ask: what is its position

15   See George Brecht, "Náhoda a obraz", p. 48, and Eugen Gomringer, "Od verše ke konstelaci", p. 224, both in *Slovo, písmo, akce, hlas* (referenced in n. 4).
16   As early as 1962, Josef Hiršal and Bohumila Grögerová presented their "Lecture on the Philosophy of Language, Statistical Aesthetics and Contemporary Literary Experiment" at Mánes in Prague. See Vít Havránek, ed., *Akce, slovo, pohyb, prostor: Experimenty v umění šedesátých let*, exh. cat., GHMP, Prague, 1999, pp. 226–257.

within them?"[17] This question, Benjamin avers, concerns the function of a work within the literary production relations of its time. In other words, it is directly concerned with literary "technique". During the liberal 1960s, socialist Czechoslovakia saw not only the rise of the avant-garde vision of programmatic art, inspired by the conquests of science and technology, but also of the new role of the creator, bringing the poet's consciousness into proximity with the machine. The concept of "technology" therefore becomes crucial for an understanding of experimental poetry and graphic music. As David Crowley pointed out, experiment in poetry and music cannot be disengaged from the political frameworks which socialism (a social experiment) was then producing.[18] Scientific socialism stimulated progressive thinking in the cultural environment, and the anticipation of future technologies had already provided a powerful seedbed for the artistic imagination since the late 1950s. Artistic experiment undeniably drew on the technological possibilities the development of which was cultivated by state policy during the 1960s. However, the social situation in Czechoslovakia after 1968, followed by the onset of normalization in the early 1970s, saw the complete removal of experimental creation from public discourse. These political circumstances marked an entire generation of progressive artists striving to become a new international avant-garde, Adamčiak among them. The situation induced Adamčiak to integrate performativity and writing into a single whole. Not being able to perform his works publicly, he further dematerialized the compositional process, ultimately realizing the potential of graphic scores and experimental poetry to be effectively played out in the mind of the performer. Only after 1989 were several of Adamčiak's scores publicly played as sonic, musical, and dance performances.

The extensive and internally differentiated archive of Milan Adamčiak's experimental work is dislocated, scattered. It is only in the past few years that his work has been published in book form.[19] One of the reasons for this situation is that Adamčiak sent out or gave away a large part of his production on various occasions. A second more prosaic reason is his eviction from his apartment, homelessness, and subsequent departure from Bratislava in 2005. Ultimately it is only because of the artist's work typology, more than the medium, that there can be any question of an archive, because its coherence is imaginary. We can interpret the "archive" as

---

17   Walter Benjamin, "The Author as Producer", trans. Anna Bostock, *Understanding Brecht*, Verso, London, 1998, p. 87.
18   See Daniel Muzyczuk, David Crowley, and Michał Libera, "Sounding the Body Electric: A Conversation", *ArtMargins Online*, October 9, 2012, http://www.artmargins.com/index.php/5-interviews/689-sounding-the-body-electric-a-conversation (accessed July 29, 2016).
19   Milan Adamčiak, *Archív I (Expo): Experimentálna poézia 1964-1972*, ed. Michal Murin, Dive Buki, Košice, 2012. Works by Milan Adamčiak are in collections of Michal Murin, Jozef Cseres, Linea Collection, Marinko Sudac Collection, and the Slovak National Gallery.

a system of categorization of experimental poetry, action art, and graphic scores. It emerges from the artist's goals and intentions, and, at the same time, is a kind of instruction for reading the articulated complex of what he produced. Adamčiak's work ranges between intricately structured scores and spontaneous sketches; parts that amount to jottings encounter a conceptual analysis of variations in the positions and sound variations of the performer. On the one hand, documentation appears as a figure in the complex of the artist's self-historicization, a very frequent phenomenon in the former Warsaw Pact countries of Eastern Europe.[20] As reasons for self-historicization, we might point to insufficient institutional reflection, or the distrust of the institution, and the associated effort to organize and communicate the closed quality and private character of artistic activities.

It is possible, using the example of Milan Adamčiak's work, to pursue archival strategies with the help of which artists create an autonomous context for their own artistic production. A fundamental expression of these strategies is the collection or accumulation of documents, often accompanied by the construction of personal mythologies and retrospective auto-interpretations. In an otherwise heterogeneous production that is scattered among genres, and ranges across a number of media, one can detect analogous processes at work in the case of such artists and their attempts to newly define themselves and their art in society – after many years of real socialism, and then in the subsequent era of political and social transformation.

Numerous publications have addressed the question of action art in the Czech Republic and Slovakia, elucidating the differing forms of action art and their historical context. Hitherto, however, little attention has been paid to the modes and strategies of documentation on which the forms of action art are mostly dependent. In the case of Slovak artists such as Alex Mlynárčik, Stano Filko, Július Koller, Peter Bartoš, and Milan Adamčiak, the procedures of self-historicization correspond with these artists' exclusion from the public sphere. Documentation from their archives, apart from reflecting and materializing the particular artist's aesthetic project, are also important personal testimonies on their life situations and the cultural politics of the time. Precisely for that reason, it is important to pay attention to the medium and form of documentation which artists chose in order to communicate their works, and what methods they used to preserve them and communicate them further.

Between today's viewer/reader/performer, historical time, and the performative work of artists of this generation stands the record, the documentation. Often it is automatically identified with the work as such, even though in many cases it amounts to mere traces, remains, relics of performances. In what sense do we today become performers of these performative works and by which methods can these works subsequently

---

20   See Zdenka Badovinac, *Prekinjene zgodovine: Arteast razstava / Interrupted Histories: Arteast Exhibiton*, exh. cat., Moderna galerija, Ljubljana, 2006.

be communicated to the public? Philip Auslander has used the term "performativity of documentation" to define documents that are not simply an indicative access point to a past event. Instead, these documents themselves are performances that fully reflect the sensibility or the aesthetic project of the artist. At the moment of reading these documents, we become an active public.[21] Therefore the unique presence of performance in real time, its disappearing "now", is not necessarily in contradiction with the archive, the logic of which is enduring repetition. Rebecca Schneider points out that if we perceive performance as an act of enduring and repeated manifestation, we need not approach it as something that vanishes after its completion.[22] In the work of an artist such as Milan Adamčiak, the document or object does not merely contain isolated relics of performance: these documents anticipate and generate further performances.

Adamčiak has followers in present-day Slovakia in literary, musical and artistic circles. Apart from scholarly reflection on his work, his charisma and his unconventional perception of language and the world does not cease to inspire young artists and poets with. One of the most moving scenes in the film *Muzikológ a tvorca* (*Musiocologist and Creator*, 2008) by Arnold Kojnok, the young Slovak documentarist, shows Adamčiak walking beside a stream in the forest. He steps into the current and alters the arrangement of stones in order to change the sound of the flowing water. He perceives the landscape as an active score; he intervenes in the landscape to make it "ring out". The motifs, techniques, and processes that Adamčiak applied and recorded remain relevant to this day. He returns to them, reconnects them again to life situations, and tests them in new conditions and settings, which is exactly what he expected the receiver/realizer of his work to do as well.

Translated from Slovak by John Minahane.

21 Philip Auslander, "The Performativity of Performance Documentation", *PAJ: A Journal of Performance and Art*, vol. 28, no. 3, 2006, p. 9.
22 Rebecca Schneider, *Performing Remains: Art and War in Times of Theatrical Reenactment*, Routledge, Abingdon and New York, 2011, p. 101.

Sabine Hänsgen

Polaroid – Link – Means for a Series

Three Performances from the Videotheque of the Collective Actions Group: Dedications to Inspection Medical Hermeneutics

The German art historian and curator Sabine Hänsgen has been involved with the conceptualist performances of the Moscow-based Collective Actions Group in various capacities since 1985. Among other things, she introduced the use of video into the group's documentary practice and set up their video archive, or videotheque, as a space not only for housing videos and other related materials but also for exploring the artistic aspects of documentation. Her contribution here is a "secondary" journey through the layers of documentation of three performances from the videotheque in which reception and interpretation are seen as part of the performance and aesthetic process. The performances took place in the early 1990s and were dedicated to another Moscow conceptual group, Inspection Medical Hermeneutics.

Since the late Soviet era, the performances of the Collective Actions Group have made an important contribution to the development of an alternative space of communication. The Collective Actions Group creates an intimate public of its own, beyond state culture and also beyond the market economy and mass media circulation. *Trips out of Town*, an ongoing project of the group since 1976, share the common objective of collaborative journeys made by a number of participants to the countryside around Moscow – often to a field far from the intensive semiotic sphere of the metropolis, that is, to an "empty" zone in nature. A field of untouched snow at the edges of the city, a park, or a forest have all served as stages for the group's minimalist actions, which delve into the elementary spatio-temporal structures of perception, and whose enigmatic nature provokes a range of different interpretations. The white field – referencing the Suprematist tradition of Kazimir Malevich, Martin Heidegger's *Lichtung* (clearing), and the Buddhist conception of *shunyata* (void) – becomes a demonstration zone creating new perspectives of contemplation and reflection for the participants. These journeys are a kind of experiment that allows for the exploration of the mind in relation to changing mythological, cultural, and political contexts.

The performances of the Collective Actions Group cannot be reduced to the immediate perception of a situation. Visible phenomena are always related to an invisible dimension of meaning, whereby the performative gesture in the situation more closely corresponds to a new impulse in an endless interpretative spiral in which situation and documentation enhance each other again and again. The process of aestheticizing extends into documentation, commentary, and theoretical discourse. In a later stage of development, the group began to compile documentary volumes about its actions in which a range of materials – descriptive texts, narratives by the participants, theoretical commentary, discussions, diagrams, photographs, video, etc. – form a descriptive-narrative-interpretive artwork of documentation.[1]

In the mid-1980s, I introduced the medium of video into the documentary discourse of the Collective Actions Group. At a time when the Soviet state strictly controlled all media of technical reproduction, I managed to bring a Blaupunkt video camera from Germany into the Soviet Union. From my point of view, video was the ideal medium for archiving aesthetic practices that were usually excluded from official cultural memory.

---

[1] The first five documentary volumes of the Collective Actions Group, which first appeared in *samizdat*, were republished in the volume *Kollektivnye deistviia: Poezdki za gorod (Collective Actions: Trips out of Town)*, Ad Marginem, Moscow, 1998. Further reading in English: *Empty Zones: Andrei Monastyrski and Collective Actions*, ed. Boris Groys, Black Dog Publishing, London, 2011; *Collective Actions: Audience Recollections from the First Five Years, 1976-1981*, trans. and ed. Yelena Kalinsky, Soberscove Press, Chicago, 2012. Documentation of the performances of the Collective Actions Group can be found on the website: http://conceptualism.letov.ru/KD-ACTIONS.htm (accessed on August 17, 2016).

In this respect, it was important for me to build up a video archive or a videotheque – a space in which not only video recordings as such are collected and preserved, but also the accompanying materials, texts, and images.² The intention of the videotheque was for the meditative recordings of the Collective Actions Group, in which almost nothing happens, to allow viewers to go on a "secondary" journey through the multiple layers of documentation, and thus to be able to reconstruct events and explore their own attitudes towards them.

The following selection from the videotheque is comprised of documentation from three performances by the Collective Actions Group dedicated to members of Inspection Medical Hermeneutics, a group of artists from the next generation of Moscow Conceptualism whose practices were characterized by hyperbolizing principles of commentary and interpretation, as well as by play with discourses from East and West, psychedelia, and pseudo-scientific methodology.³ These three performances and the related documentation date back to the time of transition when a shift from a specifically Soviet to a global context was taking place in the art world. For the Collective Actions Group, it was also a time when the *Trips out of Town* were expanded to include travel abroad, a change that provided a new impulse to reflect on the perception of other cultures, one's own culture in contact with other cultures, and the processes of translation between the cultures.

The video recordings also offer a reflection on the potential of various other media to represent these processes. *Polaroid: For Pavel Pepperstein* focuses on instant photography, thus emphasizing the moment of presence, i.e. contemporaneity. *Link: For Sergei Anufriev* demonstrates the use of new digital media, the structure of the video recording being determined by the course of a computer game. *Means for a Series: For Yuri Leiderman* represents a restaging of the *samizdat* typescript book, a medium that was characteristic of the hermetic communication among members of the Soviet underground.

---

2   Individual videos were included in many exhibitions on Moscow Conceptualism. A selection in the form of the videotheque was shown for the first time in the exhibition *M.A.N.I. Museum Video Archive* at the Gallery Obscuri Viri, Moscow, 1996, and is now part of the collection of the National Centre for Contemporary Arts (NCCA) in Moscow. See also http://artkladovka-ru.1gb.ru/ru/artists/10/kollektivnye-deystviya/works/185/ (accessed August 17, 2016).

3   The art collective Inspection Medical Hermeneutics came into being in December 1987 in a squat in Furman Lane in Moscow. The founding members were Pavel Pepperstein, Sergei Anufriev, and Yuri Leiderman. The group produced texts, installations, and performances dealing with questions of language and meaning during *Glasnost*, an era when Soviet culture was going through a process of transformation. The term *glasnost* has several meanings in the Russian language. In the 1980s, the meaning of *glasnost* as "publicity" in the sense of "the state of being open to public knowledge" was revived and made popular again by Mikhail Gorbachev as a slogan for increased government transparency.

I would now like to invite the reader on a journey through the documentation. The process of reception should be understood as part of the performance. In terms of ways of making meaning, I would emphasize the open-endedness of interpretation: interpretation as movement, as being-in-transit between languages, cultures, and media, interpretation as an event more rather than as a final result.

Conceptualizing interpretation as a performance between artists and spectators enables us to recognize that, in contrast to the complete world models of any ideology, interpretation as aesthetic process is always fragmentary, contingent on personal interests and motivations, giving us the opportunity to reflect on how meaning is made through language between and across subjects.

Documentation of the three performances *Polaroid*, *Link*, and *Means for a Series*

Each performance is documented by a short descriptive text, information about the performance, a dialogue/recollection by the authors and participants, and a series of video stills and photographs of the performances.

I
POLAROID
For Pavel Pepperstein

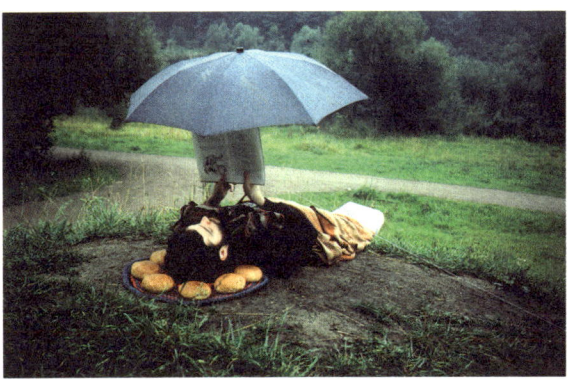

fig. 1

Sabine Hänsgen and Andrei Monastyrski,
POLAROID – For Pavel Pepperstein, 1990, photography.

Courtesy of Collective Actions Group.

We asked Pavel Pepperstein to lie on a hill by the Yauza River in the vicinity of Losiny Ostrov. He lay down on his back and we arranged six bread buns around his head to form a "nimbus". We then took a photograph of him in this position using a Polaroid camera. We attached the Polaroid image to a long string, which we tied around his finger, and hid the picture under an umbrella at the foot of the hill. At the conclusion of the action, he was supposed to pull the string and thus the photograph toward himself.

We next handed him the score of the action, which was comprised of two identical children's books of Russian fairy tales sewn to each side of a piece of cardboard. The books were attached in such a way that you could read only one of the fairy tales: *The Terrible Goat*. We glued the pages from a book about Johann Gottlieb Fichte over the beginning of the second fairy tale.

We asked Pepperstein to read the fairy tale into a radio microphone and then to comment on the texts about Fichte. After communicating these instructions to him, we walked over to the video camera, located on another hill about forty to fifty meters from the hill where Pepperstein lay. Andrei Monastyrski would receive through a set of headphones the transmission of Pepperstein's reading and commentary and repeat aloud what Pepperstein said while standing next to the video camera. In other words, the video camera would record Pepperstein's text as performed by Monastyrski. However, the radio microphone did not work, probably because of a high-voltage electric power line running between the two hills.

Nevertheless, Pepperstein read the fairy tale and made his commentary on Fichte in his assigned position, and afterwards, he pulled on the string and thus retrieved the Polaroid photograph, discovering an image of himself surrounded by a "nimbus of bread".

Moscow
22. 8. 1990
Sabine Hänsgen and Andrei Monastyrski (with Joseph Backstein)

Performance and video
Sabine Hänsgen – Andrei Monastyrski

Sabine Hänsgen: The performance *Polaroid: For Pavel Pepperstein* was designed for one participant, Pavel Pepperstein, and used elements that took into account a single viewer's aesthetic tendencies and interests.

Taking this performance as a model, it would be interesting to trace how the plot unfolds at various stages, and what relationships emerge between these stages. Specifically, there is the conception stage, which is a bit like an "ideal" plan, then comes the action, and finally, the documentation, which could also be considered a stage of the performance. It is mainly between these stages that a coherent picture of the aesthetic phenomenon emerges. In my view, the interpreter, in order to obtain this coherent picture, needs to know how to read "between" the stages of the action, since the phenomenon of performance is not depleted by having occurred in the field of vision. It is in these "in-between" intervals that we find hidden the thing that has not yet become text in its informational completeness: the live impression of the event as a whole.

Andrei Monastyrski: Yes, these intervals exist. They have a cascading character, and gradually, step-by-step, they are filled with interpretation. In the case we are discussing, one final "cascade" is the actual video recording, which is processed in a certain way and thus is open to outside interpretation. It is this ultimate aesthetic outcome that the external viewer faces. But still, we must consider all the different stages of the work.

Sabine Hänsgen: The first stage is the conception. We devised the project together. I saw a volume of Russian fairy tales with the title *Kolobok*[4] in a bookstore window. The cover featured an illustration of a scene from the fairy tale: a *kolobok* running away from home. On the one hand, I was attracted by this book simply as a collection of Russian fairy tales that I wanted to read, while on the other hand, I knew that the term *kolobok* is frequently invoked in the Moscow Conceptualist school's discourse as a metaphorical term signifying a particular image of the author-character, i.e. the author distancing himself from his or her position by taking on the perspective of a character. But I had never read the fairy tale itself. It was then, in that moment, that I had the impulse for the idea. I immediately purchased several copies of the book. The same day, I stopped by the bakery and bought two or three small round buns. I placed them in the bag where I had the books. When I got home, I took the books and buns out of the bag, and I saw that the buns resembled the *kolobok* that appeared on the cover of the book of fairy tales.

A connection formed between these objects as elements of the performance. It is worth noting that the addressee of the intended performance was immediately imagined to be Pepperstein, probably because his work features the theme of children's books and their characters, including the *kolobok*, and Inspection Medical Hermeneutics' has done various actions with bread. A plot quickly developed from these elements and took on a specific arrangement: to lay Pasha[5] down on the ground on his back, to arrange six *kolobok* buns into a "nimbus" around his head without him noticing (the book had exactly six images of *kolobok*), to photograph him in this position using a Polaroid camera, and to ask him to read the score of the action in this same prone position using a wireless microphone so that the reading could be recorded by a video camera some distance away. The score consisted of a two-sided object sewn together from the two books of Russian fairy tales. Each side allowed you to turn the pages of only one fairy tale: *The Terrible Goat*. The beginning of the next fairy tale, located further down on the same page, was covered over with pages from a book about Fichte. Pasha was invited to read the entire tale of *The Terrible Goat* out loud, but not to read the text related to Fichte, rather to just add some improvised commentary after the fairy tale. Then, with the help of a string tied to his finger, he had to pull the Polaroid image toward himself and look at it. That's when he would discover in what kind of "nimbus" he had been arranged while laying on the hill and reading the fairy tale. In other words, on the event-level of the performance, the most significant thing

---

4   *Kolobok* "refers to a baked dough ball, a character in many Russian fairy tales. *Kolobok* rolls down the road, running away from everyone who wants to eat it: the fox, the wolf, the bear, etc. *Kolobok* is a good image for someone who does not want to be identified, named, or regarded as attached to a particular role or place, for someone who is slipping away from all of this." From *Dictionary of Moscow Conceptualism*: http://www.conceptualism-moscow.org/page?id=198&lang=en (accessed July 21, 2016).

5   Pavel Pepperstein's nickname.

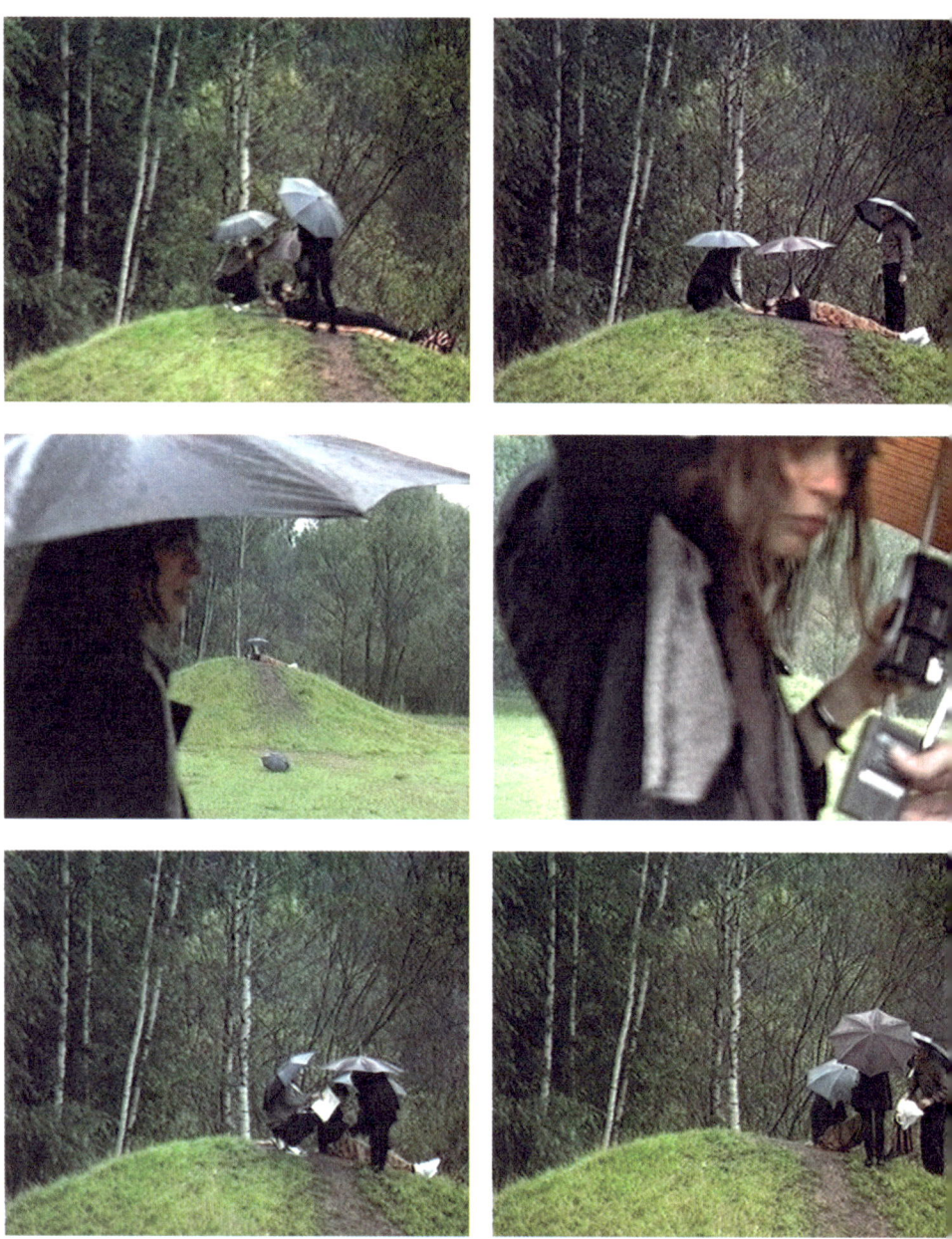

fig. 2

Sabine Hänsgen and Andrei Monastyrski,
POLAROID – For Pavel Pepperstein, 1990, video stills.

Courtesy of Collective Actions Group.

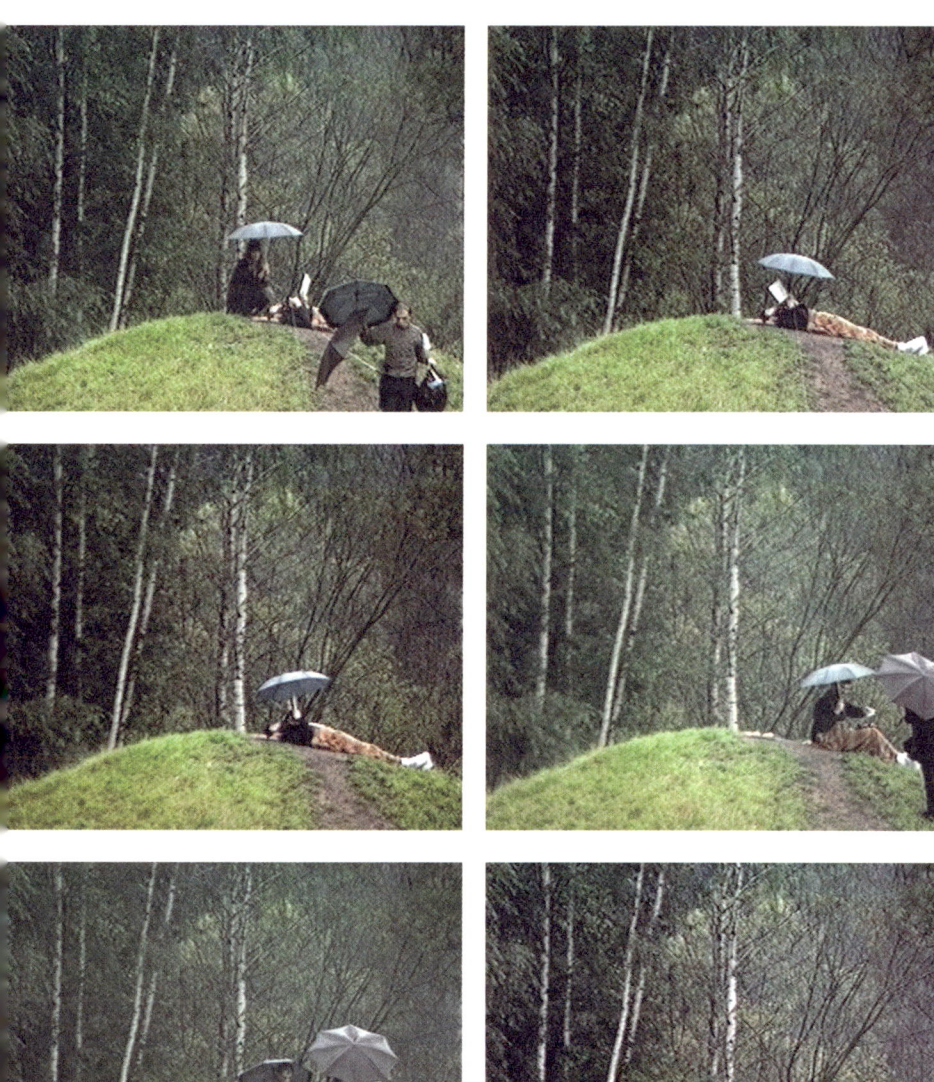

for Pasha should have been the discovery of his own image in this rather strange arrangement. This is what took place by the Yauza River in the vicinity of the Rostokino Aqueduct.

Andrei Monastyrski: When you watch the video recording of Pasha's preparations for the action – where we are wrapping him in a blanket, surrounding him with bread buns, photographing him using the Polaroid, tying the string to his finger, etc. – an image emerges of some kind of ritual activity around a dead body, a folkloristic image, archaic in its vividness and specificity. This archaic vividness is easily discernible in the Polaroid picture in which Pasha assumes the form of some kind of Bread God. Then, after a pause in the action (in the video recording, this takes the form of Pasha lying motionless on the hill for fifteen to twenty minutes), the scene changes abruptly. Pasha lifts himself up, holding the umbrella, and suddenly, there emerges a figure of a person seated on a hill beneath an umbrella clothed in some sort of ancient Chinese dress garb – that's how the blanket that initially resembled a funeral shroud appears. We then approach this figure, carrying our own umbrellas, sit down beside him, and converse about something. In any case, the video recording of this scene is very reminiscent of the meditative spaces of strolling in old Japanese engravings: tiny figures beneath umbrellas, stripped of the vividness and serious event-ness of archaic, folkloristic subjects. In other words, I discovered the stylistic transgression from a folkloristic space to a meditative-cultural one in the documentary stage, beyond the borders of the action itself, at its margins. And this is when the meaning of the score, already present at the moment of conception, became clear. A not entirely comprehensible juxtaposition of two contrasting texts – one folkloristic and vividly emotional, the other philosophical-cultural and distanced – was aesthetically articulated through the stylistic transgression in the documentary material of the video recording. However, the meaning that revealed itself in the video recording did not immediately become apparent when provided in such direct documentary form; it did not yet consolidate itself into a genre. This stylistic transgression, as a live aesthetic impression, needed to be fixed on a new level of documentary elaboration. We had to introduce the element of freeze-frames into the documentary recording, making the recording aesthetically open and self-sufficient, and introduce the still pictures, already completely generic in their character, during the preparation and post-action stages. Thus, some parts of the video recording are transformed from documentation into work of art. And it is only in this state that the work transcends the frame of the three stages of performance about which you spoke and can be considered open to outside interpretation.

Sabine Hänsgen: It turns out that the end result, or the aesthetic resolution, takes place simultaneously through the performance of the idea laid out in the score and through the unpredictable "marginal" effects that appear in both the action and the documentation. Specifically, I have in mind the fact that it was raining during the action and so umbrellas had to be used. In some sense, the umbrellas turned out to be the main protagonists of the stylistic transgression from archaic-folkloristic imagery to the freely meditative non-necessity of images in the Japanese style. And another unpredictable detail that influenced the documentation turned out to be the presence of a high voltage electric power line at the place of action. It blocked the transmission of Pasha's reading into the radio microphone for the video camera that was located on another hill. And since the audio series didn't work, the treatment of the video material focused entirely on visual documentation and, in my opinion, your idea of introducing freeze-frames was to some degree determined by the wish to correct the failed audio series, to transform it into a background of rhythmic noise background. The use of the freeze-frame device introduces a significant change into the temporal regime of the documentary event. By itself, the documentation reflects the real time spent at the place of action. The freeze-frame permits the emergence of pieces of "arrested time" relative to the event. In the rhythmic series of "arrested" time and real time, in their interplay, we discover the effect of free aesthetic time, the very *Luft* of live impression, directed toward the external viewer who does not take part in the action. In other words, this free time is one of the genre-generating factors that transform documentation into artistic material. On the one hand, the freeze-frame produces a framing effect and a kind of falling-out of the constant flow of video into a static tableau; on the other hand, the freeze-frame takes away the framing of the action event itself, refocusing the viewer's attention on incidents that were completely foreign to the plot. In other words, they take away the frame provided by the action's plot and discover the aesthetic self-sufficiency of the event before the start of the performance and after its conclusion.

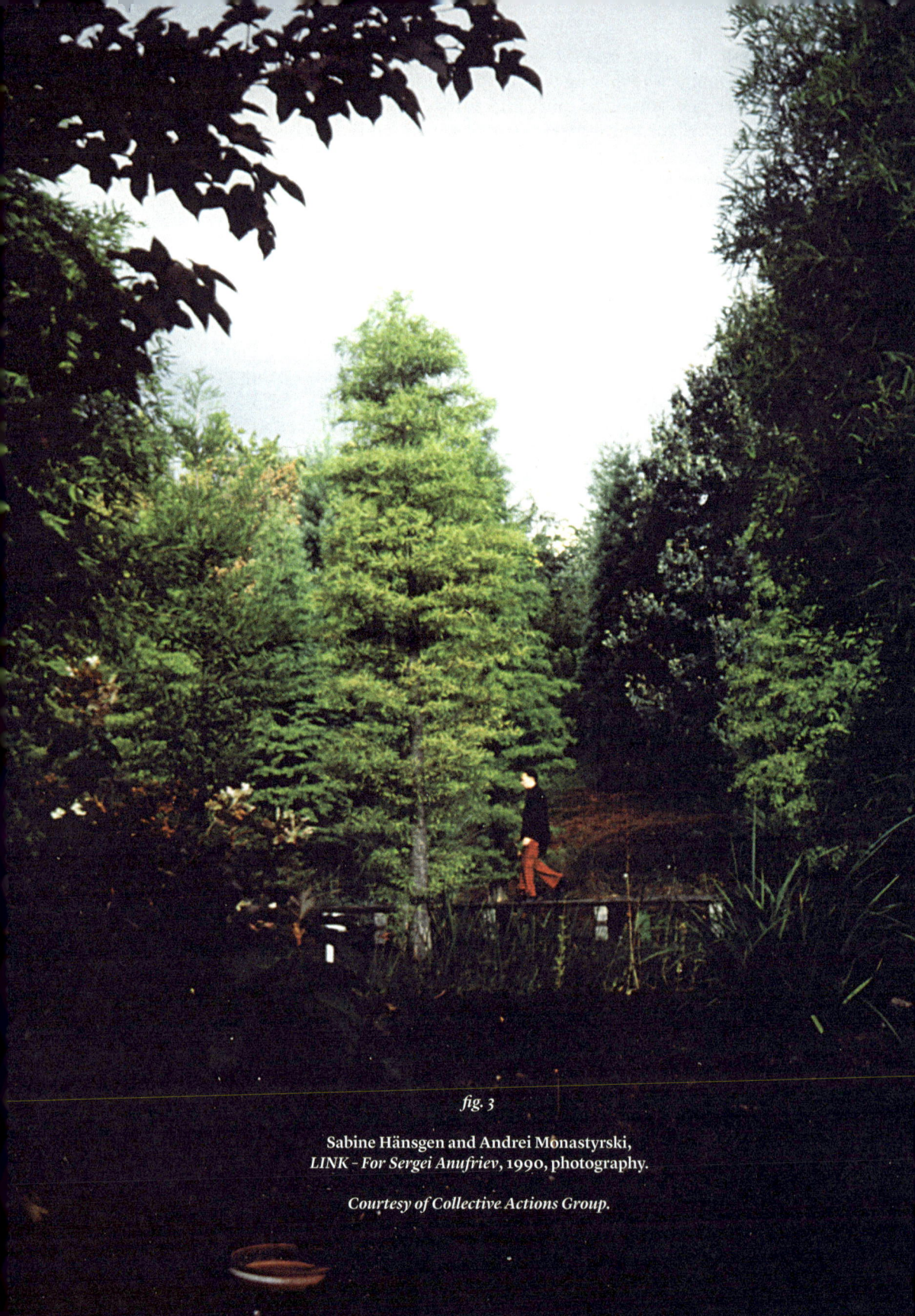

fig. 3

Sabine Hänsgen and Andrei Monastyrski,
LINK - For Sergei Anufriev, 1990, photography.

Courtesy of Collective Actions Group.

II
LINK
For Sergei Anufriev

This action took place in the Botanical Garden of the Ruhr University in Bochum on a small wooden bridge that spanned a pond in the ancient plants section.

At one end of the bridge, we assembled a structure out of a light blue vase set on a tape recorder with a pile of little cards placed on top of the vase. Glued to the cards were pictures with scenes from various computer games that had been cut out of magazines. On the other end of the bridge was a video camera switched on to play. A scene from the Nintendo computer game Zelda 2, which had been recorded the previous evening, could be observed in the viewfinder. The tape recorder beneath the vase contained a cassette tape of music from the same computer game and was also switched on to play.

We handed Anufriev a purse and invited him to walk back and forth between the vase and the video camera, where he could watch the recording in the viewfinder, but for no more than one minute. Each time he reached the vase, he had to take one of the cards and place it in the purse. Beneath the twentieth card was a set of instructions inviting Anufriev to take a hammer out of the vase, shatter the vase, and gather the broken pieces into the purse. And that is what he did.

Bochum
21. 9. 1990
Sabine Hänsgen and Andrei Monastyrski

Abroadness
Sabine Hänsgen – Andrei Monastyrski

Sabine Hänsgen: The action *Link* serves as an example of how technology from abroad has influenced the aesthetic development of Moscow Conceptualism. First we turn our attention to the location of the action, the botanical garden of the Ruhr University. It is not a "hot" place like the border zone in Berlin that attracts artists. In other words, the botanical garden is not a part of the local artistic infrastructure. There is no illusion of culture in this place, but neither is there an illusion of pure nature, since the garden is artificial. Thus, the chosen location simulates a primitive biotope – horsetails, fiddlehead ferns, etc. equipped with scientific labels and plant classifications. The action took place on a little bridge over a pond. In essence, the action came about exclusively as a result of the spatial separation of the representations of sound and image of representation in the computer game. It was within this split that Anufriev ran back and forth. How can this action be related to minimalist aesthetics? Anufriev performed movements analogous to those of the computer game character, walking back and forth like the Link character in the transitional periods in the game, which made up the majority of what was presented in the video recording.

Andrei Monastyrski: Minimalism is always relative. In this case, the "margins" of minimalism were heaped with two piles of complicated combinations of different forms and meanings. I am talking about the video camera and the structure with the tape recorder, vase, hammer, pictures, and instructions. Each of these piles contained hundreds of details. In this way, minimalism is organized by the most maximalist means in this action. It is hard to say whether Anufriev was more submerged in the visual and auditory information, or in his own walking back and forth.

Sabine Hänsgen: Let's take a closer look at the game. In a certain sense, we discover in it a continuation of the action for Pepperstein. Pepperstein read aloud a Russian fairy tale. Here we also have a fairy tale. And also, the purse that Anufriev carried while he walked back and forth had a picture attached to it of the place where Pepperstein's action took place. In the plot of the game, Link's task is to save the kingdom of Hyrule. Along the way, he battles with the forces of evil – in a forest, in a field, in a desert, etc. This game contains not only dramatic episodes related to the plot, but also purely meditative, rhythmic ones that are related to earning points. The more points earned, the more successfully you have submerged yourself into the rhythmic program embedded in the game. In the action, we placed an accent not on the old-fashioned fairy tale episodes of battle and drama, but rather on the transitional periods of rhythmic time-passing.

Andrei Monastyrski: Yes, that is exactly right. The start of the game was magnificent. It always contained two levels that transitioned smoothly from one to the other: the meditative earning of points and then, with new powers, a battle on a new level. These meditations in the course of a lighter battle were a kind of analgesic and did not permit excessive jolts or dramatics during the task. In the concluding parts of the game, when I encountered Link's double in the form of a shadow, I experienced the game with greater discomfort due to the absence of the meditative level – the analgesic – and it seems to me that the game's creators somehow miscalculated this concluding step. The simplification of the game's structure, the bringing together of the two levels into one, exclusively battle, has an extremely jolting and dispiriting effect. A new level of archaism seems to arise, not at the level of the image, but on a structural level: the convergence of all of this into the dull dramatism of confrontation without the gentle intermezzo of meditative practice, which normally makes a greater degree of resistance to new dramatic conflicts possible. The meditative phases were a kind of game with oneself. The last, dramatic step, on the other hand, is no longer a game with oneself, but with the game's creators who are hidden behind the figure of the player, in his own image: Link's shadow. Here, the creators of the game seem to have become confused. It is possible that they got carried away by the successful image of the "double" and forgot the strategic structure of the entire game, i.e. the necessary presence of two levels of action, the meditative and dramatic.

Sabine Hänsgen: Let's put aside the discussion of the game for now. If we consider the video recording of the action as a whole, we can see that a framing of live action has materialized around the video game that Anufriev watches like a film through the camera's viewfinder. The first image shows the vase on top of the tape recorder where Anufriev collects the little printed cards. The last frame shows the shattering of the vase and Anufriev's recollection of the action as an immediate impression that was produced right there on the garden bridge. The weather is important in this part of the recording, its abrupt changes from sun to hail and back again. These changes were unpredictable, and within this unpredictable, unmediated frame there is the contrasting computer game. This contrast and collision reveals that the screen is not all. That the game is finite. In other words, the contrast reveals the boundaries of simulation and focuses attention on the physical articulations that are outside the frame of the game.

Andrei Monastyrski: Nevertheless, the jolts of physical articulations, much like the jolts of dramatic obstructions in the game, caused me a great deal of discomfort. The hail was entirely unpleasant for me, as was the strong rain. I perceived it in the same way as the poor planning in the game, a disturbance in the balance of comfort and discomfort in the direction of the latter. I cannot value this as an image for imitation. And anyway, the psychic bleakness that I began to experience starting around 1988 was very rarely balanced by positives. One positive experience was going out skiing along the Zvezdnyi (Star) Boulevard in Moscow after eleven at night when the streets were virtually empty. I would first improvise for forty-five minutes on the piano and then get dressed, take the skis, and go to the boulevard. I would go out on the skis there, counting the laps I made, for probably about an hour. Then I would climb the staircase by the hardware store and walk along the courtyards past that strange tower on Tsander Street. Arrive home. It is nice after this kind of exertion to take a cold shower. It is a kind of glance off to the side, where there is nothing but snow, trees, stars.

Sabine Hänsgen: Perhaps it is with the same kind of curative aims that Anufriev suggested the action's title, *Link*. After all, Link is not just the

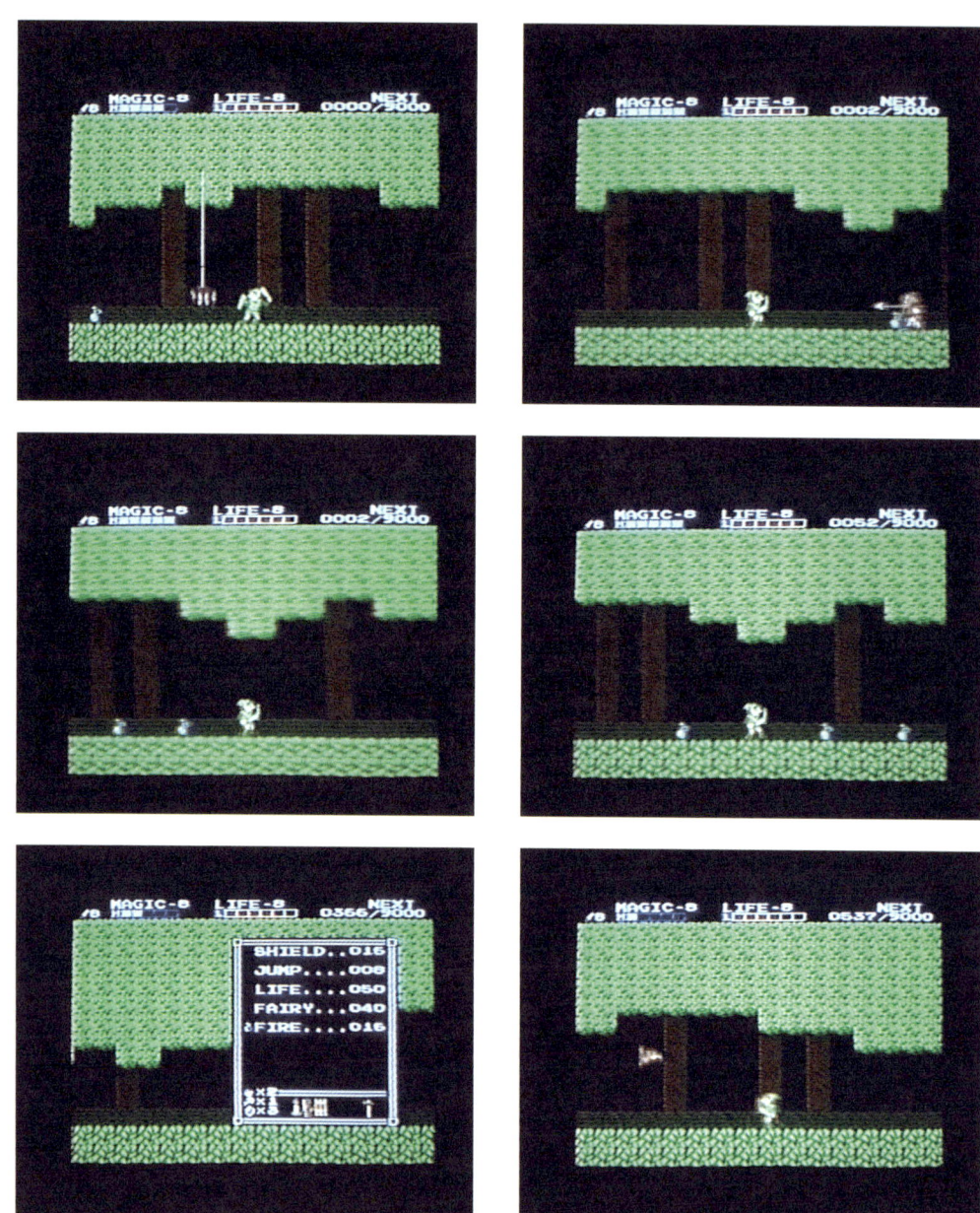

fig. 4

Sabine Hänsgen and Andrei Monastyrski,
LINK – For Sergei Anufriev, 1990, video stills.

Courtesy of Collective Actions Group.

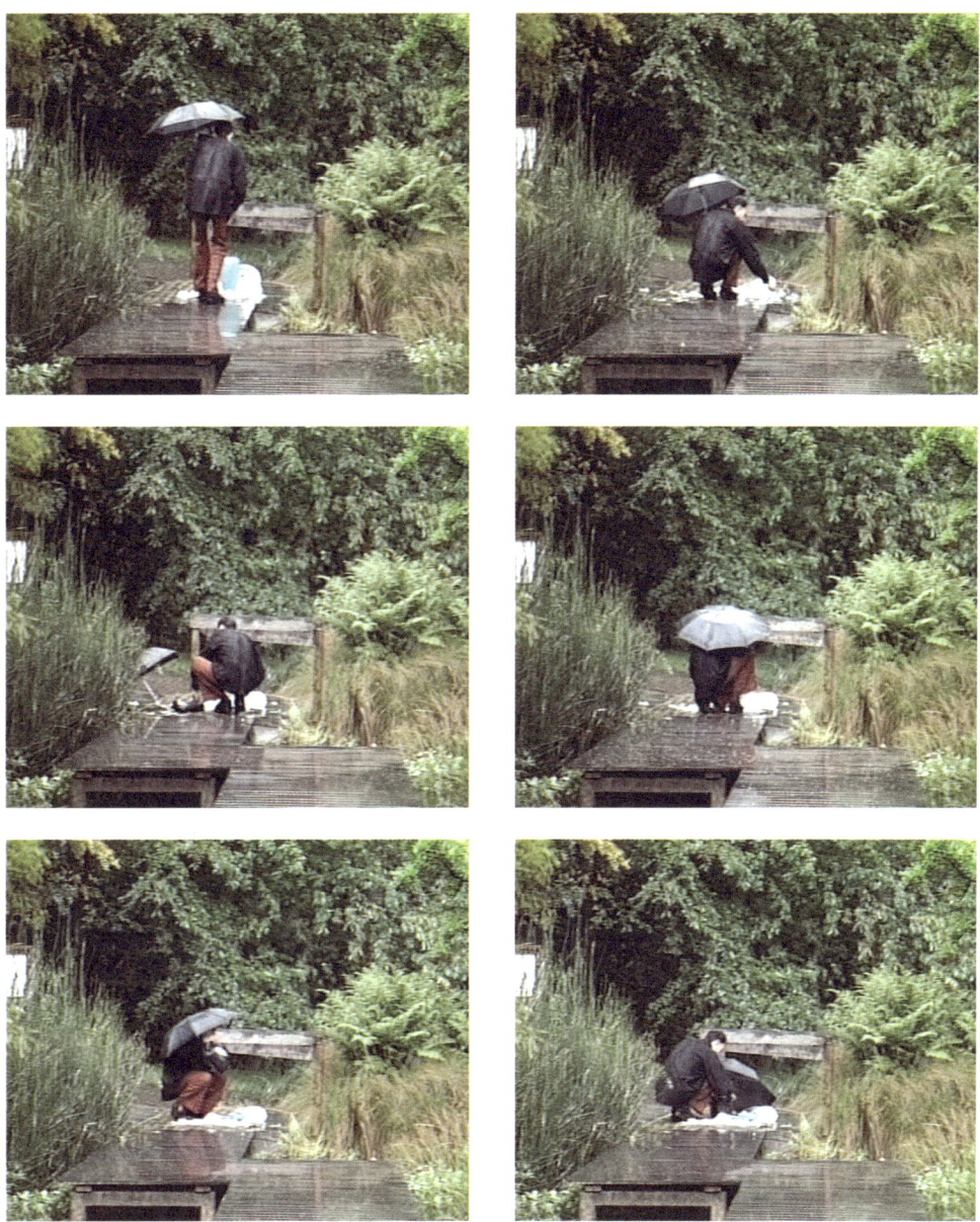

fig. 5

Sabine Hänsgen and Andrei Monastyrski,
LINK – For Sergei Anufriev, 1990, video stills.

Courtesy of Collective Actions Group.

name of the main protagonist in a computer game, but "link" in English means "connection". Perhaps Anufriev meant to imply the schizoanalytic method in which different systems of thought are randomly associated by chance, blurring the boundary between different systems of movement "there and back," like a unique kind of feedback when a microphone is held up to a loudspeaker. This is the beginning of a game on academic territory, and just as there were unexpected changes in the weather, there may be unexpected results.

Andrei Monastyrski: For me, unexpected results are only tolerable within the confines of tradition. They can only be tolerated to a certain point. The principle at the heart of the idea cannot be limitless tolerance. In my beloved *Magic Mountain* by Thomas Mann, Castorp also undertakes an important outing on skis. We all also loved *Journey to the West* and certain episodes of the *Dream of the Red Chamber*. For example, the stroll of Bao Yu in the garden with his father and entourage, and the dragging of Bao Yu along the snowy field by two monks. It is these snowy fields that are somehow unusually effective. There is in them some kind of not-yet-beginning, a constant newness and possibility. It seems to be here that we get Ilya Kabakov's love for empty white surfaces and Heidegger with his "possibilities". All of this is rooted in my childhood impressions of living in the north.

Sabine Hänsgen: Now we should make a postscript relating to the end of the Zelda-2 game. The end of the game produced a kind of unexpected turn from fairy tale to film, a real Hollywood happy ending. Link saves Zelda. Zelda comes alive and rises from the sheets. The curtain falls and from behind the curtain – a kiss. And then the words "The End" appear.

Andrei Monastyrski: Exactly right. I also found it interesting to suddenly discover the names of the team that made the game, to feel the disclosure of anonymity as the most erotic event of the entire game structure.

Sabine Hänsgen: I would prefer not to speak right now about the game, but rather about the perspective of computer games in general. For you, it was important to discover the names of the authors at the end. But if we take into account the more complex possibilities of computer games, the text-generating capacities of the computer keyboard, and the capacity of the viewer to participate in the composition, then in these interactive computer games, the player becomes the author and will already experience authorship as an erotic event. He can, for example, take pieces from different existing situations and use them to arrange new episodes or entire sequences. He can construct a scene of the romantic meeting from *Gone with the Wind* or the farewell from *Doctor Zhivago*. Moreover, the viewer can become not only the author of his own composition, but a character as well, if we take into account the possibilities of new technical methods for creating virtual reality – gloves, headphones, headsets with two small screens.

Andrei Monastyrski: I view this with less psychologizing and more detachment, as in the realm of literature, video, film, etc. Everything takes place somewhere in the distance, including everything inside the computer game regardless of its degree of virtuality. It has nothing to do with me.

Sabine Hänsgen: Why are you so interested in the names of the authors?

Andrei Monastyrski: Naming is an important discursive figure. That's why I perceive it as part of a series of traditional points of contact with worked-out situations already recorded in history. Neither the booklet, nor the game's opening titles make any mention of the authors. It is possible that they consider themselves a kind of gift similar to what players get for other achievements, the receiving of various magical items in the course of the game as a result of the battles, and finally, the magic of their names, the names of the creators of the entire game as the concluding and most significant gift at the end, when the player is victorious. Only then does the player partake in authorship, what you spoke about earlier. In other words, the discursive partaking comes before the technological. In any case, it is in this way that we can interpret the appearance of the authors' names only after the game's conclusion.

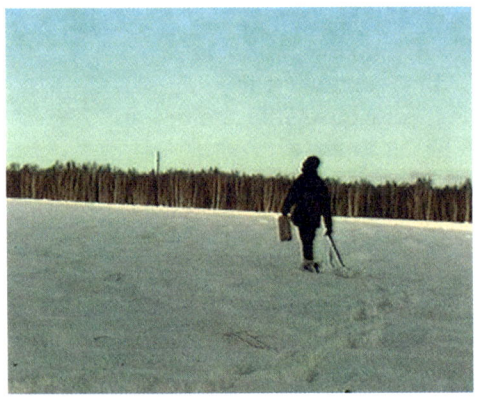 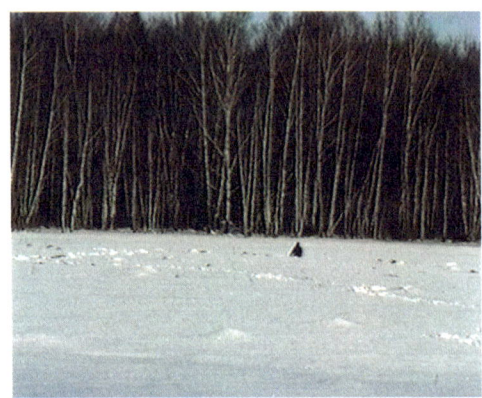
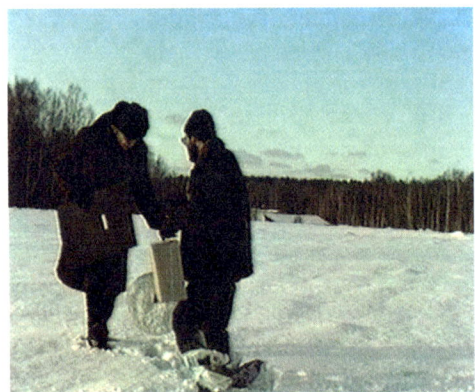 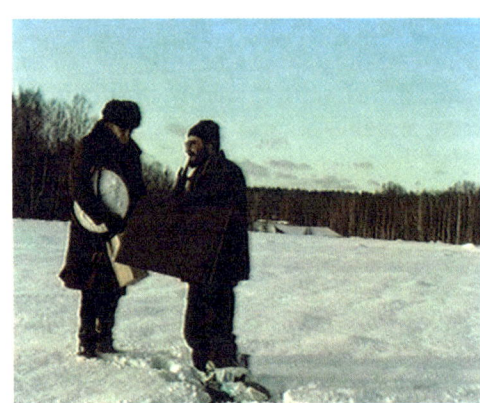
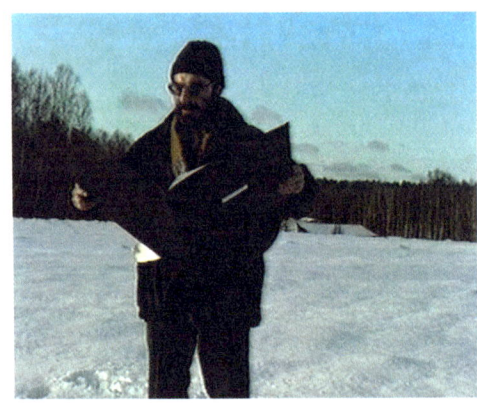 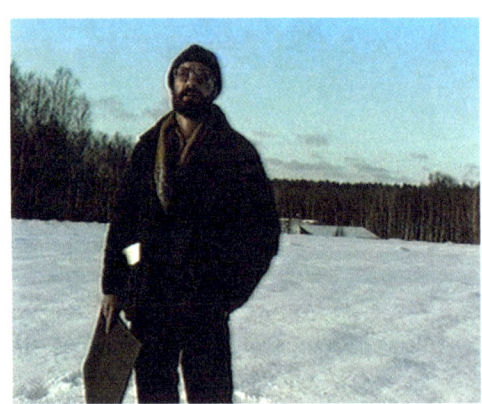

fig. 6

Sabine Hänsgen and Andrei Monastyrski,
MEANS FOR A SERIES – For Yuri Leiderman, 1991, video stills.

Courtesy of Collective Actions Group.

III
MEANS FOR A SERIES
For Yuri Leiderman

We arrived at the snow-covered Kievogorsky Field and invited Leiderman to move through the field while dragging a heavy plaster rosette on a strap behind him. In this way, he would trace a line in the snow indicating the zone from where the hangars, located in the north-west corner of the field could not be seen (see the preface and "Hangars in the North-West" from volume five of *Trips out of Town*).[6] As he occupied himself with this tracing, Leiderman carried in his other hand a sealed cardboard box. Each time it tilted, a subtle tingling of bells could be heard from within.

After marking out the prescribed zone with the trace of the rosette in the snow (this was possible due to the sloped form of the field), Leiderman was instructed to approach us. We were standing closer to the centre of the field with the hangars in the background, and Monastyrski gave him a large black notebook with the inscription "For Yuri Leiderman" on the cover.

Inside the notebook was a set of magnified images from a small notebook entitled "On the Roof" (from Hänsgen's videotheque), as well as two photographs. One was of Hänsgen standing on the pedestal of the Soviet sculptor Vera Mukhina's 1937 sculpture *The Worker and the Collective Farm Woman*, beside the heel of the collective farm woman, to which she had affixed cards with Chinese hieroglyphs. The second was of Leiderman's briefcase placed on the pedestal of another one of Mukhina's sculptures, entitled *We Demand Peace*, located on Prospekt Mira in Moscow, not far from *The Worker and the Collective Farm Woman*. Also inside the notebook was a sheet containing a fragment of Monastyrski's letter to Hänsgen concerning ideas of tradition and continuity in NOMA, the circle of Moscow Conceptualists.

Then Hänsgen posed several questions to Leiderman as he stood before the camera. Monastyrski asked him to step away from the place of action (i.e. to leave the field). Monastyrski placed the rosette down on the snow, removed a plastic doll containing a musical mechanism from inside from the box (Leiderman did not know what he had been carrying in the box, or what the part of the action described here entailed), placed the doll on top of the rosette, and read the text of the Hrdaya-Sutra aloud into the camera's microphone while the video image showed the doll on top of the rosette.

Moscow Region, Savyolovskaya Railway Line, Kievogorsky Field
26. 12. 1991
Andrei Monastyrski and Sabine Hänsgen

---

6   See *Kollektivnye deistviia* (*Collective Actions*). Hangars in the North-West are storage depots built at the end of the 1980s on the edge of Kievogorsky Field. They were used [by the Collective Actions Group] as figures for initiating an architectural discourse in the empty field, which then started being covered in dachas.

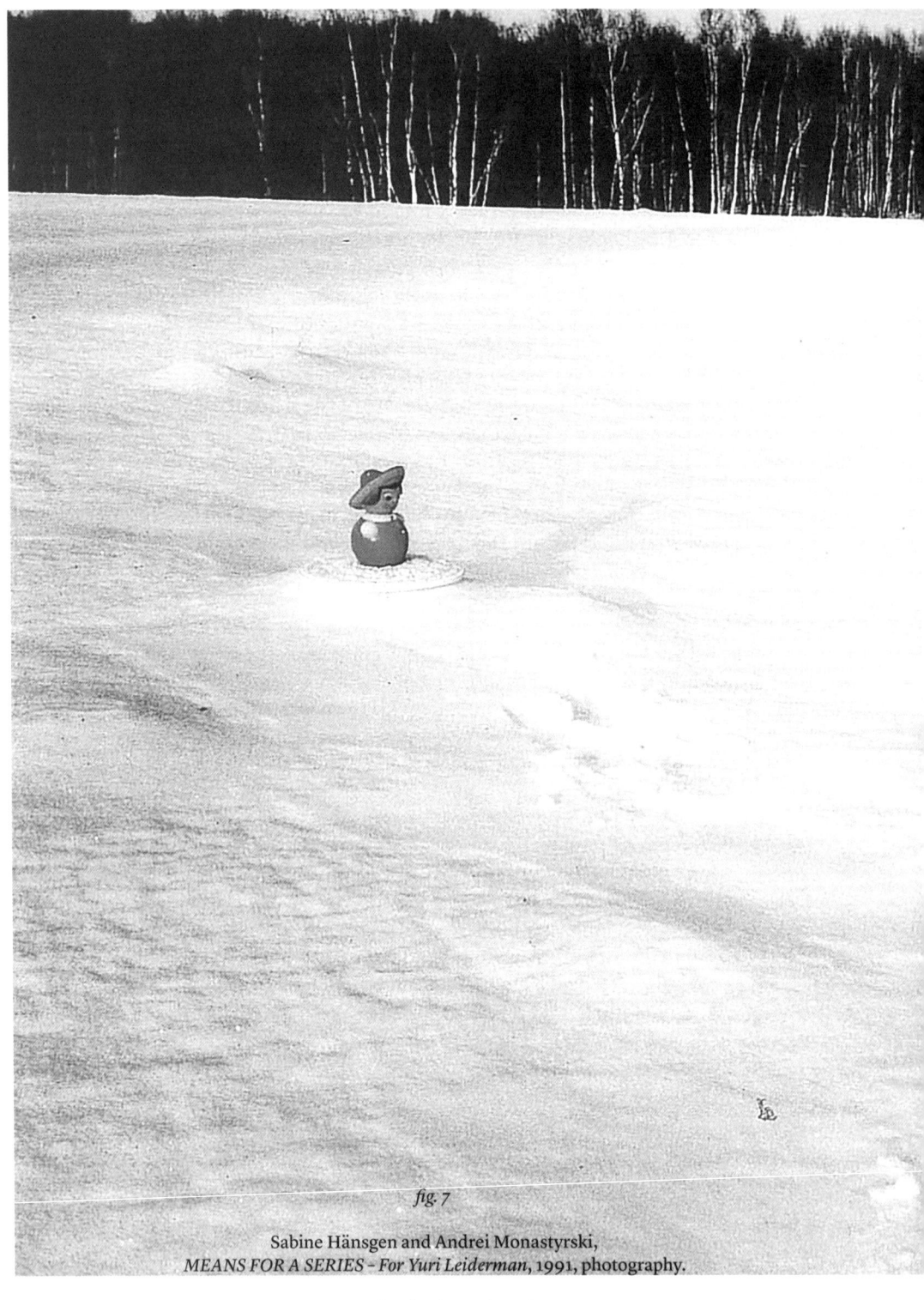

fig. 7

Sabine Hänsgen and Andrei Monastyrski,
MEANS FOR A SERIES - For Yuri Leiderman, 1991, photography.

Courtesy of Collective Actions Group.

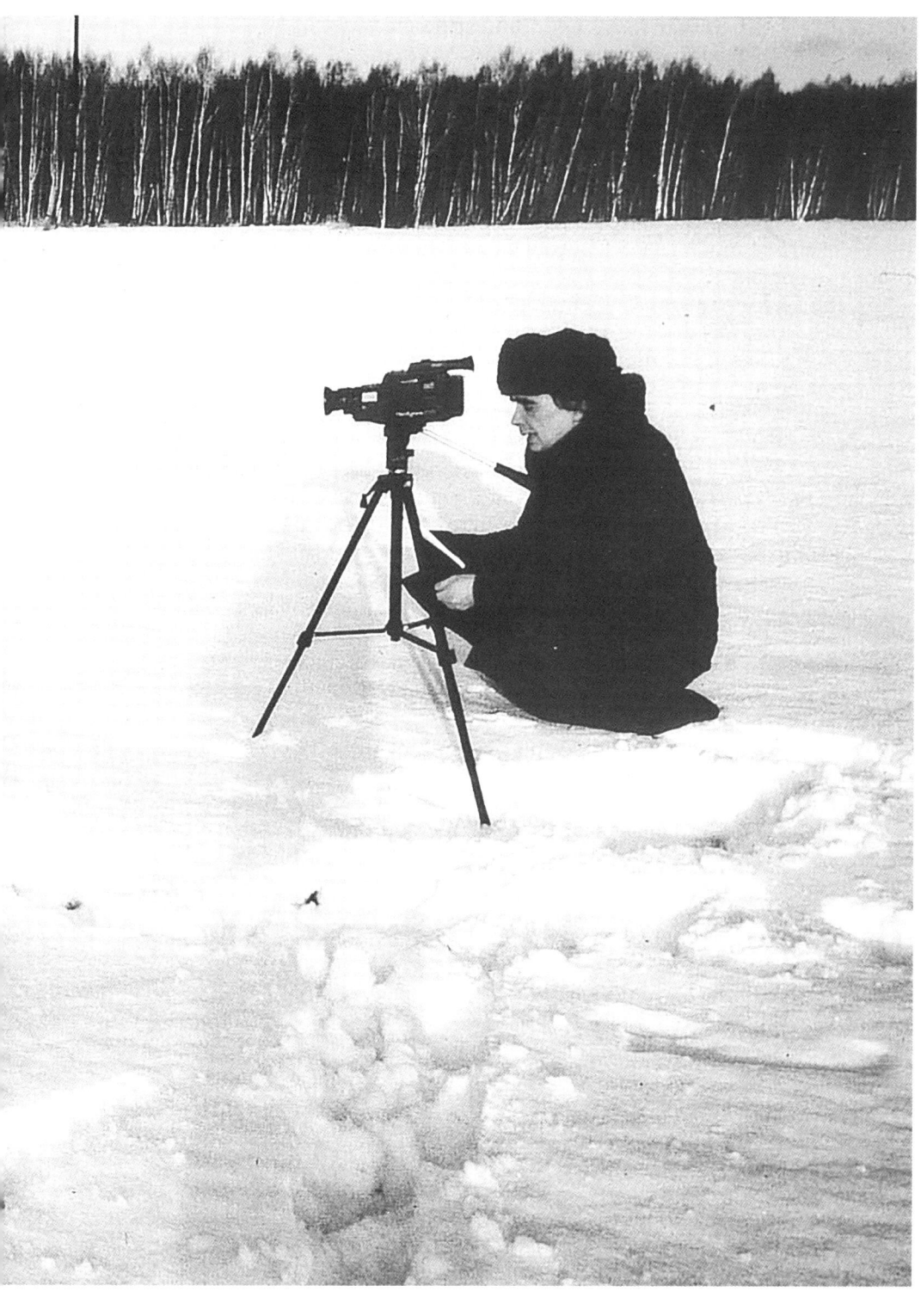

Indian Lotus and Chinese Shield
Yuri Leiderman's Recollections of the Action Means for a Series

We came out to the edge of the Kievogorsky Field and Andrei explained to me what my task would involve. I was somewhat nervous at first, since my near-sightedness and the difference in our heights made it difficult for me to see the hangars. Or more precisely, I could see them, but their white roofs looked like another snow-covered hill. Still harbouring some doubts, I took the box and rosette that were offered to me and started walking across the field with them, dragging the rosette on a strap behind me. I should say right away that the moulded ceiling in the form of a decorative rosette with a hole in the middle immediately reminded me of an ancient Chinese shield.

Everything became much clearer when I entered the field. I could see the edges of the hangars, and, following the instructions and trying not to tear my eyes away from them, I traced their outline across the field. In principle, this was supposed to make a more or less ideal arc, but, due to irregularities in the field, my path turned out to be complicated, more like a wobbly line made by a shaky hand with all manner of small loops and zigzags. I should say that the walking was pleasant and the simple yet engaging task brought me a lot of pleasure. I understood this thing as a kind of return to Collective Actions' pure, topographic, vector-like actions such as *Gazing at the Waterfall*, or, for example, *Description of Action*, which held a lot of significance for me. It was the first action of the third volume when Kabakov observed as Panitkov used his "peripheral vision" to direct the movements of Monastyrski and Romashko along the edges of a field, a special kind of "walking hangars". It was precisely in observing these movements that Kabakov had the illusion of a non-existent rope connecting Monastyrski and Romashko, an illusory rope that accepted with it all the intensifying discursive ascensions and stabilizations of actions in the third volume.

However, to return to my itinerary, it would probably be more correct to speak not of a retrospective return, but of a distinction: I seem to have separated an earlier, paranoid-topographic section of the field from a later "hangar-related" schizoid-interpretational one. This separation coincided completely with my prognosis of that time, according to which "our situation" in the future would appear less interpretational and more graphic, and simultaneously, more existentially charged, as its graphism would be based not on collective analysis, but on certain individual states and affects. As I moved along the field, a zone of hangar visibility appeared to my left like a zone of an already fading situation, while to my right was the zone of the past, half-forgotten, but sure to return to us "on a different level". Occupied with these ruminations, I scrupulously observed the hangars, always trying to walk in a way that I could see the edge of their rooftops, all the while mumbling to myself about "the return to linearity!" When I stumbled in the snow, a soft jingle-jangle wafted up from the box that I held in my left hand. I supposed that there must be some sort of German music box hidden inside. I was also absorbed by the constantly changing position of my own head. At the beginning of my journey, I was looking straight ahead and to the side. Later, my head was turned sharply to the side. Finally, I ended up having to walk backwards in order not to lose sight of the hangars. It was amusing that, despite the meanderings of the completed path, in the end, I nevertheless came out exactly at the far right corner of the field at the termination of the recently built fence.

When I reached the edge of the field, I heaved the rosette onto my back, partly so that it would more closely resemble a shield, and went in search of Sabine and Andrei. Due to certain circumstances, my mind was constantly occupied in those days with the subject of the battle between the ancient Chinese Wu and Yue kingdoms described in the book *Guoyu*, an ancient Chinese text from the 4th century BC that describes the history of various warring states. I imagined myself as a Yue warrior, wandering around with my round shield on my back. Several days prior to the action, I'd had a strange idea for a plot for a video that would feature a young woman wearing a Yue cap while I read an excerpt from *Guoyu* off-camera. There is a wonderful convergence between this idea and the third part of the video shot on the field. There turned out to be, inside the box that I had been carrying around the field, a wobbly figurine wearing a strange little cap (identified later by Andrei as Sariputra, the recipient of the *Hrdaya Sutra*). In the third part of the video, Andrei reads the text of the *sutra* off-camera while the figurine stands in the centre of the rosette, associated here with the Buddhist lotus. Everything happened roughly the way I had imagined it, the only differences are the forms of the caps and the traditions of the texts read off-camera: Buddhism and Confucianism. The key similarities are the traditionalizing allusions to the round ceiling rosette (the Indian lotus and the Chinese shield) as a "means for a series," which I used to separate the fading schizoidness of references and glances from the renewed paranoidality of experiences and affects.

The documentation sections translated from Russian by Yelena Kalinsky.

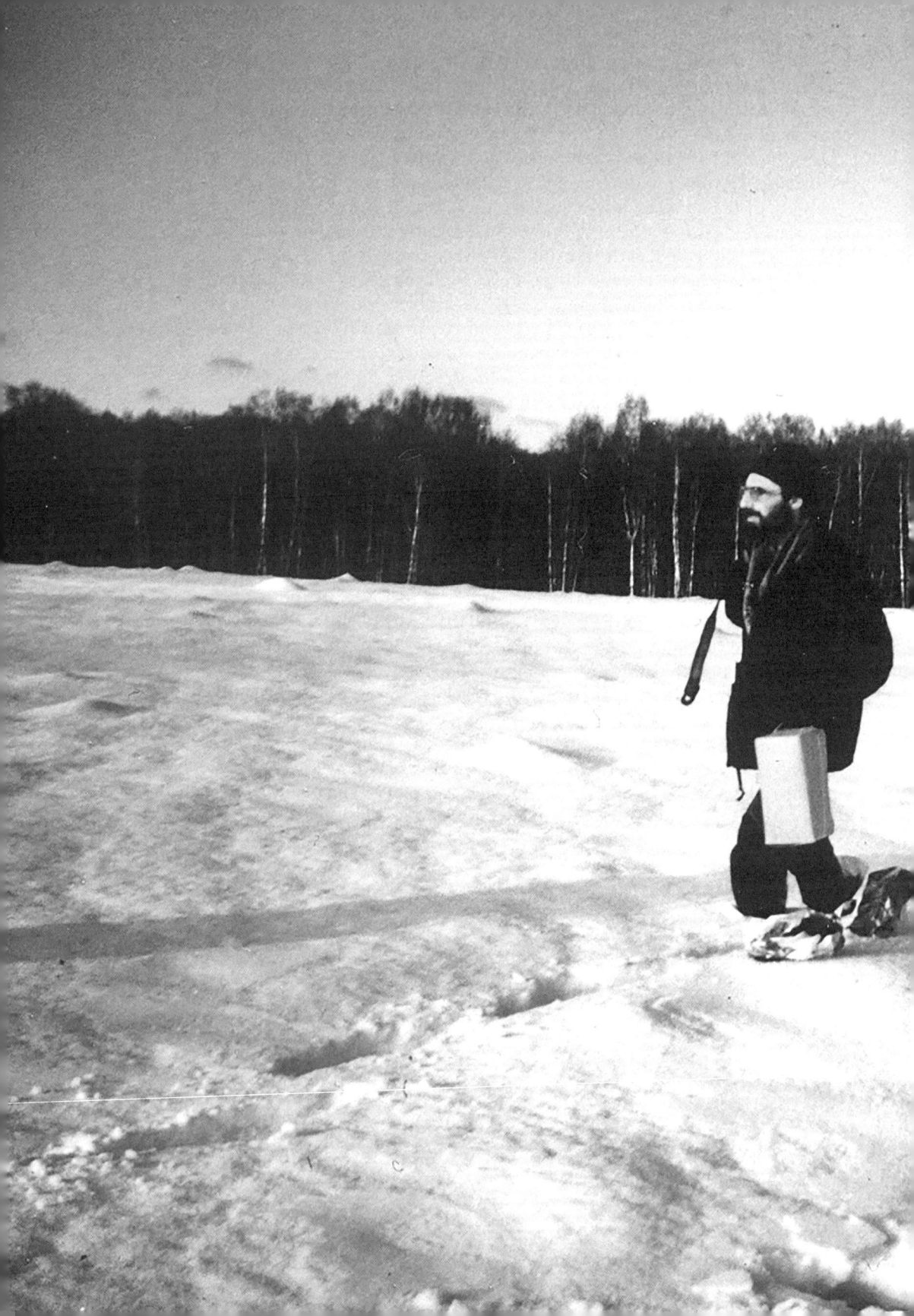

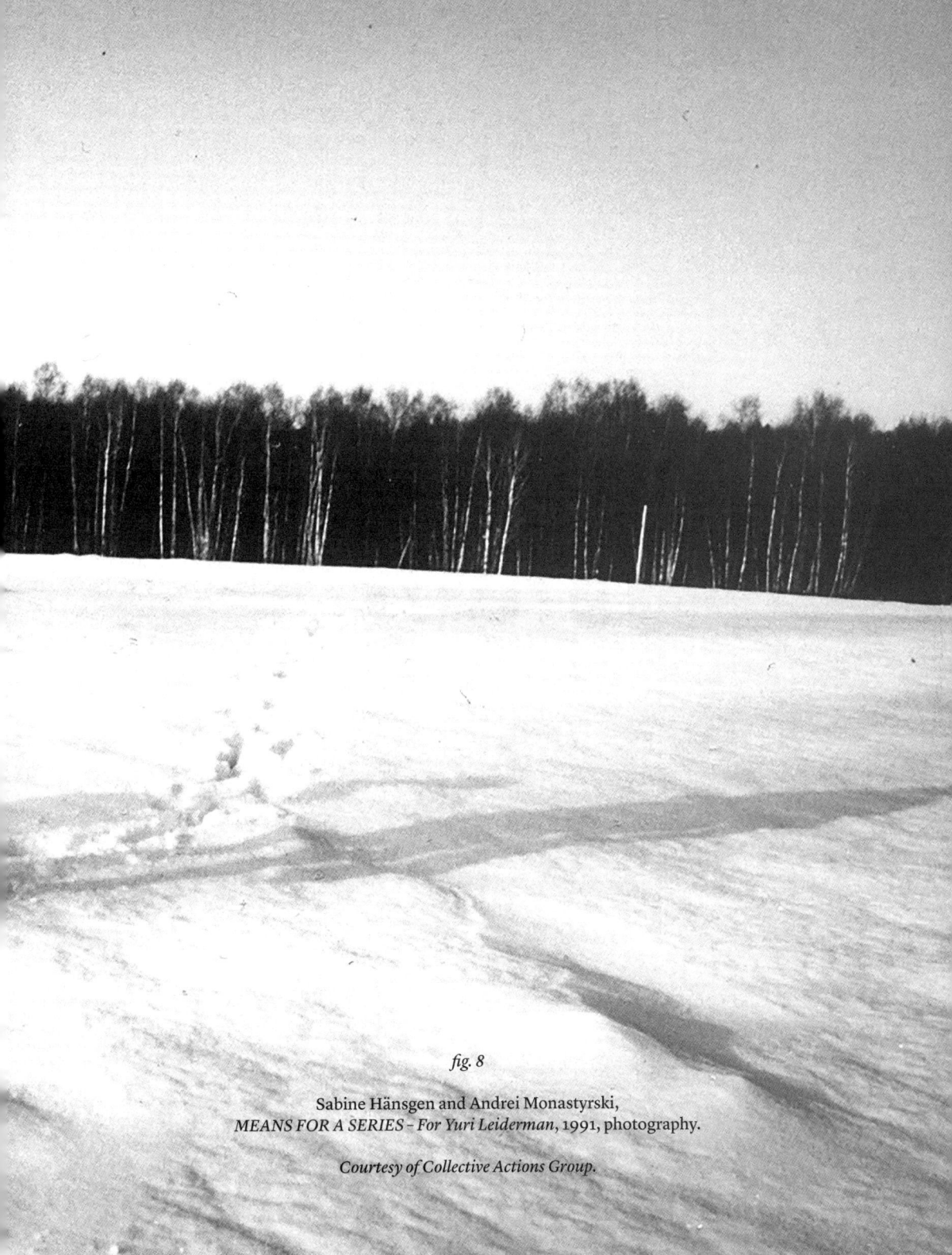

fig. 8

Sabine Hänsgen and Andrei Monastyrski,
MEANS FOR A SERIES - For Yuri Leiderman, 1991, photography.

Courtesy of Collective Actions Group.

Ekaterina Degot

Russian Art at the Rendezvous

Post-Soviet Russia at the Venice Biennale

Art historian and curator Ekaterina Degot is based in both Moscow and Cologne, where she is the artistic director of the Academy of the Arts of the World. In her research, she is interested in, among other things, artistic and socio-political issues in Russia, particularly in the post-Soviet era. Her contribution here presents a critical review of Soviet and Russian national exhibitions at the Venice Biennale from the late 1980s on. She captures the eventful history of the exhibitions in the national pavilion and notes especially the changing role of the curator, all in the context of the political, economic, and socio-cultural shifts from the decline of communism and the rise of capitalism to the present day, when Russia's pavilion exhibitions have become fully incorporated in the market economy.

First published in *Russian Artists at the Venice Biennale: 1895–2013*, ed. Nikolai Molok, Stella Art Foundation, Moscow, 2013. The version published here has been revised.

The Venice Biennale took shape at the meeting point of two 19th-century idées fixes – the nation state and the pre-modernist European art canon. But the USSR, at the time of its creation, radically rejected both these ideas. The state that inherited the Russian pavilion at the Venice Biennale with its stylized "old-fashioned" architecture did not conceive itself as a nation state made up of Russians (or even Russians in alliance with other nationalities), but as a state of workers and peasants, who needed a completely different kind of art. The new cultural hierarchy was dominated by public art, architecture, design, books, do-it-yourself theatre (performance, in today's understanding), educational displays (what we today would call "installations"), cinema, and collective art.

Coming from these positions, the USSR might have taken a very special – an alternative – place at the Venice Biennale. But this did not happen because, in the mid-1930s, the USSR experienced a kind of neo-bourgeois "Thermidor"[1] in art, as well as in other spheres.

Instead, in international contemporary art – and particularly at the Venice Biennale after 1968 – a certain "imaginary USSR" took shape: an alternative to the capitalist order in the art field, and this idea has not faded even today. This alternative "imaginary USSR" is characterized by a progressive anti-capitalist art dominated by the non-traditional media listed above, by exhibitions that are didactically structured by theme, and art practices that are to a greater or lesser extent instrumentalized for the benefit of social action. In spite of the Cold War, the culture of the West (not to mention its politics) needed the Soviet element; Western culture always remembered that the Soviet Union, although it had somehow gone astray, could look forward to a transformation (a kind of *perestroika*) that would restore its true essence, and in no sense would this be a turn toward capitalism.

But the USSR itself had completely different plans, and they are what determined the history of the pavilion in Venice.

1990–1993
Last Chance for the USSR

In the 1980s, the Soviet pavilion still paid homage to the Communist artistic hierarchy; the exhibitions of 1984 and 1986 presented theatre and cinema artists and book illustrators. But in 1988, at the start of Gorbachev's perestroika, or restructuring programme, the hero of the Soviet pavilion was none other than the classic Soviet painter Aristarkh Lentulov (1882–1943), one of the most bourgeois artists in the history of Soviet art. His

---

1 Alluding to the coup that brought down the radical wing of the French Revolution in 1794 in the month of Thermidor (according to the French Republican calendar), the term "Thermidor" is used by historians to describe a retreat from the more radical goals and strategies of a revolution.

tame cubist paintings with their national motifs and sales potential made Lentulov a key figure in the incipient era of the new Russian national capitalism in the late 1980s, and indeed he remains one of the most desirable artists for Russian collectors today.

The second exhibition of the new era (1990) – although still in the context of the USSR – was *Rauschenberg to Us, We to Rauschenberg,* which was prepared by a group of young artists close to the First Gallery (Guram Abramishvili, Sergei Volkov, Evgeny Mitta, Aidan Salakhova, Alexander Yakut, and Andrei Yakhnin). The First Gallery was not a commercial gallery in the full sense, nor was it an underground artist-run space that set itself in opposition to the establishment. Rather, it was a toy for the USSR's "gilded youth". The gallery was owned by Mitta, Salakhova, and Yakut, all young members of the Soviet Artists Union whose family connections gave them a certain privileged status – this is how they were able to make the acquaintance of Robert Rauschenberg, who had hurried over to the "new-look" Moscow in 1989 to put on a solo exhibition. The show at the Soviet pavilion in Venice consisted of paintings and silk-screen prints by the young Moscow artists in dialogue with a large work by Rauschenberg himself, who apparently had also funded the exhibition.

The long-standing commissioner of the Soviet pavilion, Vladimir Goryainov, writes of the exhibition using a unique rhetoric that characterizes the brief historical moment in which it took place. With a naivety that today sounds surprising, he takes pride in the fact that the young Soviet artists of the 1990s would be like Rauschenberg in the 1960s: "Rauschenberg came into an atmosphere that was thirty years old, from the time when the same ideas were preached by him and his friends."[2] As one might expect, this fact in itself doomed the exhibition to a fairly cold reaction from Western art professionals, for whom Rauschenberg was hardly a discovery. The professional public measured innovation using the criteria of historical novelty and originality (the criteria of the capitalist market, which requires artists to always be producing something new).

By contrast, Goryainov, a true son of the communist art-historical tradition, praised the new generation of artists for their quest as such, for their youth and their constant "restlessness". His idea of innovation was untainted by the rhetoric of competition, where the key is to be newer than others – or rather, to always be new with reference to oneself. As Goryainov writes: "In the context of today's Moscow life, Dadaism, Surrealism, Conceptualism and Hyperrealism assume a completely different colouring."[3] As if foreseeing that Soviet and Russian art would soon be accused of a lack of originality, he announces that what is important in art is the figure of the artist. "A street fair turns into a performance. It is not serious … Only one thing is seriously thought through here – the personality

---

2   Vladimir Goryainov, commissioner's statement on the Soviet pavilion, in *The 44th International Art Exhibition: La Biennale di Venezia,* exh. cat., Venice, 1990, p. 240.

3   Ibid.

of the artist, and his right to be himself."[4] This right to be oneself, the right to individualism, Goryainov links with the image he has inexplicably produced: that of a street market (which is "not serious"), the romanticized art market. The two ideas of individualism and the market have been the obsession of post-Soviet art for more than two decades, but never were they spoken of so directly as here.

Most surprising, Goryainov supposes that the young Soviet artists stand out from their Western peers by being more political: "The target of their ironical ideology is not the 'consumer society', but rather the socio-virtual structures of society as a whole. Socio-political passions are transformed into more or less generally recognized creative decisions, and this alone is what distinguishes the young art of our country from the many currents in foreign art."[5]

Here the apparent (and somewhat idealistic) thinking is that the young artists of the perestroika period were changing the image of the state and the society (for example, by organizing a commercial gallery) and that their actions carried much more weight than mere critique, which is what artists in the West were doing. This was a thoroughly Soviet logic.

The exhibition *Rauschenberg to Us, We to Rauschenberg* presented itself as an expression of the renewal inside the USSR, which earned it a special mention from the Biennale jury. But this internal renewal – perestroika – was very short-lived, and instead of the light, invigorating shake-up that was intended, it led to nothing less than the complete disintegration of the USSR. Consequently, when the next Biennale was held, in 1993, the country that was now simply Russia, a name that had suddenly reappeared on the world map, had neither the money nor the will to organize its own exhibition. Through some political manoeuvring and with the support of a foreign gallery, a project by Ilya Kabakov was held in the pavilion. His *Red Pavilion* (figs. 1–2) closed the chapter on the Soviet exhibitions some two years after the USSR itself had ceased to exist.

It is interesting to note that this was the only site-specific installation in the pavilion's entire history, from the Soviet exhibitions to today. Strangely enough, nobody else ever questioned the raison d'être of this highly ideological building – the work of Aleksey Shchusev, one of the Soviet Union's most ideological architects, who also designed the Lenin Mausoleum. Kabakov left the pavilion in the same ramshackle state in which he had found it in the summer of 1993: he put a fence round it, placed tokens of a pretended repair operation inside, and laid a barely discernible path through the rooms to the balcony. From the balcony, there was a view onto the true *Red Pavilion* – an intentionally primitive, laughable take on the Rodchenko theme of "radio operators" from the 1920s, issuing the chaotic sounds of a May Day parade (the sound recording was made by Vladimir Tarasov).

---

4   Ibid., p. 241.
5   Ibid.

Russian Art at the Rendezvous

The question Kabakov poses in the text that accompanies the installation comes not from the artist himself but from an imagined viewer who wonders: "Is it possible that the Biennale is showing an image of totalitarianism?"⁶ As we know, not only was this possible, but such displays had received the approval of the West at other international exhibitions as well: *Red Pavilion* was a natural continuation of the tradition of "export" installations by El Lissitzky in the late 1920s and 1930s and other Soviet "export" pavilions at international exhibitions. At the time of the Venice installation, Kabakov had already shown *Red Wagon* (1991), *Toilet* (1992), and *Big Archive* (March 1993), and was producing metaphorical images of "Sovietness" that were designed to pay tribute to the historical existence of the USSR and in a certain sense justify its existence – by the presence of a thinking, critical subject. In *Red Pavilion* the West saw what it had so long been waiting for – an original work with the Soviet tradition behind it that placed the Russian artist on equal terms with the West by his ability to be critical of "his" socialism, just as the Western artist is critical of capitalism.

Using the outmoded term "the West" is legitimate here because the West still existed in 1993; the era of global art had not yet begun. But Kabakov, who in 1989 had participated with African artists in the exhibition *Magiciens de la Terre* (*Magicians of the Earth*), stood at the beginnings of global art. In the eyes of the international public at the Venice Biennale, he was "original" because he made reference to his own origins and nobody else's. At this historical moment, when after the fall of the Berlin Wall economic and political confrontation was interpreted as cultural diversity, the international scene was ready to accept the USSR but only as a local exotic culture, a kind of specific nationality, enriching the market of identities with yet another original dance with a tambourine, or in this case a hammer and sickle.

Such historical hopes were not to be realized. Instead of a socialism with a human face Russia soon acquired a capitalism without one. The chaotic situation offered chances to people of a quite different stamp from Commissioner Goryainov (who in 1993 surrendered his authority due to lack of financing) or even Ilya Kabakov (who later took part only in the Biennale's main exhibitions). For the newcomers – the curators and artists of Russia's new capitalist era – the total lack of a budget, the complete indifference of the state, and a strong dependence on sponsors represented opportunities.

At the start of the 1990s, the arrival of the new generation of Russian artists on the world's art scene, and at the Venice Biennale in particular, was accompanied by certain typical misunderstandings. These artists, like many Russian critics and curators, believed they had made contact with the "real West", with that English lawn, which, as the joke goes, is

---

6   *Ilya Kabakov: Installations 1983–1995*, exh. cat., Centre Georges Pompidou, Paris, 1995, p. 188.

easy to grow – you just have to water and mow it regularly for four hundred years. But in fact what they were seeing had only just started to take shape at the end of 1980s and to a large extent was a product of their "arrival".

The birth of the international and, soon after, the global contemporary art scene (defined by the sociologist Pascal Gielen as a mobile and hyper-communicative transcontinental community[7]), the growth in the prestige of contemporary art, the appearance and importance of the freelance curator, the secondary importance accorded to the history of art in comparison with theory, the accent on installations and huge video projects – all things that made such an impression on the Russian artists who were coming to the Venice Biennale for the first time – were connected in large measure with the end of socialism (in Western countries as well as in the East), the post-Fordian turn, liberal metaphors of freedom, and the substitution of a "cultural" problematic for the previous political-economic problematic. Also, the relational aesthetics and participatory approach of the 1990s brought to art the same type of horizontal and social bonds based on solidarity that had, until recently, been the norm in the USSR and that for artists coming from the former USSR had not yet fully dissolved.

1995–2005
Curatorship as an Added Value

When the Russian Ministry of Culture invited me to serve as curator for the Russian pavilion at the Venice Biennale in 2001, I was informed that two artists, Leonid Sokov and Sergei Shutov, had already been confirmed, since their projects had financial backing. It was suggested to me that I incorporate their projects into a general concept, but I said I could only curate my own project and proposed another artist, Olga Chernysheva. Each of these three artists is remarkable in their own way and each of them deserved to have a solo show, but because Sokov's and Shutov's presentations did not have a curator, I was often referred to as the curator of the entire pavilion, both during the exhibition and afterwards. What is more, Chernysheva and I felt a certain pressure from the fact that, for some unknown reason, her solo project – a series of photographs – did have its own curator: although the photographs were expressive in themselves (fig. 3), we felt obliged to display them in some special way, in the form of an installation with live trees and the sound of birdsong – things that Chernysheva did not repeat in later exhibitions.

---

7   See Pascal Gielen, *The Murmuring of the Artistic Multitude: Global Art, Memory and Post-Fordism*, Valiz, Amsterdam, 2009.

So questions arise: why was the situation of a group exhibition created, and why did it need a curator – one to whom, ultimately, no real authority was given other than selecting one of the artists? To find the answers we have to go back to the 1990s. Throughout the decade Russian cultural journalists had drummed into the heads of their readers, who included officials at the Ministry of Culture, that what the national pavilion needed most of all was a curator, that the curator was of the utmost importance and should be appointed first and then she or he should select the artist to be exhibited. In fact, many countries, including France and the United States, do the opposite: the "national" artist is chosen first, and then, as a more or less ancillary figure, the curator is matched to the artist. The usual pattern in national pavilions is a solo exhibition by a "classic" artist of the older generation or an emerging artist who has already exhibited at the international level and then after the Biennale goes on to be a fully fledged star. There were no artists of the second type in Russia in the 1990s – although there was an attempt to present Sergei Bugaev-Afrika in such a light in 1999. Russia did have artists of the first type, particularly among the émigrés, but they did not always receive backing from major galleries and collectors and, until the mid-2000s, confirmed financing was a condition for having a project accepted.

In 1997, there had been the idea of presenting Komar and Melamid's *People's Choice* project, but the money could not be found so at the last minute the pavilion was occupied by the conservative artist Maxim Kantor, who received financial support from Deutsche Bank. Kantor tried to present himself as a "national classic", but in doing so he only intensified the feeling on the Russian art scene that solo projects at the pavilion were by their very nature reactionary.

Indeed, strange as it may seem, opposition to mounting a solo exhibition in the pavilion came not so much from the Ministry of Culture as from the art community itself, which wanted to advance conceptual curatorial projects and believed passionately in the figure of the curator as the guarantor of a project's intellectual potential. From the mid-1990s to 2011, we tend to see the big names of Russian art appearing in the main exhibition at the Biennale, while the Russian pavilion regularly offered group exhibitions of young or mid-career artists as curatorial projects or, more often, as imitations of curatorial projects.

The international enthusiasm in the 1990s for the freelance curator is directly related to the post-Fordian turn towards "immaterial labour", the dominance of the "idea", the end of the universal welfare state (including the Soviet state), and greater prestige accorded to personal and even voluntaristic choice.

In the post-Soviet conditions the curator was assigned responsibility for the "good quality" of the event, to ensure that it was "Western-style" and "presentable" – in other words, "capitalist" as opposed to "amateurish". In the USSR, there had been no curators and the selection of works for the exhibition was made by the artists themselves (acting as

fig. 1

Ilya Kabakov, *Red Pavilion*,
sketch for the Russian pavilion, Venice Biennale, 1993.

Courtesy of Ilya and Emilia Kabakov.

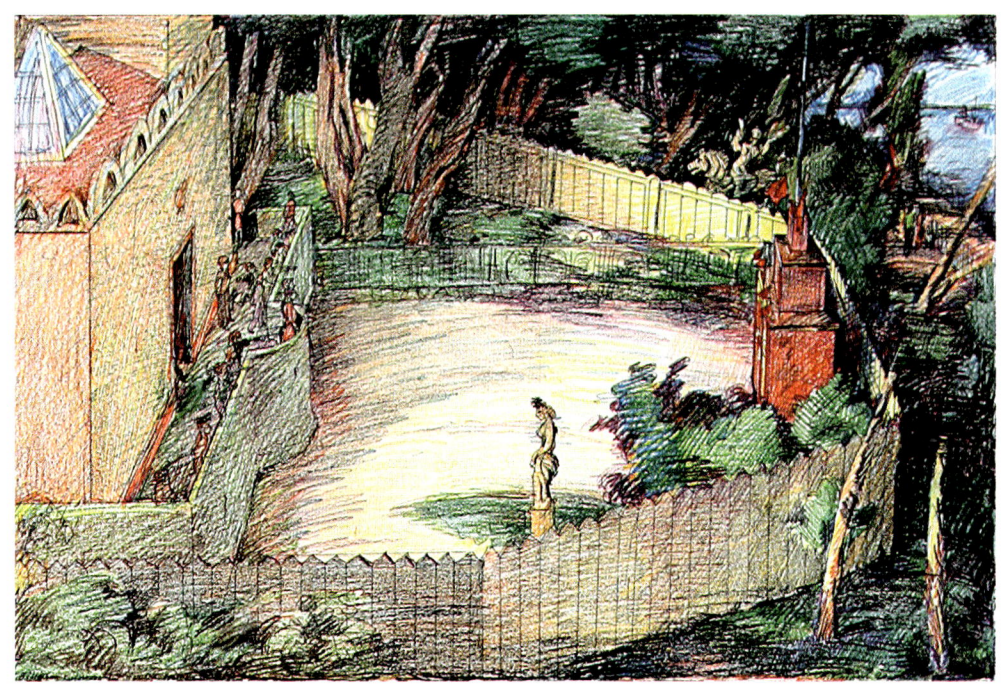

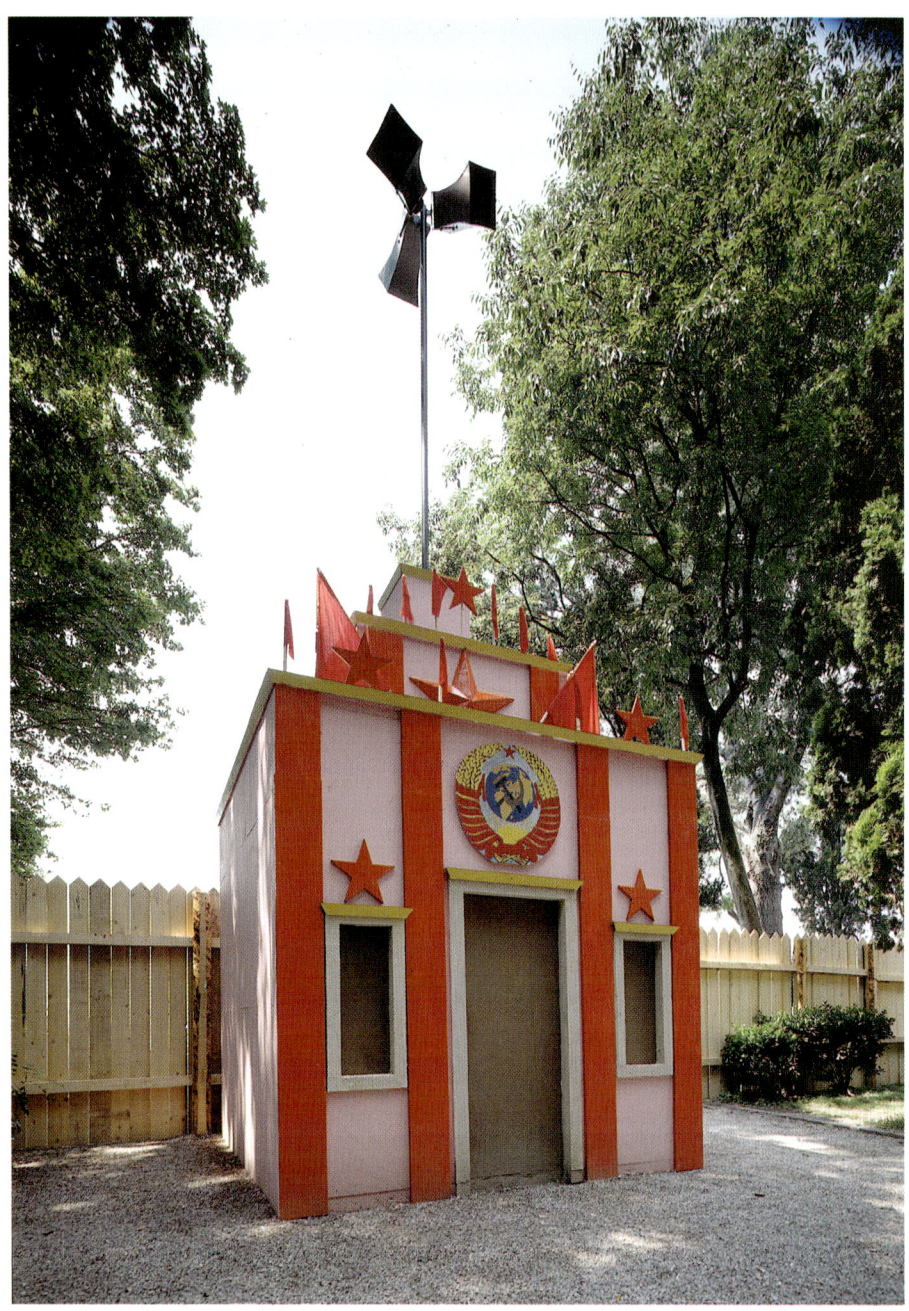

fig. 2

Ilya Kabakov, *Red Pavilion*, installation view,
Russian pavilion, Venice Biennale, 1993.

Photo by Emilia Kabakov. Courtesy of Ilya and Emilia Kabakov.

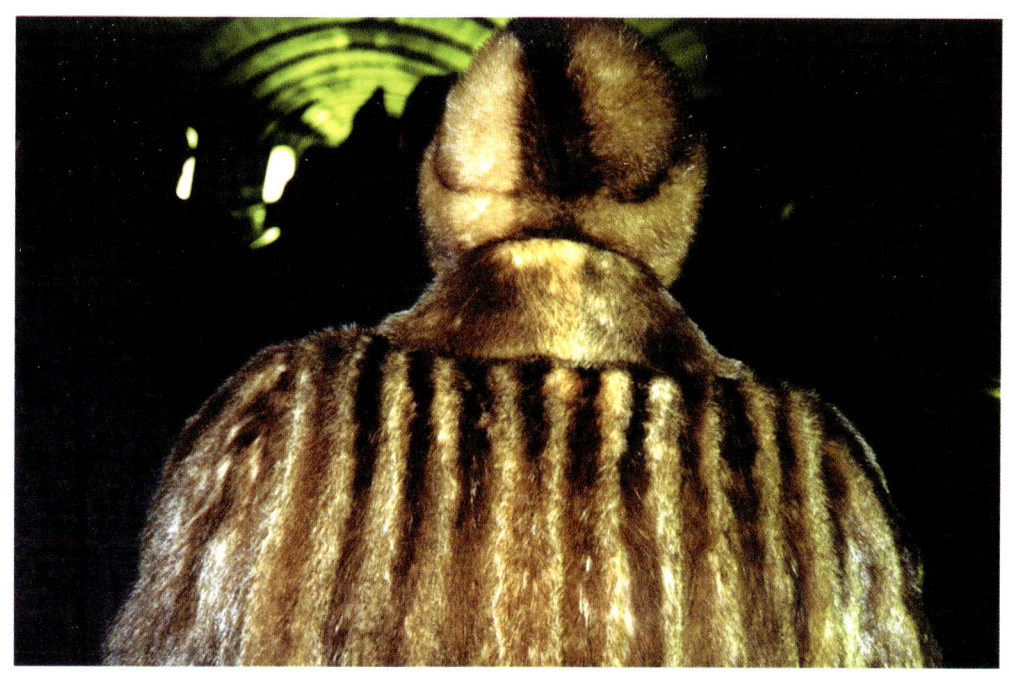

fig. 3

Olga Chernysheva, *Second Life*, 2001,
photography series, 100 cm x 150 cm x 15 cm.

Courtesy of the artist.

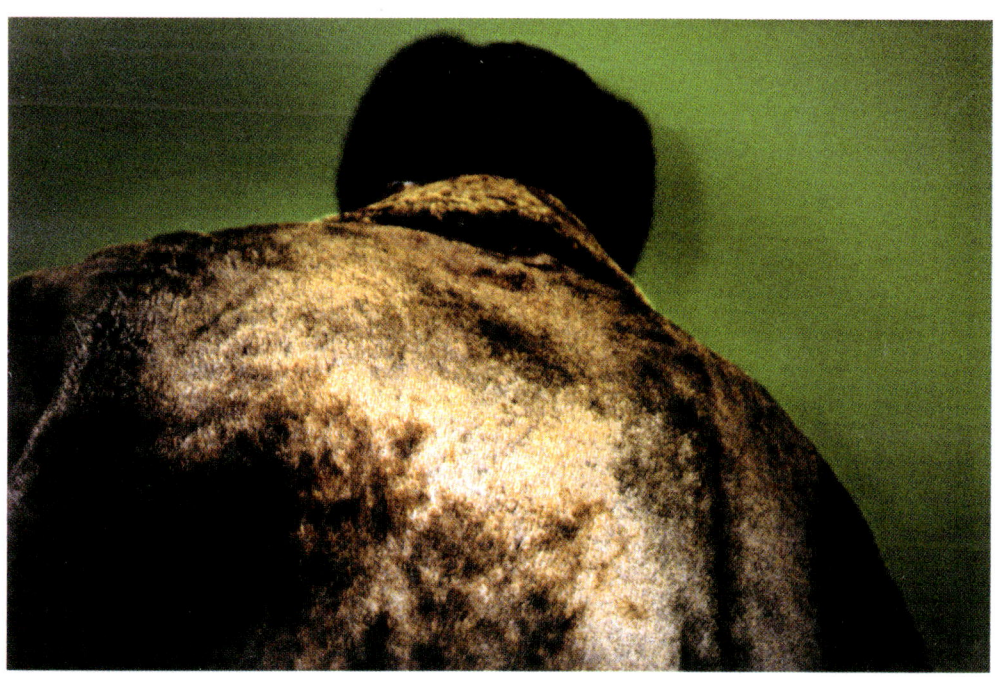

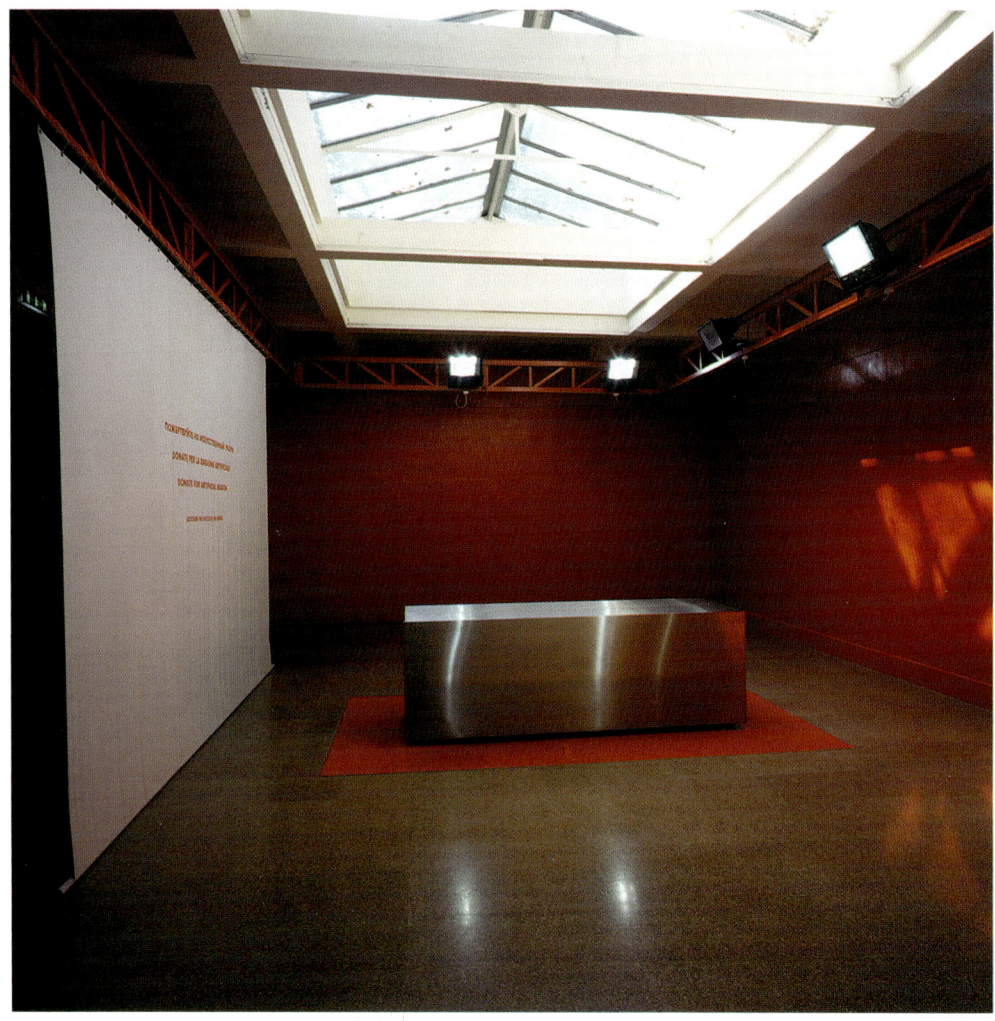

fig. 4

Reason Is Something the World Must Obtain Whether It Wants To or Not,
exhibition project by curator Viktor Misiano and the artists
Evgeny Asse, Dmitry Gutov, and Vadim Fishkin, detail of the
installation, Russian pavilion, Venice Biennale, 1995.

Photo from Viktor Misiano's private archive.

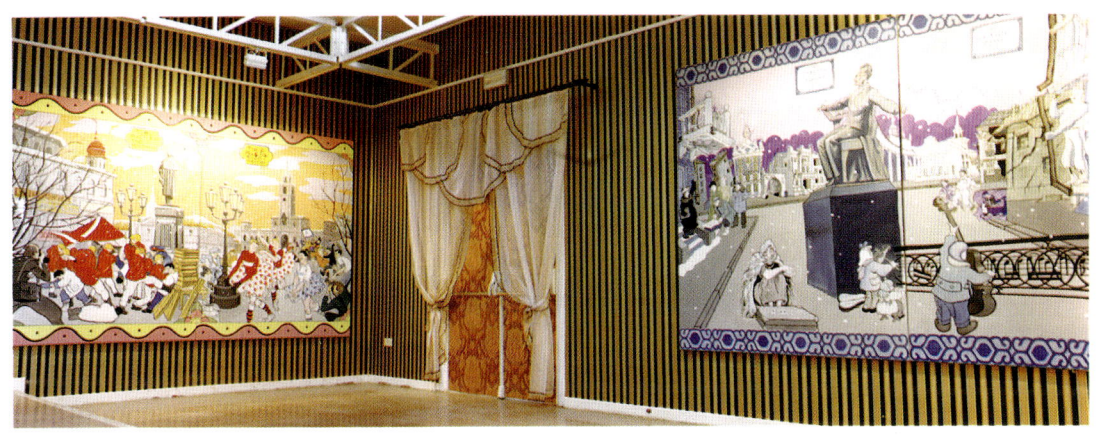

fig. 5

View of the Konstantin Zvezdochetov room with the series
Moscow Types, Russian pavilion, Venice Biennale, 2003.

Photo from Viktor Misiano's private archive.

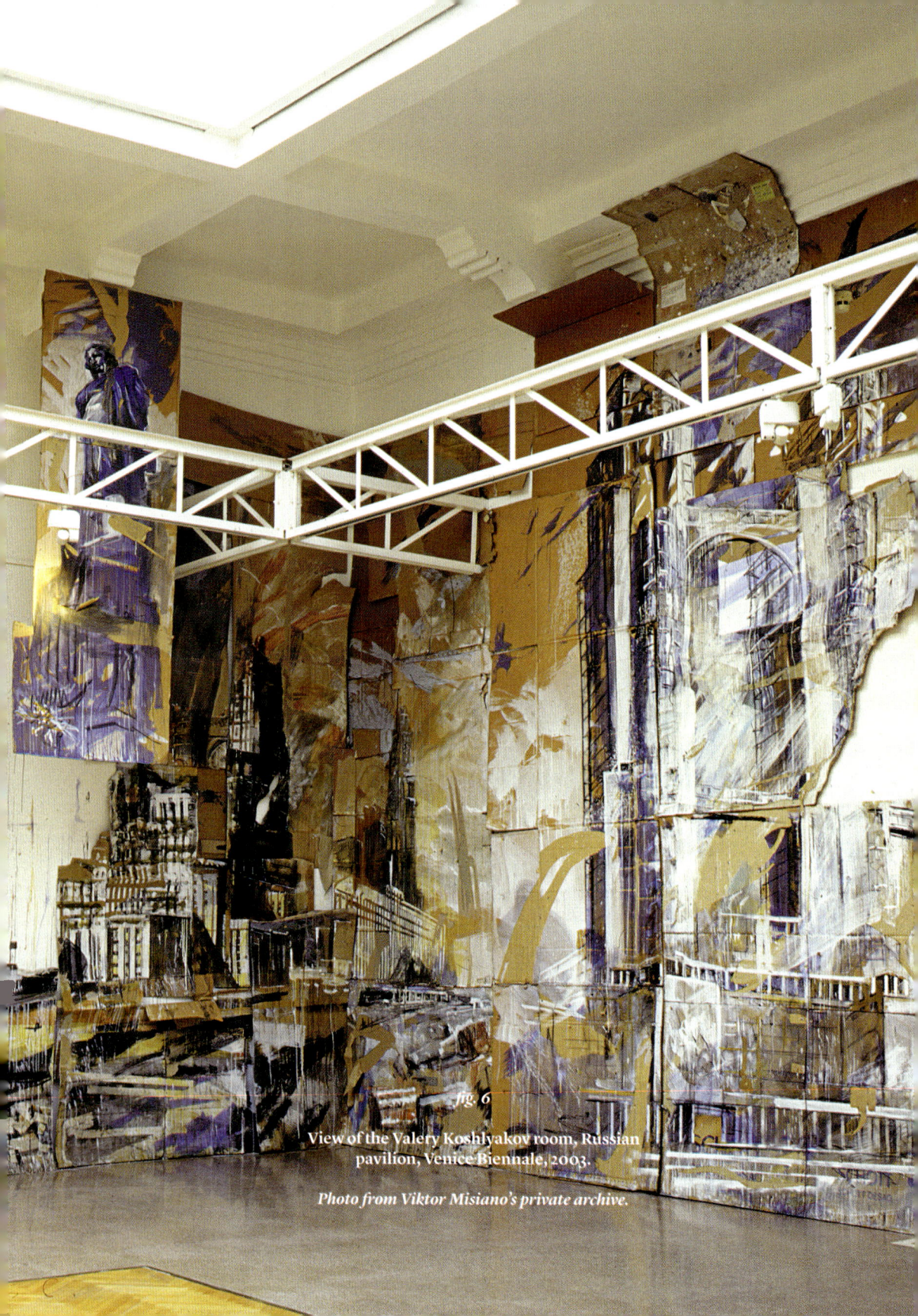

fig. 6
View of the Valery Koshlyakov room, Russian pavilion, Venice Biennale, 2003.

Photo from Viktor Misiano's private archive.

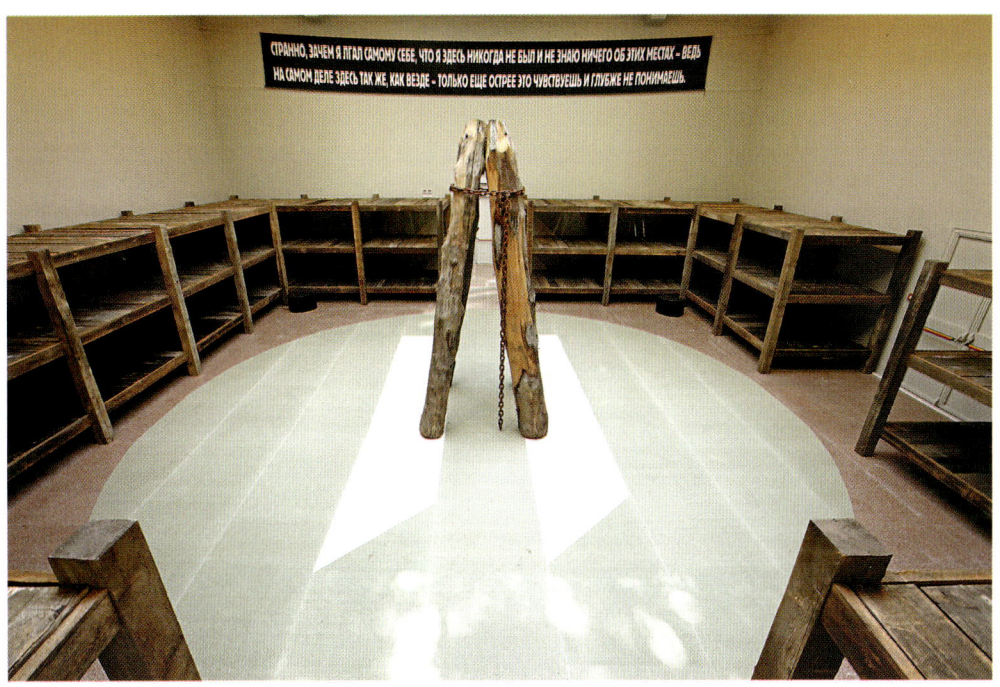

fig. 7

Andrei Monastyrski, installation view, Russian pavilion, Venice Biennale, 2011.

Photo by Daria Novgorodova. Courtesy of the Stella Art Foundation, Moscow.

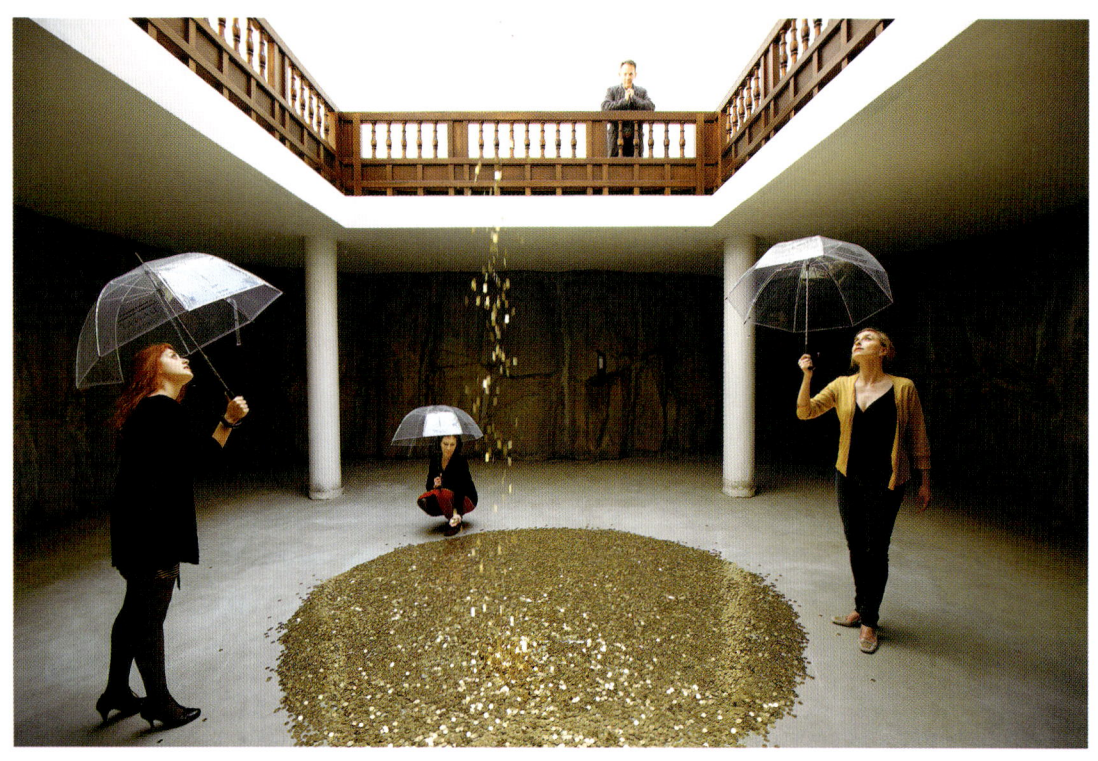

fig. 8

Vadim Zakharov, *Danaë*, installation view,
Russian pavilion, Venice Biennale, 2013.

Photo by Daniel Zakharov. Courtesy of the Stella Art Foundation, Moscow.

art-community bureaucrats). To be sure, the procedure was hardly democratic, but the final exhibition often looked like an array of everything and anything. So in the neo-capitalist era, a hierarchy of names emerged as a more contemporary and, paradoxically, fairer approach, offering everyone that famous "chance" – one of the main fetishes of the period. In principle, this hierarchy of names could have been embodied by a normative history of art, but due to the perilous condition of academic scholarship in post-Soviet Russia its place was taken by the "creative will" of the curator, a mass-media manipulator of ideas who was capable of fitting any set of artists into the shiny envelope of "the concept". At least that is what came to be expected of the curator in the 1990s and 2000s.

In Russia, the unequal relationship between artist and curator was, and is, accentuated by the fact that the curator is, as a rule, more educated, more adept at foreign languages, and has more international experience than the artist, so that they are the one who, for example, can deal with sponsors and other backers. Throughout the 1990s and 2000s, the Russian art bureaucracy took completely different attitudes toward curators and artists, and the differences were marked by a class distinction. The curator was always perceived as "one of us", while the artist was considered an irrational wild creature who needed to be seated at the far end of the table at formal banquets. The curator was a far more acceptable and reliable partner for the Ministry of Culture and, essentially, agreed to assume the role of censor and bureaucratic manager, taking responsibility for the paternalistic state power and serving as its proxy.

Meanwhile, the future "creative class" and the intellectual producers – the curators, critics, and journalists, who in the 1990s were usually out of work or in precarious positions – sought to impose the idea of prestige on the nascent system, where, as they already sensed, the only value would be money. The only possible criterion for prestige was "conceptuality", the presence of an "added ingredient" over and above the "mere display" of individual works. And the creative intelligentsia was willing to go far to protect its monopoly, for example, by insisting on the impossibility of understanding contemporary art without the help of expert appraisal.

The beginning and end of this era are marked by two paradigmatic projects by the curator Viktor Misiano. The first project, in 1995, established for many years the notion that every exhibition in the Venice pavilion required, first and foremost, a curator with some "concept" accompanied by an "explanation". Titled *Reason Is Something the World Must Obtain Whether It Wants To or Not*, it was a group project by Evgeny Asse, Dmitry Gutov, Vadim Fishkin, and Misiano himself, in which the authors discussed long and hard what, in principle, could be shown in a pavilion where the name "Russia" was inscribed on the façade for the first time; they wanted to ensure that the exhibition at least did justice to the powerful social reality of the moment (fig. 4). This "process of thought" found its reflection in the collective project. The Chechen war, the political killings, the grotesque types of people who emerged in the initial accumulation of capital, and the comical sexual freedom of the media were all documented. The chief metaphor of the powerlessness of art and language in the face of the brutal reality was a fragment of archival footage (from 1932, at the height of Stalin's ruthless industrialization) in which a village musician, with his fingers in his mouth and with great diligence, whistles Tchaikovsky's *Neapolitan Song*. The insouciance and meaninglessness of art, embodied in the figure of the mute performer, presented a stark contrast with the external reality.

The title of the project, which was undoubtedly one of the key works of Russian art in the 1990s, is a quote from Marx. In his catalogue statement, the curator (although the text is unsigned the style is Misiano's) wrote that the source of the title was unimportant – he apparently wished to to break the link with the Soviet period and demonstrate openness to the indefinite future. In a kind of parallel to the Russian pavilion, the main project at the Venice Biennale in 1995 was an art-historical exhibition by Jean Clair, which gave a great deal of space to Soviet realism as an alternative to Western modernism. At the time, however, few critics made any connection between the two exhibitions, as Soviet history was judged to be over.

Misiano had planned to hold several successive exhibitions in the pavilion, but his next project there did not in fact occur until 2003, culminating the era of the precarious "creative curator". The name of the 2003 exhibition, *Return of the Artist*, in itself underscored the idea that the curator had decided to withdraw into the background, giving centre stage to the artists, or more specifically, the painters: Konstantin Zvezdochetov, Valery Koshlyakov, and the duo Vladimir Dubossarsky and Alexander Vinogradov. A fifth participant, Sergei Bratkov, was initially invited to play a somewhat different, secondary role – as portrait photographer.

Misiano said that in the project he was trying to "simply show good, viewable art"[8] – which, however, does not mean that the curator's role was reduced to zero. As in 1995, we were given a group exhibition, but even more than in the earlier project, which involved the work of a self-organized collective, bringing these artists together was a wilful and, to some extent, forcible decision on the part of the curator.

On this occasion, the power of the curator was manifest in the fact that he declared as "fashionable" a large-scale, viewer-oriented style of painting that was also attractive to collectors; in this way, he used the pretext of the zeitgeist to absolve himself of the sin of commercialism. The curator, then, was still the key figure, embodying prestige, intellectual superiority, and connections, but he very likely lacked any real power (such as control over the budget) and so, in a sense, was held hostage to the prestige of his position.

---

8   Quoted by Sandra Frimmel, "50th Biennale 2003: The Russian Pavilion", in *Russian Artists at the Venice Biennale: 1895–2013*, ed. Nikolai Molok, Stella Art Foundation, Moscow, 2013, pp. 594–597.

In 2003, the Russian pavilion received its first Russian sponsor – the Bank of Moscow, of which the largest shareholder at the time was the City of Moscow. The pavilion projects thus began taking on an official character and no longer had the appearance of a quirky gesture by representatives of a little-known community of "narrow" professionals. And important guests were more frequently in attendance at the openings. The bank's sponsorship also had an indirect impact on the 2003 exhibition, which started off with a series of enormous paintings by Zvezdochetov. The series presented a highly complex narrative that mixed the ideological and metaphoric rhetoric of Stalin-era caricatures with 19th-century and present-day imagery to depict various "Moscow types" of people (fig. 5). I remember how surprised everyone was that something so local, including jokes that were completely incomprehensible to foreigners, was being shown at an international event. But the reason was simple: for the first time, the exhibition was addressed primarily to our own Moscow elite, who wanted to know what the government and the sponsor were spending their money on.

The aesthetics of the 2003 exhibition was also very "Muscovite", combining a thoroughly Soviet love of figurative painting with the Russian taste for bright colours, narrative, and large proportions. A monumental panel by Vinogradov and Dubossarsky, which showed post-Soviet rich kids at play (underwater, as if in an aquarium), flirted with glossy magazines and the art of the classic Soviet painter, Aleksandr Deineka, while the section with paintings by Valery Koshlyakov was reminiscent of Renaissance and baroque sources, from which Soviet art as a whole had drawn inspiration (fig. 6).

Although not entirely successful, Misiano's 2003 project would become a reference point for the Russian pavilion exhibitions in the late 2000s, which were characterized by an overabundance of isolated art objects, a conservative populist aesthetic, a refusal to put the pavilion itself in question, and an orientation toward the local elite/consumer rather than the international context. Whether by accident or not, the projects in 2007 and 2009 also had an organizational connection with Moscow and presented the city's traditional cultural image – one of generosity, garishness, wealth, and simple-heartedness. Misiano was a diagnostician of his time and there was probably a touch of irony in his attitude to the work in the 2003 show, but the irony got lost along the way.

2007–2015
Marriage Market or Museum of Patriarchs?

In 2005 the Russian pavilion hosted the last curatorial project that was "genetically" linked to the image of the freelance curator from the 1990s era of immaterial production. Curators Olga Lopukhova and Lyubov Saprykina presented the Moscow group Escape, along with an artist duo from Nizhny Novgorod, Sergei Provorov and Galina Myznikova, who work under the name Provmyza. Escape had always leaned toward a "non-spectacular" art, ephemeral interventions, and performance gestures, and for this occasion, Provmyza presented something in a similar spirit.

But the 2005 exhibition was already behind the times: by the mid-2000s, Russian capitalism had reached the point where it required images of its own prosperity; there was a modest but steady market demand for Russian art, and the figure of the freelance curator-entrepreneur engaged with immaterial projects no longer fitted the bill. What was needed was the institutionally integrated curator-collector, who could produce not only real market values but also "icons of ownership" that valorized the sculptural, physical and space-filling qualities of artworks (as objects of attention) and offered a strong expression of individual authorship.

The 2007 Russian pavilion opened in a completely new context. The sponsor was the Moscow luxury goods store, TsUM; the opening was on a grand scale and attended by a crowd of cultural ministry officials, sponsors, and their friends, including Roman Abramovich, who came to the Venice Biennale for the first time. Later that year, the opening of the Garage Museum of Contemporary Art in Moscow was announced, a major prize for contemporary art (the Kandinsky Prize) was awarded in Russia for the first time, and Russia's first Larry Gagosian Gallery opened in a luxury shopping mall near Moscow. Meanwhile, the International Olympic Committee chose the city of Sochi as the venue for the 2014 Olympic Games. In this new context, the Russian elite began to see Venice as a place where countries come to compete and show off their resources.

The 1990s tradition of grass-roots, self-organized initiatives was now interrupted for the first time: the pavilion was put at the disposal of institutions that operated on a museum logic, specifically, the logic of the neo-capitalist museum, where the main purpose was the accumulation of entertaining exhibits rather than research and where the criterion of successful work ("efficiency", in the new terminology) was the number of visitors. The pavilion commissioner was Vassili Tsereteli, the director of the Moscow Museum of Modern Art, and the position of curator was given, for two successive Biennales, to Olga Sviblova, the influential director of the Multimedia Art Museum in Moscow, who had a reputation for working successfully with both city officials and sponsors.

In both her pavilion shows, Sviblova continued the tradition of group projects, and in fact took the "genre" to the limit: in 2007, she presented five artists and, in 2009, seven artists. The 2007 show, *Click I Hope*, took its name from an internet project by the young artist Yulia Milner, about whom hardly anything was known, either before or after the Biennale, except that she was a former model, a photographer, and the wife of the owner of Russia's largest internet mail server. Milner was not alone in her transformation into a contemporary artist – by now, the prestige of contemporary art had risen so high, and a certain kind of artistic production had come so close to everyday life, that a year later Russia's best-known socialite, Ksenia Sobchak, also decided to become an artist and held an exhibition of her own footwear in a Moscow gallery.

The 2007 pavilion projects were all technically very complex; they included a 3D-animation by the AES+F group; LEDs in a mirror tunnel by Andrei Bartenov; a glass construction with an automatic wave generator and a video by Alexander Ponomarev; a composition of 235 monitors with non-stop broadcasting by Ponomarev and Arseny Meshcheryakov; and, on a huge monitor, Milner's internet project. Never before had the exhibition at the Russian pavilion been so expensive, which helped to show that Russia was a country with huge potential, a country of the future, hope, and a positive attitude.

The title of the 2009 exhibition, *Victory Over the Future*, seemed to affirm the reverse, heralding a certain neo-conservative aesthetic: the silhouette of the Nike of Samothrace on the cover of the catalogue could easily have been calling for a return to classicism. But the chain of associations, perhaps not fully recognized by the curator herself, was more complex. The future in the title was a reference to futurism, which was associated with the transformation of political power, with the USSR and its communist rhetoric, which Sviblova undoubtedly wished to reject. To conquer the future, to stop chasing the future, as the title implies, was to proclaim an "end to revolutions", including artistic revolutions, and "the end of history"; it was to express satisfaction with neo-capitalism as the ideal world system – undoubtedly the position of the institutions and sponsors who stood behind the pavilion.

But to dispense with the idea of the future did not entail a desire to dispense with the idea of victory: in his statement in the catalogue, Commissioner Vassili Tsereteli said again that the Venice Biennale was the Olympic Games of contemporary art[9] – in these years, the state rhetoric was all about Russia "rising from its knees". The pavilion artists were described as "young and successful", borrowing terms from the all-powerful Russian marketing world that meant triumphant, positive, breaking with the communist past, fully self-sufficient in the capitalist sense, and able to

---

9   See Vassili Tsereteli, commissioner's statement, in *Victory Over the Future: Russian Pavilion, 53rd International Art Exhibition: La Biennale di Venezia 2009*, Multimedia Art Museum , Moscow, 2009, p. 6.

produce a valid product. The last sentence of Sviblova's introduction to the catalogue put it like this: "As the production of an oeuvre that outlives the creator, artists' activity by its very nature represents a victory over the future."[10]

The real heroes of the 2009 show, then, were not the artists but the objects: a sculpture of a fountain made from multicoloured oilcloth (Irina Korina); a phosphorescent multi-figure fresco (Alexei Kallima); a labyrinth of boards with paintings that moved, a ringing telephone, and an automated drawing device (Gosha Ostretsov); an installation made of glass balls (Anatoly Zhuravlev); three full-size Nikes of Samothrace with oil and blood bubbling inside them (Andrei Molodkin); a large dark hall with illuminated drawings scattered around the space and rap music (Pavel Peppershtein); and a foam rubber motorcyclist "zooming out" from the pavilion onto the street (Sergei Shekhovtsov). Any one of these large-scale installations would almost have been enough for the pavilion, and to make them all fit (or not fit, as in the case of the motorcyclist) the interior had to be divided into separate narrow corridors.

In both 2007 and 2009, the Russian exhibitions were presented in darkness with spotlights on the individual videos or objects, like treasures displayed in a jeweller's shop. In this context, the curator's main concern was that each of these autonomous objects, isolated as they were from each other, should be presented in "the most favourable light". The purpose of the exhibition, as Sviblova repeatedly emphasized, was to allow young artists to "show themselves" in the West, which is why she considered it justified to show the maximum number of works. What we were looking at, then, was a marriage market.

By 2009, it had become established practice that oil-rich Russia would, along with the pavilion exhibition, present a large programme of parallel projects at the Biennale, mainly with private support. All demonstrating the same taste and aims, these projects also pursued the same polemic (whether covertly or openly) against the idea of a critical and social art, which in the view of many Russians was being imposed by the international art establishment. In 2009, the parallel programme included the exhibition *Danger! Museum* (a polemic against the idea of contemporariness) by Vladimir Dubossarsky and Alexander Vinogradov, in which the authors reinterpreted a number of classic European paintings, and the group exhibition *Unconditional Love* (a polemic against the idea of criticism), which was designed principally to show the enormous video installation *Trimalchio's Feast*, by the AES+F group.[11]

All of this feverish self-promotion evoked a fairly negative reaction from the Russian art community, which around this time split into several parts. At first, it appeared that the Russian art world had divided in two:

10 Olga Sviblova, "Victory Over the Future", in *Victory Over the Future*, p. 10 (see previous note).
11 The name Trimalchio, from a character in Petronius's *Satyricon*, has become a byword in Russia for the worst excesses of the nouveau riche.

a "nouveau riche" party associated with the tastes of the new capitalism and another, "civilized", Westernizing party that had developed from the unofficial art of Soviet times, particularly the conceptualists. In 2007, concurrently with the new-media circus in the Russian pavilion, the main Biennale project, curated by Robert Storr, showed a very different kind of art from Russia – not only a large project by Ilya and Emilia Kabakov (their contribution at the Biennale had already become a tradition) but also an installation by Andrei Monastyrski and a project by Dmitry Gutov and David Riff, who documented the work of Russia's "unofficial" school for the study of Marxism. In the same year, Russian artists were represented for the first time at *documenta 12*, as part of the independent publishers' programme, and they were nearly the same ones as in Venice: Gutov, Monastyrski, Anatoly Osmolovsky, Kirill Preobrazhensky, and the collective Chto delat'? ("What is to be done?"), of which David Riff is a member. The wheel seemed to have come full circle: as in Soviet times, art dissidents were being recognized only in the West, while art for domestic consumption was favoured by local sponsors.

But in fact, matters were more complicated. From the second half of the 2000s, when hopes disappeared for a legitimate transfer of presidential power, and even for any kind of historical development in Russia, a variety of activist groups and platforms appeared in the country: Chto delat'? assumed its final shape in 2004, as did Voina ("War") in 2008, while various self-organized projects by artists and activists appeared at every possible opportunity. The first May Congress of Creative Workers was held in Moscow in 2010, Voina held its best-known actions that same year, and a guilty verdict was delivered in a high-profile court case against the curators and artists from the exhibition *Forbidden Art*. It became clear that Russia now had an oppositionist art movement, which had developed even before the appearance of any genuine political opposition.

At the same time, the Moscow Conceptualist circle was becoming an object of interest and respect from medium and big businesses. In 2005, the artist Vadim Zakharov – himself a member of the circle – and I put together the book *Moscow Conceptualism*, which was produced by the small private publishing house WAM; Zakharov insisted that the book, an enormous volume with glossy photographs, should have gold edging. This seemed like a joke at first, but it soon became clear that he was asking the Russian business world to embrace the conceptualist unofficial art tradition as its own – to identify with it just as, decades before, it had identified with Russia's *art moderne* (and in any case, there were not enough paintings by Aristarkh Lentulov to satisfy the market).

The first person from this world to take an interest in the conceptualist circle, as early as 2004, was Stella Kesaeva, the founder and president of the Stella Art Foundation. In 2006, with the foundation's support, an exhibition of Zakharov's work was held at the State Tretyakov Gallery in Moscow; other exhibitions of the conceptualist circle were then held in museums outside Russia – at the Kunsthistorisches Museum in Vienna in 2008 and the Ca' Rezzonico in Venice in 2009. When Kesaeva was appointed commissioner of the Russian pavilion for three consecutive Biennales, it was perfectly natural that her first exhibition, in 2011, was a retrospective (curated by Boris Groys) of the key conceptualist artists Andrei Monastyrski (fig. 7) and the Collective Actions Group, while her second and the third pavilion shows were solo projects by Zakharov (fig. 8) (in 2013, curated by Udo Kittelmann) and Irina Nakhova (in 2015, curated by Margarita Tupitsyn). Independently, the first Monastyrski retrospective in Russia was held in the autumn of 2010 by the Victoria – The Art of Being Contemporary Foundation; it was curated by Teresa Mavica. The conceptualist circle also gained the support of the private publisher and art patron German Titov, who launched the enormous publication series *The Library of Moscow Conceptualism*.[12]

As unlikely as it might have first seemed, the conceptualists' hope of winning such support was never completely unfounded, since in Russia the representatives of medium and big capital often come from the old Soviet technical and scientific intelligentsia, or they have friends and acquaintances from that background. This is an environment where you find people who respect knowledge and share common ground with the intellectual art elite, including the highly theoretical conceptualist circle. Such business people find the same value system in this art that they themselves espouse – one of individualism as opposed to Soviet communitarianism. What allows the former unofficial artists and today's agents of the neo-capitalist economy to understand each other is an ideology that derives from the liberal pro-Western, anti-communist spirit that was characteristic of the Soviet intelligentsia as early as the 1970s. The apolitical aspect of Moscow Conceptualism, its escapism, and its pointedly private character, in contrast to the repressive monolithic culture of the time, retain their charm and relevance (and even acquire new relevance) in the contemporary political environment. The self-referentiality of these projects was a guarantee of their political independence, which is now underwritten by private foundations to which the state delegates its international representation in the sphere of contemporary art.

As a result, for the first time in its history, the Russian pavilion in Venice began to show the "patriarchs" of the country's contemporary art, putting special emphasis on the historical nature and museological quality of the exhibitions. We can take this as an indication that Russian capitalism has now finished with both the period of initial accumulation in the 1990s and the commodity-wealth exhibitionism of the 2000s and has entered a "normal", "civilized" capitalism, one that does not need to advertise itself – that it has integrated itself in the world system of the division of labour (which means, incidentally, that foreigners, by virtue of their intellectual superiority, must serve as curators) and legitimized itself through a con-

---

12   See the project's web site, http://www.conceptualism-moscow.org/page?id=404&lang=en (accessed May 17, 2016).

vertible historical tradition – which is how the tradition acquires its meaning: retroactively. Moscow Conceptualism thus appears as the historical and like-minded predecessor of a properly organized market economy in Russia. And this, in turn, creates a completely new balance of forces and ideologies, by reference to which young artists will define their positions.

Translated from Russian by Ben Hooson.

Karel Císař

Modernology

Art after Postmodern Art

The Prague-based philosopher, curator, and art theorist Karel Císař studies attempts to re-evaluate and revitalize the project of modernity and modernism in contemporary art. Beginning with Foucault's and Deleuze's understanding of modernity as an approach to the present that can be adopted in any period whatsoever, Císař's essay examines contemporary artworks and exhibitions – including his own exhibition *Memories of the Future* – that demonstrate the relevance of modernity and modernism for our own time, not as historical developments but as the unfulfilled possibility of our relationship to the present.

First published in Czech and English in *Between the First and Second Modernity 1985-2012*, ed. Jiří Ševčík and Edith Jeřábková, exh. cat., National Gallery and Academic Research Centre of the Academy of Fine Arts in Prague, Prague, 2012, pp. 49-65. The version published here has been revised and abridged.

If we want to understand the changes that took place in contemporary art at the turn of the 20th and 21st centuries, we must first examine the transformation in the concept of the "contemporary". If during the 1990s, the typical concept of contemporaneity was the pure presence of a post-historical stage of history, in which everything was permitted, the beginning of the new millennium ushered in a contemporaneity as heterochrony, a situation in which, at first glance, everything seems possible, whereas in fact almost nothing is. Instead of the neo-liberal dream of the ultimate generalization of economic laws to encompass all human activity, a sobering up took place on first the political and later the economic level, which revived an interest in the project of modernity. According to ideas propounded by Michel Foucault and Gilles Deleuze in their later works, modernity should not be interpreted as a historical epoch between a kind of archaic premodernism and an uncertain postmodernism, but as an approach to the present which can be adopted in any period whatsoever. According to Foucault's analyses, modernity presupposes the discontinuity of time, in which the present always necessarily differs from tradition. However, modernity is not passively reconciled to this discontinuity but, on the contrary, attempts to capture its "heroic moment" within every present.[1]

According to the first version of Foucault's text "What Is Enlightenment?", which appeared in English in 1984, the modern individual adopts this stance not only in respect to the period in which they live, but also in respect to themselves. Above all they become the subject of investigation, discovery, and future change, for which purpose art is one of the possible spheres of experimentation.[2] In the second version of the text, published in French in May of the same year, Foucault abandons the individual model of "care of the self" and instead emphasizes the political aspect of allegiance to what "we" are now in our present and what we could be.[3] And this is what Foucault and, after him, Deleuze call the "actual" (*actualité*):

> The actual is not what we are but, rather, what we become, what we are in the process of becoming – that is to say, the Other, our becoming-other. The present, on the contrary, is what we are and, thereby, what already we are ceasing to be. We must distinguish not only the share that belongs to the past and the one that belongs to the present

---

1   See John Rajchman, "The Contemporary: A New Idea?", in *Aesthetics and Contemporary Art*, ed. Armen Avanessian and Luke Skrebowski, Sternberg Press, New York and Berlin, 2011, pp. 125–144, which sets this "resistance to the present" within a wider tradition leading from Agamben's recently published text "What Is the Contemporary?" via the later work of Deleuze and Foucault all the way back to Nietzsche's *Untimely Meditations*.
2   Michel Foucault, "What Is Enlightenment?", in *The Foucault Reader*, ed. Paul Rabinow, Pantheon Books, New York, 1984, pp. 32–50.
3   Michel Foucault, "Qu'est-ce que les Lumières?", *Dits et écrits II: 1976–1988*, Gallimard, Paris, 2001, pp. 1498–1507; in English as "The Art of Telling the Truth", trans. Alan Sheridan, *Politics, Philosophy, Culture: Interviews and Other Writings, 1977–1984*, ed. Lawrence D. Kritzman, Routledge, New York and London, 1988, pp. 86–96.

but, more profoundly, the share that belongs to the present and that belonging to the actual. It is not that the actual is the utopian prefiguration of a future that is still part of our history. Rather, it is the now of our becoming.[4]

As well as historical time, which proceeds in accordance with the logic of "before" and "after", according to Deleuze there exists a time of "the event" or "becoming", in which different spheres of time coexist. Instead of rules of sequence, in this "stratigraphic time" the laws of layering apply, which see events and phenomena emerge as the actual, which from the point of view of history we regarded as long past. The present thus appears more as the contemporary: as the joint occurrence of heterochronic spheres of time in which it is always necessary once again to highlight what is genuinely actual in this or that present. From this perspective the relationship to modernism cannot henceforth be entered on an axis with two fields in which the antithesis of modernity is antiquity, but must be given in the form which Foucault, in the second version of the text "What is the Enlightenment?", calls "the 'sagital' relation to our own present": "What is my present? What is the meaning of this present? And what am I doing when I speak of this present? This, it seems to me, is what this new questioning on modernity means."[5] From this Foucault deduces that more important than revolution, which is still burdened by the linear time of history, is "the enthusiasm for the Revolution": "Revolution will always run the risk of falling back into the old rut, but as an event whose very content is unimportant, existence attests to a permanent potentiality that cannot be forgotten: for future history it is the guarantee of the very continuity of progress."[6]

This discussion forms the framework for artistic tendencies most clearly articulated in the 2007 *documenta 12* exhibition, curated by Roger Buergel and Ruth Noack, which as one of its three main leitmotifs (making direct reference to the texts quoted from Foucault) chose the question of whether modernity is our antiquity. As is clear from the more extensive text on the theme by Roger Buergel with the symptomatic title "Source", the starting point for the exhibition's concept was the work of Arnold Bode, who founded *documenta* in 1955, and Catherine David, who curated the *documenta 10* exhibition in 1997.[7] According to Bode, the purpose of *documenta* was to answer the questions: "Where does art stand today? Where do we stand today?" Catherine David, aided by a genealogy of contemporary art rather than the factual state of contemporary art, entitled her exhibition *Retroperspectives*. In addition, David set aside

---

4   Gilles Deleuze and Félix Guattari, *What Is Philosophy?*, trans. Hugh Tomlinson and Graham Burchell, Columbia University Press, New York, 1994, p. 112.
5   Foucault, "The Art of Telling the Truth", p. 89.
6   Ibid., p. 94.
7   Roger Buergel, "Source", *Documenta Magazine: Modernity?*, no. 1, 2007, pp. 13–27.

a key place in her exhibition for artists whose work was brought to a sudden end by premature death, such as Marcel Broodthaers, Öyvind Fahlström, Gordon Matta-Clark, and Hélio Oiticica. Ten years later, Buergel continued in a similar vein, this time selecting female artists who had abandoned their artistic path prematurely, Lee Lozano and Charlotte Posenenske.

In "Source", Buergel interprets Bode's intention of locating an exhibition of contemporary art in the ruins of the bombed Fridericianum Museum as an attempt to revive civil society amidst the ruins of the enlightenment project. According to Buergel, the exhibition as a medium represents the discontinuity of the history of modernity by means of it "being staged". This permits viewers to feel (not just metaphorically but also physically) the experience of pure contingency, which opens hitherto unknown forms of ethical and aesthetic relationships. The fragility and nakedness of "things that we don't understand" – i.e. the works of art – corresponds precisely to the fragility of the bare lives of those who visit the exhibition. The fact that, due to the condition of the building and construction site, most of the works were not hung on walls but instead located in open spaces, meant that they occupied the viewers' surroundings and forced the viewers to share the space with them. Once on the premises of the exhibition, observers thus had no option but "surrendering" their own identities and subjecting themselves to the gaze of others. The works of art, in contrast, were deprived of their supposed autonomy and presented simply as items among other items. Buergel believed that a new configuration of the conditions for shared reciprocity could be created in this experimental space where the boundaries between the observer and the observed, between the subject and the objective, were destabilized.

With his concept for the 2007 *documenta* exhibition, Buergel attempted to revive this aspect of the opening year of 1955. The question of modernity within the medium of an exhibition assumed a semblance that Buergel called the "migration of forms". He was convinced that globalization as a traceable movement between countries, places, and artistic means of expression goes back much further than many think. Buergel wanted to achieve, through a deliberately anachronistic and highly speculative combination of apparently different artistic positions, immediate contact with the works of art, a contact unmediated by the history of art or any one-dimensional politics. Like Bode and David before him, he expanded the concept of what is usually considered contemporary art by including in the exhibition examples of Persian rugs or Indian aquarelles from the end of the 18th century, as well as the work of non-canonized artists, such as lesser-known neo-avant-garde artists from the former Eastern bloc.

In certain cases, this type of "migration of forms" became the structure of an individual work of art, such as in the installation *Modernology (Triangular Atelier)* by the Austrian artist Florian Pumhösl, with whom Buergel had already collaborated on his previous project *How do we want to be governed* at the Barcelona Museum of Contemporary Art (MACBA) in 2004. The title of Pumhösl's installation was inspired by the research project "Kogengaku" ("Modernology"), the 1920s work of the Japanese architect and anthropologist Kon Wajiro in which he applied archaeological methods previously used exclusively on ancient monuments to popular culture and the lifestyle of the present.[8] In his work (fig. 1), Pumhösl displays the complex internal dependencies between the *Triangular Atelier* (1926) by Japanese avant-garde artist Murayama Tomoyoshi, the black panelling used in the exhibition *Der Sturm* (1914) in Tokyo, and the unique technology of glass painting developed by Walter Dexel in Germany in the 1920s. The resulting installation was composed of black panels (arranged in a triangular space) upon which were affixed paintings on glass, formally reduced to geometric abstraction, and "reliefs" (as the artist terms them) – wall vitrines containing archival material, mostly samples of graphic design and Japanese textile art from the mid-20th century. Pumhösl claimed that with this work he wanted to make a break with the previous interest in the manifestations of Western modernity under the different sociocultural conditions of the Far East or Central Africa and return to an elementary examination of the grammar of modern art. He thus turned his back not only on the postmodern ideas regarding unified global art that emerged during the 1990s, but also on the purely documentary-oriented artistic practice that sees critical potential in the act of reference itself.[9]

Pumhösl's conception represents a liminal form of a broader artistic current that flows through exhibitions such as *Formalism: Modern Art, Today* (curated by Yilmaz Dziewior, Hamburger Kunstverein, 2004), the above-mentioned *documenta 12*, and *Modernologies* (curated by Sabine Breitwieser, MACBA, Barcelona, 2009), among others. *Modernologies*, which was named in reference to Pumhösl's work, explicitly thematized the efforts of artists of the younger and middle generations to find a new evaluation and actualization of the project of modernity as a possible site of resistance against the growing influence of neo-conservative tendencies in economics, politics, and culture. These artists' enquiries do not take the form of a nostalgic return to a world condition that never really existed but, to the contrary, represent modernity as a completely actual project. This coincides precisely with the understanding of the term "modernity" as formulated by Michel Foucault and Gilles Deleuze. Therefore, formal reduction as conceived by these artists does not mean a return to a politically indifferent post-war abstract painting; likewise, the search for the boundaries of a selected medium is not intended to lead to the

---

8   Tom Gill, "Kon Wajiro, Modernologist", *Japan Quarterly*, vol. 43, no. 2, 1996, p. 199. The term Kogengaku (meaning modernology, or in its Esperanto equivalent, to which Wajiro gave priority, *modernologio*) was created by replacing the syllable "ko" (old) in the word Kokogaku (archaeology) with the syllable "gen" (contemporary).

9   See Sabeth Buchmann, "Abstract Characters? Reference and Formalism in the Works of Florian Pumhösl", in *Florian Pumhösl*, ed. Christopher Müller and Silvia Sgualdini, Buchhandlung Walther König, Cologne and London, 2007, pp. 113–122.

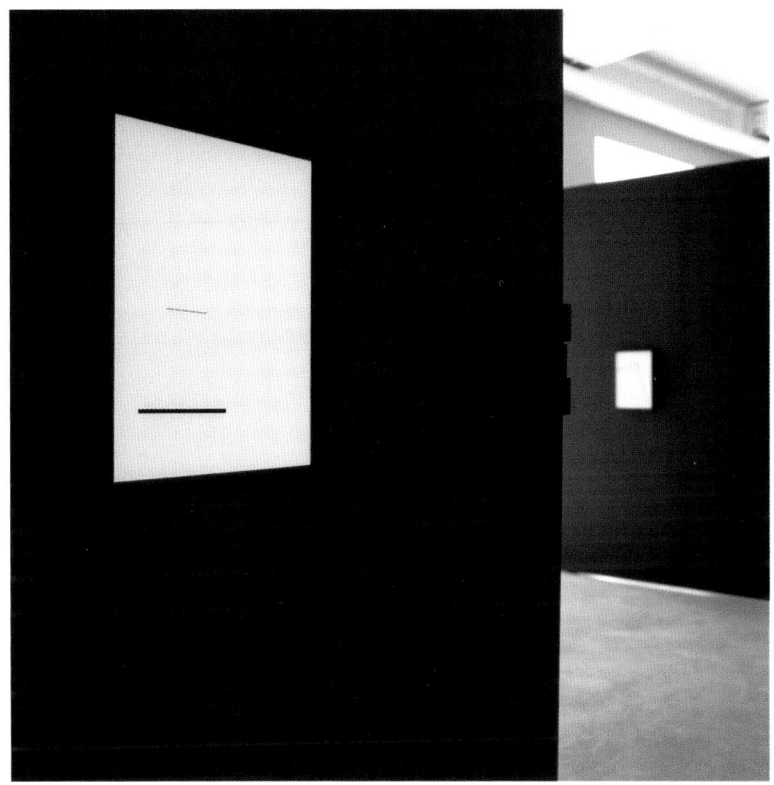

fig. 1

Florian Pumhösl, *Modernology* (*Triangular Atelier*), installation view from *documenta 12*, 2007, Kassel.

Photo by Hannes Böck.

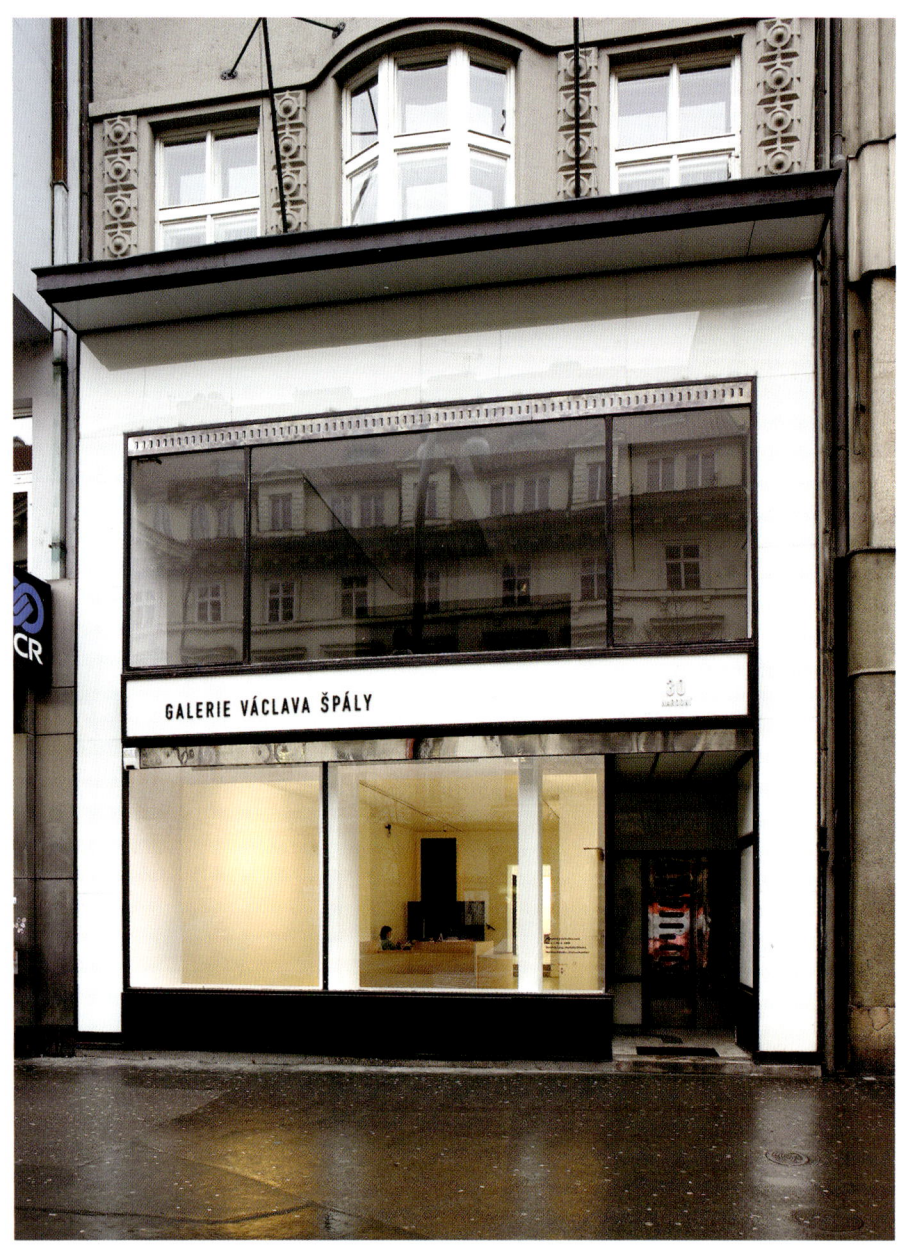

fig. 2

Florian Pumhösl, *Untitled*, 2009, Václav Špála Gallery, Prague.

Photo by Martin Polák.

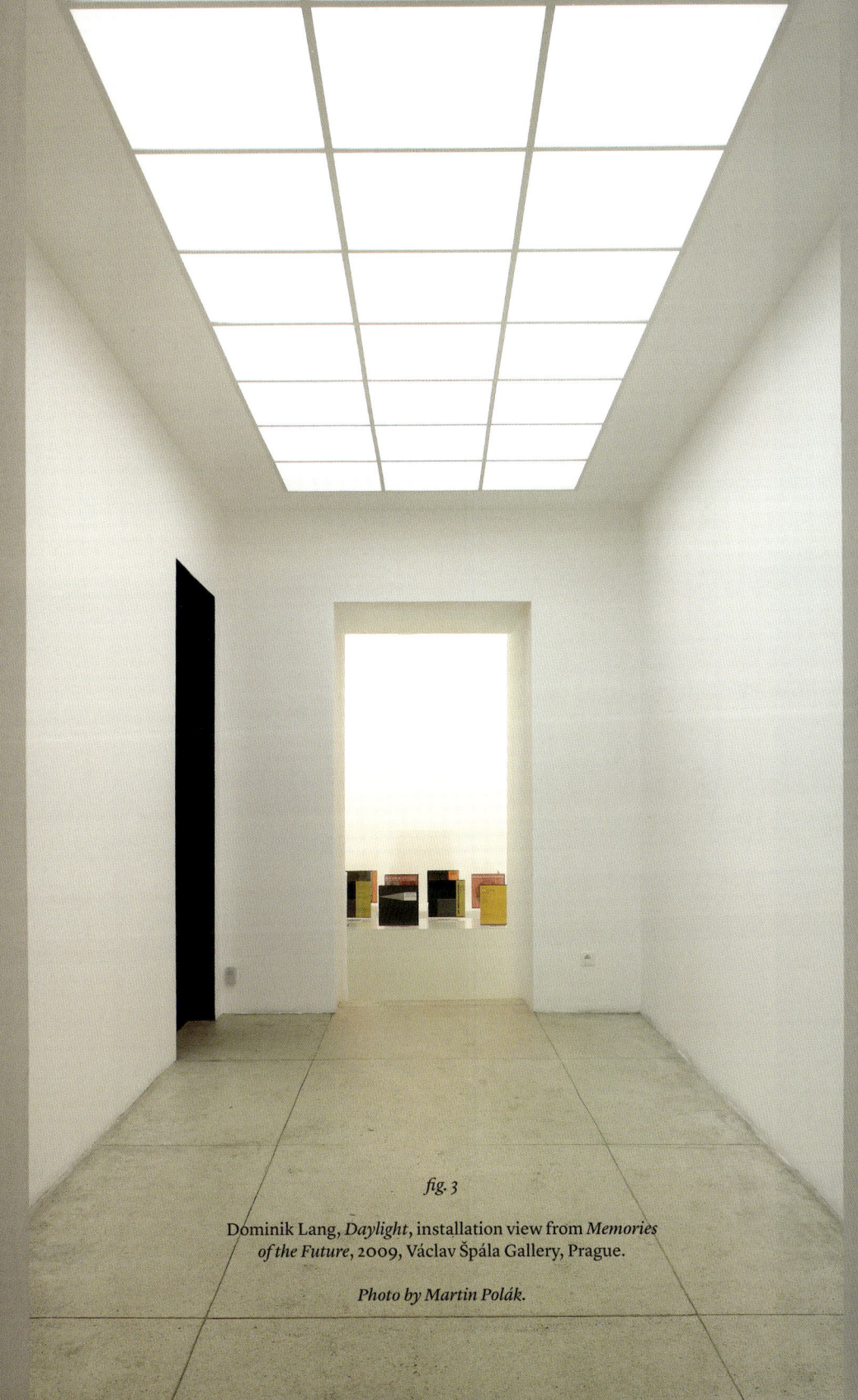

fig. 3

Dominik Lang, *Daylight*, installation view from *Memories of the Future*, 2009, Václav Špála Gallery, Prague.

Photo by Martin Polák.

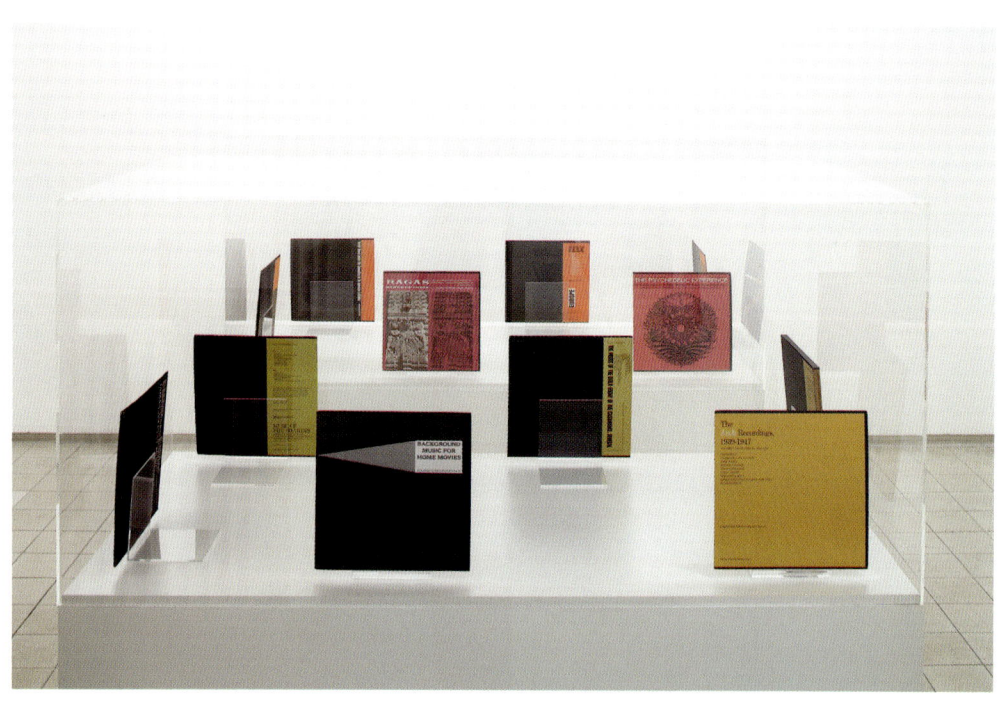

fig. 4

Mathias Poledna, *Untitled*, 2006, installation view from
Memories of the Future, 2009, Václav Špála Gallery, Prague.

Photo by Martin Polák.

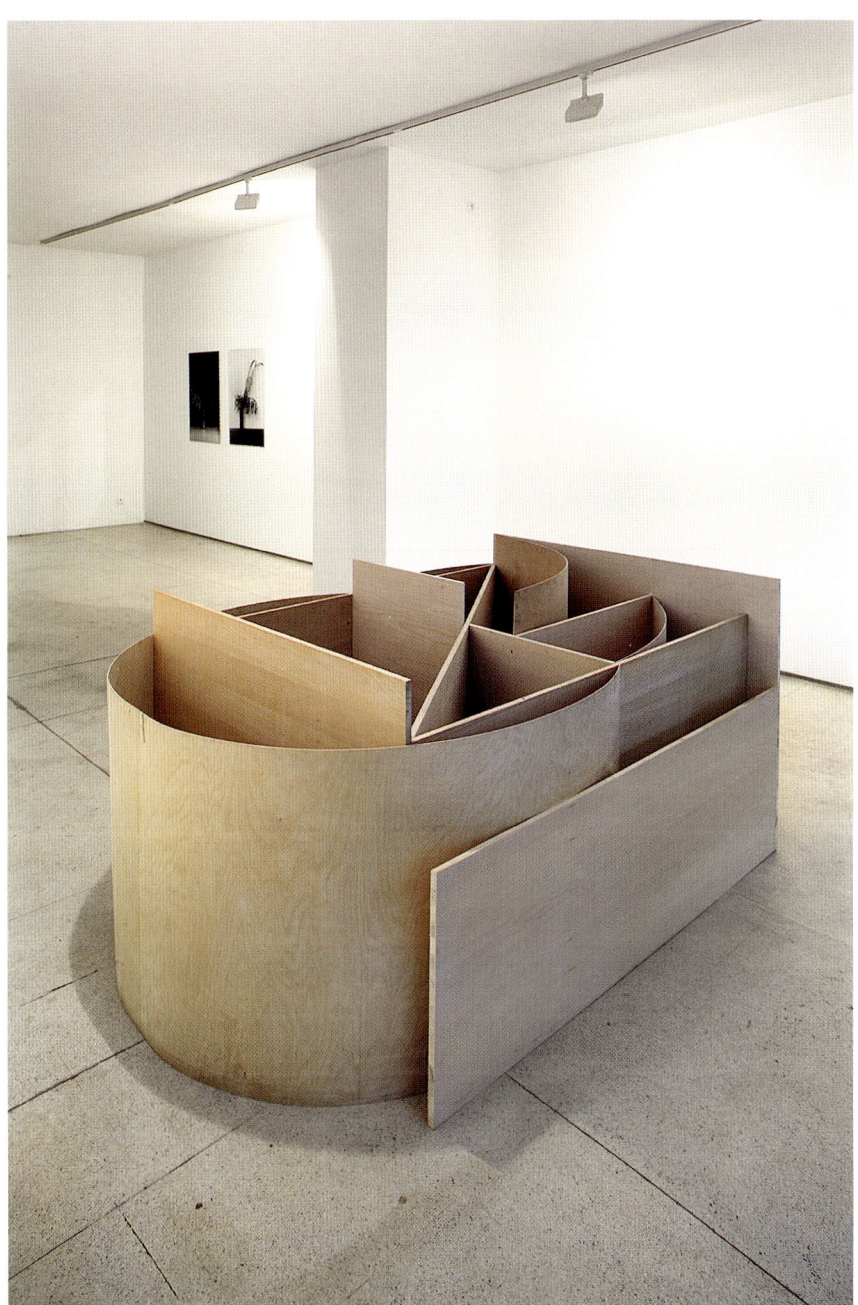

fig. 5

Dominik Lang, *Stanislav Kolíbal: Construction II*, 2005, installation view from *Memories of the Future*, 2009, Václav Špála Gallery.

Photo by Martin Polák.

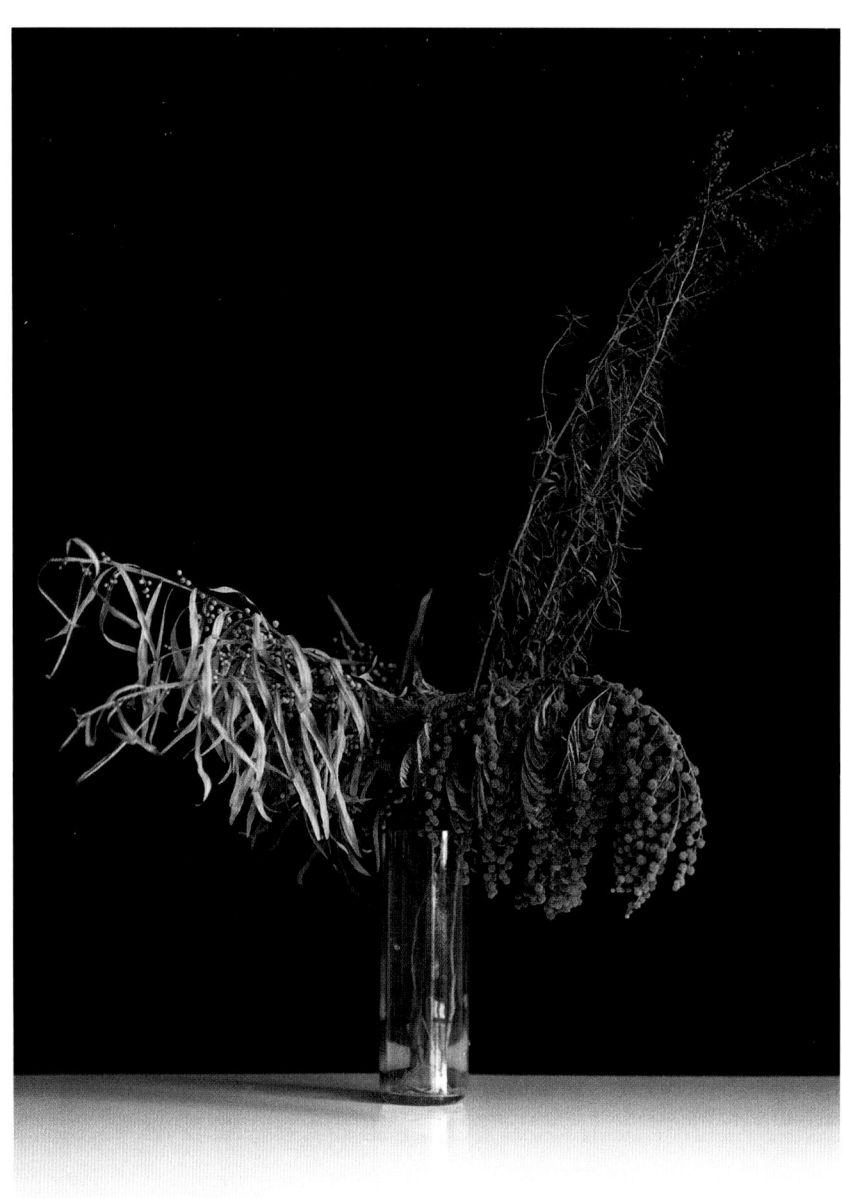

fig. 6

Markéta Othová, *Untitled*, 2008, 2 gelatin silver prints.

Courtesy of the artist.

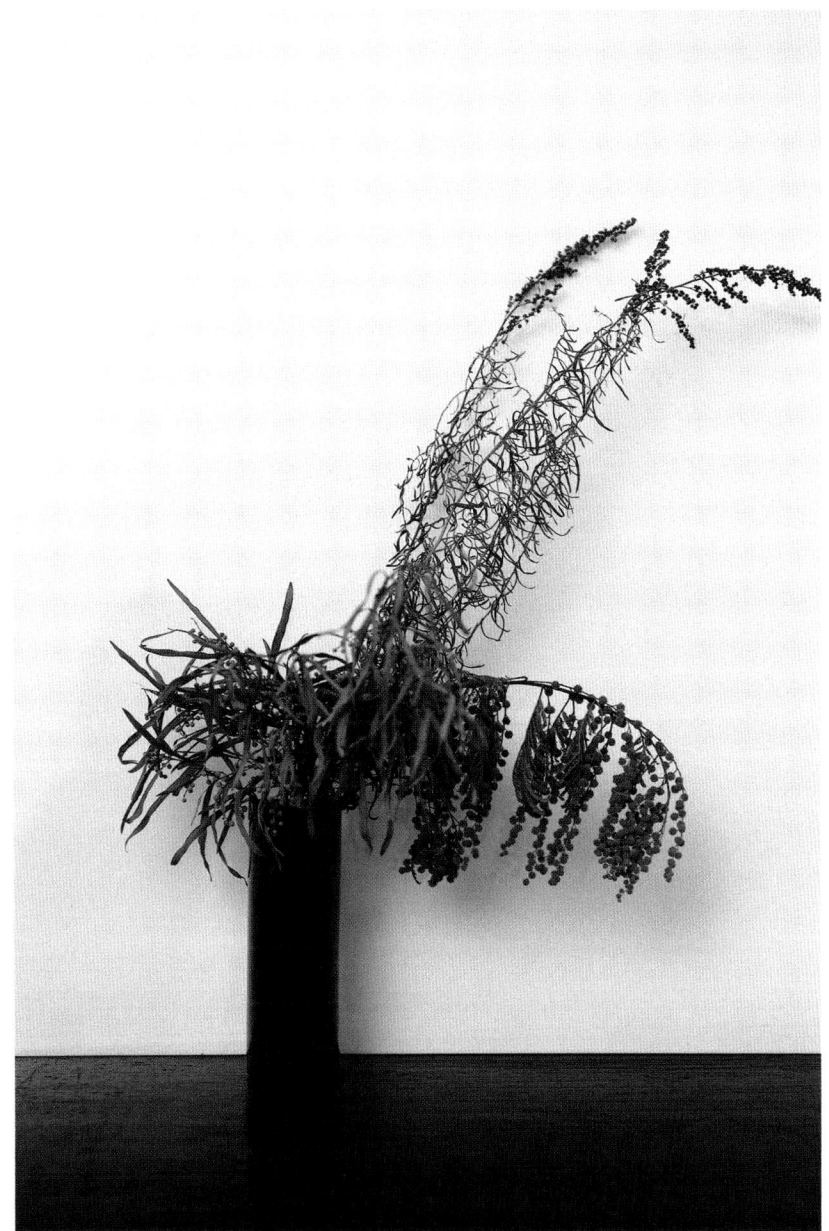

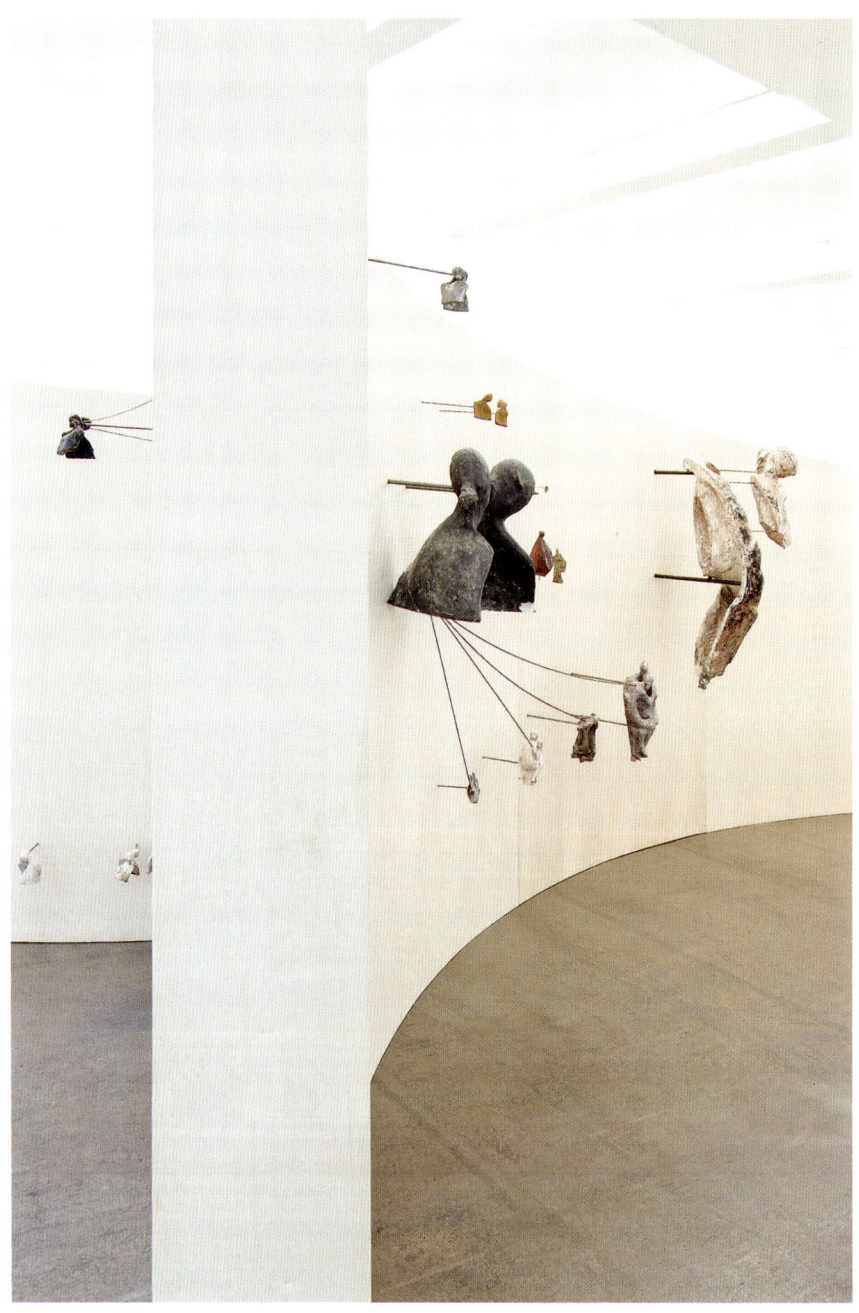

fig. 7

Dominik Lang, *The Lovers*, 2012,
installation view, Galerie Krobath, Vienna.

Photo by Lisa Rastl.

crystallization of its purity. Rather, the "monochrome" of the exhibited works refers to the pulsing movements between states of complete excess and evacuation corresponding to the sudden changes of the current post-Fordist economy, and the thematization of the affinity between film and painting refers to the essentially hybrid character of each medium.[10]

The work of David Maljković and Paulina Olowska, artists from Central and Eastern Europe, enjoyed a prominent place at the *Modernologies* exhibition. These artists, with their interest in the incomplete project of modernity, combine the politically enforced loss of the dominant interpretation of history with the need to create the conditions of one's own creative output. For this reason, they often combine the role of artist with that of exhibition architect or curator in their activities. In this respect, the choice of historical period with which these artists work is of special significance. The 1930s and 1960s, two waves of modernization in Central and Eastern Europe, predominate. Just as the processes of modernization during these periods were of a marginal character (compared to the West), so too the figures on whom these artists focus their attention often occupy a marginal status with respect to the main artistic trends of the time. This was the case with the art deco painter Zofie Stryjeńska, whom Paulina Olowska made the subject of her work, while the Croatian sculptor Vojin Bakić performed the same role for David Maljković.

The exhibition *Memories of the Future*, which I curated for the Václav Špála Gallery in Prague at the beginning of 2009, included two participants from the *Modernologies* exhibition, the Austrian artists Florian Pumhösl and Mathias Poledna, as well as Markéta Othová and Dominik Lang, Czech artists of the middle and younger generations. The exhibition attempted to introduce into the Czech cultural environment debates on the actuality of modernity in contemporary art. The exhibition was inspired by the specific institutional and spatial conditions of the Václav Špála gallery. The glass façade of the functionalist building evokes the modern utopia of physical and metaphorical transparency characteristic of the 1920s and 1930s. On an institutional level, the gallery represents a place of renewed interest in avant-garde artistic trends, which culminated in Prague during the 1960s not only with exhibitions by the Japanese group Gutai (1967) and Marcel Duchamp (1969), but above all with the emergence of the important contemporary Czech neo-avant-garde artists of that time. *Memories of the Future* thus strategically made reference to the physical and institutional features of the gallery both through interventions in

---

10   See Sabine Breitwieser, "Modernologies: Or What Makes Contemporary Artists Investigate Modernity and Modernism", in *Modernologies: Contemporary Artists Researching Modernity and Modernism*, MACBA, Barcelona, 2009, pp. 11–23.

the gallery's architecture and by virtue of the fact that most of the works exhibited made reference to the avant-garde and neo-avant-garde periods.[11]

These elements were also present in concentrated form in the work *Untitled* (2009) by Florian Pumhösl. After detailed archival research, Pumhösl decided to design a new visual identity for the gallery, which would correspond to its constructivist architecture. Given the fact that the space was not originally the site of the gallery, but of the Vilímek bookstore, Pumhösl's design represented the reconstruction of something that had never existed. The gallery's Czech name and address, "Galerie Václava Špály" and "30 Národní", made with black and grey metal letters respectively, was mounted on a milky white glass surface on the gallery's façade, which corresponded to Pumhösl's practice of reductive drawings (fig. 2). In terms of its functional design, the inscription was completely unobtrusive because it matched the character of the architecture better than the logo that the gallery used at that time. (I should note that this radical gesture of denial of the existing gallery's visual identity recalled the institutional critiques of the 1970s.) Like other works in the exhibition, Pumhösl's installation drew attention to the general problem of the "distribution of the visible", as Jacques Rancière, who was influenced by Foucault, calls it: namely, the internal dependency between what can be perceived within a given regime and its own power organization.[12]

Works by Dominik Lang entitled *Daylight* and *Large Glass* (both 2009) occupied a similar role in the exhibition. The first (fig. 3) comprised an artificial skylight that created the impression of the diffuse daylight common to traditional museums; the second installation involved the walling-off of two identical rooms by a sheet of transparent glass, which both opened up the isolated spaces to the viewer's gaze and prevented physical access to them. In both cases, Lang highlighted the organizing power of apparently neutral enhancements of visibility, which, in addition to the fact that they allow one to see, can also be a method of closing off and separating. The installation *Untitled* (2006) by Mathias Poledna (fig. 4), comprising two hermetically sealed vitrines containing LP album sleeves from the American recording company Folkways Records & Service Co., functioned in a similar way. Between 1948 and 1986, Folkways released more than two thousand titles of authentic recordings of ethnic music and other sounds, everything from Jamaican cult music and the voices of satellites to recordings of the testimony given by Bertolt Brecht before the House Un-American Activities Committee. Not only did the selection of LPs thematize the social and political conditions of cultural production during

---

11   Pumhösl's interest in the tradition of "marginal modernities" was also manifested in his exhibition *678* at the Museum Moderner Kunst (MUMOK), in Vienna in 2011, in which he included works by Czech avant-garde artists such as Karel Teige and Ladislav Sutnar, among others. See *Florian Pumhösl: 678*, ed. Matthias Michalka, Buchhandlung Walther König, Cologne, 2011.

12   Jacques Rancière, *Le partage du sensible: Esthétique et politique*, La Fabrique, Paris, 2000 (especially pp. 12–25).

the Cold War, but the installation of the vitrines itself (which the viewer could hardly move around in order to see the archival content) reflected manipulative tendencies similar to those emphasized by Dominik Lang in his architectural interventions in the gallery's space.[13]

In the exhibition *Memories of the Future*, Lang's sculptural object *Stanislav Kolíbal: Construction II* (2005) and the photographs by Markéta Othová *Untitled* (2008) and *Untitled* (2009) referred to a specific cultural memory of place. By using book reproductions to reconstruct the work of Kolíbal, an important representative of Czech neo-constructivist art, whose work was shown in the Špála Gallery for the first time in 1966 and for the last time in 1999, Lang made visible the difference between the original and a copy, highlighting the temporally and spatially absent quality of Kolíbal's work, which Lang had never seen (fig. 5). In the diptych *Untitled* (2008), Markéta Othová developed her interest in exhibiting a photographic image with references to modernist photographic experiments more than she ever had before. Under studio conditions, she photographed identical floral still lifes against a dark and light background in order to create the erroneous impression of positive and negative (fig. 6). By exploring the photography medium's specificity, the artist's intention was not to cast doubt on the indexical character of this means of expression but, on the contrary, to show with what fidelity photography is able to capture the instability of the visual world.

Pumhösl again addressed systems of visibility with his installation on the upper floor of the Špála Gallery. Called *Untitled* (2009), it consisted of three simple black-and-white drawings of lines painted directly on the wall, a reference to Wassily Kandinsky, and the projection of a 16mm film, *OA 1979-3-5-036* (2007). He also made crucial use of the light from a street lamp in the immediate proximity of the gallery window. Pumhösl decided to rid the space completely of any other source of light and to amplify the entire situation by using the variable lighting conditions of the film projection and the street lamp. Together, the two works created an integrated cinematographic space that completely surrounded the viewers. They first encountered the projection of the film *OA 1979-3-5-036*, the title of which comes from the registry of the British Museum and refers to an album of wood engravings of kimono designs by Take Hiratsugi, one of the masters of late-17th-century Japanese textile art. The film presents Pumhösl's transformation of a number of these kimono patterns: floral, geographical, and military motifs are replaced by a smooth fall of light and extremely reduced geometrical motifs. The trio of black wall drawings, meanwhile, was arranged so that there was a diptych on the right-hand side of the gallery and only a solitary drawing on the left. The apparent contradiction between these two parts of the upper floor of the gallery

---

13   See Julianne Rebentisch, "Deconfigurations of Community: Mathias Poledna's *Version*", in *Mathias Poledna: Version*, ed. Christopher Müller, Galerie Daniel Buchholz, Cologne, 2010 [unpaginated].

– static drawings and moving film – was further accentuated by the positioning and references of the drawings. The constant movement of the projected image was, in the case of the drawings, replaced by their repetition and juxtaposition, which transformed the abstract diagrams into a sort of serial pattern. In addition, movement was inserted into the isolated drawing, since its shape derived from diagrams by Wassily Kandinsky, according to which every line is the result of movement in the sense of "force and direction".[14] The migration of forms here not only takes on the form of "the stratigraphic history" of abstraction between the 17th and 20th centuries, but also shifts between the hybrid media of drawing, painting, and film as well. These elements were bathed in the warm light from the streetlamp, the quality of which corresponded to the light emanating from the projector lamp. The historically autonomous art of abstraction was thus exposed to the external influences of "public space", and the gallery was revealed to be an experimental space, only a thin membrane of glass separating it from everyday experience.

The selection of the two Czech participants in the exhibition was not accidental. The work of Markéta Othová represents a portent of the later interest of Czech contemporary artists in the project of modernity. *The Sleeping City* (2011), a more recent work by Dominik Lang, embodies the culmination of this evolution. The metaphorical "movement" described by the work of Markéta Othová resembles an intuitive descent into the history of photography, the starting point being her 1990s archive. Othová compiled photographic installations from an extensive collection of her own photographs dating back to 1994, in which the significance of individual photos was determined by the syntax of the whole. At the beginning of the 21st century, she moved from these works to time series recorded by sequenced camerawork, which recalled conceptual art from the 1970s. In *Leçon de photographie* (2007) and *Mayday* (2004–2007), a series of abstract photographs, she began a self-reflection upon the employed media, and, in the movement through the history of photography, found herself on the same level as the experimental work of the photographic avantgarde at the beginning of the 20th century. Likewise, Dominik Lang started from the position of the institutional critique of the 1970s and arrived at the most explicit reflection of the Czech cultural memory in *The Sleeping City* and *The lovers* (fig. 7) – his installation for the Pavilion of the Czech and Slovak Republics at the 54th Venice Biennale in 2011 and for *curated by_vienna* in 2012 – where he became a radical interpreter of the late modernist sculptures of his father, Jiří Lang. In this way, Othová and Lang reveal very accurately the actuality of modernity, not as a historical event, but as the unfulfilled possibility of a relationship to our present, which Deleuze calls experimentation:

---

14   Wassily Kandinsky, *Point and Line to Plane*, Dover Publications, New York, 1979, pp. 57–59.

To think is to experiment, but experimentation is always that which is in the process of coming about – the new, remarkable, and interesting that replace the appearance of truth and are more demanding that it is. What is in the process of coming about is no more what ends than what begins. History is not experimentation, it is only set of almost negative conditions that make possible experimentation of something that escapes history. Without history experimentation would remain indeterminate and unconditioned, but experimentation is not historical. It is philosophical.[15]

15   Deleuze and Guattari, *What Is Philosophy?*, p. 111.

What, How & for Whom / WHW

"There is something political in the city air"*

The curatorial collective What, How & for Whom / WHW, based in Zagreb and Berlin, examine the interconnections between contemporary art and political and social strata, including the role of art institutions in contemporary society. In the present essay, their discussion of recent projects they curated highlights the struggle for access to knowledge and the free distribution of information, which in Croatia also means confronting the pressures of censorship and revisionism in the writing of history and the construction of the future.

Contemporary art's attempts to come to terms with its evasions in delivering on the promise of its own intrinsic capacity to propose alternatives, and to do better in the constant game of staying ahead of institutional closures and marketization, are related to a broader malady in leftist politics. The crisis of organizational models and modes of political action feels especially acute nowadays, after the latest waves of massive political mobilization and upheaval embodied in such movements as the Arab Spring and Occupy and the widespread social protests in Southern Europe against austerity measures – and the failure of these movements to bring about structural changes. As we witnessed in the dramatic events that unfolded through the spring and summer of 2015, even in Greece, where Syriza was brought to power, the people's will behind newly elected governments proved insufficient to change the course of austerity politics in Europe. Simultaneously, a series of conditional gains and effective defeats gave rise to the alarming ascent of radical right-wing populism, against which the left has failed to provide any real vision or driving force.

Both the practice of political articulation and the political practices of art have been affected by the hollowing and disabling of democracy related to the ascendant hegemony of the neoliberal rationale that shapes every domain of our lives in accordance with a specific image of economics,[1] as well as the problematic "embrace of localism and autonomy by much of the left as the pure strategy"[2] and the left's inability to destabilize the dominant world-view and reclaim the future.[3] Consequently, art practices increasingly venture into novel modes of operation that seek to "expand our collective imagination beyond what capitalism allows".[4] They not only point to the problems but address them head on. By negotiating art's autonomy and impact on the social, and by conceptualizing the whole edifice of art as a social symptom, such practices attempt to do more than simply squeeze novel ideas into exhausted artistic formats and endow them with political content that produces "marks of distinction",[5] which capital then exploits for the enhancement of its own reproduction.

The two projects visited in this text both work toward building truly accessible public spaces. *Public Library*, launched by Marcell Mars and Tomislav Medak in 2012, is an ongoing media and social project based on ideas from the open-source software movement, while *Autonomy Cube*, by artist Trevor Paglen and the hacker and computer security researcher Jacob Appelbaum, centres on anonymized internet usage in the post-

---

* David Harvey, *Rebel Cities: From the Right to the City to the Urban Revolution*, Verso, London and New York, 2012, p. 117.
1 See Wendy Brown, *Undoing the Demos: Neoliberalism's Stealth Revolution*, Zone books, New York, 2015.
2 Harvey, *Rebel Cities*, p. 83.
3 See Nick Srnicek and Alex Williams, *Inventing the Future: Postcapitalism and a World Without Work*, Verso, London and New York, 2015.
4 Ibid., p. 495.
5 See Harvey, *Rebel Cities*, especially pp. 103–109.

Edward Snowden world of unprecedented institutionalized surveillance. Both projects operate in tacit alliance with art institutions that more often than not are suffering from a kind of "mission drift" under pressure to align their practices and structures with the profit sector, a situation that in recent decades has gradually become the new norm.[6] By working within and with art institutions, both *Public Library* and *Autonomy Cube* induce the institutions to return to their initial mission of creating new common spaces of socialization and political action. The projects develop counterpublics and work with infrastructures, in the sense proposed by Keller Easterling: not just physical networks but shared standards and ideas that constitute points of contact and access between people and thus rule, govern, and control the spaces in which we live.[7]

By building a repository of digitized books, and enabling others to do this as well, *Public Library* promotes the idea of the library as a truly public institution that offers universal access to knowledge, which "together with free public education, a free public healthcare, the scientific method, the Universal Declaration of Human Rights, Wikipedia, and free software, among others – we, the people, are most proud of", as the authors of the project have said.[8] *Public Library* develops devices for the free sharing of books, but it also functions as a platform for advocating social solidarity in free access to knowledge. By ignoring and avoiding the restrictive legal regime for intellectual property, which was brought about by decades of neoliberalism, as well as the privatization or closure of public institutions, spatial controls, policing, and surveillance – all of which disable or restrict possibilities for building new social relations and a new commons – *Public Library* can be seen as part of the broader movement to resist neoliberal austerity politics and the commodification of knowledge and education and to appropriate public spaces and public goods for common purposes.

While *Public Library* is fully engaged with the movement to oppose the copyright regime – which developed as a kind of rent for expropriating the commons and reintroducing an artificial scarcity of cognitive goods that could be reproduced virtually for free – the project is not under the spell of digital fetishism, which until fairly recently celebrated a new digital commons as a non-frictional space of smooth collaboration where a new political and economic autonomy would be forged that would spill over and undermine the real economy and permeate all spheres of life.[9] As Matteo Pasquinelli argues in his critique of "digitalism" and its celebration of the

---

6   See Brown, *Undoing the Demos*.
7   Keller Easterling, *Extrastatecraft: The Power of Infrastructure Space*, Verso, London and New York, 2014.
8   Marcell Mars, Manar Zarroug, and Tomislav Medak, "Public Library", in *Public Library*, ed. Marcell Mars, Tomislav Medak, and What, How & for Whom / WHW, exh. publication, What, How & for Whom / WHW and Multimedia Institute, Zagreb, 2015, p. 78.
9   See Matteo Pasquinelli, *Animal Spirits: A Bestiary of the Commons*, NAi Publishers, Rotterdam, and Institute of Network Cultures, Amsterdam, 2008.

virtues of the information economy with no concern about the material basis of production, the information economy is a parasite on the material economy and therefore "an accurate understanding of the common must be always interlinked with the real physical forces producing it and the material economy surrounding it".[10]

Public Library emancipates books from the restrictive copyright regime and participates in the exchange of information enabled by digital technology, but it also acknowledges the labour and energy that make this possible. There is labour that goes into the cataloguing of the books, and labour that goes into scanning them before they can be brought into the digital realm of free reproduction, just as there are the ingenuity and labour of the engineers who developed a special scanner that makes it easier to scan books; also, the scanner needs to be installed, maintained, and fed books over hours of work. This is where the institutional space of art comes in handy by supporting the material production central to the *Public Library* endeavour. But the scanner itself does not need to be visible. In 2014, at the Museo Nacional Centro de Arte Reina Sofía in Madrid, we curated the exhibition *Really Useful Knowledge*, which dealt with conflicts triggered by struggles over access to knowledge and the effects that knowledge, as the basis of capital reproduction, has on the totality of workers' lives. In the exhibition, the production funds allocated to *Public Library* were used to build the book scanner at Calafou, an anarchist cooperative outside Barcelona. The books chosen for scanning were relevant to the exhibition's themes – methods of reciprocal learning and teaching, forms of social and political organization, the history of the Spanish Civil War, etc. – and after being scanned, they were uploaded to the *Public Library* website. All that was visible in the exhibition itself was a kind of index card or business card with a URL link to the *Public Library* website and a short statement (fig. 1):

> A public library is:
> - free access to books for every member of society
> - library catalog
> - librarian
>
> With books ready to be shared, meticulously cataloged, everyone is a librarian. When everyone is librarian, the library is everywhere.[11]

Public Library's alliance with art institutions serves to strengthen the cultural capital both for the general demand to free books from copyright restrictions on cultural goods and for the project itself – such cultural capital could be useful in a potential lawsuit. Simultaneously, the presence and realization of the *Public Library* project within an exhibition enlists the host institution as part of the movement and exerts influence on it by

---

10 Ibid., p. 29.
11 Mars, Zarroug, and Medak, "Public Library", p. 85.

taking the museum's public mission seriously and extending it into a grey zone of questionable legality. The defence of the project becomes possible by making the traditional claim of the "autonomy" of art, which is not supposed to assert any power beyond the museum walls. By taking art's autonomy at its word, and by testing the truth of the liberal-democratic claim that the field of art is a field of unlimited freedom, *Public Library* engages in a kind of "overidentification" game, or what Keller Easterling, writing about the expanded activist repertoire in infrastructure space, calls "exaggerated compliance".[12] Should the need arise, as in the case of a potential lawsuit against the project, claims of autonomy and artistic freedom create a protective shroud of untouchability. And in this game of liberating books from the parochial capitalist imagination that restricts their free circulation, the institution becomes a complicit partner. The long-acknowledged insight that institutions embrace and co-opt critique is, in this particular case, a win-win situation, as *Public Library* uses the public status of the museum as a springboard to establish the basic message of free access and the free circulation of books and knowledge as common sense, while the museum performs its mission of bringing knowledge to the public and supporting creativity, in this case the reworking, rebuilding and reuse of technology for the common good. The fact that the institution is not naive but complicit produces a synergy that enhances potentialities for influencing and permeating the public sphere. The gesture of not exhibiting the scanner in the museum has, among other things, a practical purpose, as more books would be scanned voluntarily by the members of the anarchist commune in Calafou than would be by the overworked museum staff, and employing somebody to do this during the exhibition would be too expensive (and the mantra of *cuts, cuts, cuts* would render negotiation futile). If there is a flirtatious nod to the strategic game of not exposing too much, it is directed less toward the watchful eyes of the copyright police than toward the exhibition regime of contemporary art group shows in which works compete for attention, the biggest scarcity of all. *Public Library* flatly rejects identification with the object "our beloved bookscanner" (as the scanner is described on the project website[13]), although it is an attractive object that could easily be featured as a sculpture within the exhibition. But its efficacy and use come first, as is also true of the enigmatic business card–like leaflet, which attracts people to visit the *Public Library* website and use books, not only to read them but also to add books to the library: doing this in the privacy of one's home on one's own computer is certainly more effective than doing it on a computer provided and displayed in the exhibition among the other art objects, films, installations, texts, shops, cafés, corridors, exhibition halls, elevators, signs, and crowds in a museum like Reina Sofía.

12 Easterling, *Extrastatecraft*, p. 492.
13 See https://www.memoryoftheworld.org/blog/2012/10/28/our-beloved-bookscanner-2/ (accessed July 4, 2016).

For the exhibition to include a scanner that was unlikely to be used or a computer monitor that showed the website from which books might be downloaded, but probably not read, would be the embodiment of what philosopher Robert Pfaller calls "interpassivity", the appearance of activity or a stand-in for it that in fact replaces any genuine engagement.[14] For Pfaller, interpassivity designates a flight from engagement, a misplaced libidinal investment that under the mask of enjoyment hides aversion to an activity that one is supposed to enjoy, or more precisely: "Interpassivity is the creation of a compromise between cultural interests and latent cultural aversion."[15] Pfaller's examples of participation in an enjoyable process that is actually loathed include book collecting and the frantic photocopying of articles in libraries (his book was originally published in 2002, when photocopying had not yet been completely replaced by downloading, bookmarking, etc.).[16] But he also discusses contemporary art exhibitions as sites of interpassivity, with their overabundance of objects and time-based works that require time that nobody has, and with the figure of the curator on whom enjoyment is displaced – the latter, he says, is a good example of "delegated enjoyment". By not providing the exhibition with a computer from which books can be downloaded, the project ensures that books are seen as vehicles of knowledge acquired by reading and not as immaterial capital to be frantically exchanged; the undeniable pleasure of downloading and hoarding books is, after all, just one step removed from the playground of interpassivity that the exhibition site (also) is.

But *Public Library* is hardly making a moralistic statement about the virtues of reading, nor does it believe that ignorance (such as could be overcome by reading the library's books) is the only obstacle that stands in the way of ultimate emancipation. Rather, the project engages with, and contributes to, the social practice that David Harvey calls "commoning": "an unstable and malleable social relation between a particular self-defined social group and those aspects of its actually existing or yet-to-be-created social and/or physical environment deemed crucial to its life and livelihood".[17] *Public Library* works on the basis of commoning and tries to enlist others to join it, which adds a distinctly political dimension to the sabotage of intellectual property revenues and capital accumulation.

14 Robert Pfaller, *On the Pleasure Principle in Culture: Illusions Without Owners*, Verso, London and New York, 2014.
15 Ibid., p. 76.
16 Pfaller's book, which first appeared in German, was published in English only in 2014. His ideas have gained greater relevance over time, not only as the shortcomings of the immensely popular social media activism became apparent – where, as many critics have noted, participation in political organizing and the articulation of political tasks and agendas are often replaced by a click on an icon – but also because of Pfaller's broader argument about the self-deception at play in interpassivity and its role in eliciting enjoyment from austerity measures and other calamities imposed on the welfare state by the neoliberal regime, which since early 2000 has exceeded even the most sober (and pessimistic) expectations.
17 Ibid., p. 73.

The political dimension of *Public Library* and the effort to form and publicize the movement were expressed more explicitly in the *Public Library* exhibition in 2015 at Gallery Nova in Zagreb, where we have been directing the programme since 2003. If the *Public Library* project was not such an eminently collective practice that pays no heed to the author function, the Gallery Nova show might be considered something like a solo exhibition. As it was realized, the project again used art as an infrastructure and resource to promote the movement of freeing books from copyright restrictions while collecting legitimization points from the art world as enhanced cultural capital that could serve as armour against future attacks by the defenders of the holy scripture of copyright laws. But here the more important tactic was to show the movement as an army of many and to strengthen it through self-presentation. The exhibition presented *Public Library* as a collection of collections, and the repertory form (used in archive science to describe a collection) was taken as the basic narrative procedure. It mobilized and activated several archives and open digital repositories, such as *MayDay Rooms* from London, *The Ignorant Schoolmaster and His Committees* from Belgrade, *Library Genesis* and *Aaaaaarg.org*, *Catalogue of Free Books*, *(Digitized) Praxis*, the digitized work of the Midnight Notes Collective, and *Textz.com*, with special emphasis on activating the digital repositories *UbuWeb* and *Monoskop*. Not only did the exhibition attempt to enlist the gallery audience but, equally important, the project was testing its own strength in building, articulating, announcing, and proposing, or speculating on, a broader movement to oppose the copyright of cultural goods within and adjacent to the art field.

Presenting such a movement in an art institution changes one of the basic tenets of art, and for an art institution the project's main allure probably lies in this kind of expansion of the art field. A shared politics is welcome, but nothing makes an art institution so happy as the sense of purpose that a project like *Public Library* can endow it with. (This, of course, comes with its own irony, for while art institutions nowadays compete for projects that show emphatically how obsolete the aesthetic regime of art is, they continue to base their claims of social influence on knowledge gained through some form of aesthetic appreciation, however they go about explaining and justifying it.) At the same time, *Public Library*'s nonchalance about institutional maladies and anxieties provides a homeopathic medicine whose effect is sometimes so strong that discussion about placebos becomes, at least temporarily, beside the point. One occasion when *Public Library*'s roving of the political terrain became blatantly direct was the exhibition *Written-off: On the Occasion of the 20th Anniversary of Operation Storm*, which we organized in the summer of 2015 at Gallery Nova (figs. 2–4).

The exhibition/action *Written-off* was based on data from Ante Lešaja's extensive research on "library purification", which he published in his book *Knjigocid: Uništavanje knjige u Hrvatskoj 1990-ih* (*Libricide: The*

Destruction of Books in Croatia in the 1990s).[18] People were invited to bring in copies of books that had been removed from Croatian public libraries in the 1990s. The books were scanned and deposited in a digital archive; they then became available on a website established especially for the project. In Croatia during the 1990s, hundreds of thousands of books were removed from schools and factories, from public, specialized, and private libraries, from former Yugoslav People's Army centres, socio-political organizations, and elsewhere because of their ideologically inappropriate content, the alphabet they used (Serbian Cyrillic), or the ethnic or political background of the authors. The books were mostly thrown into rubbish bins, discarded on the street, destroyed, or recycled. What Lešaja's research clearly shows is that the destruction of the books – as well as the destruction of monuments to the People's Liberation War (World War II) – was not the result of individuals running amok, as official accounts preach, but a deliberate and systematic action that symbolically summarizes the dominant politics of the 1990s, in which war, rampant nationalism, and phrases about democracy and sovereignty were used as a rhetorical cloak to cover the nakedness of the capitalist counter-revolution and criminal processes of dispossession.

Written-off: On the Occasion of the 20th Anniversary of Operation Storm set up scanners in the gallery, initiated a call for collecting and scanning books that had been expunged from public institutions in the 1990s, and outlined the criteria for the collection, which corresponded to the basic domains in which the destruction of the books, as a form of censorship, was originally implemented: books written in the Cyrillic alphabet or in Serbian regardless of the alphabet; books forming a corpus of knowledge about communism, especially Yugoslav communism, Yugoslav socialism, and the history of the workers' struggle; and books presenting the anti-Fascist and revolutionary character of the People's Liberation Struggle during World War II.

The exhibition/action was called *Written-off* because the removal and destruction of the books were often presented as a legitimate procedure of library maintenance, thus masking the fact that these books were unwanted, ideologically unacceptable, dangerous, harmful, unnecessary, etc. *Written-off* unequivocally placed "book destruction" in the social context of the period, when the destruction of "unwanted" monuments and books was happening alongside the destruction of homes and the killing of "unwanted" citizens, outside of and prior to war operations. For this reason, the exhibition was dedicated to the twentieth anniversary of Operation Storm, the final military/police operation in what is called, locally, the Croatian Homeland War.[19]

18   Ante Lešaja, *Knjigocid: Uništavanje knjige u Hrvatskoj 1990-ih*, Profil and Srbsko narodno vijeće, Zagreb, 2012.
19   Known internationally as the Croatian War of Independence, the war was fought between Croatian forces and the Serb-controlled Yugoslav People's Army from 1991 to 1995.

The exhibition was intended as a concrete intervention against a political logic that resulted in mass exile and killing, the history of which is glossed over and critical discussion silenced, and also against the official celebrations of the anniversary, which glorified militarism and proclaimed the ethical purity of the victory (resulting in the desired *ethnic* purity of the nation).

As both symbolic intervention and real-life action, then, the exhibition *Written-off* took place against a background of suppressed issues relating to Operation Storm – ethno-nationalism as the flip side of neoliberalism, justice and the present status of the victims and refugees, and the overall character of the war known officially as the Homeland War, in which discussions about its prominent traits as a civil war are actively silenced and increasingly prosecuted. In protest against the official celebrations and military parades, the exhibition marked the anniversary of Operation Storm with a collective action that evokes books as symbolic of a "knowledge society" in which knowledge becomes the location of conflictual engagement. It pointed toward the struggle over collective symbolic capital and collective memory, in which culture as a form of the commons has a direct bearing on the kind of place we live in. The *Public Library* project, however, is engaged not so much with cultural memory and remembrance as a form of recollection or testimony that might lend political legitimation to artistic gestures; rather, it engages with history as a construction and speculative proposition about the future, as Peter Osborne argues in his polemical hypotheses on the notion of contemporary art that distinguishes between "contemporary" and "present-day" art: "History is not just a relationship between the present and the past – it is equally about the future. It is this speculative futural moment that definitively separates the concept of history from memory."[20] For *Public Library*, the future that participates in the construction of history does not yet exist, but it is defined as more than just a project against the present as reflected in the exclusionary, parochially nationalistic, revisionist and increasingly fascist discursive practices of the Croatian political elites. Rather, the future comes into being as an active and collective construction based on the emancipatory aspects of historical experiences as future possibilities.

Although defined as an action, the project is not exultantly enthusiastic about collectivity or the immediacy and affective affinities of its participants, but rather it transcends its local and transient character by taking up the broader counter-hegemonic struggle for the mutual management of joint resources. Its endeavour is not limited to the realm of the political and ideological but is rooted in the repurposing of technological potentials from the restrictive capitalist game and the reutilization of the existing infrastructure to build a qualitatively different one. While the culture industry adapts itself to the limited success of measures that are geared toward

---

20   Peter Osborne, *Anywhere or Not at All: Philosophy of Contemporary Art*, Verso, London and New York, 2013, p. 194.

fig. 1

Marcell Mars, *Art as Infrastructure: Public Library*, installation view, *Really Useful Knowledge*, curated by WHW, Museo Nacional Centro de Arte Reina Sofía, Madrid, 2014.

Photo by Joaquín Cortés and Román Lores / MNCARS.

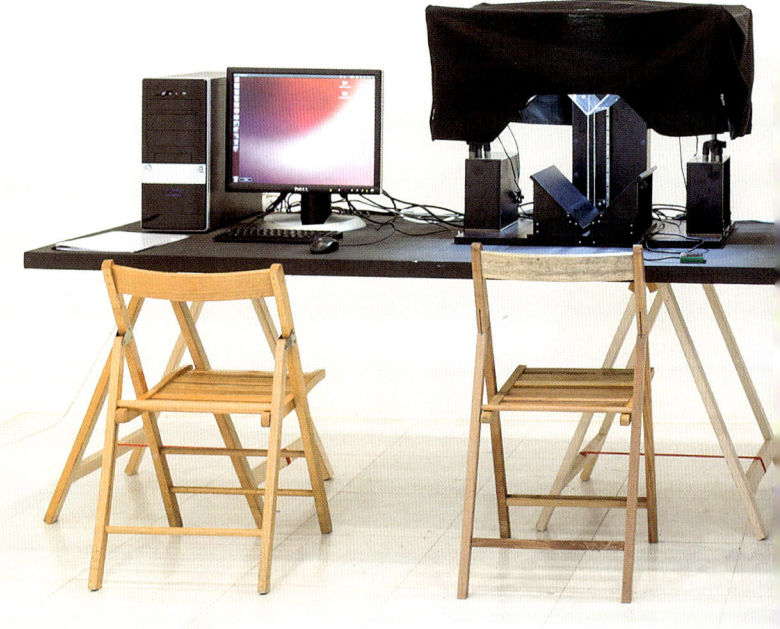

fig. 2

Public Library, exhibition view, Gallery Nova, Zagreb, 2015.

Photo by Ivan Kuharić.

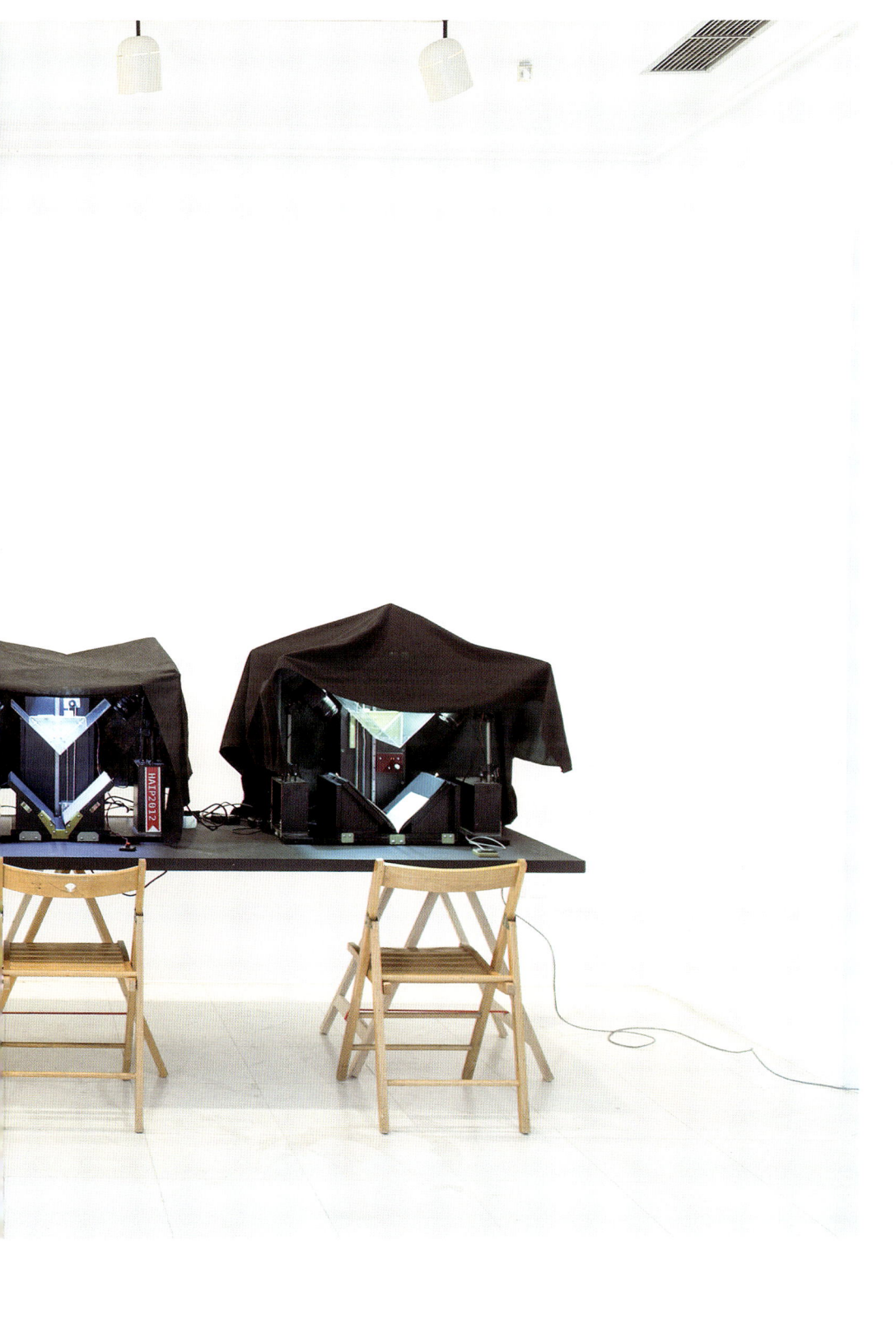

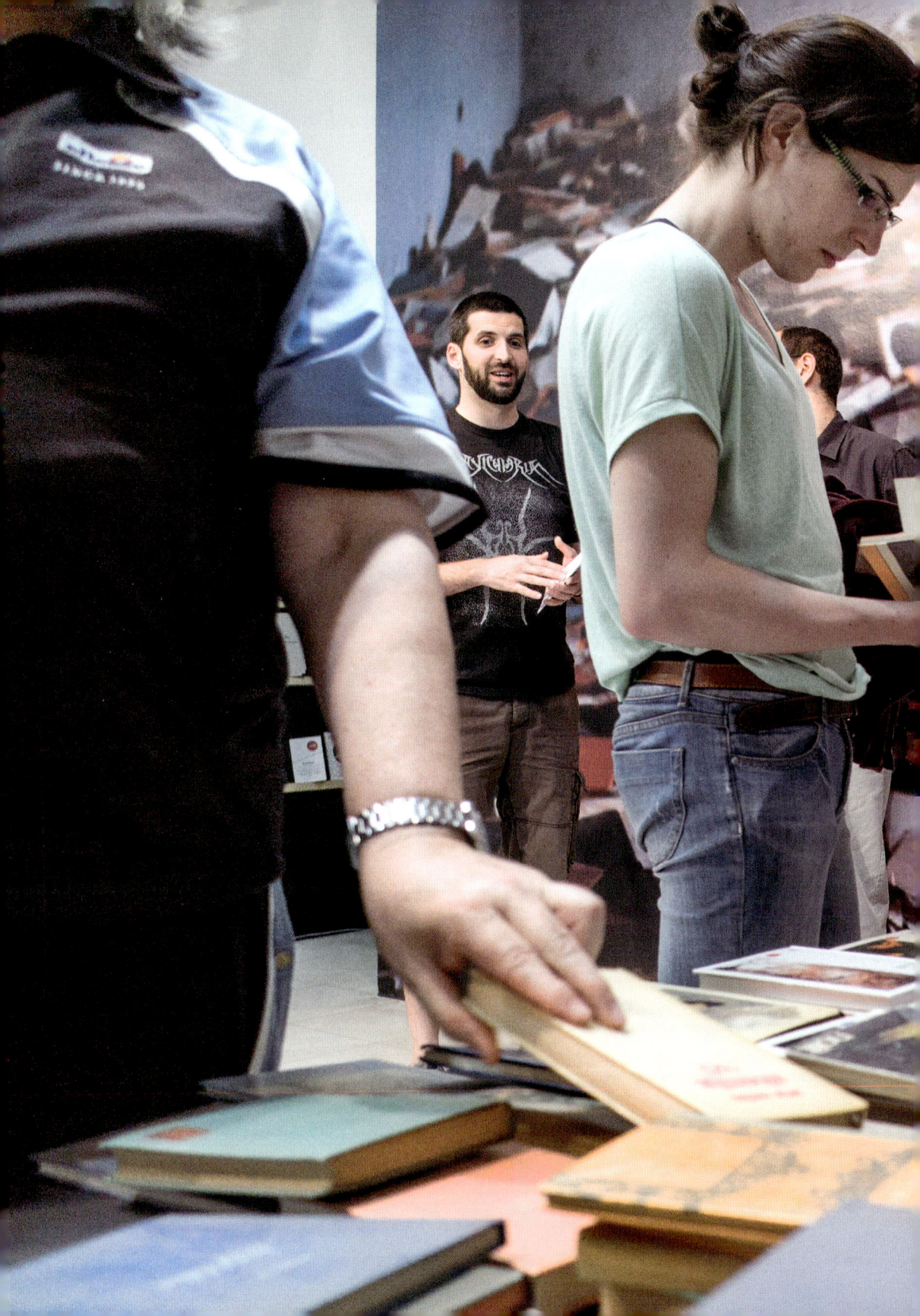

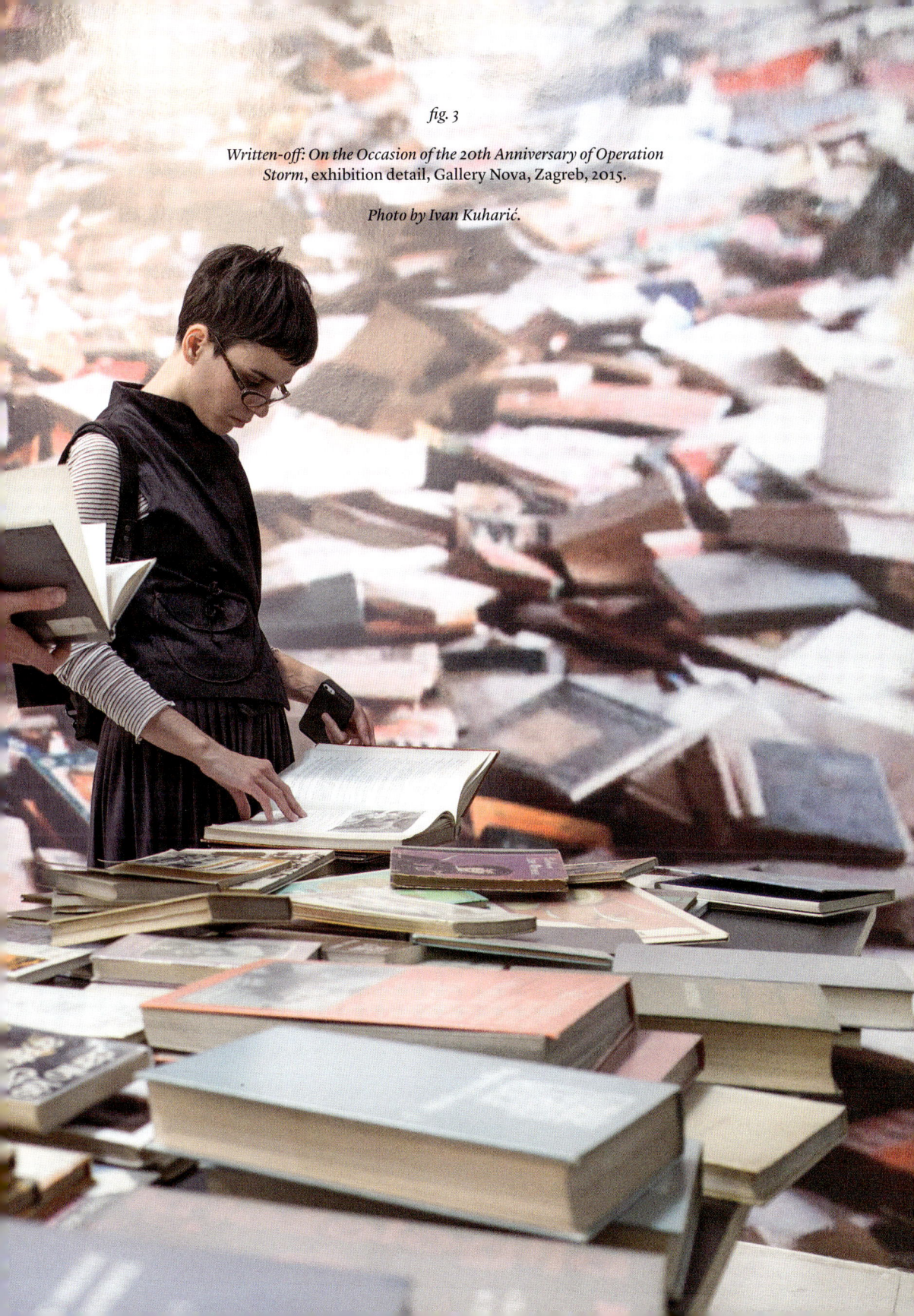

fig. 3

Written-off: On the Occasion of the 20th Anniversary of Operation Storm, exhibition detail, Gallery Nova, Zagreb, 2015.

Photo by Ivan Kuharić.

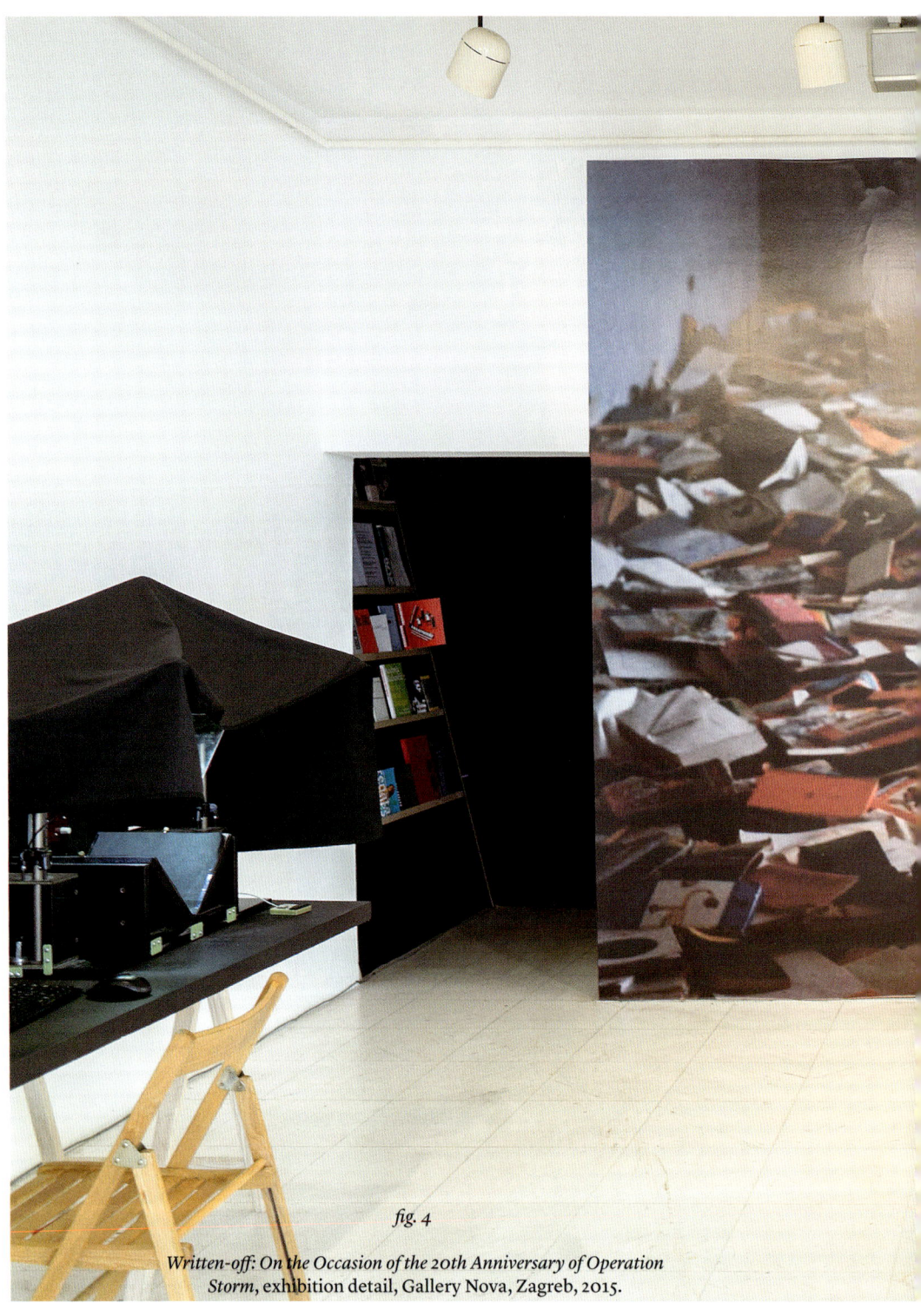

fig. 4

Written-off: On the Occasion of the 20th Anniversary of Operation Storm, exhibition detail, Gallery Nova, Zagreb, 2015.

Photo by Ivan Kuharić.

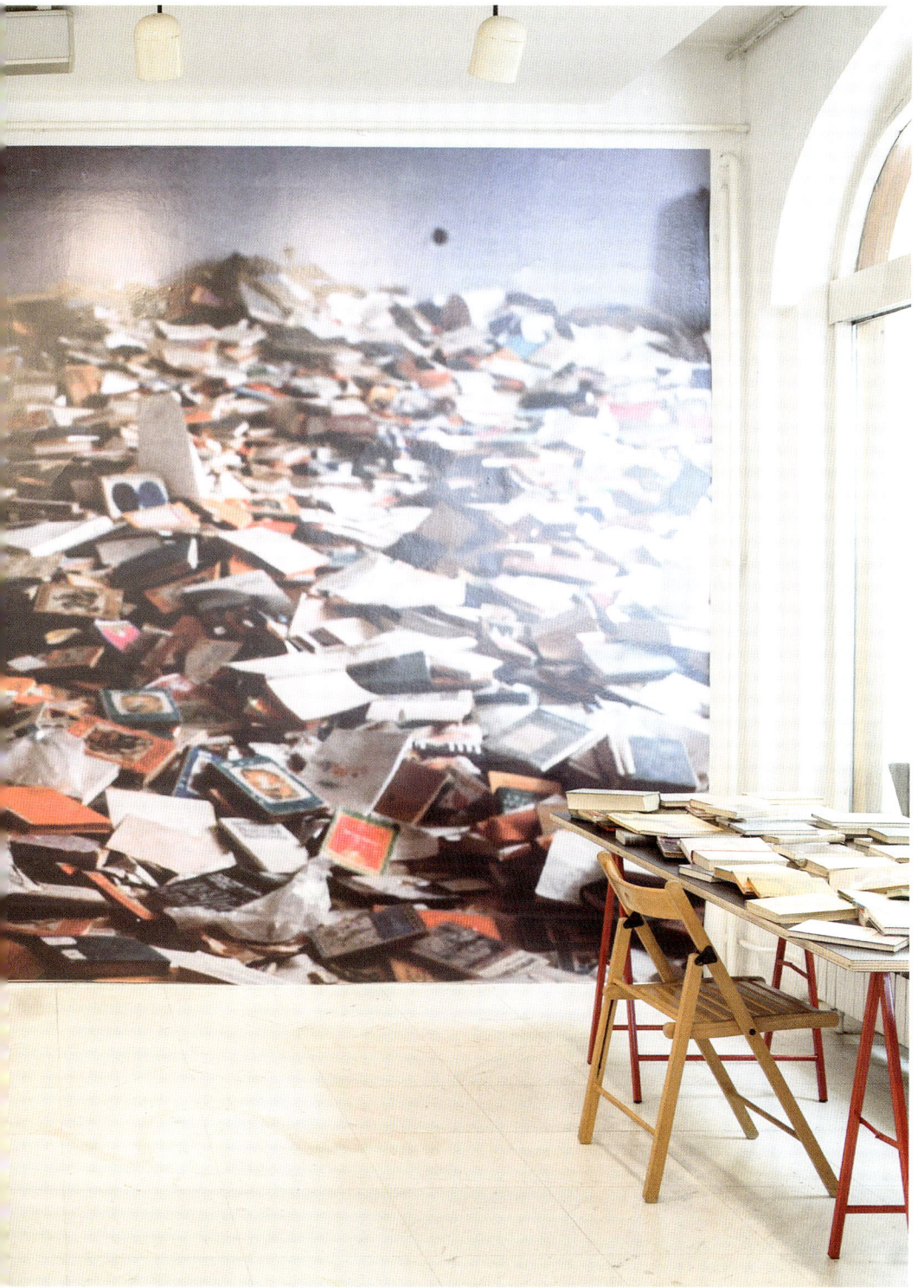

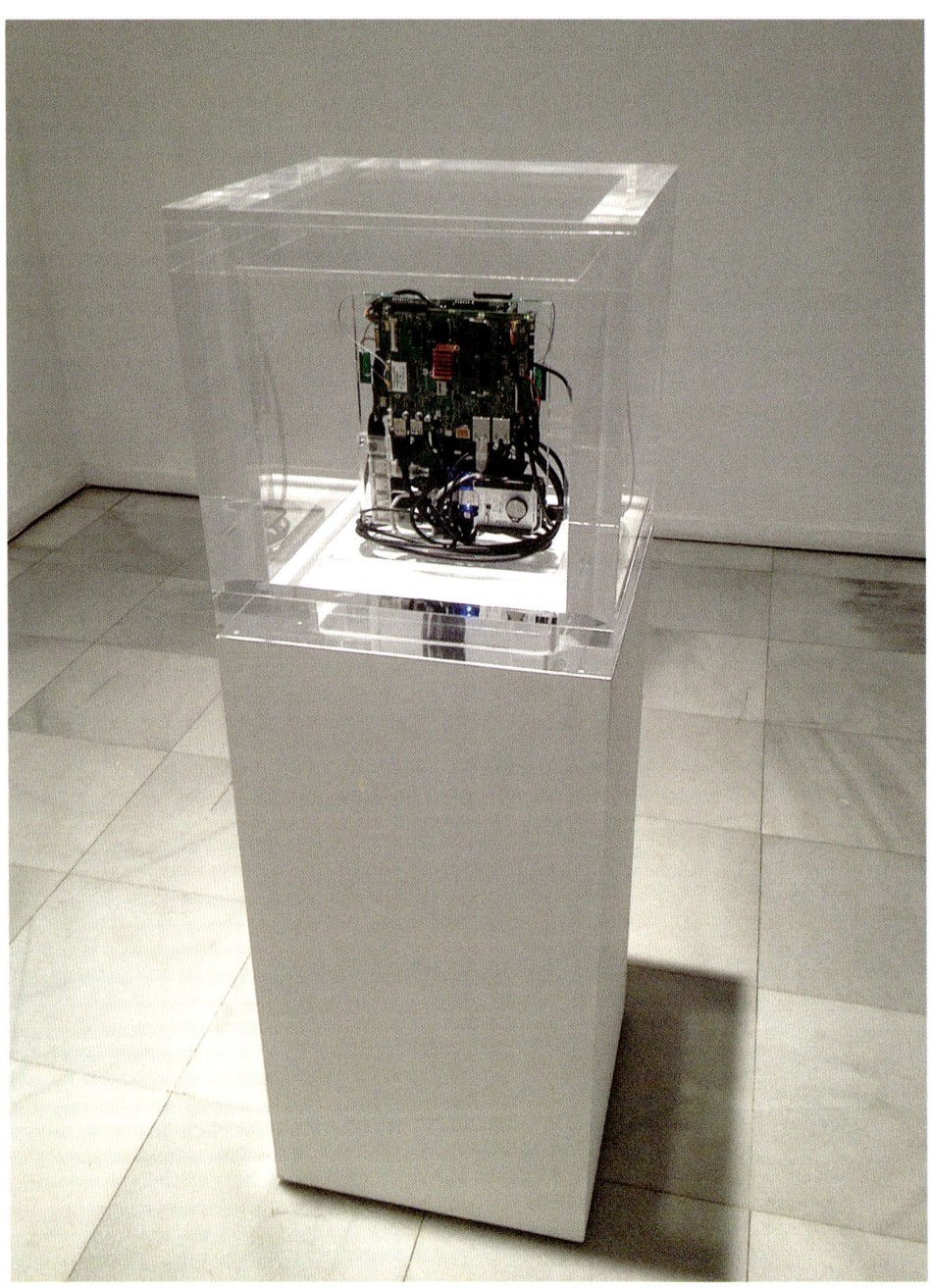

fig. 5

Trevor Paglen and Jacob Appelbaum, *Autonomy Cube*,
installation view, *Really Useful Knowledge*, curated by WHW,
Museo Nacional Centro de Arte Reina Sofía, Madrid, 2014.

Photo by Joaquín Cortés and Román Lores / MNCARS.

preventing the free circulation of information by creating new strategies for pushing information into a form of property and expropriating value through the control of metadata (information about information),[21] *Public Library* shifts the focus away from aesthetic intention – from unique, closed, and discrete works – to a database of works and the metabolism of the database. It creates values through indexing and connectivity, imagined communities and imaginative dialecticization. The web of interpenetration and determination activated by *Public Library* creates a pedagogical endeavour that also includes a propagandist thrust, if the notion of propaganda can be recast in its original meaning as "things that must be disseminated".

A similar didactic impetus and constructivist praxis is present in the work *Autonomy Cube*, which was developed through the combined expertise of artist and geographer Trevor Paglen and internet security researcher, activist and hacker Jacob Appelbaum. This work, too, we presented in the Reina Sofía exhibition *Really Useful Knowledge*, along with *Public Library* and other projects that offered a range of strategies and methodologies through which the artists attempted to think through the disjunction between concrete experience and the abstraction of capital, enlisting pedagogy as a crucial element in organized collective struggles. *Autonomy Cube* offers a free, open-access, encrypted internet hotspot that routes internet traffic over TOR, a volunteer-run global network of servers, relays, and services, which provides anonymous and unsurveilled communication. The importance of the privacy of the anonymized information that *Autonomy Cube* enables and protects is that it prevents so-called traffic analysis – the tracking, analysis, and theft of metadata for the purpose of anticipating people's behaviour and relationships. In the hands of the surveillance state this data becomes not only a means of steering our tastes, modes of consumption, and behaviours for the sake of making profit but also, and more crucially, an effective method and weapon of political control that can affect political organizing in often still-unforeseeable ways that offer few reasons for optimism. Visually, *Autonomy Cube* references minimalist sculpture (fig. 5) (specifically, Hans Haacke's seminal piece *Condensation Cube*, 1963–1965), but its main creative drive lies in the affirmative salvaging of technologies, infrastructures, and networks that form both the leading organizing principle and the pervasive condition of complex societies, with the aim of supporting the potentially liberated accumulation of collective knowledge and action. Aesthetic and art-historical references serve as camouflage or tools for a strategic infiltration that enables expansion of the movement's field of influence and the projection of a different (contingent) future. Engagement with historical forms of challenging institutions becomes the starting point of a poetic praxis that materializes the object of its striving in the here and now.

21 McKenzie Wark, "Metadata Punk", in *Public Library*, pp. 113–117 (see n. 9).

Both *Public Library* and *Autonomy Cube* build their autonomy on the dedication and effort of the collective body, without which they would not exist, rendering this interdependence not as some consensual idyll of cooperation but as conflicting fields that create further information and experiences. By doing so, they question the traditional edifice of art in a way that supports Peter Osborne's claim that art is defined not by its aesthetic or medium-based status, but by its poetics: "Postconceptual art articulates a post-aesthetic poetics."[22] This means going beyond criticality and bringing into the world something defined not by its opposition to the real, but by its creation of the fiction of a shared present, which, for Osborne, is what makes art truly contemporary. And if projects like these become a kind of political trophy for art institutions, the side the institutions choose nevertheless affects the common sense of our future.

---

22   Osborne, *Anywhere or Not at All*, p. 33.

Alenka Gregorič

Cultural Jetlag

Fact, Curse, or Opportunity?

Alenka Gregorič's recent research has focused on the institutional aspects of artistic and cultural production and the corresponding role of cultural institutions in contemporary society. In her essay here, she discusses problems facing museums of contemporary art on the territory of the former Yugoslavia, where many have been closed or stripped of political and financial support, and looks at some local initiatives that have formed in solidarity with them. She juxtaposes this situation with the model of the "starchitecture" museum (especially widespread in the West), which fosters gentrification and "touristification" and turns the presentation of art and culture into just another (private) business venture. By critically examining both realities, she opens a space for reflection on the possible future role of the art museum as a public institution.

Early in 2009, a number of art professionals from different countries of the former Yugoslavia had a chance encounter at an art opening in Ljubljana. During our casual conversation, we came to the realization that at that moment not a single national museum of contemporary art in any of the successor states of Yugoslavia was open and operating. The reasons were varied. The buildings of Moderna galerija in Ljubljana[1] and the Museum of Contemporary Art in Belgrade were being renovated. The Contemporary Art Museum of Macedonia was closed for roof repairs, as it has been before and after this conversation. The Museum of Contemporary Art Metelkova in Ljubljana and the new building of the Museum of Contemporary Art Zagreb were both under construction. Despite Renzo Piano's existing design from 2000 for the Sarajevo Museum of Contemporary Art slated to house the international *Ars Aevi* collection, perennial financial and political problems prevented the beginning of construction. Due to its unclear status and inadequate funding, the Art Gallery of Bosnia and Herzegovina was run at only half speed, with its permanent collection in the museum storage facility, no exhibition programme, and some of its galleries being leased. The Museum of Contemporary Art Vojvodina[2] in Novi Sad was awaiting a permanent move to the former Museum of the Socialist Revolution, where it had been carrying out its exhibitions programme since 2001.

At the time of our conversation, there were only two formally functioning museums of national importance in the region: the Kosovo National Art Gallery in Priština, then virtually unknown outside its immediate environment due to an extremely locally-oriented programme, and the "national" Museum of Contemporary Art of the Republic of Srpska in Banja Luka, Bosnia and Herzegovina. Of course, the whole situation and all its specificities cannot be summed up in a single paragraph; the realities of the political, social, and cultural circumstances are far too complex for that. But suffice to say that we did find a common denominator: "closed". A significant number of art collections in the region were inaccessible, kept in storage, and far from the eyes of the public (including the professional public).

Many museums in the region of the former Yugoslavia conceived and developed collecting, programming, and exhibition policies by looking at their own specificities and analysing and critically appraising established Western examples (already under the socialist regimes). Thus, they set the

1   Moderna galerija (the Museum of Modern Art in Ljubljana, established in 1948), has long functioned as a museum both of modern and contemporary art. This was formalized in its constitutional document of 2004, in which the institution was operationally divided into two units: a Museum of Modern Art and a Museum of Contemporary Art. The former is housed in the Moderna galerija original building in the city centre, and the latter, since 2011, in a renovated former military barracks on Metelkova Street.
2   The Museum of Contemporary Art Vojvodina is included here because Vojvodina enjoyed the status of an autonomous region in Yugoslavia. Thus the institution can also be considered to have national status although it officially became a museum only in 1996. Prior to that it was called the Gallery of Contemporary Art.

Cultural Jetlag

bar high. For example, since its founding in 1965, the Museum of Contemporary Art in Belgrade, among others, has followed the model of MoMA, which was prevalent during that era: a chronological permanent exhibition of the museum's collection and consequently a linear presentation of the history of art. In contrast, once it finally obtained suitable premises to exhibit its collection in 2009, the Museum of Contemporary Art Zagreb[3] adopted more recent standards, displaying its collection in themed sections and linking works by subject matter. The concept is called "Collection in Motion", and it aspires "to initiate and demonstrate improvements in the presentation, communication, and interpretation of the artworks in [the] collection" and "to emphasize the major characteristics of contemporary art: movement, change, transience, and uncertainty".[4]

Moderna galerija in Ljubljana created the concept of its *Arteast 2000+* collection in the 1990s. Including works by many eminent artists from Eastern Europe and based on dialogue between art from Eastern and Western Europe, the collection was first presented publicly in 2000. The Museum of Contemporary Art of Macedonia in Skopje, founded less than a year after the devastating 1963 earthquake, has a heterogeneous international collection assembled from the donations of world-renowned artists in solidarity with the struck town and its inhabitants. The building now housing the collection was completed in 1970. The international collection *Ars Aevi*, conceived during the war in Bosnia and Herzegovina and first presented in 1999, is composed of donations made by public museums from numerous countries to post-war Sarajevo and its inhabitants.[5]

Both the Skopje and the Sarajevo collections, assembled with international donations, remain inaccessible or only partly accessible today, because programming visions and financing that would support their (suitable) presentation have not been developed or implemented, primarily

---

3 Initially called the City Art Gallery Zagreb, the museum was founded in 1954. Since its inception, it has developed a collection and worked as a museum institution, although it only acquired premises for displaying its collection with the opening of the new museum building in 2009.

4 See http://www.msu.hr/#/en/stalni_postav/ (accessed March 25, 2016).

5 The idea of the collection emerged in July 1992 (three months after the occupation of Sarajevo) during a forum of artists and other intellectuals who devised the general concept of the *International Cultural Project – Sarajevo 2000* (hereinafter the Project). Underpinning the decision to form a collection for the Sarajevo Museum of Contemporary Art was the idea of donation-oriented group exhibitions: international museums would stage exhibitions, contributing organization and funding, and the exhibited works by international artists would be donated to the Project's collection. The first Project exhibition (followed by another four) was staged in Milan, in Centro Spazio Umano in 1994. Subsequent exhibitions took place in the Centro per l'arte Contemporanea Luigi Pecci in Prato in 1996, as well in Moderna galerija in Ljubljana during the fall of the same year. The Project, renamed *Ars Aevi* in 1997, later continued to Venice, Sarajevo, Bologna, and Vienna. The collection was first presented in Sarajevo in 1999, then exhibited temporarily in the former Museum of the Revolution, and when that had to undergo renovation, moved to another temporary location, the Skenderija Centre, where it remains to this day.

for political reasons. The unsuccessful management of these two art institutions has done more damage than merely restricting access to two internationally relevant collections; it has also led to the stagnation of large parts of the Macedonian and Bosnian art scenes. A museum, and especially a progressive one, in addition to being one of the key building blocks of the art system[6] and co-creating the national (art historical) narrative, also leads to connections with international museums and other networks vital for the positioning of local art developments and artists relative to international art (historical) trends. This is especially true in countries where other segments of the art system are precarious or not well established.

I will conclude my thoughts on the art system and, above all, on the enmeshment of art institutions with the political system and its transformations, with the following quote:

> The system of art consists of a network of diverse authorities – be it institutions and (governmental) agencies or individual professionals and experts – taking part in the definition, formation, and production of meaning and knowledge in contemporary art. All these authorities represent or relate to different institutions as well as to the institutionalized roles and responsibilities in the professional field of contemporary art. However, it should be made clear that the system of art is inextricably interwoven with the general political system, particularly in authoritarian societies.[7]

Despite the post-1991 changes in the societies of the former Yugoslavia, the involvement of politics in crucial decisions concerning public museums – in particular, the selection of the management and subsequent interference in management's decisions – continues to be the practice in most of these countries. In some, museums have stagnated or even regressed due to inexpert, politically appointed staff, unclear programming and financial objectives, and unfocussed and ineffective cultural policies. A number of museums in the region are closed, neglected, or permanently seeking new structural and programming guidelines.

For example, the impact of political reality is very obvious in Macedonia: for years, the politically appointed and professionally unqualified management of the Museum of Contemporary Art of Macedonia has been unable to keep the museum in continuous operation. As Suzana Milevska

---

6   The art system is comprised of various segments. Its integral part consists primarily of artists and their works and activities. This is followed by spaces of presentation (exhibition spaces from non-profit galleries and centres to spaces of the Kunsthalle-type and museums), systems of interpretation (curators, theorists, critics), education (pedagogic and andragogic programmes, publishing, symposia, conferences), the art market (commercial galleries, art fairs, auction houses, collectors), collections (private and public), and, last but not least, sources of funding (public and private). A summary of: Igor Zabel, *Eseji 1*, Založba /*cf.*, Ljubljana, 2006, p. 369.
7   Alenka Gregorič and Suzana Milevska, eds., *Inside Out: Not so White Cube*, Museum and Galleries of Ljubljana, Ljubljana, 2015, p. 35.

described it in an interview in 2014: "The curatorial positions in public art institutions are undermined and we have a situation where most of the important curatorial decisions are made directly by the Prime Minister, the Ministry of Culture (by the Minister of Culture), or by the institutions' directors who mostly haven't been educated or had any previous experience in the field of art and were appointed by the Government directly. It is a direct autocracy in the Macedonian way."[8] Constant repairs to the museum building only serve as an excuse for the semi-functioning of the museum and its obscure programming policy.

The barely open, non-operational museums in Bosnia and Herzegovina can be cited as the most drastic example of the impact of social reality and unstructured politics at the state, canton, and municipal levels. During recent years, the indifference of national politics and the subsequent unclear legal status and funding of the museums have forced the National Museum of Bosnia and Herzegovina, the Art Gallery of Bosnia and Herzegovina, and five other museums to close their doors. This unbearable state of affairs prompted the artist Azra Akšamija to co-found the *CULTURESHUTDOWN* platform,[9] the most resounding project of which was the *Day of Museum Solidarity* in 2013, involving the participation of 225 institutions in 40 countries. In a gesture of solidarity and protest, participating institutions worldwide blocked the entrance to their exhibition rooms, or covered parts of their collections or individual exhibits for a day, in order to raise public awareness of the insufferable conditions in which cultural institutions in Bosnia and Herzegovina find themselves. The action's international success triggered public debate in Bosnia and Herzegovina on the issue of the status of the closed museums.

The degree to which art systems are (non)functioning varies as the systems in each successor country evolved alongside the new economic, political, and social order in the 1990s after the breakup of Yugoslavia. The process of transition took on a different shape in each country. In a few, transition became an almost permanent condition, relegating visions of cultural policies to last place in public considerations of the future of the new states. In others, the transition from the old order to some kind of "normalcy" – parliamentary democracy and the free market – happened virtually overnight, and, as a result, certain cultural institutions changed their strategies of operation without proper reflection, uncritically adopting segments of the Western art system model (e.g. implementing the market model of culture in a society that was unused to paying, and unwilling to pay, for certain public services) or sometimes even neglecting their primary mission.

---

8   See Kristina Kulakova, "Interview With Macedonian Curator Suzana Milevska", *Viennacontemporary* web site, March 14, 2014, https://viennacontemporarymag.com/2014/03/14/interview-with-macedonian-curator-suzana-milevska/ (accessed July 20, 2016).

9   See project's web site http://www.cultureshutdown.net/ (accessed July 7, 2016).

Artists played an important role in defining new orientations for art institutions during this turbulent time and this also overlapped with so-called New Institutionalism. New Institutionalism "describes a series of curatorial, art educational as well as administrative practices that from the mid 1990s to the early 2000s endeavoured to reorganize the structures of mostly medium-sized, publicly funded contemporary art institutions, and to define alternative forms of institutional activity".[10] The more progressive among them critically assessed the institutions, trying to co-create some general guidelines for the future with their knowledge and experience of various models of art systems and art institutions. For the most part, their suggestions concerning the restructuring of institutions went unheeded, which induced a number of artists to use the ideas that emerged from their critique of institutions as platforms for the foundation of their own "private" institutions, from galleries and artist-run spaces, to art collections, museums,[11] associations, institutes, and other organizations for the production and presentation of art.

Thus a system for founding parallel art spaces was defined at the same time as the visions and programmes of national institutions aimed at establishing their place and role in the new states were being (trans)formed. With the introduction of a new legal and economic framework, the formalization of existing and newly established art spaces and organizations became possible, as well as new options for systemic public funding, the long-term acquisition of spaces, and the financing of operations.

In the 1990s, existing and newly founded NGOs played a significant role in the effort to create new cultural institutions, including the establishment of new guiding principles for museums and international connections, and the development of local scenes. The role of NGOs was so important that they continue to maintain their position as incubators of the scene and important agents in international networks. The Soros Centers for Contemporary Art (SCCAs) were an essential agent on the non-governmental scene during the 1990s; the financial, technical, and logistic support they provided fostered the development of local art scenes and, in particular, new media art. The latter would not have flourished so quickly had the SCCAs not been there, because museums were technologically underequipped, and their programming visions often lagged behind in a figu-

10 Jonas Ekeberg introduced the term New Institutionalism in the homonymous first issue of the publication-series *Verksted*, published by the Office for Contemporary Art Norway in 2003. See Lucie Kolb and Gabriel Flückiger, "New Institutionalism Revisited", *Oncurating.org*, no. 21, December 2013, pp. 6-15 or http://oncurating-journal.de/index.php/issue-21.html#.V8lxaDV8vow (accessed July 7, 2016).

11 There are many museums in the region that have been founded by artists as antipodes to existing national museums and their collecting, evaluation, and exhibition policies, e.g. Tadej Pogačar's *P.A.R.A.S.I.T.E. Museum of Contemporary Art* in Slovenia, Vladimir Dodig Trokut's *Anti-Museum* in Croatia, Goran Đorđević's *Museum of American Art, Berlin*, Mrđan Bajić's *Yugomuseum*, Dragan Papić's *Inside of Artists Brain Museum*, Vladimir Perić's *Talent Museum of Childhood*, Nikola Džaf's *Museum of the Rabbit or the Rabbit that ate the Museum* (the last four in Serbia), etc.

rative Stone Age. The SCCA network brought its own value system, co-creating, as Miško Šuvaković put it, a unique visual idiom – "Soros realism".[12] The SCCAs and the artists associated with them effectively linked the local scenes with regional and international developments in art. Nonetheless, they found themselves criticized and even politically attacked in some countries despite, or because, of that. And, while the cooperation between the SCCAs and the museums was above reproach, no real synergy developed in any of the countries in the region. In 2000, Hungarian billionaire and philanthropist George Soros' Open Society Foundation ceased financing the SCCAs, and they gradually reorganized, forming new local and regional networks and collaborating more closely with public institutions.

Collaboration between public institutions and NGOs became the new norm and even a necessity in some places, in particular during the post-2008 recession. When speaking about the importance of collaboration between museums and NGOs, it needs to be pointed out that the art system is rather rudimentary in most countries in the region; parts of it have never fully developed. This is particularly evident in the commercial aspect of the system – a network of internationally present and recognizable commercial art galleries, which, with a few exceptions, are virtually non-existent in the region. Not only do commercial galleries act as promoters of local scenes internationally, but they also, and more importantly, encourage and co-finance the production of art projects, positioning them in international currents through commercial networks and art fairs. The absence of this part of the system hampers the entire sector, as public institutions and NGOs must shoulder many of these tasks, something that is often difficult due to meagre public funding.

Now, several years after the start of the financial downturn and the implementation of austerity measures, most NGOs remain active, although many find themselves on the brink of survival and some have been forced to close down. Due to vague and undefined cultural politics – and, in some countries, the completely ignored public appeals of cultural professionals – certain segments of the system have started to collapse. A case in point is the non-governmental cultural sector in Macedonia, which virtually disappeared at the end of 2000s.[13] All of the countries in the region have been facing the problems of alarmingly low financial support to the entire cultural sector and especially NGOs, and they also share the problem of the unregulated status of self-employed professionals in the field of culture.

---

12   Miško Šuvaković, "The Ideology of Exhibiting: On the Ideologies of Manifesta", *PlatformaSCCA*, no. 3, SCCA-Ljubljana, 2002, p. 17; available at www.ljudmila.org/scca/platforma3/suvakoviceng.htm (accessed July 7, 2016).
13   Jadro, an independent cultural association was established in 2012 with the aim of uniting the NGO sector in its fight against the elimination of financing for the non-governmental scene, which had been deprived of all support due to the national project *Skopje 2014*.

Cases of cooperation between the public and the non-governmental (or civil) sectors in the region include initiatives for supporting public museums. One such action was *Hosting Moderna galerija!*, organized by personal initiative[14] during the renovation of Moderna galerija in Ljubljana (2007–2009), when the museum, in addition to having its building temporarily closed, found itself without resources for its programme, since programming funds had been channelled into the renovation and the renting of substitute offices. Twenty governmental and non-governmental organizations from across Slovenia united in support of the main national institution of modern and contemporary art, hosting and co-producing exhibitions, panel discussions, screenings, and other kinds of programmes that the museum would have otherwise been unable to carry out because of the renovation and reductions in its programming budget. Thus the Moderna galerija was taken under the wing of other institutions that provided support in terms of venues, organization, and above all financing (which the institutions participating in the action received from public sources), and was able to maintain some continuity in its programme. Moreover, the action was also a show of support to the museum at a time when there was an attempt to politically discredit its management and curatorial staff. Government policies were also trying to influence the programme strategy of Moderna galerija's new unit, the Museum of Contemporary Art Metelkova, the facilities of which were still under construction. Of course, this action is just an example and should not become a model for aiding public institutions that are subject to political pressure and/or underfunded. The main accomplishment of this action of solidarity was to raise awareness of crucial cooperation between various agents in the field of culture in terms of programme, space, and financing, as well as the importance of a national museum for the entire art scene.

#JaSamMuzej in 2015 represents another case of supporting a (closed) national museum, and revealed how artists and art professionals can strive to provide the basic conditions for the operation of a national institution that is deprived of state support. *#JaSamMuzej* was a joint action that brought about the reopening of the National Museum of Bosnia and Herzegovina after three years of closure.[15] Because of its ambiguous legal status, the museum had been receiving no funding and was closed to the public. Its employees kept coming to work for three years with no salary so that the museum, and above all its collection, would not fall into ruin. The Akcija (Action) Association issued an appeal to the citizens of Bosnia and Herzegovina to volunteer as attendants in the museum during opening hours and in this way show solidarity with the unpaid museum staff, while also underscoring the absurdity of the oldest cultural institution in Bosnia and Herzegovina, supposedly the property of all citizens, being closed to

---

14 The action was initiated by Jadranka Plut and myself, and coordinated by the Škuc Gallery. More on the action at http://old.mg-lj.si/node/154 (accessed March 27, 2016).
15 See the initiative's web site http://jasam.zemaljskimuzej.ba/ (accessed March 25, 2016).

the public. Over five thousand people responded: cultural figures, public servants, media personalities, athletes, inhabitants of Sarajevo as well as citizens of other countries in the region: Croatia, Slovenia, and Serbia.

The need for artists, art professionals, and other concerned citizens to get involved in maintaining the physical premises of galleries and museums and keeping them open to the public is the harsh reality in some countries of former Yugoslavia. Closed museum buildings surrounded by scaffolding (the National Museum of Serbia, located in the centre of Belgrade) and inactive or even neglected construction sites (the Museum of Contemporary Art in Belgrade) convey an important message at a symbolic level. A museum that is closed, unmaintained, or in a state of permanent renovation shows the "other" side of society because culture and its institutions are indicators of not only the economic, but also the social standards of a country.

Despite the austerity measures introduced after 2008 by all governments in the region, art institutions managed to avoid, at least formally and conceptually, many of the pitfalls of the Western, primarily American, model, in which museums are largely in the hands of private capital. Art museums in the region remain national institutions, or, occasionally, under the patronage of a city (e.g. the Museum of Contemporary Art Zagreb), which is still a form of public ownership. In accordance with the spirit of austerity measures, national governments allot a decreasing amount of resources to art institutions and the cultural sector in general. As a result, contemporary art museums seek various ways of staying afloat without excessively cutting their programmes. One way to do this is to include content prepared and produced by organizations in the non-governmental sector. In this way, museums fill the gaps in their programmes, while NGOs and self-employed professionals in culture have the opportunity to present their work in reputable art spaces. In short, museums outsource the contents they cannot consistently produce as part of their programmes because of underfunding or understaffing. In this way, museums attempt to keep their programmes diverse, showing content mostly financed by external producers. Collaborations of this type have as their aim the common good and a spirit of mutual support, and thus tend to be publicly presented as examples of good practice, and are also increasingly favoured by public grant givers. The downside is that this form of inter-institutional cooperation plays into the neoliberal paradigm of the "lean state", which, in the final analysis, is based on the principle of exploiting the weakest.

Despite the underhanded incursion of the neo-liberal model into art institutions, the countries in the region have not engaged in the privatization of museums in the form of an actual change of ownership, or even representatives of private capital serving on administrative or supervisory boards. In this context, we might claim that the prolonged process of transition, incessant financial difficulties, and the asynchronocity of the region with the rest of Europe – a sort of "cultural jetlag" – could be interpreted in a positive way. Namely, it has allowed time for reflection about the potential future of museums as public institutions.

The basis for the professional working of a museum is a coherently conceived vision – from the collecting policy to the programming and exhibition activities to public communications, publishing, education, and marketing. But in the new era, during which museums seem to focus principally on ways and means of marketing their collections and collection-related contents, it is necessary to be aware of the dangers of marketing-based approaches in the conception of museums. Claire Bishop, in her discussion about exhibition practices at the London Tate Modern and the Paris Pompidou Centre, which represent ideal models for many museums in our region and farther afield, writes: "the apparatus is multiculturalism, seen in the equation of contemporaneity with global diversity; its structure of mediation is marketing, addressed to the multiple demographics of economically quantifiable 'audiences'".[16]

Looking at the pitfalls of the Western models of art institutions, let us mention the most conspicuous element – museum architecture, which, since the 1990s, has triumphed over museum content. The 1990s was a decade when star architects – spawning the coinage of the term "starchitecture" – designed museums that led to the paradigm of architectural predominance, namely architectural design as an envelope that, instead of complementing, competes with or even overpowers what is inside the building. Terry Smith describes this type of architecture as destination architecture, architecture as entertainment or amusement park, the goal of which is to transform both contemporary architecture and art into attractions.[17] According to Smith, minimum criteria represented the maximum standards of the museum architecture, especially during the 1990s. But the trend did not stop in the twenty-first century, which has seen numerous new buildings constructed as echoes of the "Bilbao effect",[18] with the main purpose being to foster cultural tourism and the main focus on profitability. The wording of the text on the Guggenheim Bilbao website – "… the city planned to build a first-class cultural facility"[19] – is indicative of the commercially oriented logic behind a movement of gentrification that significantly includes museums and contemporary art.

The idea of reviving post-industrial cities with new-fangled architectural attractions spread throughout Western Europe like a virus. Of course, ambitions to build bombastic pieces of architecture, and indeed actual projects of this type, also exist in Eastern Europe, but projects by "starchitects" tend to be financially too formidable to realize. There are other examples of the Western model of urban revitalization of cultural content that have

---

16 Claire Bishop, *Radical Museology: Or What's Contemporary in Museums of Contemporary Art?*, Walther König Verlag, Cologne, 2014, p. 43.
17 Terry Smith, "Bilbao afekt: kultura kao industrija", in *Savremena umetnost i muzej*, ed. Jelena Stojanović, Muzej savremene umetnosti, Belgrade, p. 25.
18 Also the term "Bilbao factor" is used. Both terms denote prestige and the spiking financial growth of towns that draw masses of tourists with architectural attractions, on a par with what occurred in Bilbao after the opening of the Guggenheim Museum in 1998.
19 See http://www.guggenheim.org/bilbao/history (accessed March 11, 2016).

influenced cities in Eastern Europe over the last fifteen years: one example is the ubiquitous ambition to win the laurel of European Capital of Culture. This cultural "circus" with its focus on international stars and megalomaniac projects makes use of its flattering and lucrative title to latch onto a city like a leech. In most cases, the aftermath of this year long cultural hyperventilation and over-activity resembles the situation in Bilbao – a local scene that has been marginalized and financially set back even further than it was before.

Analysing "starchitecture" and in particular its impact on the cultural landscape, Smith refers to Margaret King's article "Theme Park Thesis". King writes that the present-day museum is a theme park with four attractions: an attractive building, a good permanent collection, primary and secondary temporary exhibitions, and ancillary amenities such as a store and a restaurant. In this context, we can think of museums as gravitational centres that replace a trip to the mall for consumers of cultural content. Put another way, museum complexes can be seen as high-end contemporary shopping malls with a touch of class. And just as shopping malls are architectural complexes with highly elaborate and well-thought-out interiors, so are the museums of the past few decades pieces of architecture with extremely well thought out exteriors. In many cases, the interior of the museum is of secondary importance rendering collections and exhibition activities subordinate to architectural spectacle. Here I would like to mention Zaha Hadid's MAXXI in Rome, where additional walls or panels must be erected for the exhibition of art because drilling holes in the museum walls is not permitted. In addition to attractive, "selfie-friendly" architecture, such "wow-factor" museums also offer admission-free amenities as an important part of the interior: spaces for socializing, restaurants, stores. The latest such example is the extension to Tate Modern in London where as many as three stories out of eleven are dedicated to "public or social spaces". These spaces for socializing and spending free time are described as follows: "The top three floors of the new building are spaces dedicated to the enjoyment of all our visitors," while the architect of the extension points out in the promotional video that "walking or moving through the building itself is an interesting experience."[20]

In all of this, we see a direct link between present-day museums and shopping malls, deliberately planned and designed environments dedicated to consumption, market exchange, luring visitors by offering pleasure and amusement. In his book *Life Inc.*, Douglas Rushkoff writes about what made Americans enjoy spending their free time in the first shopping malls as early as the mid-1950s. His description of shopping malls could also be applied to new trendy museums:

> While individual mall stores offered their own theme environments, the design of the mall as a whole proved even more compelling to early

---

20   See http://www.tate.org.uk/about/projects/tate-modern-project/social-spaces (accessed March 14, 2016).

mall-goers. Studies showed that shoppers went to the mall for the mall itself. They thought malls were beautiful, and wanted to behold the spectacle. Many people said they enjoyed the sense of the escape they felt there. Stimulated by sound and light, they were distracted from their daily worries. Lonely suburbanites said they felt less isolated, and the overworked experienced a pleasurable loss of time.[21]

In the West, museums were built as a new type of amusement parks, following the model of shopping malls. In the countries of the former Yugoslavia, shopping malls were built as the new amusement parks. Due to the perennial lack of funds for museum construction, most museums in the region have paradoxically avoided the hazards of Western trends: the model of the museum as infrastructure for leisure-time activities and the reckless policies of urban renewal of degraded areas with attractive museum complexes in the role of new amusement parks. Except for the building of the Museum of Contemporary Art Zagreb, which opened in 2009 and whose colossal form looks like a belated echo of the grand architectural attractions of the 1990s, the region tends to restrict itself to renovations, reconstructions, and extensions to existing museum buildings. For the most part, museums thus remain "trapped" in old or out-dated pieces of architecture, which do not allow for contemporary expansiveness or spectacular approaches in architecture, and force museums to focus instead on their collections, exhibition activities, and the topicality of content. In terms of King's definition of a successful museum, most museums in the region can boast only collections and exhibitions, having unwittingly managed to avoid the other trends in the Western planning, managing, and marketing of museums. As a result, they are relatively uninteresting for international art tourism and its growing audience, although some of them occupy conspicuous places on the world map of significant art institutions as a result of their outstanding programmes and the conceptions of their exhibition policies.[22]

Therefore, I daresay yet again that, despite its drawbacks, "cultural jet-lag" on the territory of the former Yugoslavia has a positive side when we reflect on the possible future of museums. Especially since the opposite picture in the region is not difficult to imagine: megalomaniac works of architecture that, despite their shine, remain empty – due to the lack of programming vision, state support, public funding or the interest of private capital.

Translated from Slovene by Tamara M. Soban.

21   Douglas Rushkoff, *Life Inc: How Corporatism Conquered the World, and How We Can Take It Back*, Vintage Publishing, London, 2010, p. 78.
22   A noteworthy example is Moderna galerija in Ljubljana as the co-founder of the international museum network *L'Internationale*, which currently represents one of the most prominent and important models of intermuseum collaboration. The Zagreb and the Belgrade Museums of Contemporary Art also collaborate with some of the most preeminent international institutions of contemporary art.

Kirill Medvedev

Live Long, Die Young

What happens when two young Marxists in 21st-century Moscow interview a sentimental (former?) Communist who made a world-famous monumental film about the Holocaust? This is the situation Kirill Medvedev – poet, political activist, and the co-founder of the Free Marxist Press – presents in his poem "Live Long, Die Young". Inevitably, it all comes down to politics, "the wound on the body of history ... that will not heal".

Lots of time, lots of cars,
Lots of money, so much love,
Very cold and very hot.
But now it's freezing out,
The director Lanzmann is giving us an interview,
Without, it must be said,
Much passion.
This man was intimate with
Simone de Beauvoir
And worked alongside Sartre.

But that's later. For now
Channel One
Is filming him *en face*
In the next room
And we can make out
A few scattered remarks.

His nine-hour film
About the Holocaust
Played in every
Country –
People nodded off,
And in their dreams
They saw the horrors
And the voice of our famous guest
Faded in and faded out.

It fades in, fades out,
In the hall
The beautiful
Camilla comes and goes.
She perches on the sofa
Then she walks away.

The assistant to the cultural attaché
Of the French Embassy
Is also here. She's the one
Who signed up me and Kolya
For this interview with Lanzmann.
She's also beautiful and young.
A little older than us
But she looks younger.

Live Long, Die Young

Whereas me and Kolya,
We don't want to look younger.
One of us is thirty-three,
The other's thirty-four.
Not yet at the peak
Of our powers,
We're gathering force
And preparing to strike.

We're like Lanzmann
Who at the age of eighteen
Joined the French
Communist Party.

He joined not because
He read Marx or Lenin
But because he was asked
By his friends
In the Resistance.

We are like Lanzmann
Who cried when he learned
Of the death of Stalin.

He cried not because
He loved Stalin
But because he was
Sentimental:
He saw Soviet
Sailors
Lowering their flags to half-mast,
And thought about how
The Soviet people
Had absorbed,
During the war,
The most terrible
And frightful blows.

We are like Lanzmann
Who in 1949
Made the acquaintance
Of Sartre and Simone
De Beauvoir.

He began to work with them
On the magazine
Les Tempes modernes.
And today he is
That publication's
Editor in chief.

We are like Lanzmann
Who in 1972
Made the film
Why Israel?,
Which, in the words
Of the online encyclopedia,
"Did not shy away from
Difficult questions."

We discussed all our questions
In advance of the interview.
Inside us it was as if
Some keys, cold and hot,
Were rattling. It's nearly freezing out.

Meanwhile I was thinking about how
Kolya is a *rude* artist.
In the sense that
There are radical artists
Everywhere you look,
But not so many
Genuinely rude artists.
The rudeness of an artist,
I thought,
Is an interesting quality.

But now Channel One is leaving,
Kolya takes off his jacket with its skulls
And sets up our cameras.
"We are the representatives of the left," we say.
Lanzmann lowers his gaze wearily:
Now they're going to start in about Israel.

But Kolya, having explained a bit
About his art collective,
Asks Lanzmann instead
About monumental
Art:

"Monumental
Art. What might it look like
Right now?"

"How should I know?"
says Lanzmann.
"There could be no
Monumental
Art
Today.
The world is scattered. For
A monumental
Work you need
A unified sense
Of the world."

"But you yourself
Filmed a monumental
Work. Surely you have
Some ideas on this score?"

"I didn't think about
That. I'm an artist,
Understand? I don't
Think in such
Categories. What are you,
Communists?
Your task is
The Revolution.
Why are you asking
Me about
Monumental
Art?"

We're the ones asking the questions

We're the ones asking the questions

We
Here
Are the ones
Asking the questions.
In the iron air
Of Moscow.

Eidelman, Markelov,
Pechersky are with us.[1]
Medvedev the Bear Jew and Jeff
"The Snowman" Monson –
That's what they call us
Around town.

"In what capacity
Did you make that film –
As a Frenchman, a Jew,
An intellectual?
Or as a member
Of the Resistance?"

"I repeat,
I wanted…
…"

"Does the term
The 'Holocaust Industry'
Mean anything to you?"

"What's that?"
Asks Lanzmann.
(I warned Kolya
That Lanzmann wouldn't
Understand
Or would pretend
Not to understand
What that means.)

"The Holocaust Industry
Usually means
The use of the memory
Of the destruction of the Jews
During World War Two
To legitimate, in part,
The State of Israel."

---

1 Marek Edelman (1919–2009) was a Jewish socialist and one of the leaders of the Warsaw Ghetto uprising in 1943; Stanislav Markelov (1974–2009), a labour and human rights lawyer, was murdered by neo-Nazis in Moscow in 2009; and Alexander Pechersky (1909–1990), a Ukrainian Jew and officer in the Red Army, was captured by the Germans and sent to the Sobibor death camp, where he led an armed uprising against the guards, which resulted in several hundred prisoners escaping, of whom approximately fifty survived the war. – *Translator's note.*

The translator starts
To worry.
She suspects us
Of anti-Semitism.

But we are like Lanzmann
Who came
to Moscow
To do this strange interview,
Without revealing his secrets.
He won't talk,
He's hard as a rock,
This man whose youth
Is reflected
In our cocky
Faces.

Lanzmann himself has conducted
Many interviews:
With Franz Suchomel,
The SS Unterscharführer,
With Jan Karski,
And others.
He knows very well
How to walk
His subjects
Into this or that
Confession
Or experience,
All while leveraging
His moral authority.
And here, gradually,
In the words of this master
Of the interview,
We begin to detect
The artistic position
Which we so oppose.
"I, you know, just
Slapped together this
Thing.
I was interested
In the human aspect.
As for ideas
And theories
That's not my bag."
…

Of course, many artists
Take this stand.
They don't interest us at all.
But Lanzmann, on the one hand,
Enjoys this status
As an artist who works with
Emotions, memories,
His own and other people's
Experiences, that is, more with
Emotions than with documents.
On the other hand, he knew
Full well that his film
Would be received
As a political proclamation,
That it would quickly occupy the heart
Of intellectual and socio-
Political debates.
To work on people's feelings,
As an artist, while at the same time
Refusing to engage in rational
Explanations, of the sort
Demanded of intellectuals – really
This is the same stuff as using the
"Incomprehensibility" of Hitler
Or the destruction of the Jews
As a form of political argument –
And this is the shameful
Hypocrisy of our friend Lanzmann.

How to save himself
From this disgrace
The old man Lanzmann
Does not know.
But we know, and we'll tell:
You need to speak about Israel
You need to speak about Israel
In this is the key to immortality
This is the burning wound
And it is Lanzmann who understands this
He knows that politics is the wound
On the body of history.
An unnecessary, unwanted wound
That will not heal.

To refuse to forget politics
To refuse to tear Israel
From one's heart –
Because politics is
Always here,
And Palestine is a bloody wound that says:
Politics is
Always here.
You can't hide from it
At the supermarket,
You can't run from it
With beautiful words.
And old man Lanzmann
Understands this,
He knows that
Politics is the wound
On the body of history.
In its inability to process its own
Information,
A rejection of politics
Leads to senility.

(Only later would I find
This passage
In an interview Lanzmann gave
To *Der Spiegel*:

Spiegel: You write
That the Israeli military doctor
Who gave you a check-up
Before you flew in a fighter plane
Said you could live
Until a hundred and twenty.
Are you worried about
Death right now,
At your age?

Lanzmann: I have no age.
I constantly think
Of death, including
My own.
At the same time
This remains totally
Unreal. As I said

Earlier, only life
Has any meaning.
...

"Does the term
The 'Holocaust Industry'
Mean anything to you?"

"I don't want
To talk
About Israel.
I repeat:
You are thinking
In abstract
Categories."

"Yes, but your film
Became the center
Of intellectual
Debate –
About the uniqueness
Of the Holocaust,
About the supposed
Anti-Semitism
Of the Poles. Many
Thought that your movie
Made the Poles out
To be
Anti-Semites."

"Israel exists
Under impossible
Pressure.
Its army must be judged
According to different measures.
The Israeli Merkava tank
Was created
In impossible conditions.
Israeli tank officers
Love their Merkavas,
They are obliged
To have them always
At the ready.
And you, instead of

Building up
Abstract
Theories,
Should try harder
To create artistic works ...
An artist has his own
Way of seeing."

And so on.

The director is tired.
It's time for a rest.
"Communists? I know your path.
First, revolution; then firing squads."

A warning from the attaché –
Our time
Is almost up.
This will be
Our last question
And our judgment of the gray
Old man
Will be simple.

He has just one moment left
To die young.

But what did the fog of those eyes
Communicate?
Vague sentence fragments,
A dry, unpleasant refusal?

...

"Hang in there, boys.
Be strong just one more time.

Communists never surrender."

Translated from Russian by Keith Gessen and Michael Robbins.

Miklavž Komelj

Partisan Art Revisited

The question that interests the Ljubljana-based poet, art historian, and cultural theorist Miklavž Komelj is how to produce a new field of the possible out of the confrontation with the impossible. To this end, he examines historical turning points that set new coordinates for thinking about art. One such turning point is found in the revolutionary struggle that emerged with the anti-Fascist partisan resistance in Yugoslavia during World War II. In the present essay, Komelj revisits ideas from his comprehensive study *How to Think Partisan Art?* (published in Slovene in 2009), discussing as well changes in attitudes about the partisan movement that have appeared in Slovenia since his monograph was published.

One of the most profoundly moving artefacts from the Yugoslav partisan movement of World War II is a cyclostyle booklet of poems by the Slovene partisan poet Karel Destovnik – Kajuh,[1] produced by the cultural group of the 14th Division of the partisan National Liberation Army. Printed in an edition of only thirty-eight copies (of which, probably, only two are preserved), the booklet was produced in a provisional shelter in a snowstorm during the German offensive of November 1943. The poet dictated his poems by heart to dancer Marta Paulin – Brina (fig. 1),[2] who did the typing. The blizzard was penetrating the shelter and the paper was wet with snowflakes during the printing. As a result, the print is blurred and the pages hard to read; in many places the text is almost illegible (figs. 2–3). Reading this beautiful booklet, we have to read this unreadability: the very erasure of the text inscribes something onto the pages that must be read as carefully as the text itself. Equal attention must be given to both the human words and the snowflakes, which have written themselves onto the pages as something most fragile but also most brutal – the inscription of the impossible material conditions of production.

This fragile partisan booklet can be seen as a kind of symbol in my re-examination of certain theses from my book *Kako misliti partizansko umetnost?* (*How to Think Partisan Art?*), which was published in 2009.[3] In the common view, partisan art has generally been viewed as one-dimensional, as poster-like propaganda, a formulative simplification of art conditioned by the need to subordinate art to politics for the practical purposes of armed struggle. But a closer examination of the materials convinced me that even in cases where such simplifying efforts were manifested on the declarative level, we cannot accept any sort of simplification in our reading. In order to truly grasp the internal tensions and complexity of this art, we must trace certain very subtle nuances, like the inscriptions of the snowflakes in Kajuh's booklet. My extensive study of the concrete formulations of partisan art from Yugoslavia, and especially from Slovenia, revealed many manifestations of this art as something subtle, fragile, and

---

1   Karel Destovnik – Kajuh (1922–1944) is regarded in Slovenia as the prototypical partisan poet. Nevertheless, almost all his partisan poems were written before he actually joined the partisans in 1943. He died during the 14th Division's march to Styria, an almost "suicidal" war operation. He was posthumously awarded the Order of National Hero.
    (Here we follow the common practice in Yugoslavia and its successor states of placing partisan *noms de guerre*, such as "Kajuh", after a dash; we make an exception, however, for Josip Broz, whose partisan name "Tito" is now usually treated as a single name in English or merged with his birth name. – *Editors' note*.)
2   Marta Paulin – Brina (1911–2002) performed experimental contemporary dance among the partisans (see fig. 1); she once very beautifully described what she felt during these performances in nature, that she found new forms of expression and developed a new feeling for her body, as if her arms were reaching past the treetops. She said that her dance experiments were attempts to articulate her thoughts through her body. Sadly, during the march of the 14th Division, her feet became frostbitten and she was never able to dance again. After the war, she became a renowned dance teacher; she also created choreographies and published dance criticism.
3   Miklavž Komelj, *Kako misliti partizansko umetnost?*, Založba */cf.*, Ljubljana, 2009.

fugitive, full of nuances and silences. It is very characteristic that Matej Bor,[4] who in 1942 wrote the first book of partisan poetry in Yugoslavia and titled it *Previharimo viharje* (*Let's Outstorm the Storms*)[5] – which might be read as an ecstatic excess of combative revolutionary pathos – later reproached his critics by saying that in the midst of the storms they were unable to hear his silence.[6] And what is more, it was this subtle formulative level of art that often allowed the partisans to address the most brutal inner tensions of their time. As with the Kajuh booklet, we are confronted with the specific mode of existence of an art that requires us to invent new ways of reading it.

The partisan movement in Yugoslavia emerged in response to the aggression of Germany, Italy, and Hungary after Yugoslavia's withdrawal from the pact of accession to the Axis Powers in April 1941. The army of the Kingdom of Yugoslavia was quickly defeated and the occupying powers rearranged the political map of the region. The anti-fascist forces began organizing under the guidance of the Communist Party of Yugoslavia, led by Josip Broz Tito, in a movement that has inscribed itself onto some of the most heroic pages in the history of the European resistance.[7] Nevertheless, this movement was not limited to mere resistance; it grew into a full-scale revolution that created the basis for the socialist transformation of the country after the war. The Yugoslav partisans were fighting not only against foreign occupation but also against (real or imagined) fascists and collaborationists within the Yugoslav nations themselves; they called these enemies "national traitors" or the "White Guard", and the conflict assumed some of the most brutal elements of civil war.

To establish their ideological position, the partisans faced a complicated task: they had to reinvent everything they were defending; their concept of national liberation, for example, presupposed a completely new definition of nation, one based on the class concept of the "working people". In *Slovenska revolucija* (*The Slovene Revolution*), the bulletin published by the Christian Group in the Liberation Front (the name of the Slovene partisan movement),[8] we read: "The Slovene people's forces are creating

---

4   Matej Bor (born Vladimir Pavšič, 1913-1993) expressed his wish to be "the court poet / of Her Majesty Revolution" (*Let's Outstorm the Storms* – see following note). Besides being a poet, he was also a playwright, novelist, and translator of Shakespeare.
5   Matej Bor, *Previharimo viharje*, Glavno poveljstvo slovenskih partizanskih čet (Chief Command of the Slovene Partisan Units), 1942.
6   Matej Bor, "Iz avtobiografije", unpublished typescript, National and University Library archives, Ljubljana, p. 121.
7   Not even the last surviving witness from Hitler's bunker could write his memoirs about the war's final stages without mentioning the "hopeless battle against Tito's partisans" in the Balkans. See Bernd Freytag von Loringhoven, *In the Bunker with Hitler: The Last Witness Speaks*, written with François d'Alançon, Phoenix, London, 2007, p. 118.
8   Unlike other parts of Yugoslavia, where the partisan movement was directly under Communist Party control, in Slovenia the anti-fascist forces formed a kind of coalition, known as the Liberation Front (*Osvobodilna fronta*). One of the founding groups was

a new Slovene nation."[9] The leader of the Christian group, the poet and thinker Edvard Kocbek,[10] contributed a formulation to the Liberation Front programme about the "transformation of the national character" as one of the aims of the struggle. Here it is worth noting that the emblem of the Slovene Christian Group consisted of a cross and a sickle, which were linked visually in a way that resembled the Communist hammer and sickle – a very unorthodox symbol, indeed, from both the Communist and the Christian points of view. Even when they tried to achieve a kind of "orthodoxy", the basic position of the Yugoslav partisans was, in a way, "heretical".

The first partisan detachments were formed right after Germany invaded the Soviet Union and the symbolic indebtedness of the Yugoslav partisans to the latter was enormous; one Slovene song in its original version celebrated the future "Soviet" Slovenia and many partisans died with Stalin's name on their lips. Ironically, however, the revolutionary dimension of the partisan struggle meant, in practice, disobedience to the Soviet demand for a much more moderate ideological expression and even for reconciliation with the government-in-exile of the Kingdom in Yugoslavia. It is not surprising, then, that the Cominform resolution that attacked "Tito's Yugoslavia" in 1948 reproached the Yugoslav leadership for having always been essentially "Trotskyites".

The situation of the Yugoslav partisans was unique on the international level. After the Yugoslav king and his government fled the country in 1941, the partisans declared that Yugoslavia now in pieces, but they still managed to create a new federal Yugoslav state, one that emerged from the revolutionary process itself: in 1943, the Anti-Fascist Council of People's Liberation of Yugoslavia – known by its Serbo-Croatian acronym AVNOJ – established itself as the first revolutionary government, with Tito as leader, who now assumed the title Marshal. Nevertheless, not long before the end of the war a temporary compromise was reached with representatives of the kingdom that facilitated a legal transfer of authority; in this way, they imposed the conditions of the new revolutionary power

---

made up of "cultural workers". The Liberation Front proclaimed itself as the only legitimate power in Slovenia and branded all those who opposed it as "national traitors".

9   *Slovenska revolucija: Glasilo krščanske skupine v Osvobodilni fronti*, no. 1, July 20, 1942, p. 3.

10 Edvard Kocbek (1904–1981) declared his intention to reconcile Marxism and Christianity, actuality and the cosmos, revolutionary man and the man of sainthood, the rings of Ptolemy and the rings of Galileo. After 1943, tensions between his Christian Group and the Communists came to surface; that same year, he became minister of popular education in the first revolutionary government of Yugoslavia (the Anti-Fascist Council of the People's Liberation of Yugoslavia, known by its Serbo-Croatian acronym AVNOJ). After the war, from the early 1950s on, he had the ambiguous status of semi-dissident. Although one of Slovenia's most important poets, he published no poems when he was a partisan. It was only later that he developed drafts of poems he had made during the war; Boris Paternu calls these works "non-canonical partisan poetry". His war diaries are one of the most important sources for understanding the spiritual dimension of the partisan movement. In what was probably his last poem he wrote: "Liberty is the terrible liberty of Nothing."

on the former state's representatives. In such a complicated situation, the symbolic dimension of the struggle became at least as important as the physical weapons. The very word "partisan" acquired a strong symbolic charge with a completely new meaning, one that cannot be reduced to the technical term for guerrilla fighter; it became the name of a new revolutionary subjectivity. The partisan units in Yugoslavia represented the initial stage of a popular uprising that grew during the war into a regular army with various divisions and corps – the army of the newly established state. Nevertheless, the word "partisan" remained an effective term for designating the transformative dimension of the struggle: a *partisan* was the prototype for a "new human being" engaged in the building of "the new world", and this obliged him or her to be creative in a variety of fields; it was even said sometimes that poetry-writing was one of the distinguishing features of the true partisan. In a parody of the song "Lili Marleen" that was sung in the Slovene partisan marionette theatre (with a beautiful, long-legged marionette ballerina dancing to the music) (fig. 4), the partisans mocked Nietzsche's *Übermensch*, but when I was researching partisan publications, I came across a demand that the partisan must be a "Superhuman".[11]

In this atmosphere, art was ascribed enormous importance. It was considered a crucial component in the field of culture, which was of such importance for the partisan struggle that on occasion the partisans even spoke of "cultural revolution"[12] as indispensable for achieving the social revolution. Nevertheless, despite the enormous role of art in the field of culture (which was remarkably well organized, especially in Slovenia), there was also an awareness that art could not be subsumed under culture. Art was seen, in its very essence, as related to the mode of existence of the revolutionary struggle itself, perhaps in the sense of Lenin's idea that insurrection must be treated as an art.[13] This is one way to read one of Kajuh's most ecstatic poems, "Preko smrti stopamo v svobodo" ("Through Death We Enter Freedom"), in which the collective "we" of the participants in the revolutionary movement becomes "we modern Raphaels".[14] Here it is not art as an autonomous field of creativity, but the struggle as such that gives the partisans such an epithet. In Kajuh's poem, the struggle

---

11 As of this writing, I have not been able to find again the specific source for this demand and am quoting from memory (I believe it was expressed in an article by the partisan Dušan Hreščak, who was himself later executed by partisans). At their most extreme, the aspirations of the partisans even extended to the realm of ecstatic mysticism, as we find in words Kocbek spoke at the funeral of the national hero Ivo Lola Ribar, in the presence of Marshal Tito: "We are a force that strives to overcome the death itself. We are a force that assails eternity itself." (Edvard Kocbek, *Osvobodilni spisi II*, ed. Peter Kovačič-Peršin, Društvo 2000, Ljubljana, 1993, p. 10).

12 Matej Bor wrote an unpublished brochure with this title.

13 V. I. Lenin, "Marxism and Insurrection", *Collected Works*, Progress Publishers, Moscow, vol. 26, 1972, pp. 22–27, published online at https://www.marxists.org/archive/lenin/works/1917/sep/13.htm (accessed July 10, 2016).

14 Karel Destovnik – Kajuh, *Zbrano delo*, ed. Emil Cesar, Borec, Ljubljana, 1971, p. 303.

is seen as the creation of "bloody canvases" that will be exhibited in the "pavilion of the New Times"; at the same time, the poem stages a kind of "theatre of cruelty". For the partisans, art was never merely part of the "superstructure"; it was related to the very core of their struggle.[15]

In Kajuh's poem, art with its specific way of existing becomes a paradigm for grasping the essence of the struggle itself, but at the same time this process questions the boundaries of art: in order to think partisan art, we must constantly go beyond the limits of art as some pre-established field of creativity. In partisan documents, we even find formulations about how the revolutionary struggle surpasses art by being the realization of its highest tensions more completely than any work of art. Perhaps the most ecstatic articulation of such a stance are the words the poet Ivan Goran Kovačić[16] addressed to fighters at the partisan academy held in honour of the poet Vladimir Nazor[17] in Bihać, in Bosnia and Herzegovina, in 1943.[18]

The fundamental connection between art's specific way of existing and that of the revolution can be seen in the way both were presented as breaking through their own impossibility.[19] That is to say, the essence of

15 Significantly, some partisan brigades were named after poets. It is also emblematic that in the very first report we have from a partisan camp, written by Matej Bor, we meet a commander in the snow-covered forest who says that "contemporary" art should be a synthesis between the actual and the cosmic. See "In a Partisan Camp", *Political Practices of (Post-)Yugoslav Art*, ed. Zorana Dojić and Jelena Vesić, Prelom kolektiv, Belgrade, 2010, pp. 44–49.

16 Ivan Goran Kovačić (1913–1943) wrote one of the masterworks of partisan poetry, the poem "Jama" ("The Pit"), about a massacre of partisans by the Ustaša, the Croatian fascist militia. Kovačić himself was killed by Chetniks, Serbian nationalist units who were initially a resistance movement serving the Yugoslav government-in-exile but who later collaborated with the Germans. After the war, Paul Éluard wrote the poem "The Tomb of Ivan Goran Kovačić".

17 As a celebrated Croatian poet, Vladimir Nazor (1876–1949) enjoyed a special status among the partisans. His partisan poems in praise of Tito are very well known, but he also published a poem (censored in post-war editions of his poetry) dedicated to the Renaissance poet Lodovico Ariosto where he says that it is not Tito, but the goddess Avantura (Adventure) who guides him through the forest, and not the Idea, but Angelica who he seeks among the pines. And then: "Messer Lodovico with an ambiguous expression / on your lips, I am not afraid of your smile" (Vladimir Nazor, *Pjesme partizanke (1943)*, Zemaljski odbor USAOJ, [1944], pp. 42–43).

18 "With your struggle … poetry came to life, making poetry has become a reality, embodied every single moment in its most sophisticated nuances, words and deeds. The dreamt brotherhood, the dreamt equality, justice, goodness, the highest meaning of human life has been transformed from here and now, right before us, transformed into reality … I stand in trepidation with the desire to artistically encompass this reality in all its beauty, a trepidation similar to what I would feel if someone told me to grab the shining sunny beams and wave them like golden swords of justice and freedom." Quoted (in English translation by Jelena Bajić) in Miklavž Komelj, "Partisan Art Obliquely", in *Art as Resistance to Fascism*, ed. Marija Vasiljević, Museum of Yugoslav History, Belgrade, 2015, p. 27, n. 14.

19 This internal tension can already be detected in the first partisan poem in Slovenia, "Pojte za menoj!" ("Sing After Me!"), written by the most celebrated Slovene poet of the day, Oton Župančič (1878–1949), who, however, never joined the partisans. In the poem, published anonymously in 1941 under the non-name "Neznani" ("The Unknown

both the partisan movement and partisan art was often conceptualized by the partisans as a breaking through impossibility, as something impossible turned possible. It was as if the title of the famous pre-war almanac of the Belgrade Surrealists *Nemoguće / L'impossible* (*The Impossible*, 1930) was being brought into action.

One of the most surprising "artistic" components of the Yugoslav partisan revolution – its "subterranean" connection with the pre-war surrealist revolution[20] – cannot be grasped within the scope of the art field itself; to understand it, we must examine how art transcended itself. The very fact that the brilliant and multifaceted intellectual and poet Koča Popović[21] – who with Marko Ristić[22] was a key theorist of the Belgrade surrealist group in the early 1930s (together they published the philosophical treatise *Outline for a Phenomenology of the Irrational*[23]) – became one of the military leaders of the partisan movement demonstrates the unique position of the Yugoslav surrealists. While the international surrealist movement declared itself inseparable from the social revolution, it was only in Yugoslavia that any surrealists played an active role in such a revolution.[24] But this engagement occurred through a rupture; Popović had made his decision as early as the 1930s: "It makes no sense to scribble some half-understandable poems; I must become active."[25] Consequently, he joined the organized Communist movement and the revolutionary struggle. In 1971, however, shortly before renouncing all political leadership positions,

        One"), someone demands that the poet write a poem "for today's use". But to perform such a task, the poet must face his own impossibility of singing; he regains his voice only when he has positioned himself outside the symbolic, identifying with the howling wolf. The whole poem can be seen as a kind of regression; it even reminds us of the *berserkers* in the Scandinavian Odin cult. The ambiguity between the "avant-garde" and regressive impulses is characteristic of many articulations of partisan art.

20 I discuss this topic extensively in my book *Jugoslovanski nadrealisti danes in tukaj*, Moderna galerija, Ljubljana, 2015 (in Slovene).
21 Koča Popović (1908–1992) was interested in all fields of human knowledge, from the theory of relativity to psychoanalysis. After fighting in the Spanish Civil War, he became the commander of the legendary First Proletarian Brigade in the partisan army in 1941 and went on, after liberation, to become Chief of the General Staff of the Yugoslav People's Army. From 1953 to 1956, he served as the Yugoslav minister of foreign affairs.
22 Marko Ristić (1902–1982) was a leading figure in Yugoslav surrealism (his masterwork *Bez mere* [*Without Measure*, 1928] is superb). Ristić was a very subtle poet and brilliant thinker and had many international connections. Before the war, Tito accused him of Trotskyism. Although he never joined the partisans, in 1945 Tito appointed him as the Yugoslav ambassador to Paris.
23 Koča Popović and Marko Ristić, *Nacrt za jednu fenomenologiju iracionalnog*, Nadrealistička izdanja, Belgrade, 1931.
24 René Char, of course, also led a unit in the French Resistance; the difference is that the partisans in Yugoslavia were engaged in full-scale revolution.
25 Aleksandar Nenadović, *Razgovori s Kočom*, 2nd rev. ed., Delo, Ljubljana, and Globus, Zagreb, 1989, p. 13.

he exclaimed to an astonished journalist who had received no answers to his interview questions: "Don't you understand? I'm a surrealist!"[26]

In 1932, at the height of political tensions within the surrealist movement, after the final break between André Breton and Louis Aragon, part of the Belgrade surrealist group (including Oskar Davičo,[27] who would also become a partisan) proposed a radical "third solution" to the alternative "surrealism or Communism?": they declared the self-abolition of the group in the name of the paradoxical inner logic of surrealism itself and for the sake of an *obsession* with the social.[28] The very act of self-abolition, then, was underscored as a paradoxical way of remaining surrealists; what seemed to be the end of the surrealist movement in fact became a never-ending "subterranean" current.

In his partisan diaries, Koča Popović criticized some of his own surrealist ideas, such as those about suicide,[29] but even so, for him the partisan experience was directly connected to some of the central concerns of his earlier surrealist writings.

One of grand themes of the Yugoslav surrealists was the question of "living the unliveable". In his answer to a surrealist survey on humour and morality,[30] Popović put forward the argument that humour was unliveable, that it belonged to the realm of death, which is incompatible with the realm of morality and action, which belongs to life; in the realm of death, humour has the same value as morality in the realm of life. Popović thus distinguished between action and humour, seemingly abandoning humour in the name of action. But during the war, it was the revolutionary action itself that required him to live the unliveable, to be alive in the realm of death. Significantly, in his private partisan humour, Popović used the same example he had cited in his theoretical discussion of humour and its connection with death and the ethics of the unliveable, namely, the fact that before going to war the Japanese sign themselves as "the dead"; Popović, with partisan humour, referred to himself as "the deceased Koča".[31]

26   Koča Popović, *Nadrealizam i postnadrealizam*, Prosveta, Belgrade, 1985, p. 185.
27   Oskar Davičo (1909-1989) was one of the greatest Serbian poets and novelists; among the surrealists, he represented the tendencies toward extreme radicalism.
28   See [Oskar] Davičo, [Đorđe] Kostić, and [Dušan] Matić, *Položaj nadrealizma u društvenom procesu*, Narodna štamparija, Belgrade, 1932.
29   Koča Popović, *Beleške uz ratovanje (dnevnik, beleške, dokumenti)*, Beogradski izdavačko-grafički zavod, Belgrade, 1988, pp. 123-125.
30   Koča Popović, "Da li je humor moralan stav?", *Nadrealizam danas i ovde*, vol. 1, no. 1, June 1930, Nadrealistička izdanja, Belgrade, pp. 17-19.
31   See Nenadović, *Razgovori s Kočom*, pp. 80-81. Speaking as if already dead was a frequent theme in partisan poetry. What are probably Kajuh's most famous lines (in the poem "Materi padlega partizana" ["To the Mother of a Fallen Partisan"]) are spoken by a fallen partisan who exclaims to his mother that he would like to die again for the cause for which he died. But another version of these lines (published, among other places, in the cyclostyle booklet of 1943) is even more radical: the partisan says that, for the cause for which he died, it was *too little* merely to die. This is yet another example of the unbearable inner tension and astonishing openness to the impossible in partisan art. See

In fact, the conceptualization of subjectivity proposed by the Yugoslav surrealists before the war can help us grasp certain features of the specific partisan revolutionary subjectivity (as reflected in numerous works of art that were far from any surrealist methodology) much better than, for example, some simplified doctrinaire Soviet-style articulation. For example, if we truly want to understand the contradictions of the new collective subjectivity of the "modern Raphaels", it is not enough to use standard disciplinary expressions about subordinating the individual to the collective – the new collective subjectivity was created rather from the notion that it was everyone's task to become more than themselves, to become greater-than-one in the process of multiplication through an internal rupture, an internal split within their own subjectivity. As we ponder this conception of an uncountable multitudinous subjectivity, certain formulations by the Yugoslav Surrealists can be of great assistance.

The meaning of Kajuh's phrase "the modern Raphaels" is, of course, multivalent; it designates the new collective subjectivity as a condensation of the "old" and the "new". It can also be read in relation to Karl Marx and Friedrich Engels's idea, in their book *German Ideology*, that in the communist society everyone who has a "Raphael" within themselves will be allowed to develop this aspect.[32] "The modern Raphaels" can also be understood in relation to the conviction that the specific nature of the partisan revolution has awakened the creative potential of the "popular masses". What is more, the intense inner tensions of art helped people orient themselves in a terrible, unliveable situation; they helped them confront a situation that even uneducated fighters perceived as a "break between two worlds" (to quote the title of a poem written by a partisan named Mimi), when the very coordinates of the symbolic reality had to be posited anew.[33]

The creativity of the "popular masses" was supported systematically by the partisan leadership; nevertheless, it emerged from an inner urgency that expressed itself in enormous quantities of artworks, especially poems, written by known and unknown authors, by famous poets and anonymous fighters alike.[34] This awakening appeared as a sudden realization

Komelj, *Kako misliti partizansko umetnost?*, p. 376.

32 Karl Marx and Friedrich Engels, "Saint Max", chap. 3 in *German Ideology* (1845–1846), Progress Publishers, Moscow, 1968; transcription available at https://www.marxists.org/archive/marx/works/1845/german-ideology/ch03l.htm (accessed October 11, 2016). See in particular the subsection III.2, "Organisation of Labour".

33 There were moments when everything seemed possible. Juš Kozak writes about how the partisans were able to convince a Catholic priest to bury a fallen partisan with his dog – also a fallen comrade (although he had in fact first belonged to the Gestapo) – with a church ceremony as if the dog was a human being. See Juš Kozak, "Mutasti so spregovorili", in *Slovenski zbornik 1945*, ed. Juš Kozak, Državna založba Slovenije, 1945, p. 542.

34 An extensive research project led by Boris Paternu collected some twelve thousand poems, in Slovenia alone, written in the years 1941–1945 and connected with the people's liberation struggle and revolution. A selection was presented in the four-volume anthology *Slovene Resistance Poetry: Slovensko pesništvo upora: 1941–1945*, ed. Boris Paternu

of Lautréamont's famous dictum, that poetry must be made by all. It was this dictum, so dear to the Yugoslav Surrealists as well, that I chose to put on the dust jacket of my book *How to Think Partisan Art?*

In my book, I was interested not only in the fact that this enormous surge of creativity did not fit into the already established art realm, but also in the way it set new coordinates for itself. This process cannot be grasped simply as the opposition of the "new" to the "old"; in these new conditions, even old works could assume unexpectedly new symbolic values. For example, in temporarily liberated Republic of Užice in Serbia in 1941,[35] the actors in the local theatre symbolically opposed the threat of German invasion by studying Goethe's play *Egmont*.[36]

My investigation was focused mainly on materials from Slovenia, which are especially rich in texts and drawings by anonymous fighters. Unlike some other parts of Yugoslavia, there was a very low rate of illiteracy in Slovenia, so while partisan units elsewhere were organizing basic classes for eradicating illiteracy, writing classes in Slovenia tended to support more advanced forms of writing; for example, one finds partisan manuals on metrics and poetic rhythm for "simple talents from among the people". As for partisan publishing efforts, Koča Popović praised the Slovene press in his war diary as the finest in all of Yugoslavia.[37] Especially rich materials from the liberated Slovene territory have been preserved from the last two years of the war, when the partisans organized creative opportunities for many different artists (poets, writers, composers, musicians, painters, sculptors, architects, actors, and others), who came mainly from Ljubljana. The newly established power structures on the liberated territory even included a department of the arts (it was led by Mile Klopčič,[38] a communist poet who once proclaimed in a communist newspaper that beauty itself is militant and revolutionary[39]). Autonomous art institutions were founded, such as the Slovene National Theatre on the Liberated Territory (*Slovensko narodno gledališče na osvobojenem ozemlju*) (fig. 5) and even a marionette theatre for children; art exhibitions were organized and bibliophile editions of collections of partisan linocuts were printed, while the partisan radio station also served as an important medium for the artistic programme. Important, too, was the self-organization

(with Marija Stanonik and Irena Novak Popov), Mladinska knjiga, Partizanska knjiga, and Znanstveni institut Filozofske fakultete, Ljubljana, and Dolenjska založba, Novo Mesto, 1987–1997.

35 The first liberated territory in Yugoslavia, in western Serbia, the Republic of Užice existed for a few months in 1941.

36 Classical works were an important part of the repertoire in partisan theatre: the Slovene National Theatre on the Liberated Territory, for example, staged Molière's *Le Malade Imaginaire* with splendid baroque-style costumes made out of parachute silk (see fig. 5).

37 Popović, *Beleške uz ratovanje*, p. 213.

38 As a partisan, Mile Klopčič (1905–1984) also wrote the very popular short play *Mati* (*Mother*).

39 See Komelj, *Kako misliti partizansko umetnost?*, p. 509.

of artists from different fields – this led to an intense informal artistic life, which Vitomil Zupan described[40] as "the partisan bohème".[41] But at the same time, I was interested in juxtaposing such art manifestations with borderline cases such as the splendid illegal action that took place occupied Ljubljana in 1943, which, if we can trust Zdenka Kidrič's laudatory description,[42] the whole city was transformed into a kind of partisan theatre – in which even the occupiers with their panicked reactions played their parts.[43]

We need to consider the preserved works of art in conjunction with such borderline manifestations – and to consider both with the understanding that, for the partisans, the dimension of "not-yet-existing" was already inscribed on their present. In this sense, unrealized works of art were no less important than realized ones;[44] what is more, even the realized works were often consciously conceptualized as manifestations of something "not-yet-existing".[45]

It is this evasive dimension of partisan art that seems hardest to grasp.

In post-war Socialist Yugoslavia, partisan art became an object of pride; it formed a basic part of primary and secondary school education, was presented in numerous exhibitions, and so on. But such glorification could also block a deeper reception of this art. On the one hand, its celebration often prevented more serious analytical attempts, while on the other, it could lead to the feeling that partisan art was "boring". When in the late 1960s, for example, certain young artists wanted to oppose the generation of their fathers, they did so by mocking partisan poems.

With the bloody disintegration of Yugoslavia and the restoration of capitalism in the early 1990s, there was a complete turnaround in the public assessment of the partisan movement and, consequently, partisan art. From the new revisionist perspective, the partisan movement was seen as highly problematic and even criminal. In some parts of Yugoslavia, and especially in Croatia, even the post-war monuments to the partisan movement were systematically destroyed, including such masterpieces as

---

40   Vitomil Zupan (1914–1987), an extremely prolific novelist, playwright and poet, constantly attacked the taboos of society in his search for inner freedom. After 1948, he spent several years in prison, where he created an astonishingly large body of poetry.
41   See Jože Javoršek, *Radio Osvobodilna fronta*, Partizanska knjiga, Ljubljana, 1979, p. 276.
42   Zdenka Kidrič (1909–2008) led the Security and Intelligence Service of the Liberation Front.
43   Zdenka Kidrič, "A passage from an article 'Our Revenger'", in *Political Practices of (post-)Yugoslav Art*, p. 50 (see n. 15).
44   One paradigmatic example is Edvard Kocbek's reverie about his own partisan movie, which he describes in his partisan diary; see Edvard Kocbek, *Listina: Dnevniški zapiski od 3. maja do 2. decembra 1943*, 2nd ed., Slovenska matica, Ljubljana, 1982, pp. 515–516.
45   A paradigmatic work in this regard might be "Sutrašnja pesma" ("Tomorrow's Poem") by Radivoj Koparec (1919–1943); see Milan Bandić, *Cvet i steg: književnost narodnooslobodilačke borbe*, privately printed, Belgrade, 1975, p. 51.

Vojin Bakić's[46] giant abstract modernist *Monument to the Revolutionary Victory of the People of Slavonia* (1957–1968), in Kamenska, Croatia. On the other hand, even cases of an "affirmative" approach to the revolutionary past were often merely attempts to assimilate it to purely nationalist goals while erasing the transformative revolutionary dimension from the memory of the liberation struggle. At the time I was writing my book (2008–2009), it was almost considered taboo to openly and affirmatively discuss the revolutionary dimension of the partisan struggle. Nevertheless, my efforts toward a new evaluation of this dimension were not completely isolated. I should mention such groundbreaking texts as the essay "Symbolic Policy of Partisans",[47] by the Slovene theorist Rastko Močnik, and contributions by the Belgrade-based collective Prelom ("Break").[48]

The social developments of recent years have completely changed the situation. Seven years after the publication of my book, we can observe in certain circles, at least in Slovenia, both a revival of Marxism and renewed, and very intense, interest in the partisan movement. The new permanent exhibition of the national collection, titled *Continuities and Ruptures*, at the Moderna galerija in Ljubljana now includes a presentation of partisan art (which I curated) (fig. 6). Young people on the left are using such partisan paraphernalia as the red star, and the partisan movement itself has become an object of mass identification.

And yet, this revival has also brought new misunderstandings. The obsession with partisan iconography does not represent any serious questioning about the possible lessons of the partisans for our time; rather, it simplifies the present situation, transposing it into the terms of World War II, as if we are fighting in the same conflict today. And such attitudes can sometimes generate a shockingly stupid insensitivity. For example, the idealization in Slovenia of the partisans as people incapable of committing war crimes and atrocities means that most "leftists" who hold this affirmative view accept as normal and reasonable, and without any problematization, even such crimes as the mass slaughter of war prisoners from the collaborationist units (as well as many civilians) by the Yugoslav People's Army immediately after the war. But on the other side, those who are denouncing such monstrosities regularly end up in a total apology of collaborationism, denouncing the "Communists" as the only true occupiers, and so on.

---

46   Vojin Bakić (1915–1992), a pioneer of post-war modernist sculpture in Yugoslavia, created many monuments to the partisan movement.
47   Rastko Močnik, "Partizanska simbolna politika / Symbolic Policy of Partisans", in *Partizanski tisk / The Partisans in Print*, ed. Breda Škrjanec and Donovan Pavlinec, MGLC – International Centre of Graphic Arts and National Museum of Contemporary History, Ljubljana, 2004, pp. 20–40.
48   Branimir Stojanović, "Politika partizana", *Prelom*, no. 5, spring–summer 2003, pp. 48–50; and Ozren Pupovac, "Project Yugoslavia: The Dialectics of the Revolution", *Prelom*, no. 8, fall 2006, pp. 9–22; both articles are available online at http://www.prelomkolektiv.org (accessed July 11, 2016).

Today in Slovenia we see such bizarre situations as when one group of adults (including, perhaps, a renowned historian) dress up as partisans while others dress as Home Guardsmen (the *domobranci*, the Slovene collaborationist anti-partisan units who were trained by the Nazi SS) and perform their ceremonies like children in kindergarten, one group being killjoys to the other. I cannot stress enough my disgust for such cheap identifications. And what is worse, I'm horrified to think that some of the people playing out their cheap identification with the partisans might even consider my book a source of inspiration for them.

What irony! The basic theme of my book was precisely the problematization of identitary logic as such. Throughout the book, I tried to establish, not the logic of identification in relation to the partisan movement, but rather, to use the Brechtian term, a certain *Verfremdung*, or defamiliarization.[49] My aim in using this device was not to contest the greatness of the movement; on the contrary, my thesis is that only a radical *Verfremdung* can present its unbearable internal tensions. When we try to identify ourselves with the partisans, we become blind to exactly this dimension. What interested me in the partisan movement was, indeed, not something that would enable identification but rather what makes it impossible: total implacability, pure contradiction, unbearably heightened tensions. Only by reflecting on this dimension, we can approach the partisan movement's aim to "live the unliveable" and their confrontation with the impossible. And it was out of this dimension that partisan art emerged.

The Kajuh poem I mentioned earlier, "Through Death We Enter Freedom", which offered the paradigm of partisan revolutionary subjectivity as "modern Raphaels", was written in the most ambiguous situation possible: not at a moment of militant euphoria, but, on the contrary, at a time when Kajuh, who was part of the partisan intelligence service, was accused by his comrades of being a German spy. He barely managed to prove his innocence and avoid being shot by one of his comrades.[50] The poem, which was originally dedicated to the comrade who had come to interrogate and eventually kill him, articulated the new revolutionary subjectivity out of the unbearable inner contradiction. It is not by chance that, in this poem, the "bloody canvases" produced by the new collective revolutionary subject present this subject in a highly ambiguous position: the collective subject "we" gives its own skins to be used as canvases and, at

---

49 The *Verfremdung* technique was used by the partisans themselves; their poetry often tries to make their struggle visible in cosmic terms and across enormous temporal distances. They explicitly rejected the notion that they would be evaluated solely in a local context. Significantly, whenever someone tries to inscribe partisan art into one of the Yugoslav "national cultures", a great part of this production seems to be a regression from modern art to pre-modernity; but when we try to view it from a planetary perspective (the partisans insisted on planetary coordinates for their struggle for the "new world"), this work reveals itself as a condensation of the most extreme inner tensions of the 20th century.

50 See Emil Cesar, *Karel Destovnik Kajuh*, Društvo piscev zgodovine NOB Slovenije, 1993, pp. 127–128.

the same time, paints these canvases with its bloody actions. This position of being on both sides of the action is what distinguishes Kajuh's portrayal of bloody revolutionary struggle as a form of creating art from any "aestheticization of politics", if I may use Benjamin's (too often abused) term.[51]

The very essence of the partisan revolution can be seen as a contradiction of the most extreme sort. Long after the war, Vlatko Velebit,[52] who had symbolically obtained the rank of reservist general in the partisan army, declared himself to be a total anti-militarist who rejects armies as such.[53] These were truly extraordinary words for a person of such high military rank, but they were by no means at odds with the essential idea of the partisan struggle, which was meant to be nothing less than a "war against war".[54] Koča Popović, too, who after the liberation became the Chief of the General Staff of the Yugoslav People's Army, was described by the British military deputy F. W. Deakin as a military genius who hated war.[55] (Similarly, the Slovene painter France Mihelič, in a speech at the founding assembly of the Slovene Artistic Club on the Liberated Territory in 1944, tried to represent partisan art as essentially anti-militaristic.[56]) This basic contradiction was linked to many others: for example, the partisans declared their struggle as being both for establishing new Yugoslav borders and for "a world without borders". Such contradictions and strong tensions were constantly inscribing themselves into the formulations of partisan art: from Matej Bor's exclamation that you must suppress the love in your heart if you love the new world,[57] to articulations of the basic temporal paradox: the partisans were constantly referring to the future, but the future was supposed to already reside in their contemporaneity as the real presence of the not-yet-existing; in a way, this reference to the future in itself demanded of the partisans a kind of life without the future. On the level of art organization, in their attempts to create a wholly "new art", we find tensions between anti-institutional impulses and their founding of new art institutions.[58]

51 Images of explicit violence in Kajuh's war poetry are often directed not toward the enemy but toward the transformation of "our" (the reader's) subjectivity; for example, when Kajuh describes his verses metaphorically as bayonets (much like a well-known line by Mayakovsky), the bayonets are not intended to kill the enemy but to awaken a flame in the heart of the reader.
52 Vladimir (Vlatko) Velebit (1907–2004) was a Croatian lawyer, politician and diplomat.
53 Mira Šuvar, *Vladimir Velebit: Svjedok historije*, Razlog, Zagreb, 2001, p. 501.
54 Ironically, Franjo Tuđman (1922–1999), who in the 1990s would become the nationalist right-wing leader in Croatia, wrote a book with this title in the 1950s. Despite his later rightist views, Tuđman had been a partisan in World War II.
55 See Nenadović, *Razgovori s Kočom*, p. 100.
56 See Komelj, *Kako misliti partizansko umetnost?*, pp. 530–533. France Mihelič (1907–1998), who was one of Slovenia's most original 20th-century painters, created an important oeuvre of partisan linocuts.
57 Matej Bor, *Previharimo viharje* (1942), p. 5.
58 The partisans' attitudes could be extremely paradoxical toward the cultural heritage as well: Bogdan Osolnik, himself a partisan, told me the following anecdote about the

It is only by being aware of such contradictions that we can grasp the relationship between partisan art and the partisan movement as such. Of course, it was an art both *within* and *of* the movement. Still, it cannot be reduced simply to the service of the movement. Partisan art in its essence was not an accommodation to the given situation, however revolutionary might it be; rather, it was often the explicit expression of non-accommodation, reflecting itself as something that emerges *despite* the war. Words like "despite", "nevertheless", "and yet" echo as a refrain throughout partisan poetry. "And yet, I could not in my heart / smash this poem!"[59] – we are told in Kajuh's partisan love poem, which is written at a time, he says, when he should not be writing love poems but only howling like an animal. And yet, this love poem can be perceived as a directly revolutionary message far more than some sort of "agitprop" work. It was this emerging of art *despite everything*, despite the given situation, that connected partisan art most intensely with the internal tension of the revolutionary situation itself.

Awareness of these inner contradictions raises new questions about art and the political, beyond the recent and too often oversimplified understanding of "political art". In his 2004 essay, mentioned above, Rastko Močnik presents partisan art as a prototype of "political art", one that offers contemporary art a very difficult choice: "Contemporary art is political art, or else it is just aestheticizing kitsch."[60] But the question is: what is political? In partisan art, Močnik sees the presumed annihilation of the bourgeois autonomy of art as something liberating; he also declares his sympathies with certain practices that have usually been interpreted as demands for the direct subordination of art to the revolutionary struggle (such as the directive to painters to avoid still lifes, and also the so-called "partisan birch" position, namely, the demand by some propagandists that motifs such as trees be painted only in relation to attributes of the partisan struggle). As for me, I was trying in my book to elaborate a distinction between the political and politicization, as well as between the aesthetic and aestheticization. This distinction allowed me to discern in the partisans' problematizing of the relative autonomy of art in bourgeois society also articulations of a different, non-bourgeois, intrinsic autonomy of art as the specific way that art exists by making a new field of possibility from the very encounter with the impossible. I shifted my focus away from the declarative politicization of art (although partisan art was highly politicized) to the political impact of (self-)questioning the very (im)possibility of art as conceptualized within the partisan movement.

    national hero Vinko Paderšič – Batreja (1916–1942): after partisans devastated the medieval Hmeljnik Castle in Slovenia in a true orgy of destruction, Batreja rescued an original 1584 edition of the first Slovene grammar from the castle library and carried it with him as part of his equipment – as a symbol of what he was fighting for.
59 Kajuh, *Zbrano delo*, p. 212.
60 Močnik, "Partizanska simbolna politika / Symbolic Policy of Partisans", p. 39. In 2016, one is tempted to ask: what about political kitsch?

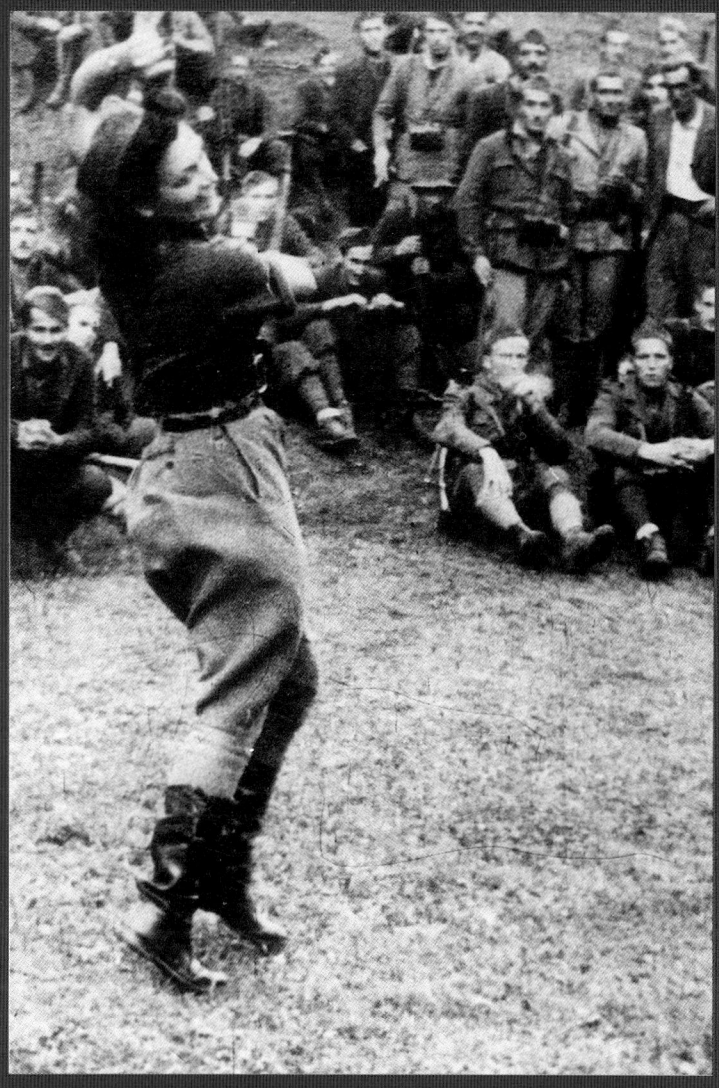

fig. 1

Dancer Marta Pavlin - Brina, a member of the cultural group of the 14th Division, performs at a partisan gathering after the oath-taking of the Rab Brigade on September 23, 1943.

Photo by Jože Petek. Courtesy of the National Museum of Contemporary History, Ljubljana.

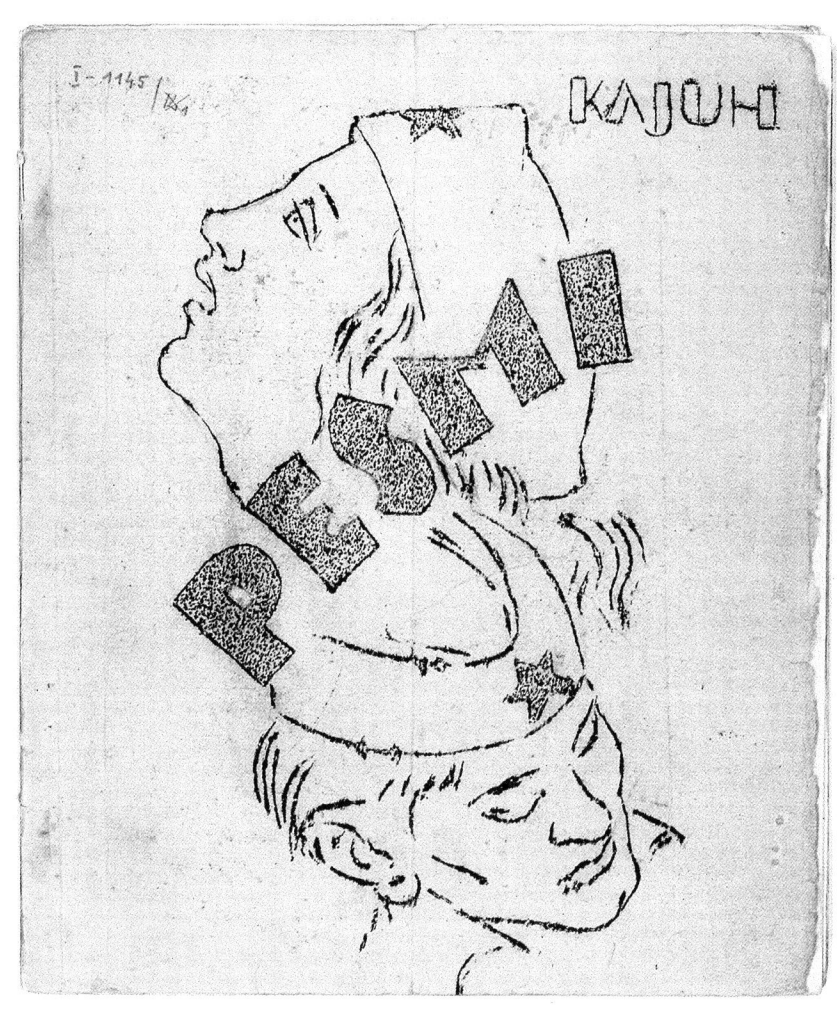

fig. 2

Karel Destovnik - Kajuh, *Pesmi* (*Poems*), cyclostyle booklet, cover, 1943.
Produced by the cultural group of the 14th Division.

Courtesy of the Archives of the Republic of Slovenia.

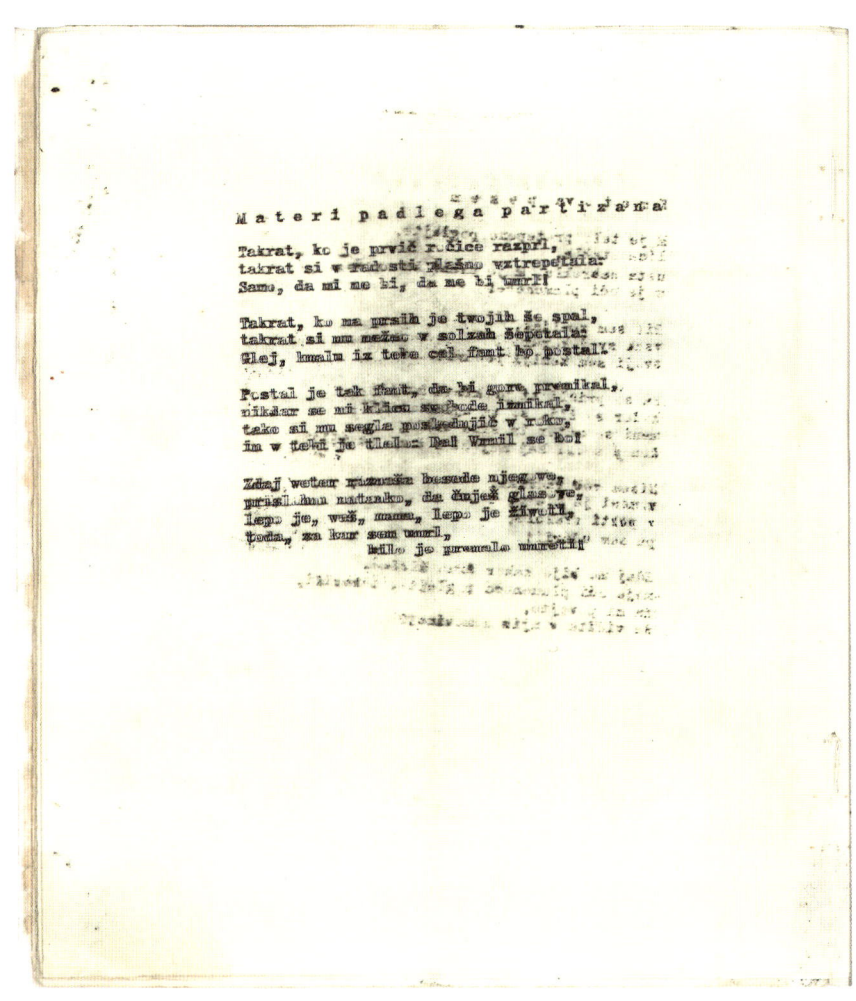

fig 3

Karel Destovnik – Kajuh, "To the Mother of a Fallen Partisan",
Pesmi (Poems), cyclostyle booklet, 1943.
Produced by the cultural group of the 14th Division.

Courtesy of the Archives of the Republic of Slovenia.

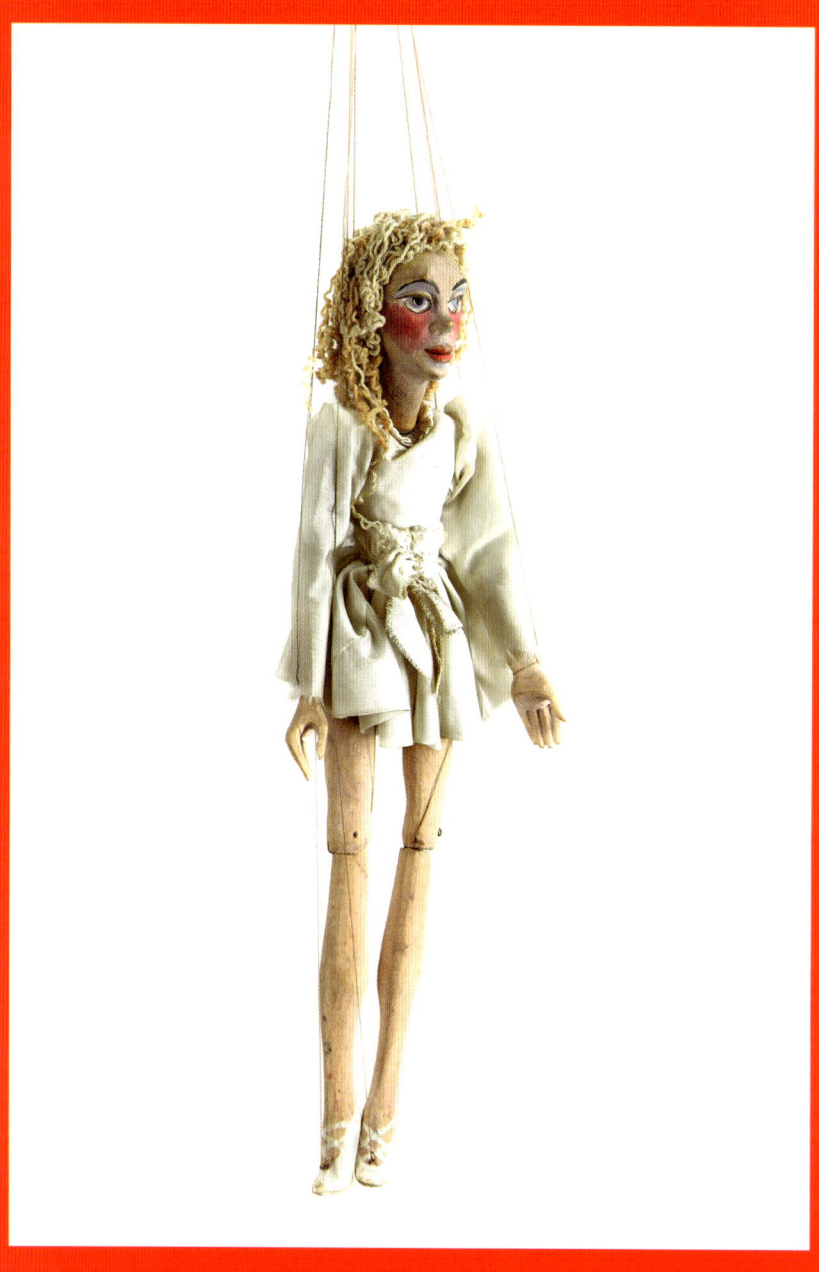

fig. 4

Lili Marlen puppet, Slovene partisan marionette theatre.

Photo by Sašo Kovačič. Courtesy of the National Museum of Contemporary History, Ljubljana.

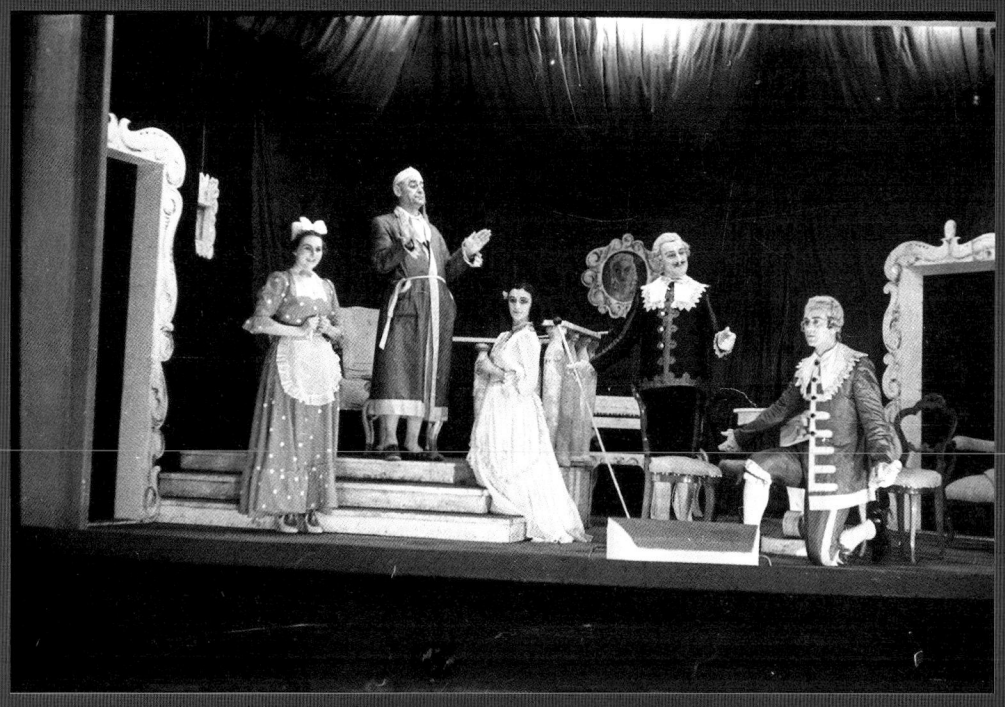

fig. 5

Molière's *Le Malade Imaginaire* staged by the Slovene National
Theatre on the Liberated Territory in Črnomelj in 1944.

*Photo by Alfred Kos. Courtesy of the Archive of the Theatre
and Film Studies Centre at the Academy of Theatre, Radio,
Film, and Television, University of Ljubljana.*

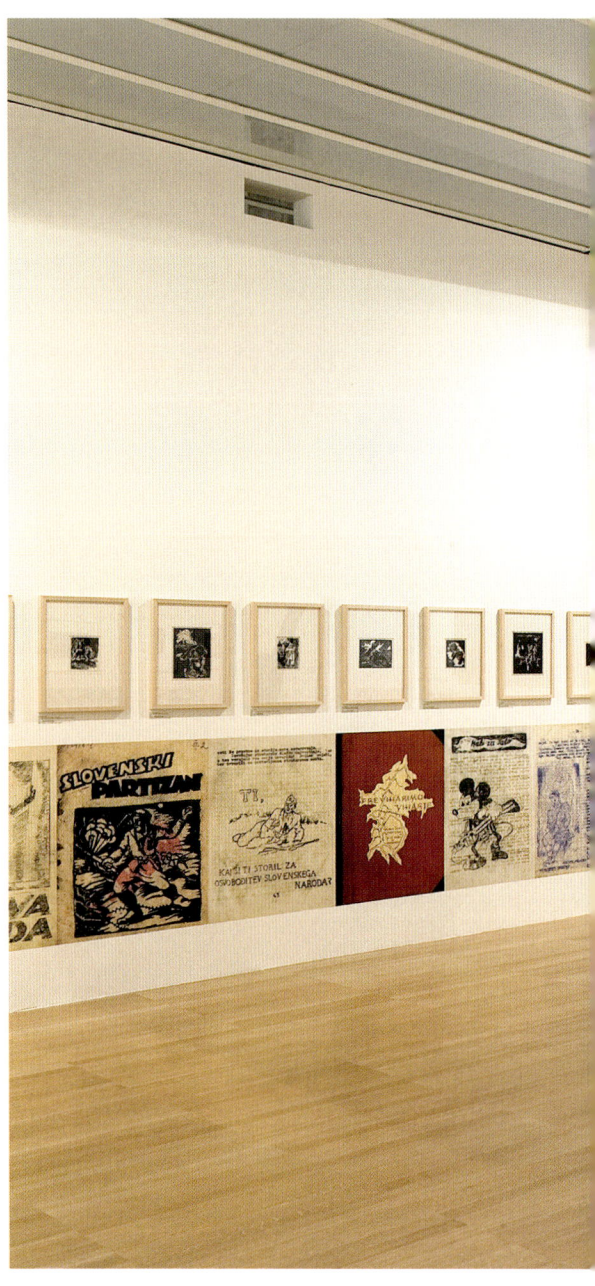

fig. 6

Partisan art installed in the permanent exhibition of the national collection of 20th century art, *Continuities and Ruptures*, Moderna galerija, Ljubljana.

Photo by Dejan Habicht. Courtesy of Moderna galerija.

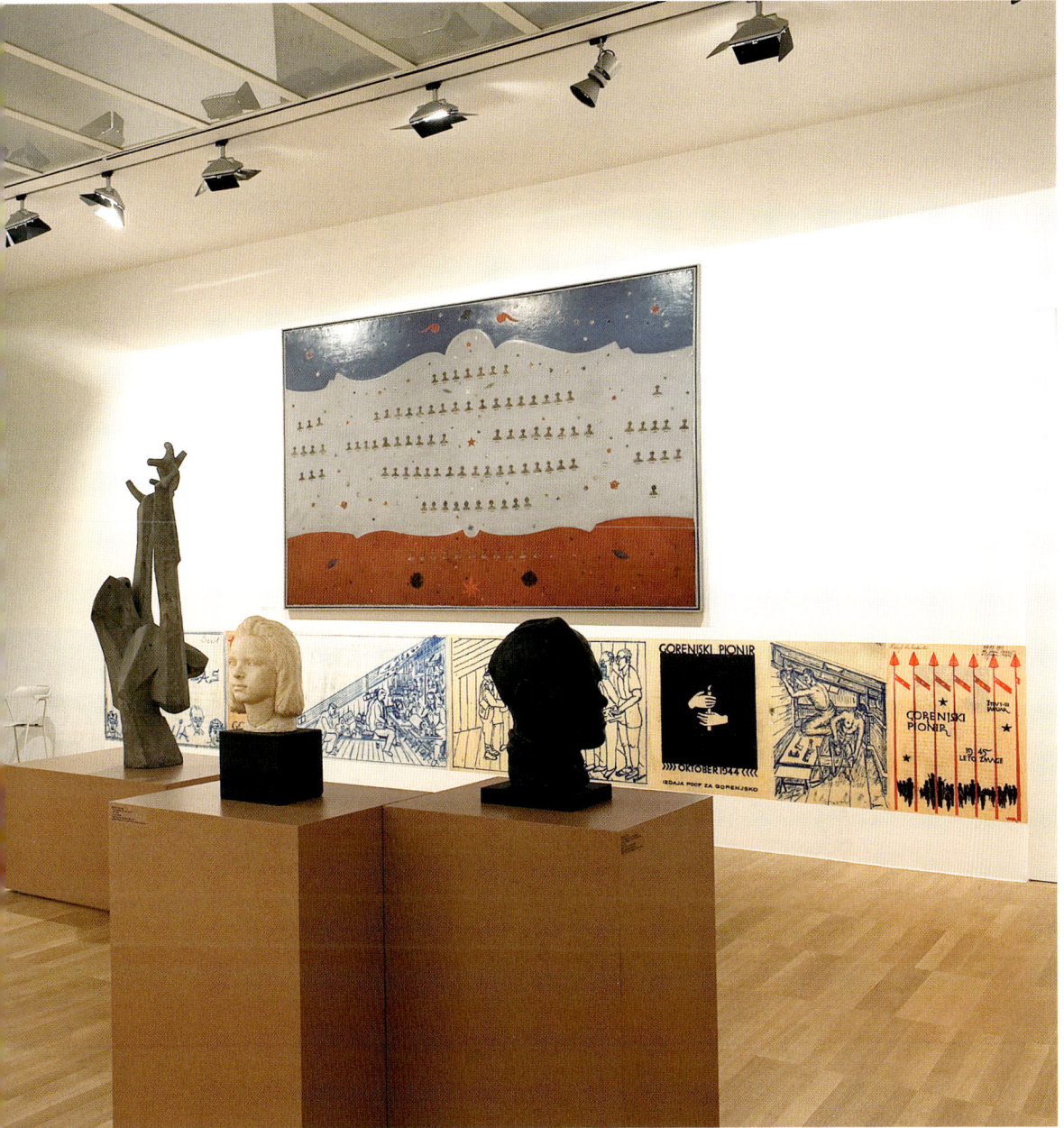

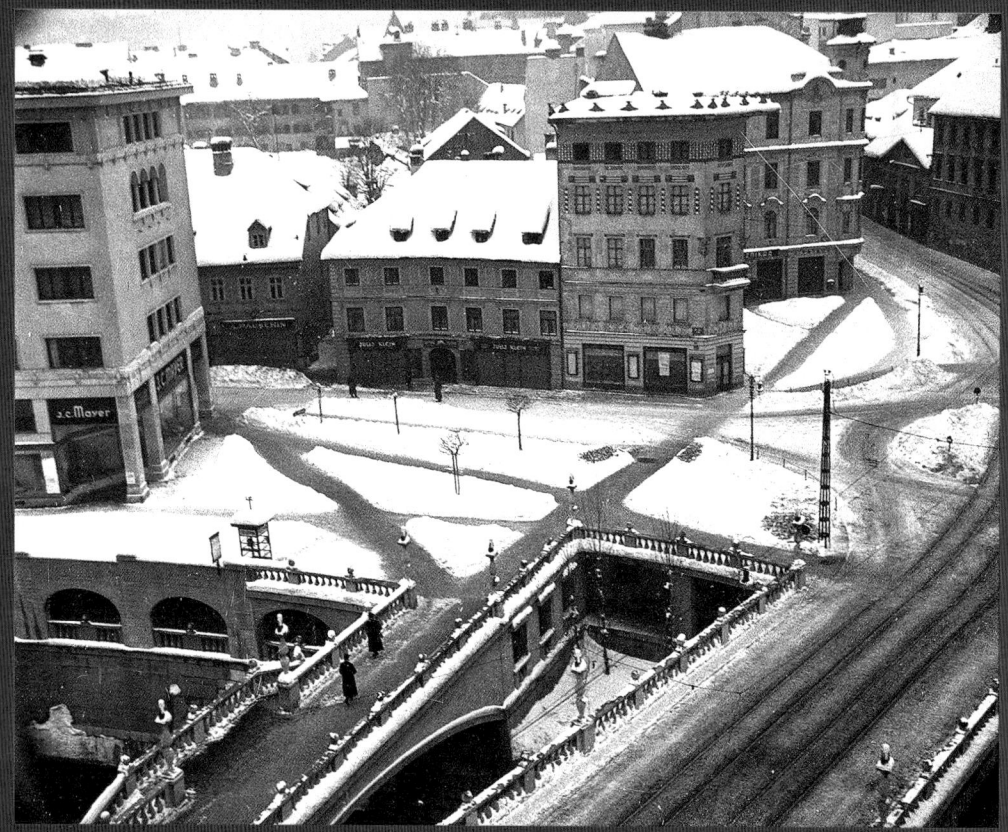

fig. 7

Two views of St. Mary's Square in Ljubljana (today's Prešeren Square; it bore the earlier name from 1876 to 1949). The photographs were taken at 4:45 p.m. on February 11, 1942, when the square was already completely empty. A daily curfew from 5:30 p.m. to 6:30 a.m. was in place for the entire Province of Ljubljana from February 7 to February 16, 1942. The empty streets were due to an administrative order issued by the occupying forces in response to the Liberation Front's "silent actions". According to the photographer, Jakob Prešeren, the order meant he had to take his photographs through rooftop windows or from behind front doors.

Photos by Jakob Prešeren. Courtesy of the National Museum of Contemporary History, Ljubljana.

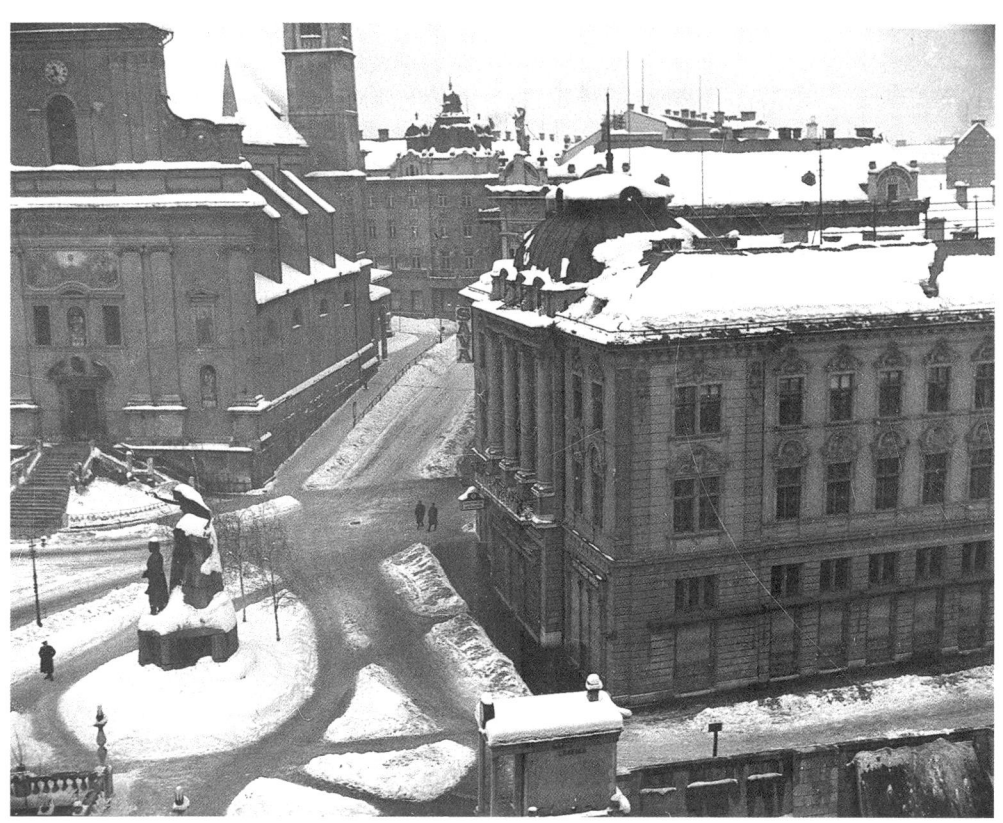

Partisan art could be seen as a politically committed art par excellence[61] – and yet *this was not enough*. The Argentinian poet Alejandra Pizarnik once said in an interview that a "political poem" was not only bad poetry but also bad politics.[62] We find an astonishingly similar statement by Boris Kidrič,[63] one of the leaders of the partisan revolution, in a discussion with the poet Božo Vodušek.[64] When Vodušek objected to applying propagandistic logic in art by arguing that if a play, for propaganda purposes, showed "our" side as good and the "enemy" as bad, it would be a bad play, Kidrič at once replied that it would "not only be artistically bad, it would also be politically bad".[65]

Such a statement does not need to be seen as explicitly revolutionary. Even Giuseppe Bottai,[66] the minister of public education in Fascist Italy, was well aware that "art which is directly controlled by the state, as an instrument of propaganda, not only results in illustration or documentation; but, owing to its lack of expression, loses all its efficacy as propaganda".[67] What is paradoxical in partisan art is that some of its formulations could even be seen as directly opposed to propaganda. Bor's *Let's Outstorm the Storms* is full of direct mobilizing exclamations, but we also encounter the kind of excesses that could seem appalling to the ordinary public with its pre-established values.[68] Bor's poetry was by no means seeking to

---

61 Nevertheless, in his unpublished autobiography Matej Bor wondered if *Let's Outstorm the Storms* really was an example of "committed poetry"; he preferred to consider the book "an explosion" (Bor, "Iz avtobiografije", p. 120). The difference between Bor's poetry and French "committed poetry" was noted by Marc Alyn in his introduction to Matej Bor, *La trace de nos ombres: poèmes*, trans. Marc Alyn and Victor Jelesnik, Seghers, Paris, 1966, pp. 7–8.
62 Alejandra Pizarnik, *Poesía completa*, Lumen, Barcelona, 2002, p. 308.
63 Boris Kidrič (1912–1953), was one of the central figures in the Slovene Liberation Front and a leader of the Yugoslav revolution. In 1945, he became prime minister in the first government of the People's Republic of Slovenia (a constituent republic of Socialist Yugoslavia), and in 1946, he became the Yugoslav minister of industry and the head of the Yugoslav Economic Council.
64 Božo Vodušek (1904–1978) was one of the most important Slovene poets. During the war, he tried to write a partisan play in verse in the solemn style of Greek tragedy.
65 See Komelj, *Kako misliti partizansko umetnost?*, p. 570.
66 Despite his Fascist convictions, Giuseppe Bottai (1895–1959) was a highly cultivated man who supported artistic experimentation and was openly opposed to "sterile conservatism". In 1942, as a result of his cultural policies, the National Gallery in Ljubljana received a donation from the Italian occupying administration in the form of a small collection of works by the best Italian painters of the time, such as Morandi, De Pisis, and others.
67 From Bottai's speech at the opening of the 1940 Venice Biennale, quoted in Simonetta Fraquelli, "All Roads Lead to Rome", in *Art and Power: Europe under the Dictators 1930–45*, ed. Dawn Ades et al., Thames and Hudson and the Hayward Gallery, London, 1995, p. 135.
68 For example, Bor exclaims that "red engineers" should place dynamite at the very foundations of the "old word" and asserts, in the spirit of internationalism, that even Arabs are to be found among the Slovene partisans. Significantly, in the last period of war, poems from *Let's Outstorm the Storms* were no longer being reprinted in partisan anthologies; they were apparently too "wild" for the cultural policy at the time.

persuade people by accommodating to their expectations; rather, it was the unsparing explosion of an "exceptional state of consciousness",[69] which was addressing the already transformed collective subjectivity.

Bor was well aware of this; in his text "In a Partisan Camp"[70], in 1941, he describes how, when he first read his poems to the partisan fighters, he was thinking of Mayakovsky's lines:

> I want to be understood by my country,
> but if I am not understood –
>   so what?
> I must pass by my homeland
>   off the side,
>   just like the slanting rain.[71]

The choice of these lines was significant. Mayakovsky's biographer Bengt Jangfeldt makes the following comment about them:

> Just as interesting as Mayakovsky's doubts about whether his poetry had any place in the new society is the fact that he later deleted these lines – on the advice of Osip [Brik], who thought that a poet "for whom the goal of his whole work, his life, is at any price to be heard and understood by his country" could not write in this way. Although Mayakovsky was very attached to these lines, he agreed to delete them. By doing this he also annulled the contrast between ambivalent feelings, which is so characteristic of his best poems.[72]

Bor didn't avoid this ambivalence; on the contrary, he reopened it, using Mayakovsky's deleted lines as the starting point for his self-questioning. In the same text, he designated the partisan fighters as the "new critics".[73] Criticism and self-criticism were understood as an irreducible component of the creative process itself. Not only did the partisans in the woods write poems; they even wrote poems about why they wrote poems.[74]

The entrance of the "popular masses" into the field of art was seen at the time as an enormous tectonic shift, but nevertheless it was not evaluated

---

69 Bor's formulation in his preface to the 1961 edition of *Let's Outstorm the Storms*; see Matej Bor, *Previharimo viharje*, Cankarjeva založba, Ljubljana, 1961, p. 5.

70 Bor, "In a Partisan Camp", p. 45.

71 The lines are quoted in Bengt Jangfeldt, *Mayakovsky: A Biography,* trans. Harry D. Watson, University of Chicago Press, Chicago and London, 2014, p. 343.

72 Ibid., pp. 343-344.

73 Bor, "In a Partisan Camp", p. 45.

74 One of the most poignant documents of partisan poetry was discovered in a German archive: these were German translations of poems found in the knapsack of the eighteen-year-old Slovene partisan Franc Pintarić – Švaba, who had been murdered. One of the poems was titled "Warum Lieder?" ("Why Poems?"). See *Slovensko pesništvo upora: 1941–1945*, vol. 1, p. 297.

in the sense of any cheap "democratization of art". The appreciation of this shift did not mean that everything created by these "new talents from the people" should be accepted as art; rather, their creative work was an opportunity for the established artists to reconsider their own position and, indeed, the nature of art itself. In 1944, in a discussion of the Slovene Artistic Club on the Liberated Territory, the painter Nikolaj Pirnat[75] posed the self-critical question: "Who confers on us the authority that we are art?"[76] And what is more, along with assertions that the entrance of "the people" into the art field marks the beginning of a new era that will lead to the creation of unimaginable great artworks in the future, we also find statements saying that partisan art does not yet even exist. So we can say that partisans considered their art as being literally between nothing and everything – which, if we remember the lyrics of *The Internationale* ("Nous ne sommes rien, soyons tout" – "We are nothing, let us be everything"), we can understand as the revolutionary tension par excellence. To think partisan art, then, we have to think its existence and non-existence simultaneously.[77]

It is this specific way of (non-)existing that remains outside the reach of any (simple) identification with partisan iconography and rhetoric, which at most can merely inscribe partisan art into the artistic tradition Pasolini criticized in a letter to Allen Ginsberg in 1967:

> Who gave us – both young and old – the official language of protest? Marxism, whose only poetic vein is the record of Resistance, Vietnam and Bolivia. Why do I lament this official language of protest which the working class, through its (bourgeois) ideologists, has given me? Because it is a language which doesn't ever leave out the idea of power and is therefore always practical and reasonable. But aren't practicality and reason the same goddesses who have made our bourgeois fathers MADMEN and IDIOTS?[78]

75 Nikolaj Pirnat (1903–1948) was a sculptor, drawer, illustrator and caricaturist; as a partisan, he created an important oeuvre of linocuts.
76 See Komelj, *Kako misliti partizansko umetnost?*, p. 561.
77 Among the partisans, something of this elusiveness was transferred as well to the new perception of the art of the past. In his book *The Eagle and the Roots*, the Slovene-born American writer Louis Adamic (1898–1951) records a conversation with the great painter Božidar Jakac (1899–1989), whose body of work as a partisan is important not only artistically but also for its documentary value – it includes many photographs as well as film recordings. Jakac told Adamic about an experience he had in an underground bunker: after several days spent in fear of death, a ray of light penetrated the bunker and shone on the faces of his comrades; Jakac called this moment the most intense experience of his war years and tried to capture it with the words: "It was an El Greco!" See Louis Adamic, *The Eagle and the Roots*, Doubleday, Garden City, NY, 1952, pp. 192–197; published in Slovene as *Orel in korenine*, trans. Mira Mihelič, 2nd ed., Državna založba Slovenije, Ljubljana, 1981, pp. 218–222.
78 Pier Paolo Pasolini, *Vita attraverso le lettere*, ed. Nico Naldini, Einaudi, Turin, 1994, p. 277 (I have slightly modified Ginsberg's translation so it corresponds more closely to the original Italian).

At the same time, Pasolini was critical of poets who opposed the idea of power and who, fighting against the world of practicality and reason, "have done nothing but prepare the ground, like prophets for the god War, whom society invokes: a God exterminator".[79]

How do we think partisan art within this constellation? Of course, it can be seen as a paradigmatic example of the art of resistance. But given that in Yugoslavia the resistance grew into revolution, it is much more than this. The real connection of partisan art with the partisan revolution lies not in the invention of a new language,[80] but rather in a new intensity of reading, in a self-criticism of language, in the constant turning of language against itself. Partisan art must be thought as a break, a discontinuity within the field of art caused by revolution, which shifts the very coordinates of art and, indeed, reopens the question "What is art?" This break cannot be reduced to any positive message articulated by partisan art, although this art constantly inscribed itself into its messages. If we accept Paul Klee's idea that the highest act of creativity is to create a void, one of most beautiful symbols of this specific way of (non-)existing can be seen in the so-called "silent actions" of the Liberation Front in occupied Ljubljana, when at an agreed time the streets of the city would remain empty for an hour (fig. 7). This "minimalist" act produced a maximum feeling of insecurity among the occupiers as a premonition that became visible in "the silence, the quiet, and the absence", to quote the words of activist Zima Vrščaj.[81]

This specific way of art's (non-)existing within the process of social transformation is another reason why we placed partisan art within the

---

79 Ibid.
80 With regard to rhetoric, some of the partisans' formulations could be astonishingly similar to those of their enemies; in some cases this may have been a deliberate symbolic strategy of "overidentification" – not unlike what Bor calls for when he writes: "Let's outstorm the storms, / let's outmonster the monster!" (*Previharimo viharje* [1942], p. 65). The partisans' emphatic assertion that their struggle has transformed the Slovene people into a "nation of heroes" finds its counterpart in the Italian Fascist anthem "Giovinezza", which begins: "Salve, popolo d'eroi!" ("Hail, people of heroes!"). Also the partisans' insistence that the Slovene nation was a "nation-proletarian" (*narod-proletarec* – a quotation from the writer Ivan Cankar, 1876-1918) had its counterpart in the designation of Italy as the "great proletarian" (*la grande proletaria*) in official Fascist propaganda (of course, we must keep in mind Mussolini's Marxist background). The Slovene partisans' songs also included an adaptation of the "Florian Geyer Lied", a German song from World War I that was part of the repertoire of SS units. But correspondences can found at more subtle levels, too. For example, there is a poem by Kajuh about how people didn't need radio reports because their veins had become antennas and their bones radio waves "swarming with news / of the struggle of all humans" (Kajuh, *Zbrano delo*, p. 204) – a beautiful articulation of the new revolutionary subjectivity; still, we find almost the same words in Céline's novel *Nord*, when he describes the state of mind in Nazi Germany when the country is collapsing (Louis-Ferdinand Céline, *Nord*, in *Romans*, vol. 2, Gallimard, Paris, 1974, p. 528; originally published in 1960).
81 Zima Vrščaj, "Tihe akcije", in *Junaška Ljubljana: 1941-1945*, vol. 1, ed. Marica Čepe, Vladimir Krivic, and Niko Lukež, Državna založba Slovenije, Cankarjeva založba Slovenije, and Mladinska knjiga, Ljubljana, 1985, p. 292.

conceptual line of the avant-garde when we included it in the Moderna galerija's permanent exhibition – even though its formal language is far from the experimentation of avant-garde art and often even opposed to it.

And yet, this division between the rearticulation of the art field itself and the "positive content" of the art does not mean that how things were formulated did not matter. On the contrary, from this evasive perspective every line, every letter, every punctuation mark acquired an excess of meaning. In Bor's *Let's Outstorm the Storms*, one of the most powerful lines opens – in total desperation – a new field of the possible with the very intensification of the impossible, which solves the unsolvable question in a way that transforms it into an imperative, simply by changing a punctuation mark:

Kam? Kam!
(Where to? To!)[82]

A year after the publication of *Let's Outstorm the Storms*, the Italian occupiers shot the poet Ivan Rob.[83] After the war, someone pointed out that Matej Bor's pseudonym, when read backwards, formed the sentence: ROB JE TAM (meaning both "Rob is there" and "The border is there"). Bor became worried that someone aware this possible inversion had read his pseudonym as a kind of cryptogram and denounced Rob as the presumed author of his book.[84] Was Rob shot because of some unintended game of letters? Fortunately, Bor's fears were groundless – Rob, it turns out, was not shot as the presumed author of Bor's book. Nevertheless, Bor's account of his unease provides us with a final lesson about partisan art: even in the highest tensions of the revolutionary struggle, which demand total mobilization, it is not true that anything needs to be simplified, nor should such subtle levels of language as the anagrammatic be viewed as inconsequential. On the contrary, it is precisely in such situations that these levels might suddenly acquire vital importance. When subtleties such as the anagrammatic aspect of language are neglected, even a game of letters can bring death.

---

82 Bor, *Previharimo viharje* (1942), p. 11.
83 Ivan Rob (1908–1942) was a master of the genre of literary travesty. He joined the partisans and was captured by the enemy after somebody informed on him. Before he was shot, he quoted a verse from the Risorgimento to his Italian executioner: "Chi per la patria muore, / vissuto è assai" ("One who dies for the fatherland has lived long enough").
84 See Matej Bor, "Kako sem pisal Previharimo viharje", *Jezik in slovstvo*, vol. 4, no. 8, May 1959, p. 237, as well as his unpublished "Iz avtobiografije", pp. 110–111. It should be noted that the occupying forces punished anyone found carrying partisan literature no less severely than they did those found with military weapons.

Keti Chukhrov

On the Violence of the General

The Moscow-based philosopher and poet Keti Chukhrov here discusses the role and meaning of violence in the emancipatory struggle. Beginning with seminal texts by Georges Sorel (1906) and Walter Benjamin (1921), she moves on to examine the unwelcome segregated "other" in modern liberal democracy – using as illustration Michael Haneke's 1997 film *Funny Games*. Chukhrov ends her analysis with a critique of the contemporary enlightened left, warning that a solidarity confined mainly to rhetoric only widens the gap between the socially disadvantaged and the cultural and academic elites.

First published in *Invisible Violence*, ed. Zoran Erić and Blanca de la Torre, Museum of Contemporary Art, Belgrade, Artium, Basque Museum–Centre of Contemporary Art, Vitoria-Gasteiz, Spain, and Salzburger Kunstverein, 2016. The version published here has been somewhat revised.

I

Paradoxically, no state system or penal institution would use the term "violence" in its rhetoric or judicial documentation when carrying out legalized acts of coercion; in the language of authority, violent acts may only be committed by "perpetrators", who can never be the State or the Law. Meanwhile, all the theoretical works that claim violence as an indispensable component in any emancipatory struggle (such as those by Georges Sorel, Walter Benjamin, Georg Lukács, Frantz Fanon, and Slavoj Žižek[1]) insistently place this term in the foreground, although violence is far from being the only component of an insurrectionary agency or the struggle for justice.

So the Law, which tacitly applies violence in order to realize certain goals, conceals and paraphrases this application with legislative rhetoric; whereas in theoretical works that posit violence as a component of the emancipatory struggle the term "violence" is laid bare. The reason for this insistence on violence as part and parcel of emancipation lies mainly in the fact that there is no time for any gradual change. The existing system does not permit any transition, progress, or transformation; hence, violence becomes a kind of metaphor for urgency in demanding the extreme and immediate termination of the present state of affairs. The urgency in this case can be thought of as the need to block and sublate the present regime and to reject the present world of injustice, oppression and inequality – that which cannot be transformed "now" or in the near future.[2]

In *Reflections on Violence* (1906), Georges Sorel differentiates the protective and establishing force of the State from the destructive violence of strike and revolution. For him, the reason violence becomes a focalized term is the impossibility of changing the modes of production under the conditions of the capitalist state and its economy. Revolution cannot be developmental and evolutionary; it can only be eschatological or destructive.[3] Destruction is inevitable in laying claim to a new world of non-capitalist equality. Therefore, for Sorel, destruction supersedes utopia. However, the theoretical stance of revolution as destruction ignores an important part of Marxist thought which concerns the historical and transformative role of production in affecting the disposition between the

---

1   See Georges Sorel, *Reflections on Violence*, ed. Jeremy Jennings, Cambridge University Press, Cambridge, 2004; Walter Benjamin, "Critique of Violence", *Reflections: Essays, Aphorisms, Autobiographical Writings*, ed. Peter Demetz, Schocken Books, New York, 1986, pp. 277-300; Georg Lukács, *History and Class Consciousness: Studies in Marxist Dialectics*, trans. Rodney Livingstone, Merlin Press, London, 1971; Frantz Fanon, *The Wretched of the Earth*, trans. Constance Farrington, Penguin Books, London, 2001; and Slavoj Žižek, *Violence: Six Sideways Reflections*, Picador, New York, 2008.
2   Hannah Arendt subjects to critique the transgressive function of violence. While admitting the agency of riot and rebellion, she explicitly disputes the political potential of violence or its capacity to produce political power. See Hannah Arendt, *On Violence*, Harcourt, New York and London, 1970.
3   See Sorel, *Reflections on Violence*.

forces of production and the relations of production. Sorel's focus on eschatology is all the more problematic since it is unclear what would follow after the destructive and eschatological rupture: Sorel's theory stops at the moment when the syndicalist groups and the working class appropriate the means of production and sabotage the owners. Such conditions, however, are insufficient either to bring about a new general socialist order or to preserve the economic hegemony of the strikers.

Walter Benjamin's attitude, in "Critique of Violence" (1921), is also eschatological in his treatment of violence as a tool of resistance. However, by coining the term "divine violence" as a procedure that can terminate the law-making and law-sustaining conditions of the capitalist state, he provides an explanation of the reasons for such a non-political eschatology.[4] "Divine violence" is after-political, theologically termed and non-developmental. This is because insurgence cannot be seen as the continuation of the present politics that transforms it by means of democratic resistance; it must eschatologically sublate not only the present political situation, but also everything that abides by the present law. Benjamin's essay is perhaps the most articulate attempt to show that the term "violence" is not only the tool of an insurgency against bourgeois state law but that it should also enable a leap out of the world of inequality, and that this leap out of the bourgeois order cannot happen by political means, i.e. within the existing social and economic conditions; hence the term "divine" – which, on the one hand, marks the impossibility of radical social change and, on the other hand, calls for this change despite its social and political impossibility.

Unlike Sorel, who embeds violence in the immanent proletarian syndicalist struggle and the framework of a single class (the proletariat), Benjamin, when using the term "general strike", treats the act of empirical insurgency as a collateral effect. To be proletarian is not possible "in itself"; one has to become proletarian "for itself". But the issue at stake is that becoming proletarian "for itself" does not mean merely emancipating a particular oppressed class but also necessitates establishing the condition of a common cause generally and universally – for all classes, not only for the working class. So that "the general" as the condition of emancipation for the working class (the one that needs emancipation) should also become necessary for the privileged classes, which are not so greatly in need of emancipation; this implies that the common cause would entail the loss of privileges in favour of the common and general interest. Thus, what is central in the "violent divinity" of the "general strike" is the concept of "the general" rather than the actions of the strike of the proletariat as a specific social group. In other words, proletarianism is a necessary condition of generality both for the working class, i.e. the oppressed, and for the classes that are not oppressed – in other words, for everyone.

4   See Benjamin, "Critique of Violence".

According to Benjamin, then, the issue is not so much to broaden the power of the proletariat through a strike but to assert that the proletariat claims and exerts a general will and that this will is a condition for everyone, including non-proletarians. It is at this point that the general becomes extreme. Thus, the general strike is claimed as necessary not only for proletariat, not only in the name of the working class, but for the general system of equal justice.

When the political exertion of the common and of the radically equal is impossible, one applies methods and terms that accomplish political change through non-political means; hence Benjamin's reference to the "divinity" of violence. Yet the application of the term "violence" by Benjamin is fairly metaphoric. The issue is not the violence itself or its empirical, or even systemic, applications, but rather the significance of Benjamin resorting to this term in his text. As I have already mentioned, by asserting the violence of the *general* strike, the agenda is not only a radical form of proletarian resistance, i.e. the self-emancipation of a single social group, but first and foremost the immediate and ultimate installation of the common cause.

Apart from the cleavage between law-making and divine violence, Benjamin puts forth another, less evident but still very important, antagonism: the ethical difference between life as such ("mere life" or "bare life") and "the living".[5] By confronting the capitalist state, proletarian violence is equally opposed to "mere" life (*blossen Leben*) – which is nothing more than normal life as an inherent part of the capitalist state's law and force. The guilt of "mere life" is that it is confined to mere utilitarian existence. "Divine violence" – when surmounting the present social condition of inequality supported by the State – is a force that sublates not only the law of the State but also the "mere life" embedded in that law and produced by it.

Benjamin, in fact, speaks of a redemptive procedure that runs counter to the individual human life's existential intentionality. For example, when Abraham chooses to sacrifice his son Isaac, he does so out of his shame at living a mere life, which only "divine violence" can redeem. This act is meant to be a rejection of the old world of pagan servitude to gods and an opening up to the new monotheistic world. Benjamin says that the new world redeemed by "divine violence" does not *demand* sacrifice (as the old world of worship had done) but *accepts* sacrifice as the sign of ultimate fidelity. God does not demand that Abraham make such a sacrifice but Abraham nevertheless decides to carry out the act – an act that tears away the advantages and laws of a mere life to leave a life accepted by God, which is now for him the condition of universality: a life that, no matter how violent it is, can be nothing other than objective and general.

---

5   We should note that by "mere life" Benjamin means not the life of the deprived, but private life that is deprived of the dimension of common.

Interestingly, the courage and readiness to perform such a violent act ends in an act of mercy that makes the violent act unnecessary.

II

In the film *Funny Games*, by Michael Haneke, we are confronted with a Benjaminian disposition: unconditioned violence befalls a decent, law-abiding middle-class family, a couple and their child. Visitors in white – the cruel "angels" – break into the country house where the family is spending a holiday and stage their attack as a game, mercilessly bringing gradual death to all three family members. Much has been written about Haneke's visual methodology for representing violence in the film. I would like to focus, however, more on the dialectic between the unmotivated attack by the perpetrators and the inevitability of the violent invasion of the dwelling of "innocent" law-abiding bourgeoisie.

The film was made in 1997, before any major global terrorist attack. The two villains who terrorize the innocent family are not desperate jihadists or raging Third World subalterns. They are polite young yuppies who look like they could belong to a "Western" welfare democracy. Even when violent, they speak the language of neighbourly hospitality. The plot exposes an important aspect of the democratic order: although the serene life of a decent family does not harm anyone, Haneke shows us that the civic continuation of the humanist social contract, even in its frequently employed humanitarian rhetoric of goodwill, contains within itself the social colonization of the unequal "other". This might be the potential "other" of the commons, the other of solidarity and equality, the other with whom to share the dimension of the general, but it might equally be the uncanny other (whom Žižek calls "a neighbour" and Judith Butler defines as the melancholically internalized other[6]) – the one who cannot be loved but who also cannot be murdered, mourned, or dispensed with. This tacit subjugation of the unequal other by which they are kept inside us and among us in order to keep our conscience clean is an essential element of the social security of civil society and the private security of its members. Civil life is permeated by the unconscious fear of the intrusion of this tacitly eliminated unequal "other", who sooner or later might invade.

In the film, the intruders are in no way the oppressed. However, the rhetoric used by these murderers reveals two aspects of violence: on the one hand, in their communicative behaviour, they mirror the hypocrisy of the language of democracy, which manifests social empathy but simultaneously seeks to keep the evicted other at a distance and tame them. On the other hand, the cruel murderers structurally occupy the position that

---

6   This is the principal argument in Judith Butler's *The Psychic Life of Power: Theories in Subjection*, Stanford University Press, Stanford, 1997; see especially the chapter "Melancholic Gender" (pp. 132–166).

the oppressed "others" find themselves in. They are newcomers, visitors who are not welcome; they are treated like anonymous aliens, who are received hospitably only in the hope that they will leave once their requests have been satisfied. In the film, the mere private life of the middle-class family is shown as already guilty, since its social complacency automatically presupposes the *non-recognition* of the "other" and indifference to its socially evicted position. It is this tacit *non-recognition* that becomes the spark for the violent act of the intruders, which at first sight seemed unmotivated.

Recent events are increasingly revealing the conservative and clerical turn in layers of society that would have once formed the proletariat class. Benjamin's "divine violence", in this case, turns into surplus enjoyment by means of violence,[7] the difference being that this is the violence of resentment and revenge and not at all the establishing of the dimension of the general. It is pointless to enumerate such examples of reactionary insurgency, which take place today because the various forms of social assistance – allowances, subsidized education, medical care, charity – do not empower or satisfy the underprivileged. Here, democratic aid that seeks to civilize and educate the underprivileged causes even more and harsher rage. The revenge of the underprivileged against the polite and condescending non-recognition they receive from the civilized, enlightened, and privileged classes manifests itself as an outrageous, merciless, and senseless attack.[8]

III

Democracy must insistently assert civil equality and constantly display concern for the disinherited and underprivileged, but at the same time it cannot help but keep such groups away from the conditions of genuine emancipation; such a disposition tacitly affirms inequality as an insurmountable social condition even as it engages in a social and institutional concern for those who are less than equal.

---

7   See Žižek, *Violence*.
8   Commenting on the attack at the offices of *Charlie Hebdo* in Paris in 2015, Žižek emphasizes the logic of contemporary fundamentalism. Rather than fighting the sinful residents of the civilized West, the pseudo-fundamentalists are fighting their own temptation, their own inability to be believers, and the fact that they themselves are not fundamentalist enough; this leads to Žižek's assertion that the rage comes not so much from the fact that the civilized West disregards real belief or genuine values, but from the fact that the fundamentalists themselves are experiencing their own inferior status and non-recognition vis-à-vis the "civilized". In this case, the motive might in fact be envy over the enjoyment of the privileged other, and hence the attempt to retrieve some surplus enjoyment out of a violent act, as Žižek puts it. See Slavoj Žižek, "Are the Worst Really Full of Passionate Intensity", *New Statesman*, January 10, 2015; http://www.newstatesman.com/world-affairs/2015/01/slavoj-i-ek-charlie-hebdo-massacre-are-worst-really-full-passionate-intensity (accessed January 8, 2016).

Yet the question at stake not only concerns the vicissitudes of democracy or actual politics but is also about avoiding the trap of the social-democratic rhetoric found in left-leaning theory, artistic production, and cultural politics. It is obvious that the leftist stance, be it in political activism, art, culture, or social struggle, is critical of representative democracy under the conditions of the capitalist State. However, it is here that a false democracy is implemented even as it is simultaneously criticized.

The biggest problem of the enlightened left today is that a particular social group, or class, which although perhaps precarious is not necessarily oppressed, has appropriated the voice of the oppressed. The support of the dispossessed in and by emancipatory discourses and institutions is often positioned far from the grasp of the underprivileged; in short, this "other" happens to be representative of the alienated and lower social layers in its relation to the privileged bearers of critical theory and discourse. There is an explicit difference between the way emancipation discourse is applied today and the way it was applied at the end of 19th and the beginning of the 20th centuries. At that time, theories of equality were able to incorporate the dispossessed into the struggle for emancipation both practically and cognitively; today, however, the discursive and theoretical edifice of social critique cannot expand deep enough into the social field to form any political continuity with the underprivileged, a continuity that might exceed the mere rhetoric of solidarity. Anti-government emancipatory social work and politically engaged art projects are not enough to annul the class gap between the enlightened left and the socially underprivileged. In this regard, it is worth mentioning Georges Sorel's point that the bourgeoisie's shame over its privileges and its voluntary philanthropy are much more dangerous to the working class than its indifference, since the bourgeoisie's social agency for the sake of the socially underprivileged blocks the proletariat's own agency and makes it more difficult to sustain the possibility of radical change.[9]

Among the few consequences of this contradictory situation, we can mention the paradoxical outcome of the anti-Kremlin protests in Russia in 2011 and 2012. The leftists in the anti-Putin movements appeared to be socially much closer to the creative class than to the majority of the socially dispossessed, who were either supportive of Putin or politically passive. As a result, the ones producing the discourses about emancipation and the ones who in actual fact needed to be emancipated were political and social adversaries. In this case, the socially underprivileged population is being not only socially colonized by the ruling regime but also manipulated by the enlightened agents of emancipation themselves. Unfortunately, this paradox exists not only in the so-called failed democracies (the post-socialist countries, Russia included) but resides generally in the impossibility of integrating the underprivileged "other" despite anti-capitalist activities.

---

9   Sorel, *Reflections on Violence*, pp. 157–182.

Interestingly, during the transitional period of the early 1990s, despite the mass impoverishment in conditions of primitive accumulation, the formerly socialist societies (and Russia in particular) still preserved an unsegregated social continuity between the completely impoverished and the suddenly wealthy. The differences between social groups were not yet qualitative or systemic; they were ontic. Boris Mikhailov, in his photographic series *At Dusk* (1993), documented the uncanny survival of people in post-Soviet Kharkiv, depicting how the early post-socialist period paradoxically retained the dimension of the commons despite the social collapse; this was because irreversible class gaps and segregation areas had not yet been established.

Returning to the issue of class, we can observe the following paradox. Contemporary art institutions engage with the problems of oppression, migration, and neo-colonial injustices by relying on the revolutionary practices of the Russian avant-garde or the legacies of the protest movements of the 1960s. However, a solidarity confined mainly to rhetoric only widens the gap between racially or socially segregated groups and creative and academic workers.

The most uncanny effect of such a "progressive" condition arises when art institutions, with their pretensions to enlightenment, try to make interventions within social ghettos.[10] The art institution attempts, on the one hand, to research social problems and import them as research material into the art space and, on the other, to position itself as a site of applied education and cultural production for the socially deprived. The outcome of such activity is that the institution's and its workers' political responsibility for the segregated group contributes to international praise for socially engaged art and its agents, which in turn supports and justifies their funding. Consequently, by researching and exhibiting the dispossessed, proponents of emancipation both claim a bond of solidarity with the oppressed and, precisely by virtue of this pretension, increase the class gap between privileged and underprivileged social groups.

It is in this nebulous zone that two violent outcomes might emerge:

1. The first would possibly be an act of resentment on the part of the segregated that seeks to violently block the contrived discourse of solidarity, which in fact is intrinsically biased by the non-recognition of the segregated.[11] In cases where the segregated are in any way inscribed as exhibits in an art institution that claims to help "them" or even where they are participants in an activist or research project, they have incentive to sabotage the institution, to paralyse its functions and thus transcend their inferior status and non-recognition through the surplus enjoyment of this act of rage.

---

10 A frequent case for socially engaged art institutions.
11 In fact, no progressive cultural institution would acknowledge such non-recognition of the socially deprived when so much effort is invested into social work. However, the checkpoint here is not theoretical, or conceptual, it can only be practical and sensuous. For more on the *practical and sensuous* see my article "Drei Komponenten des Realismus", *Springerin*, no. 2, 2015, pp. 25–31.

Such an act would prevent intellectual agents from using underprivileged social groups as "material" that confirms the agents' own progressive and enlightening activity without them becoming *sensuously* involved in the lives, aspirations, and fates of the underprivileged and granting equal conditions to them (that is, it would prevent all false enlightening activity that does not emphasize the class gap and confess to occupying a privileged position).

2. The second option would be an impossibly miraculous situation (miraculous in the Leninist sense) when out of nowhere a general decision about equality becomes a matter of utmost urgency – a decision that would not only assert but also implement the procedures of the general: in terms of the general interest, the general will, and the common cause. Such a decision would be "divinely" violent – violent because it might cruelly expose the interests of many of us, who would then be compelled to bring the interests of all into real-life practice and not merely into discourse. Enlightenment and education would then make sense only with the presumption of general equality and overall civil recognition of this condition. To achieve equality it is not enough to equally distribute property or wealth, whether material or non-material; equality can be achieved only when the need of the general is established as anyone's personal interest. The general – whether it is property or non-material wealth – is not distributed piece by piece but is something that belongs to each of us in all its fullness. This sounds unrealistic at present.

The question then is the following: is it possible to integrate "the other" without a revolutionary procedure, without drastic and violent change? To put it another way, as Lukács asked in "Bolshevism as a Moral Problem" (1918), is it possible to attain equality via gradual democratic reforms?[12] Or should there be a decision that brings about an irreversible shift from a society of inequality to one of equality? Such a decision would presuppose a sharing of the necessity of the general by all and thus would very likely be undesirable for certain social groups. That is why it is not merely the revolutionary strike that is violent, but first and foremost the dimension of the general in its urgent demand for overall equality.

---

12 Georg Lukács, "Bolshevism as a Moral Problem", *Social Research*, vol. 44, no. 3, 1977, pp. 416–424.

Lev Kreft and Aldo Milohnić

When the Avant-Gardists Go Marching In

Philosopher Lev Kreft and theatre historian Aldo Milohnić, both based in Ljubljana, combine forces to consider the subversive role of the neo-avant-garde and alternative culture in Slovenia in the 1980s, looking in particular at the use of such "retro-garde" techniques as defamiliarization and overidentification and the important role played by "the blasphemy of amateurism". At the same time, they raise questions about the very possibility of political art in the depoliticized "anything goes" climate of today and find a tentative answer in Igor Zabel's understanding of "commitment" in art.

Prologue

In his *Journaux intimes* (*Intimate Journals*) Charles Baudelaire commented on French metaphors for art, which to his astonishment were getting more and more military: "Fighting poets. Avant-garde literature. These military metaphors denote a spirit which is not militant but ready-made for discipline, therefore for conformity, for minds which were born domesticated, Belgian souls who cannot think but in company."[1] (Apologies for Baudelaire's politically incorrect image.) The paradox of modernism, which he described elsewhere as a tension between the present moment and eternity,[2] is here repeated from another perspective. Art is autonomous and autotelic, beyond the bourgeois world and its diabolical progress. But the metaphors we use to describe its structure and movements in space and time are military, for instance, *avant-garde*, and these are metaphors that represent conformity. Conformity and autonomy are not the characteristics of two different sorts of art done by different sorts of artists but are two other paradoxical components of modernity. In the journal entry following this one, Baudelaire concludes that for the sake of our desire for pleasure we are bound to the present and for the sake of our desire for salvation we are bound to the future. *Avant-garde*, one of the many military terms he mentions, is not just a sign of desire for salvation but also a sign of its consequences: in order to represent the future of salvation in modern contemporaneity, an atmosphere of discipline and conformity is necessary, just as an atmosphere of eternity is necessary for fleeting, transient, and contingent modernity. The avant-garde does not come after modernism as its destroyer; it is one of its components, together with a desire for pleasure which has to be put aside if one wants to follow the plan of salvation.

Baudelaire knew what later became blurred: that the term *avant-garde* used in the context of art does not derive from a metaphor that compares a radical and revolutionary political group or movement with an artistic group or movement. It comes from military vocabulary, where it denotes a part of the formation of an army on the march, not on the battlefield. When marching, armies have to be divided into three parts, the *avant-garde* walking in front and the *retro-garde* marching at the rear of the main corps of *battaglia*. There is no permanent distribution of people among these parts, because the positions change every day: the *avant-garde* marches tomorrow as the *retro-garde*, the *retro-garde* becomes the *battaglia*, and the *battaglia* becomes the *avant-garde*, and so on. The military

---

1   Charles Baudelaire, *Journaux intimes: Fusées – Mon coeur mis à nu*, Les Éditions G. Crès et Cie, Paris, 1920, pp. 70–72; also available at http://gallica.bnf.fr/ark:/12148/bpt-6k206339d (accessed January 10, 2016).
2   "Modernity is the transient, the fleeting, the contingent; it is one half of art, the other being the – eternal and the immovable." Charles Baudelaire, "The Painter of Modern Life" (1863), available at http://www.writing.upenn.edu/library/Baudelaire_Painter-of-Modern-Life_1863.pdf (accessed January 10, 2016).

concept for dealing with the vulnerability of troops marching through the countryside before they reach the battleground was adopted by Saint-Simon as a metaphor for denoting the position of art in his utopian socialist scheme, which aimed to change the world for the better. In that scheme, it is not Saint-Simon, the scientist with a revolutionary politics, who represents the avant-garde, but rather the artist who aesthetically represents the future emancipation of mankind in its present. That is why Théophile Gauthier, as early as 1835, attacked the utopian socialists for their abuse of art "for a good cause", and called for an art for the sake of art, opposing all "useful" employment of art.[3] But not all the socialisms of the 19th century were revolutionary; they were not even necessarily radical, while the communists, who were radical and revolutionary and allegedly planned to abolish private property, were but a tiny minority. Up to the beginning of the 20th century, radical art – whether it was radical in artistic terms or political terms, or both – was mostly associated with anarchist movements, not with socialists or communists. At the same time as struggles between the radical left and the reformist core started to unfold in the social democratic movement, something similar happened in the art world, where the historical avant-garde started its career with Marinetti's "Futurist Manifesto" of 1909. This coincidence is understood by Peter Bürger as a sign of a causal relationship that made the historical avant-garde dependent on the fate and success of the proletarian revolution. This revolution failed on a global scale, and its moment was lost forever (in the view typical of the Frankfurt School) – which is why the avant-garde is from that point on *historical*, i.e. the avant-garde was a unique phenomenon that is now over. The neo-avant-garde is not really an avant-garde, Bürger concludes.[4] Confirmation of this idea comes from yet another, unexpected side: Clement Greenberg claimed that in the art of the 20th century, there was just one choice, between the avant-garde and kitsch.[5] But if kitsch (meaning popular culture and political propaganda like that of socialist realism) cannot possibly be a choice, then the avant-garde becomes mainstream, and if it becomes mainstream, it certainly cannot be the avant-garde. According to Bürger, the avant-garde ceased to exist historically, in time, and according to Greenberg, it ceased to exist because it occupied the whole space of art. To add insult to these injuries, postmodernist supporters have claimed that the avant-garde belongs to modernism – and with the arrival of postmodernism, modernism is dead and gone. By saying this, postmodernism dismissed the avant-garde along with modernism and, consequently, confirmed that the avant-garde belongs to the definition of modernism.

3   Théophile Gautier, "Preface", in *Mademoiselle de Maupin: A Romance of Love and Passion*, Gibbings and Co., London, 1899; available at http://archive.org/details/mademoiselledema00gaute (accessed January 10, 2016).
4   Peter Bürger, *Theorie der Avantgarde*, Suhrkamp Verlag, Frankfurt am Main, 1974, pp. 30, 79.
5   Clement Greenberg, "Avant-garde and Kitsch" (1939), available at http://www.sharecom.ca/greenberg/kitsch.html (accessed January 10, 2016).

As much as the neo-avant-garde threatened Greenberg's doctrines, Neue Slowenische Kunst (NSK)[6] did not fit well into the postmodernist agenda. How are we to understand the existence of the retro-garde in a period after modernism and an epoch at the end of art? The retro-garde was itself part of an army's marching structure in the Renaissance, doing at the rear end of the formation what the avant-garde had to do at the head: inspecting, discovering, and informing, but also accepting the fight with the enemy and, if necessary, sacrificing itself, all for the safety of the *battaglia*. The retro-garde of NSK arrived from the European Socialist East at the time of socialism's departure from life into the past tense, and at a time when people's hopes were increasingly oriented toward the First World with its shopping malls and democracy. The retro-garde's fate was to be viewed either as support for this direction and a critique of the authoritarian regime on the way out, or as a lament over the spilt milk of totalitarianism. NSK appropriated the Eastern European, and especially the Slovene, artistic avant-gardes as well as totalitarian ideology, especially the National-Socialist cultural ideology. As Laibach's "Covenant" announced in their manifesto: "All art is subject to political manipulation (indirectly – consciousness; directly), except for that which speaks the language of this same manipulation. To speak in political terms means to reveal and acknowledge the omnipresence of politics."[7] It is worth remembering that only art which speaks the language of manipulation can avoid being manipulated, and that by doing so it acknowledges the omnipresence of politics. The omnipresence of politics was the water in which art had to swim during socialism, especially during the 1980s – the period of socialism's decay and decomposition. To stay above water, and make the water be seen, art had to provoke "a static totalitarian scream".[8] This "static totalitarian scream", which speaks "the language of manipulation" to reveal "the omnipresence of politics", comes from the retro-appropriation of the languages of the avant-garde and totalitarianism. Rereading the manifesto, we can detect a tension between the totalitarian discourse and the avant-garde process or technique, or as Viktor Shklovsky called

---

6 In 1984 in Ljubljana, three previously autonomous art groups came together to establish the new art collective Neue Slowenische Kunst (NSK) – the music and cross-media group Laibach, founded in 1980; the Sisters of Scipio Nasica Theatre, founded in 1983; and the visual art group Irwin, founded in 1983 (see Zdenka Badovinac, Eda Čufer, and Anthony Gardner, "Introduction", in *NSK from Kapital to Capital: Neue Slowenische Kunst – An Event of the Final Decade of Yugoslavia*, exh. cat., Moderna galerija, Ljubljana, and MIT Press, Cambridge, Mass., and London, 2015, p. 8). NSK also included the New Collectivism design division, founded in 1984, and the Red Pilot Cosmokinetic Theatre (which carried on the work of the Sisters of Scipio Nasica Theatre), the Builders architectural division, the Department of Pure and Applied Philosophy, and the film division Retrovision, all founded in 1987. The NSK State in Time was founded in 1992.
7 Laibach, point no. 3 in "10 Items of the Covenant", available at http://www.laibach.org/data/10-items-of-the-covenant/ (accessed January 10, 2016); first published as the Laibach manifesto in *Nova revija*, vol. 2, nos. 13–14, 1983.
8 Ibid. (point no. 8).

it in Russian, *priyom*, which de-automatizes perception, so that a fish experiences defamiliarization (*ostranenie*) with the water in which it swims.[9] The "static totalitarian scream" is provoked by this device, which does not deploy the flags of a movement toward utopia, nor does it attack the politics of manipulation in the manner of a political opposition, which then is merely the counterpart of the manipulation. However, the experiences of cultural oppositionalism from the period after World War II represent the historical background of such a de-automatization of perception. Beginning in the 1950s, cultural oppositionalism attacked the socialist regime from the positions of Western humanism and cultural autonomy. But the youth subculture of the 1960s was different: it started with the desire for pleasure and, to its own surprise, was attacked by the totalitarian power, which demands the sacrifice of pleasure for the sake of ultimate salvation. In response to totalitarian pressure, both the cultural oppositionalism and the youth subculture reacted in a similar manner: with the offended cry of a culture which is beyond politics and powerless in its confrontation with political power. It was the punk movement of the 1980s which was the first to respond differently, speaking the language of politicization unknowingly, just as Molière's Monsieur Jourdain, in *Le Bourgeois gentilhomme*, spoke prose until a philosopher told him that was what he was doing. Laibach and NSK followed and systematized the difference between cultural oppositionalism and total politicization. The retro-garde represented a manipulation that exposed power's own desire to harmonize totalitarian control with cultural humanism, a desire that cultural oppositionalism and its target have in common. To accomplish this, the retro-garde installed, not Maginot lines of cultural autonomy, but open borders and an excessive politicization, and did not express any choice between the First and the Second Worlds, between communism and capital. Its "static totalitarian scream" was disturbing for both socialist power and the power of autonomous culture alike.

Do-It-Yourself Alternative Culture

The 1980s were an especially interesting era in the contemporary history of Slovenia. The decade saw the emergence of new social, subcultural, and countercultural movements, peace movements, alternative publications, women's groups, gay and lesbian movements, punk rock bands, a

---

9   Viktor Shklovsky, "Art as Technique" (1917), in *Russian Formalist Criticism: Four Essays*, ed. and trans. Lee T. Lemon and Marion J. Reis, University of Nebraska Press, Lincoln, Neb., and London, 1965, pp. 3–23; an excerpt from the essay is available at https://paradise.caltech.edu/ist4/lectures/Viktor_Sklovski_Art_as_Technique.pdf (accessed January 10, 2016).

progressive socio-critical theory, and many alternative artistic and cultural practices (fig. 1). The alternative culture, as another way to move forward, denied the dominant political power the right to appear as the only possible progressive outcome of all social, cultural, and political conflicts and asserted the right of cultural oppositionalism to appear as the only way to overcome the dominant power in culture. Its distinctive technique was to demand what the dominant political power promised but didn't believe in and never delivered. Aleš Erjavec and Marina Gržinić, who in 1991 published *Ljubljana, Ljubljana: 1980s in Arts and Culture*, the first extended "inventory" of culture and art in Ljubljana during the 1980s, explained why they were devoting so much attention to alternative and subcultural practices: "So much of this book deals with subcultural and alternative topics mainly because they brought something very new to the atmosphere in Slovenia and Ljubljana during that decade, something that had not been seen since the end of the 1960s and the beginning of the 1970s. The alternative scene obviously flourished most dramatically during the anarchic times of the 1980s, when the old system and government were slowly dying away, while the new ones had not yet been born."[10]

In socialist Yugoslavia, there was much debate about political art, and especially political theatre, at the end of the 1970s and during the 1980s, when a socially committed theatre began to confront the various traumas and taboos of late-socialist society. Representatives of this trend could be found throughout Yugoslavia. In Slovenia, an especially important role was played by the public theatre *Slovensko mladinsko gledališče* (the Slovene Youth Theatre, today known in English as the Mladinsko Theatre) in Ljubljana. Beginning in 1980, Mladinsko developed its own recognizable style, dominated by political subjects, urban (sub-)culture, collective acting, and a relatively young audience. But despite such successes and some undoubtedly superb plays, political theatre as both an idea and a practice had exhausted itself in the former Yugoslavia by the late 1980s: the paradigm was kept alive artificially thanks to the occasional solid production, but it soon lapsed into mannerism and predictability. Then a new generation emerged who made a radical break with that paradigm and introduced an entirely new mode of thinking about the concept of the political in theatre, and in art in general. Dissident grumbling was replaced by such procedures as subversive affirmation and "over-identification" – artistic techniques that are unequivocally conceptual and political. The political optics was changing radically and the subversion of art no longer resided in parables or "reading between the lines" as a way to present "social anomalies"; rather the subversion lay in the manner of treatment of political subjects in artworks and the audience's perception. Therefore, the political aspect of art was reflected in experimentation with methods of representation (even at the outermost limits) and the politics of perception.

---

10 Aleš Erjavec and Marina Gržinić, *Ljubljana, Ljubljana: osemdeseta leta v umetnosti in kulturi*, Mladinska knjiga, Ljubljana, 1991, pp. 12–13.

Today's art practices, like their predecessors, are "children of their time". Just as Politics (with a capital P) has collapsed into a vast pile of different identity politics, so contemporary art is constantly searching for political particularisms of its own, finding ever new identity niches. Besides this eclectic mode of representation, there is another difference between the "alternative" cultural practices of the 1980s and contemporary "independent" cultural production. It can be found in Bertolt Brecht's differentiation of the notions "amateur" and "dilettante". What is the difference between the two? Brecht regards amateurism as a positive term, while dilettantism represents a bad version of amateurism, one that is unable to develop its own way of producing art – in other words, it can do no more than merely mimic the art professionals.[11] Following Brecht's idea of a specific mode of production of amateur culture, the amateur (but not dilettante) art and cultural practices that were part of the 1980s alternative culture in the former Yugoslavia could be interpreted precisely in opposition to the presupposed professionalism of the cultural elites of the day. Amateur art (in the Brechtian sense) was not an inferior copy of professional art practices – it was not about mimicking elite culture, which would be the ideological ideal of dilettante actors, musicians, and painters; on the contrary, it was about participating in the spontaneous ideology of an immediate and radical intervention in the cultural, social, and political spheres of Yugoslav society. Its practitioners were aesthetically unconcerned with the means of expression and the materials used in their works; their preoccupations resided more in their resistance to the professional elitism of the cultural establishment.

Examples of such amateurism in Yugoslav cultural production might include, for instance, punk music (as opposed to various forms of professional, usually commercial, mass entertainment music, including pop-rock music), experimental 16mm film in the 1960s and 1970s and alternative video art in the 1980s (as opposed to Yugoslavia's highly subsidized professional film industry), neo-avant-garde theatre and radical performance (as opposed to both professional theatre and the apologetic dilettantism of theatre groups mimicking the aesthetic patterns of the professional theatre), alternative theory (as opposed to mainstream academic philosophy and aesthetic theory in the academic establishment), etc. These alternative cultural practices were often intertwined – punk concerts were at the same time radical visual performances, video technology was used for documenting concerts, theatre performances, and other alternative cultural events, and so on. Furthermore, "the alternative scene was not only about new art forms and aesthetic possibilities but these alternative art forms were inextricably intertwined with socio-critical and political positions."[12] Examples are numerous, far more than

---

11 See Bertolt Brecht, "Sechs Chroniken über Amateurtheater", in *Werke: Große kommentierte Berliner und Frankfurter Ausgabe*, vol. 22/1, Aufbau and Suhrkamp Verlag, Berlin, Weimar, and Frankfurt am Main, 1993, p. 594.
12 Igor Zabel, "Avtopoetike", *Eseji I*, Založba /*cf.*, Ljubljana, 2006, p. 115.

can be listed here, but let us mention at least the FV collective (or better, "conglomerate").¹³ FV began in the early 1980s as a theatre group called FV 112/15 (figs. 2–3), but its members soon spread their alternative *prijom* to other fields of art, such as video (the FV Video group) and music (the alter-rock multimedia group Borghesia, figs. 4–5), as well as alternative cultural and social clubs (Disco FV, fig. 6). Video technology was used at Disco FV for the first time in 1982, and the publishing house Založba FV issued Yugoslavia's first-ever independent videocassette, Borghesia's *Tako mladi* (*So Young*) in 1985. Just how important video technology was for the alternative (sub-)cultural scene is evident in these comments by Zemira Alajbegović, one of the founding members of FV:

> In the 1980s video had a similar role to that of the Internet in 1990s – it was at the same time a commercial technology, an artistic medium and a democratic technique of visual recording, available for instant use. It seemed the most appropriate means of expressing radical views and quick responses to the repression of the ruling ideology. It embodied the desire for a reunification of avant-garde art with the procedures and techniques of mass culture. This utopia, bluntly confronted with the inability to penetrate the mainstream mass media, was always present on the Ljubljana subculture scene.¹⁴

The alternative video production of the 1980s (as well as its predecessor, experimental film) derived from the tradition of amateur film production carried out in the numerous cinema clubs that developed in every major city of Yugoslavia, especially during the 1960s and 1970s. As curator Ana Janevski explains: "Cinema clubs were part of the socialist project to bring culture and technology closer to all citizens of Yugoslavia, and not only the professionals. ... The cinema clubs gave their members an opportunity to engage in avant-garde experimentation, in socialist, self-managed self-organisation, and in a certain form of politics."¹⁵

Under such conditions, to be radically amateurish or "unprofessional" means simply to take seriously the blasphemy of amateurism and put it in a positive context, i.e. opposed to the bare aestheticism of the cultural

---

13 For comprehensive documentation of the FV collective, and theoretical reflections on it, see *FV: Alternativa osemdesetih / FV: Alternative Scene of the Eighties*, ed. Breda Škrjanec, MGLC – International Centre of Graphic Arts, Ljubljana, 2008, especially the detailed historical overview "Alternative Dawns" (pp. 281–343) by Neven Korda, one of the founding members of FV. According to Korda, FV was more of a "conglomerate" than a "collective" (p. 322).

14 Zemira Alajbegović, "Zamrznjeni čas – osemdeseta, ŠKUC-Forum, FV Video in drugi", in *Videodokument: Video umetnost v slovenskem prostoru 1969–1998: Eseji*, ed. Barbara Borčić, OSI Slovenia and SCCA-Ljubljana, Ljubljana, 1999, p. 39.

15 Ana Janevski, "We Cannot Promise to Do Anything More Than to Experiment: On Yugoslav Experimental Film and Cinema Clubs of the 1960s and 1970s", in *Parallel Slalom: A Lexicon of Non-aligned Poetics*, ed. Bojana Cvejić and Goran Sergej Pristaš, TkH, Belgrade, and CDU, Zagreb, 2013, pp. 137, 151.

establishment. This strategy was feasible given the relative social security maintained by the Yugoslav version of the social welfare state with the Fordist mode of production as its economic base. That mode of production (including the Yugoslav version) requires a strict division between paid (working) time and unpaid (free) time. Alternative (amateur) cultural production is neither paid (or if it is, the income is rather symbolic) nor recognized as a job or regular work. The status of alternative cultural production, however, radically changed in the process of the political and economic transition that followed the dissolution of socialist Yugoslavia. An important characteristic of post-Fordism – the mode of production typical of contemporary post-industrial capitalist economies – is the incorporation of non-work (free) time into productive (paid) time. This constellation has important repercussions for the entire system as such: the transformation of voluntary (unpaid) work into professional (paid) work, i.e. the process known as the NGO-ization of voluntary work. The cultural amateurism of the Fordist era is now transforming into a kind of flexible professionalism, typically represented by the NGO cultural sphere. Cultural amateurism has nowadays become part of the professional production sphere, i.e. the sphere that contributes significantly to the reproduction of the post-Fordist society. On the level of the love-hate dialectic, which, according to Igor Zabel, is typical for "the true professional in the field of art" (one who loves art and at the same time hates it),[16] the contemporary flexible professional is an ideal cultural producer: working as a professional and being paid as an amateur, he still loves art and hates (not art but) himself – because he can't stop working even though he is completely aware of his miserable, precarious status. In the words of Mark Banks, "The love of art can lead workers to neglect the care of the self."[17] Or as Janez Janša, one of the three (conceptually and literally) renamed Slovene artists, once said in a discussion about the position of freelancers in the cultural sector (and here we're quoting from memory): "I am looking for a good exploiter, for no one can exploit me better than I can exploit myself."

The Exhibition

In 2015, NSK artworks from the collective's beginnings to its dissolution in 1992 were exhibited at the Moderna galerija in Ljubljana under the title *NSK from* Kapital *to Capital: Neue Slowenische Kunst – An Event of the Final Decade of Yugoslavia*. One of the aims of the exhibition was to make evident the fact that NSK criticized capitalism as the result of the transition just as much as they had criticized the socialism that had had to disappear

---

16   Igor Zabel, "Professionals, Dilettantes, and Amateurs", *Contemporary Art Theory*, ed. Igor Španjol, JRP-Ringier and Les presses du réel, Zurich and Dijon, 2012, p. 281.
17   Mark Banks, *The Politics of Cultural Work*, Palgrave Macmillan, New York, 2007, p. 58.

in it. The difference between the (NSK) *retro*-principle and the *avant*-principle is that the avant-principle aims to destroy the institution of art and turn from art to life in order to overturn life, while the retro-principle aims to keep the avant-garde tradition alive and to expose the desire for power involved with life through the process of self-denunciation. But what kind of grip was this?

The Slovene literary historian, critic, and philosopher Taras Kermauner detected this method when he found that there "could be no greater Dadaistic turn" than in Laibach Kunst.[18] He might have added that it concerns Berlin Dada especially. Berlin Dada was successful in some of its turns because power was in jeopardy, in a transition from one stabilized order to another. By contrast, the much more elaborate *détournements* of movements such as the Cobra group, Lettrism, and Situationism – which we can mention as one of the avant-garde movements that formed the background to NSK – were not especially effective or successful, for which they could blame the totalitarian society of the spectacle. In the case of NSK, re-routing or hijacking, as we might translate the term *détournement*, is the sort of appropriation which is antagonistic to the appropriated perception but still ambiguous, because the oppositional message is expected but not fulfilled. The void created by the lack of a clear oppositional message was, for instance, very effective in the case of NSK's Youth Day poster (1987) (fig. 7),[19] which actuated the hijacking at a moment when the central reason for the celebration, Marshal Tito, had been dead for seven years and the purpose of the event was in question. The Slovene Socialist Youth Organization had already openly called for terminating the empty ritual. Everybody was expecting an oppositional poster that expressed the organization's political position. When no direct oppositional approach could initially be detected, the NSK poster for Youth Day was accepted by authorities as a welcome surprise. However, when the secret of the poster's *détourné* Nazi background was revealed, a huge scandal ensued.[20] Still, even in the revelation there was an attempt to hide the core of enjoyment felt by positional and oppositional powers alike. The hijacking that

---

18   Taras Kermauner, "X + (-) 11=?", in *NSK: From* Kapital *to Capital*, p. 69 (referenced in n. 6); originally published in *Nova revija*, vol. 2, nos. 13-14, 1983.
19   Youth Day was celebrated throughout the former Yugoslavia on May 25, a national holiday. The day was also celebrated as Josip Broz Tito's birthday (although in fact he was born on May 7, 1892). The celebration was organized as a symbolic relay race. The participants carried a baton that symbolized young people's greetings and devotion to Tito throughout Yugoslavia. The race went through all the country's major towns and cities, ending in Belgrade at the Yugoslav People's Army Stadium on May 25 with a spectacular public ceremony.
20   The NSK's submission for the Youth Day poster competition in 1987, which was organized that year by the League of Socialist Youth of Slovenia, was based on a Nazi painting by Richard Klein titled *The Third Reich: Allegory of Heroism* (1936). NSK replaced the Nazi symbols with symbols of socialist Yugoslavia. Their entry was selected by the Slovene jury and gladly accepted by the Yugoslav authorities, but scandal erupted when it became known that it was based on a Nazi painting. The last Youth Day celebration was held in 1988.

turned a Nazi painting into a Socialist poster was not the core of scandal; the *détournement* lay in what remained unchanged throughout this turn: the image of a young male body ready to sacrifice itself for the future of a revolution of some kind or another, an expression of blind faith, which represents any power's desire to command and control youth. The scandal was twofold: first, it revealed that totalitarian control over youth is what power desires; and second, it revealed that this desire is empty, because not even power itself believed (any longer) that its ideology of totalitarian control could be realized. What kind of critique refuses to attack its object either conceptually or on the level of mass hysteria but nevertheless exposes the object's contradictory elements by making it reveal its own weakest point? We find an example of such a critique in Marx when he asks how Germans, so content with their backwardness in comparison with England and France, can be forced to move forward and abolish their shameful satisfaction with their despicable condition? Among the treatments he proposes for the Germans, Marx employs a metaphor saying that "these petrified conditions must be made to dance by having their own tune sung to them". Or in German: "Man muß diese versteinerten Verhältnisse dadurch zum Tanzen zwingen, daß man ihnen ihre eigene Melodie vorsingt."[21] This *priyom*, at first glance, could be compared to Orpheus' song, which made the rocks move, or to the trumpets that destroyed the walls of Jericho. But these are only superficially similar to Marx or NSK. Here we have this strange and uncontrollable force of self-destruction caused by the mass hysteria of the general public, and the function of the rhythmic music is to compel vibration not through its own power but through the coincidence between the rhythmic pulsations of an army on the march, of their avant-garde leadership, and the rhythm of the change of symbols from the original to its de-Nazified double. In Marx's youth and student days, the problems of the theory of resonance, which were later solved by Marx's contemporary, Hermann von Helmholtz (1821–1894), were public knowledge. A well-known case is noted by Hallwag in 1780, in which singing vowels into the strings of a piano induced them to vibrate as other, different vowels. Even more significant was an incident that occurred in the German town of Nienburg (Saale), in 1825, which became the most important example of forced vibrations for the theory of resonance and led to a new approach for building bridges and new instructions for marching across them. On St. Nicholas Day, a crowd of gawking bystanders gathered on the Nienburg suspension bridge as a military band came marching across it. Cold feet and a mass dance psychosis induced the crowd to jump to the rhythm of music. The bridge started to dance as well and collapsed. Some fifty people died in the cold waves of the Saale River.

---

21 Karl Marx, "Zur Kritik der Hegelschen Rechtsphilosophie: Einleitung", available at http://www.mlwerke.de/me/me01/me01_378.htm; the English translation, "A Contribution to the Critique of Hegel's Philosophy of Right: Introduction" is available at https://www.marxists.org/archive/marx/works/1843/critique-hpr/intro.htm (both accessed January 10, 2016).

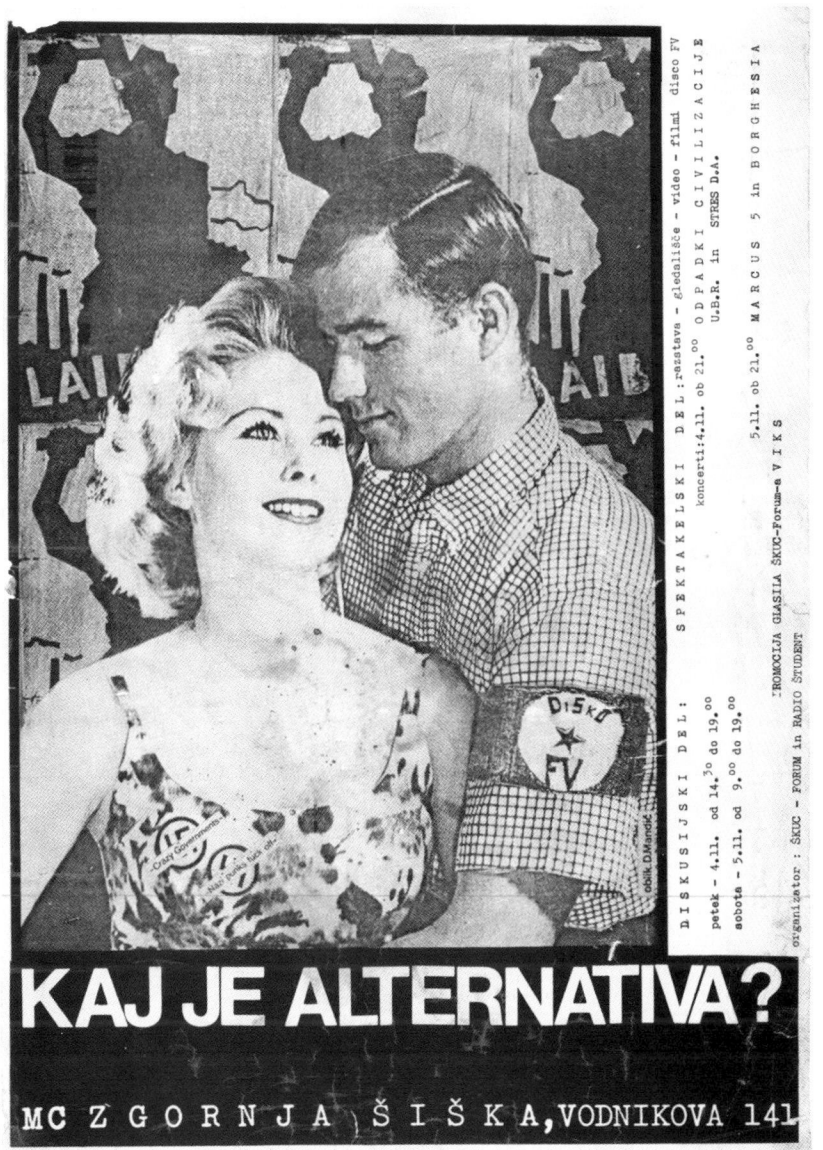

fig. 1

Dušan Mandić, *What Is the Alternative?*, 1983, poster.

Courtesy of MGLC – International Centre of Graphic Arts, Ljubljana.

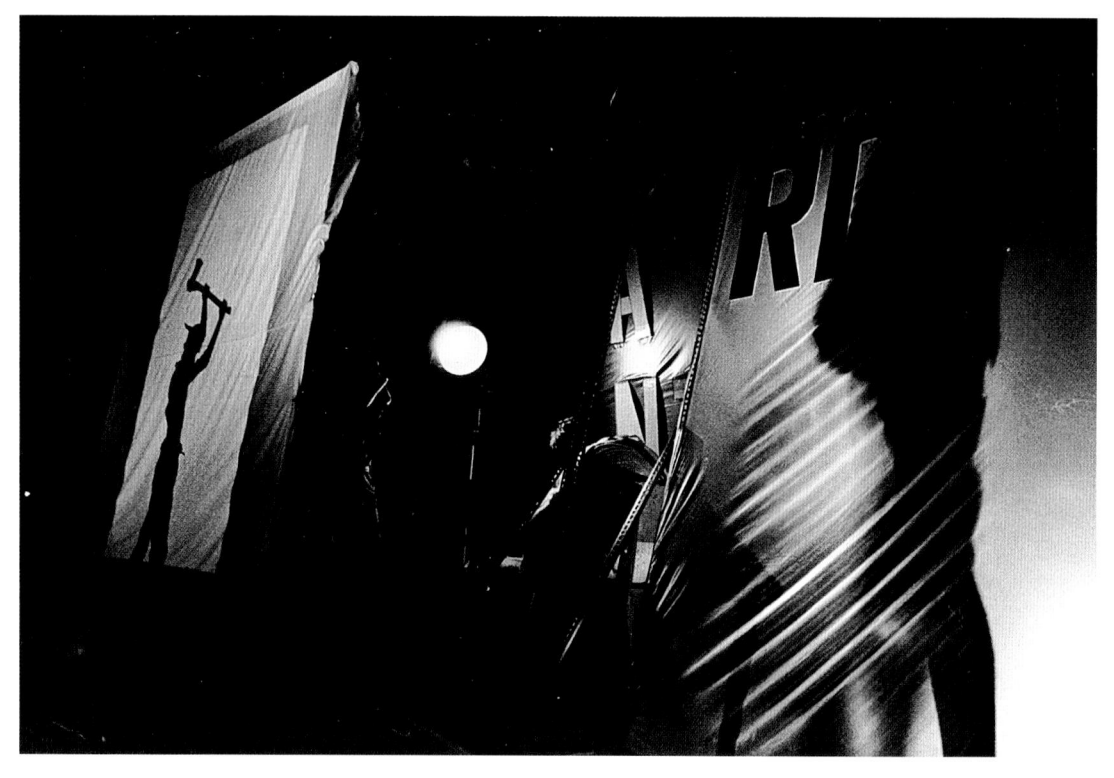

figs. 2–3

FV 112/15, *It Smelled Like Spring*, 1982, from the show at Križanke, Ljubljana.

Photo by Jane Štravs.
Courtesy of MGLC – International Centre of Graphic Arts, Ljubljana.

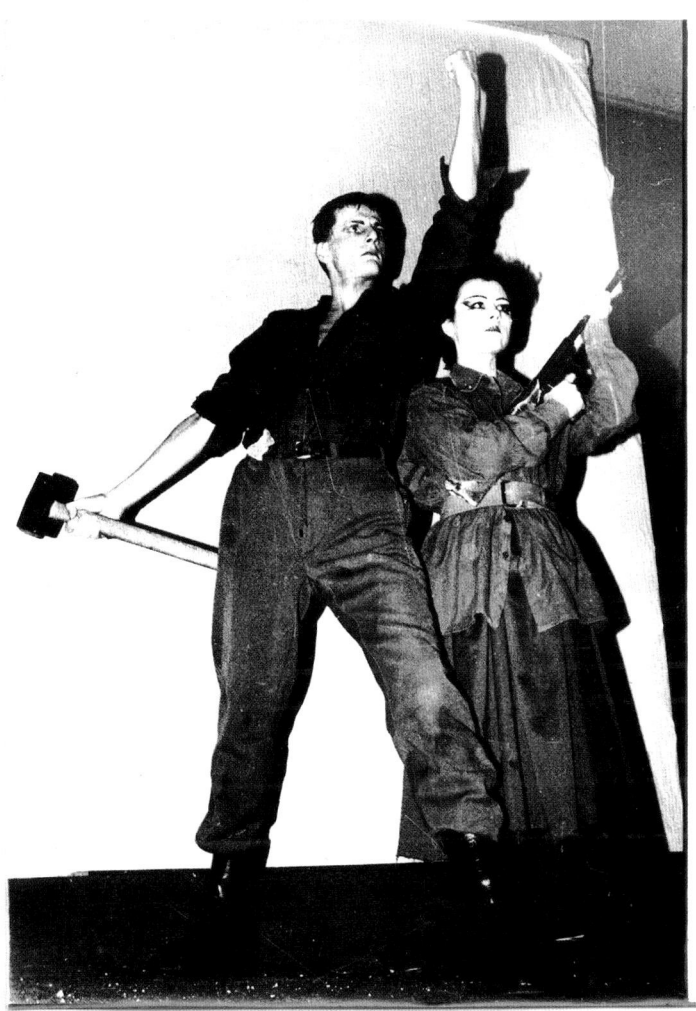

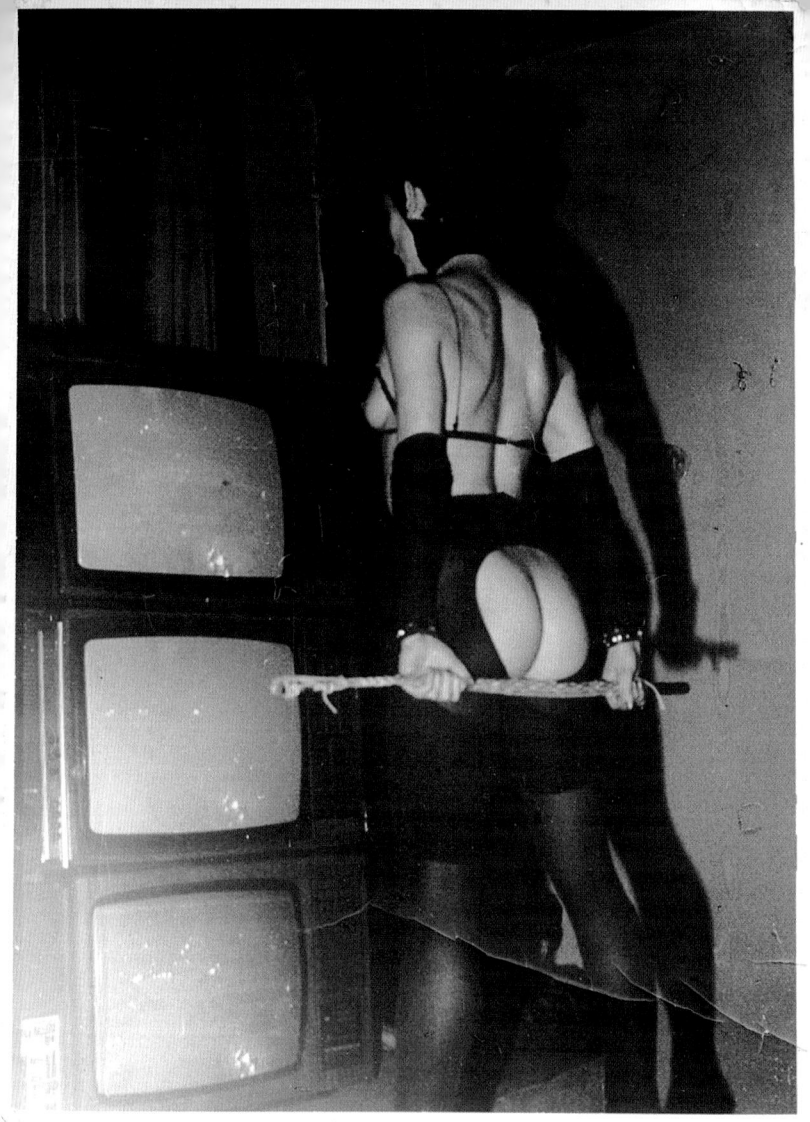

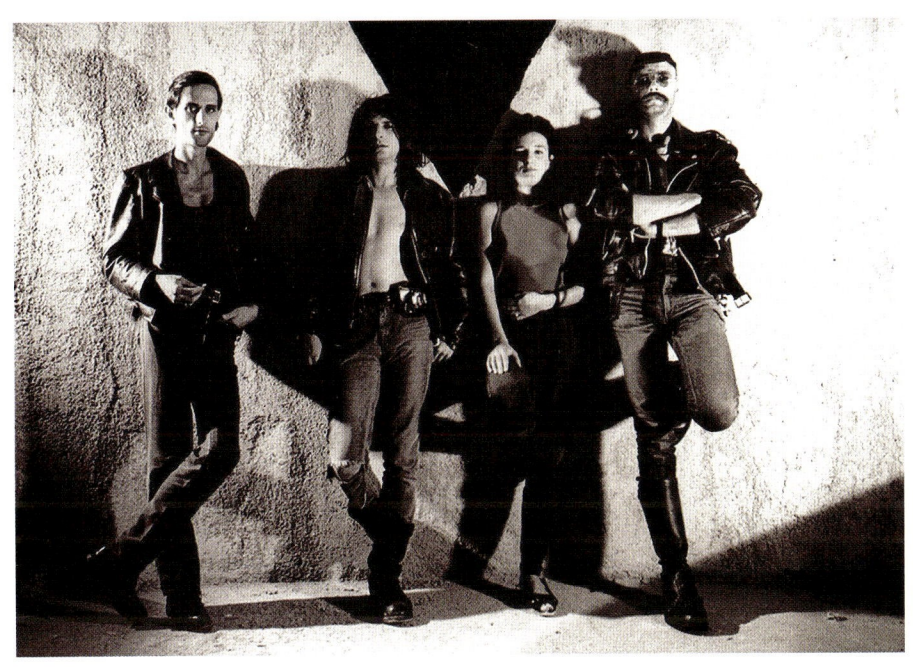

fig. 5

Borghesia, 1988.

Photo by Božidar Dolenc.
Courtesy of MGLC – International Centre of Graphic Arts, Ljubljana.

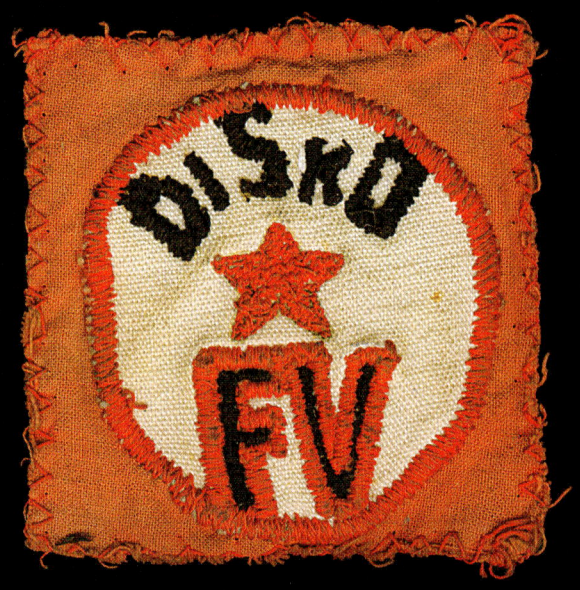

fig. 6

Handmade patch for Disco FV security guard.

Photo courtesy of MGLC - International Centre of Graphic Arts, Ljubljana.

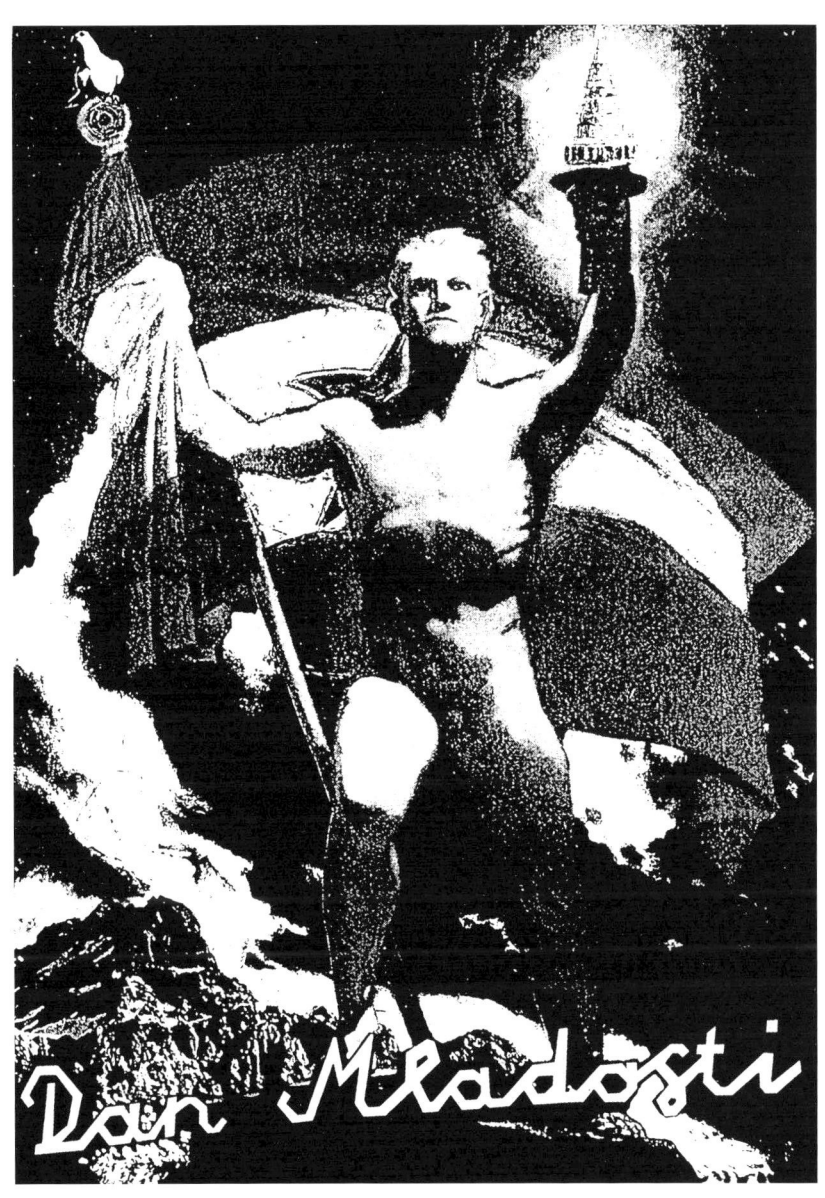

fig. 7

New Collectivism, *Youth Day*, 1987, the rejected poster proposal.

Courtesy of New Collectivism.

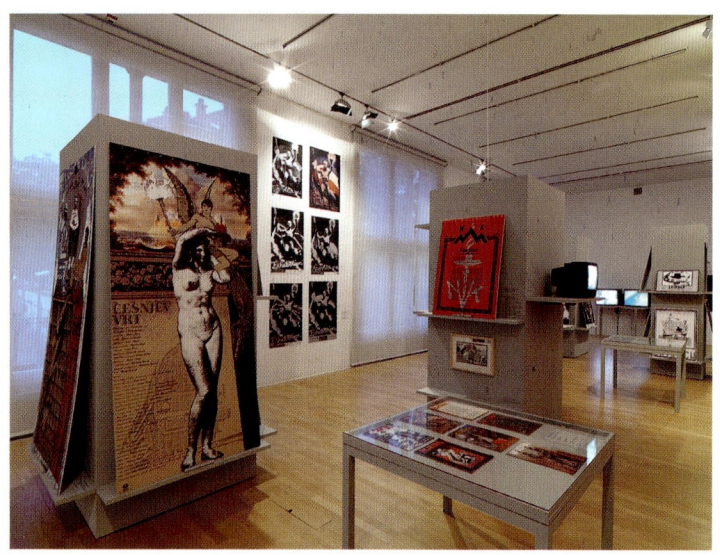

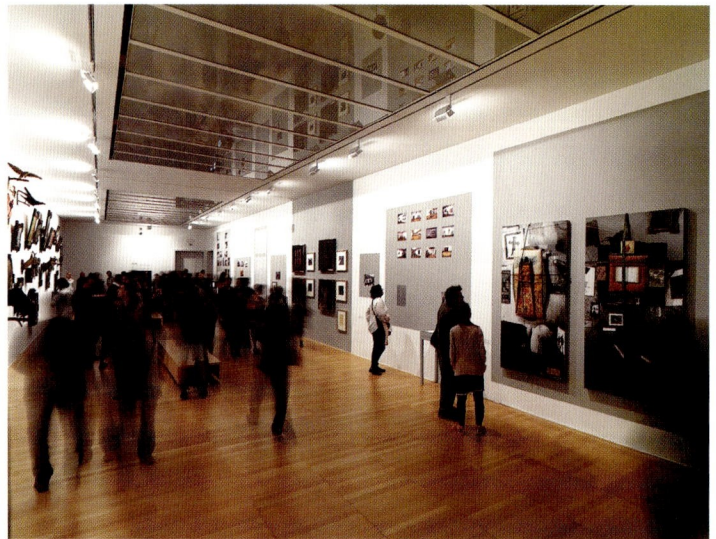

fig. 8

NSK from Kapital *to Capital*, 2015,
Moderna galerija, Ljubljana, exhibition view.

Photo by Dejan Habicht. Courtesy of Moderna galerija.

The coincidence of three rhythmic pulsations (band, crowd, and bridge), instead of building a unity of rhythm and movement, destroyed the very foundation on which they were all standing. This is a typical retro-garde effect.

But the NSK exhibition, while exhibiting this specific retro-garde *priyom* within a museum of modern art twenty-five years after NSK dissolved itself (fig. 8), raises at least two (im)pertinent questions: does the location of the exhibition prove that the political power of the past retro-garde has been again pacified into art? And why can't the example of NSK be successfully repeated in today's contemporary circumstances and by contemporary art? These questions may prove pertinent if we move from the exhibition to the collection, or rather, from The Exhibition organized as a legacy to The Collection put together by the awarding ritual.

The Collection

The year 2008, when the first Igor Zabel Awards were presented, is also the year when the book *Continuing Dialogues: A Tribute to Igor Zabel* was co-published (with the Erste Foundation and JRP-Ringier) by the Igor Zabel Association for Culture and Theory, which was established "to promote Igor Zabel's heritage and to highlight the importance and ongoing influence of his work, to enhance the exchange of knowledge and networking in contemporary visual arts and culture, and to strengthen the cultural dialogue in the Central and South Eastern European region and beyond".[22] In their essay "Commitment: A Provisional Suggestion", Maria Hlavajova and Kathrin Rhomberg explained this heritage and its theoretical orientation by quoting Zabel's summary of ideas expressed at the conference "Living with Genocide: Art and the War in Bosnia", held at the Moderna galerija in Ljubljana in 1996:

- The idea that art can seriously change the world has become questionable, utopian or even impossible …;
- Political and critical art is trapped in contradictions of its position within the art system, which permits such works only a limited audience and range of effect, and which is, furthermore, able to appropriate and use any attempt at criticism and self-criticism of art;
- Artists do not necessarily have to respond to the social reality "beyond the studio walls" in the works of art themselves …[23]

---

22 *Continuing Dialogues: A Tribute to Igor Zabel*, ed. Christa Benzer, Christine Böhler, and Christiane Erharter, JRP-Ringier, Zurich, 2008, p. 9.
23 Igor Zabel, quoted in Maria Hlavajova and Kathrin Rhomberg, "Commitment: A Provisional Suggestion", in *Continuing Dialogues*, pp. 105-106 (see previous note). See also Igor Zabel, "Commitment", *Contemporary Art Theory*, p. 74 (see n. 16).

Taken together, both these statements pregnantly describe not only the art-world locality of the award, but also, in a much broader scope, the artistic and non-artistic troubles with art in terms of the artistic geography – as troubles affecting global, Western, or Central and South European regional art. On the one hand, there is the expectation that art can and, if responsible to its aims, must change the world (including the art world, of course). On the other hand, there is the diagnosis that art cannot do or accomplish anything in "real world" and that when it tries to accomplish something it is quickly and smoothly appropriated by political and art-world institutions (so why should we care about the critical responsibility of art at all?). Speaking in terms of the "post-communist" region, this means that the best time for emancipation by means of art is long over, because the best time was the decade when communism was in its decline before its final collapse. By making the transition from socialism to capitalism and from (semi-)totalitarianism to democracy, the post-communist region entered into a world well described by W. H. Auden (his words were later quoted by Arthur Danto): "Artists and politicians would get along better at a time of crisis like the present, if the latter would only realize that the political history of the world would have been the same if not a poem had been written, nor a picture painted, nor a bar of music composed."[24] Auden's own experience of art made by means of politics and politics made by means of art was about artistic engagement in opposition to fascism (especially during the Spanish Civil War) and in the ideological struggles over the Soviet socialist-realist model of subjugating art to politics. His assertion that art cannot change anything is a personal cry of despair, not the calm and composed statement of an outsider to the art/politics embrace.

As a group, the collection of winners of the Igor Zabel Award from 2008 to 2014 shows us that the continuation of Zabel's legacy is channelled as a continuation of the Central and Eastern European experience of art's political power from the 1980s under post-transitional circumstances, including his seminal art-theoretical and art-historical contributions that opened the way to understanding contemporary art as emancipatory power. That is why the effort toward global visibility for regional art of this kind is considered to be something distinctive and at the same time globally important. Thus, fundamental and regionalized interests become one and the same. This conviction is shared by many scholars from the region, and elsewhere, including the late Piotr Piotrowski, who received the award in 2010. In 2012, in an interview with Edit András in *ArtMargins Online*, he spoke about the recognition of the Eastern European region and its identity, which is not that of "the Other" of the West but of "the close Other", the Other which shares the same *episteme* with the West but is subver-

---

24   Quoted in Arthur Danto, "The Philosophical Disenfranchisement of Art", in *The Wake of Art: Criticism, Philosophy, and the Ends of Taste*, ed. Gregg Horowitz and Tom Huhn, G+B Arts International, Amsterdam, 1998, p. 64.

sive against the centre. His views include the privileged marginal position and subversive tradition of Eastern European art, which goes back many years. On the one hand, in Piotrowski's view, this regional art, art theory, and art history must provincialize the West; on the other, it must open itself to other regions of the different Others. Piotrowski is aware that postcommunism and its art from the 1980s cannot continue to define the region, but he insists that our countries still have something in common and something to contribute to the world. As democracy today finds itself in jeopardy all around the world, the art and theory of our region have much to contribute to the critique of these troubles and the global situation because of its experience with the relationship between art and politics.[25]

The collection of award winners expresses both Zabel's and Piotrowski's programmatic idea that the region of Europe's East, Centre, and South needs European and global recognition, and that to be recognized it must continue its subversive artistic practices because they represent the distinctive legacy and experience it possesses. On the other hand, however, there is doubt that such a mission can be accomplished, a scepticism we have seen in the past, including Western postmodernist claims in the 1980s that avant-garde artistic and political activism was over.

Squaring the Circle

When we say "squaring the circle" we have in mind the way contemporary art is caught in an art world that acts as a surrogate *substitute* (*Ersatz*) of the public space. We should remember that the contemporary art world is not the kind of art world that was attacked and (potentially) left behind by the historical avant-garde; quite the contrary, it figures as a last resort that is worth defending for the sake of an art that is involved with life itself. There are major obstacles, however. First, there is a depoliticization happening where total politicization used to be in the 1980s: politics is now the continuation of the political economy in a sense never dreamed by Marx, and representation, which postmodernism so greatly criticized in art, has lost its ground in politics far more than it has in any kind of art. Without politicization it is not possible to build a case for overidentification (a typical NSK *priyom*) as a way to reveal that the politics which produces the politicization is built on a void. "Anything goes" is now taking place where there used to be total politicization with just one way allowed. It is on these depoliticized grounds and around such a void that the art world is trying to square the circle. On one side, the lines of socializing and participation in the art-world space serve as its meridians and parallels, phenomena that Bojana Kunst has thoroughly examined and critiqued

---

25 See Edit András, "Provincializing the West: Interview with Piotr Piotrowski", *ArtMargins Online*, October 9, 2012, http://www.artmargins.com/index.php/5-interviews/691-provincializing-the-west (accessed January 10, 2016).

in her book *Artist at Work*.[26] There is nothing wrong with socializing as a function of art; it was and still is important in that regard. But in contemporaneity, socializing acts as a surrogate to fill the absence of politics and public space in life: it is just a picnic on the art world's grounds. Similarly, today's participation, if compared it with older examples like Wagner's *Gesamtkunstwerk* project and William Morris's project for art in the utopian future, seems more like an attempt to make accessories out of simple bystanders who, by getting involved with art, must accept responsibility for its effects and outcomes even well beyond the realm of the art world. On the other side are activism and moralizing. Activism has appeared as a result of the lost artistic autotelism, or as Adorno put it, "It is self-evident that nothing concerning art is self-evident any more, not its inner life, not its relation to the world [in fact, he writes *das Ganze* – "the Whole", not "the world"], not even its right to exist."[27] To confirm its right to exist, art is going outside itself, looking for a good cause, and it finds it in the political economy and its critique, in ecology, in wars and militarism, in the social situation of women or any other minority, in dictatorships, in internet surveillance, etc. etc. "Anything goes!" is now understandable in its full scope. What all these activisms amount to is that art becomes morally responsible for its choice of causes, and its choice of causes becomes flimsy and slimy, which, among other things, is also a reason for the increased insistence on audience participation. Moralizing over the general results of depoliticization is given its chance despite the traditionally amoral fundament of art. Moralizing takes many different faces and approaches, but it never fails to ask why the artist is being subsidized if he or she is so critical; it notices the immorality of hanging avant-garde art on the walls of a museum; it mentions in passing that all art is in any case paid for by the taxpayers and/or tycoons; it examines a cause taken up by an artwork and measures its good and bad points with myopic puritanism – and so it confirms what Adorno said about interpretations of late style as in the work of the older Beethoven or Goya: namely, that art history or any discourse about artworks abdicates its role when it starts to put personal circumstances above the artwork as such. In the contemporary art world, this happens because moralization is one of the prevailing features of contemporaneity, and because the art world has lost its central position, which used to be rooted in art, and has assumed a position that is quite eccentric to art. For the contemporary art world, artworks are as important as cocktails are at a cocktail party – they have to be served so that mingling feels like a natural behaviour. The NSK *priyom* was not made for a situation of total depoliticization, nor is it adapted for an art world that puts art in an eccentric position.

26 Bojana Kunst, *Umetnik na delu: Bližina umetnosti in kapitalizma*, Maska, Ljubljana, 2012; published in English as *Artist at Work: Proximity of Art and Capitalism*, Zero Books, Alresford, Hants, UK, 2015.
27 Theodor W. Adorno, *Aesthetic Theory*, ed. Gretel Adorno and Rolf Tiedemann, Continuum, London and New York, 2002, p. 1.

Epilogue

Contemporary art, it seems, is expected to achieve such demanding goals that it can hardly avoid being trapped in the vagaries of political cynicism. In neo-liberal political systems the ruling caste may easily thwart subversive actions by invoking the "right to critique" and "citizens' rights and liberties", thereby ostensibly demonstrating a devotion to democracy, openness, tolerance, and other cherished values. With that banally simple manoeuvre, any subversive action may be portrayed as part of normal political life, which suggests that everything is business as usual. This, of course, is the kind of cynicism the system uses to fully protect itself from all kinds of subversive actions. Art shares the same fate as other ideological spheres in today's society, in which subversion is likewise merely a nominal possibility and its real effects are rather limited. Under such circumstances, the possibilities of artistic intervention are rather narrow, because the contemporary art system and post-Fordist capitalism are very much alike when it comes to institutional cannibalism: they are both adept at absorbing even the severest critics. The former ruling strategy of state repression has been supplanted by more elegant forms of censorship: from political and media discrediting to civil lawsuits and economic censorship. Penalties for breaking the law can be so harsh that many freelancers and smaller art collectives (NGOs and the like) do not dare risk much. Ultimately, this strategy leads to artists censoring themselves and thus blunting in advance the critical point of their work.

There is no easy way out of the vicious circle. There may, however, be at least a thin ray of hope in Zabel's interpretation of Adorno's essay "Commitment" and his understanding of the relationship between committed and autonomous art, i.e. the tension and contradictions between the two approaches. Zabel writes:

> On the one hand, in the light of critical art, we realize that a pure, autonomous art cannot remain outside political reality and that it is precisely the autonomy of this art that allows it to be appropriated by dominant – and sometimes repressive – political regimes. On the other hand, it also appears that a critical and political art (which is based on a clear awareness of its social and political position and role) cannot escape being exploited by the system.[28]

The point is not in the possible combination or synthesis of these two (negative) poles but quite the opposite, in their mutual negation. This tension remains strong today and, in Zabel's view, it is a good reason for modest optimism regarding the critical role assigned to art in contemporary democratic societies: "Such tension and contradiction ... are what still

---

28   Zabel, "Commitment", p. 75.

allow art to create values that cannot be completely absorbed either by the marketplace or by ideological functions, with the result that art continues to act as a point of resistance in society."[29] Thus, even if the structure of the contradiction changes, it is a good news that the tension remains.

---

29   Ibid.

Biographies

Authors

Edit András, PhD, is an art historian and art critic, based in Budapest and Long Island, USA. András is affiliated with the Institute of Art History, Research Centre for the Humanities of the Hungarian Academy of Sciences, Budapest, as a senior research fellow. Her main interests are modern and contemporary Eastern and Central European art, gender issues, public art, socially committed art, and art theory in post-socialist countries. She is the author of the book *Cultural Cross Dressing: Art in the Ruins of Socialism* (in Hungarian, 2009). Her most recent focus is art, politics, and nationalism. She curated the exhibition *Imagined Communities, Personal Imaginations: Private Nationalism Budapest* (2015), organized the related conference "Visualizing the Nation: Post-Socialist ImagiNations" (2015), and co-curated *Universal Hospitality* exhibition (2016) in Vienna. She is a member of the editorial board of *ArtMargins Online* and *Ars Hungarica* and has published numerous essays in books and journals (*Springerin*, *Third Text*, *e-flux*, and *Artmargins*). She served as a jury member of the Igor Zabel Award for Culture and Theory in 2010.

Fouad Asfour, art writer, editor, and linguist, works in collaborative frameworks on publications, exhibitions, performance and art exchange projects. He has worked for various art institutions and research projects, was part of the *documenta 12 magazines* project, and is a member of the Dead Revolutionaries Club artist's collective. In 2011, he initiated the independent publishing project Pole Pole Press and is the co-founder of the self-organized student support initiative Thekgo Bursary (now in collaboration with Canon Collins Trust). He holds an MA in linguistics from Vienna University and is currently completing an MA in creative writing at Rhodes University in Grahamstown, South Africa. He lives between Johannesburg and Vienna. In 2008, he was a grant recipient of the Igor Zabel Award for Culture and Theory.

Keti Chukhrov, PhD, is an art theorist, philosopher, and poet based in Moscow. She is an associate professor at the Department of Cultural Studies at the Higher School of Economics and head of Theoretical Studies in Cultural Anthropology at the National Centre for Contemporary Arts (both in Moscow). Since 2003, she has served on the editorial board of the *Moscow Art Magazine*. Chukhrov has authored numerous texts on art theory, culture, politics, and philosophy that have appeared in periodicals such as *Afterall*, *Moscow Art Magazine*, *Artforum*, *Brumaria*, *documenta magazines*, *e-flux journal*, *New Literary Review*, *Stasis*, *Problemi*, *Issues of Philosophy*, and *Springerin*. Her books include *To Be – To Perform: "Theatre" in Philosophical Criticism of Art* (2011), *Just Humans* (2010), and *Pound & £* (1999). She served as a jury member for the Igor Zabel Award for Culture and Theory in 2014.

Karel Císař, PhD, is a philosopher, curator, and associate professor of theory and history of modern and contemporary art at the Academy of Arts, Architecture, and Design in Prague. From 2009 to 2011, he was a core group participant in the Sterling and Francine Clark Art Institute's Research and Academic Program "Unfolding Narratives: Art Histories in East-Central Europe after 1989". He recently curated *Figures and Prefigurations* exhibition at Prague City Gallery (2013) that confronted works of contemporary artists with modernist exhibition design, surrealist typography, and functionalist glassware. His recently published essays (in English) include "Alphabet of Things" in *Běla Kolářová* (2013) and "Plane and Space" in *Dominik Lang: Expanded Anxiety* (2013). In 2014, he was a grant recipient of the Igor Zabel Award for Culture and Theory.

Ekaterina Degot is an art historian, curator, and art writer based in Cologne and Moscow. She is the artistic director of the Academy of the Arts of the World, Cologne, and a professor at the Rodchenko Moscow School of Photography and Multimedia. Her work focuses on aesthetic and socio-political issues in Russia, predominantly in the post-Soviet era. From 2008 until 2012, she was the senior editor of www.openspace.ru/art, an independent online magazine of art criticism and cultural analysis. She co-edited *Post-Post-Soviet? Art, Politics and Society in Russia at the Turn of the Decade* (2013) and *Moscow Conceptualism* (2005). Her recent curatorial projects include *Reports to an Academy: A Non-Academic Symposium, Performative or Otherwise*, Pluriversale I, Cologne, 2014 (with David Riff), *What Did the Artist Mean by That?*, Moscow Museum of Modern Art, 2014 (with Yuri Albert), and *Monday Begins on Saturday*, First Bergen Assembly, Bergen, Norway, 2013 (with David Riff). She received the Igor Zabel Award for Culture and Theory in 2014.

Maja Fowkes and Reuben Fowkes, PhDs, are art historians, curators, and directors of the Translocal Institute for Contemporary Art in Budapest. Their main areas of research are the art history of Eastern Europe since 1945, environmental art history, and contemporary art and ecological thought. Recent publications include Maja Fowkes's *The Green Bloc: Neo-avant-garde Art and Ecology under Socialism* (2015) and *River Ecologies: Contemporary Art and Environmental Humanities on the Danube* (2015). Reuben Fowkes is a co-editor of *Third Text*, and currently preparing a special issue on Eastern European art of the 1960s and 70s. Their forthcoming contributions include a chapter on alternative art in the 1980s in Eastern Europe for the *Afterall Exhibition Histories* series and a journal article on the Danube and contemporary art for *Geo-Humanities*. Their curatorial projects include the *Experimental Reading Room* (2014–16), the *River School* (2013–15), and the exhibition *Walking without Footprints* (2016). They are currently visiting lecturers at Central European University in Budapest, where they teach a course entitled Visual Cultures of the Anthropocene for the Environmental Humanities Initiative. In 2010, Maja and Reuben Fowkes were grant recipients of the Igor Zabel Award for Culture and Theory. www.translocal.org

Alenka Gregorič is an art historian, curator, and art writer. Between 2003 and 2009, she worked as the artistic director and curator of Škuc Gallery, Ljubljana. Since 2010, she has been the artistic director and curator of City Art Gallery Ljubljana and CC Tobacco 001 (both part of Museum and Galleries of Ljubljana). In 2009, she was curator of the Slovene pavilion at the Venice Biennale and co-curator of the Biennial of Graphic Arts, Ljubljana. In 2011, she was co-curator (with Galit Eilat) of the 52nd October Salon in Belgrade, and, in 2014, was one of the curators for the *Curated by_Vienna* project. She has curated over fifty solo and group exhibitions in Slovenia and abroad (featuring works by artists Vuk Ćosić, Jan Fabre, Omer Fast, Harun Farocki, Vadim Fiškin, Irwin, Jannis Kounellis, Ivan Moudov, Marjetica Potrč, Mladen Stilinović, Raša Todosojević, Bill Viola, Katarina Zdjelar, and others). Recently she has been focusing on the institutional aspects of art and cultural production and the role of cultural institutions in contemporary society. She served as a jury member of the Igor Zabel Award for Culture and Theory in 2012.

Daniel Grúň, PhD, is an art historian, art writer, and curator based in Bratislava. Currently, he lectures at the Academy of Fine Arts and Design in Bratislava. He published the books *Archeology of Art Criticism: Slovak Art of the 1960s and its Interpretations* (in Slovak, 2009) and *Július Koller Galéria Ganku* (2014). His main areas of research are the legacy of neo-avant-gardes, critical theory, and contemporary art. As a researcher, he was involved in the exhibition and publication series of the trans-institutional network L'Internationale. Recently he co-curated exhibitions *Mutually: Communities of the 1970s and 1980s* (tranzitdisplay, Prague, and Brno House of Arts, both 2013), *Július Koller: "?"* (Museum of Modern Art, Warsaw, 2015), and *One Man Anti Show* (MUMOK, Vienna, 2016). He is a board member and collaborator of tranzit.sk in Bratislava. In 2010, he was a grant recipient of the Igor Zabel Award for Culture and Theory.

Sabine Hänsgen, PhD, studied Slavic literature, history, and art history at the Ruhr University in Bochum. In 1984, she was awarded a DAAD grant for doctoral research at the Institute of Cinematography VGIK in Moscow. She has conducted research and taught at universities in Bochum, Bielefeld, Bremen, Cologne, and Basel, and served as a guest professor at the Humboldt University in Berlin from 2011–2014. Working as an author, curator, editor, and translator since 1985, Hänsgen has participated in the performances of the Collective Actions Group and was involved in the establishment of an audio-visual archive of Moscow Conceptualism. Currently she is a research fellow in the project "Performance Art in Eastern Europe" (University of Zurich) and is preparing a series of exhibitions under the title *Poetry & Performance: The Eastern European Perspective*. In 2012, she was a grant recipient of the Igor Zabel Award for Culture and Theory. www.sabine-haensgen.de

Tímea Junghaus, PhD, is an art historian and curator based in Budapest. She curated the First Roma Pavilion at the 52nd Venice Biennale (2007) and is co-editor of the comprehensive publication on European Roma visual art *Meet Your Neighbours: Contemporary Roma Art from Europe* (2006). She has researched and published extensively on the conjunctions of modern and contemporary art with critical theory, with particular reference to issues of cultural difference, colonialism, and minority representation. Since 2010, she has been employed as a researcher at the Institute of Art History at the Hungarian Academy of Sciences.

She received the Kairos-European Cultural Prize in 2007 and is the founding director of the European Roma Cultural Foundation, a Budapest-based NGO, which established Gallery8 – Roma Contemporary Art Space. In 2012, the European Roma Cultural Foundation was a grant recipient of the Igor Zabel Award for Culture and Theory. www.Romacult.org www.gallery8.org

Klara Kemp-Welch, PhD, is a lecturer on 20th century modernism at the Courtauld Institute of Art in London where she teaches courses on the cultural Cold War, countercultures and experimental art of Eastern Europe and Latin America. She was educated at University College London and the School of Slavonic and East European Studies in London. She is the author of the monograph *Antipolitics in Central European Art: Reticence as Dissidence under Post-Totalitarian Rule 1956-1989* (2014) and is now finishing the monograph *Networking the Bloc: International Relations and Experimental Art in Eastern Europe 1968-1989*. As a post-doctoral researcher, she was awarded fellowships from the Phillip Leverhulme Trust and the Arts and Humanities Research Council. In 2012, she was a grant recipient of the Igor Zabel Award for Culture and Theory.

Miklavž Komelj, PhD, is a poet, art historian, and translator based in Ljubljana. He has published nine books of poetry in the Slovene language (in English *Hippodrome*, 2015) and a collection of essays entitled *The Necessity of Poetry* (in Slovene, 2010). He published an extensive study on partisan art *How to Think Partisan Art?* (in Slovene, 2009) and co-curated the display of partisan art as part of the new permanent exhibition of the national collection, titled *Continuities and Ruptures*, at the Moderna galerija in Ljubljana. Komelj's main interest in the field of the history and theory of art is dedicated to the question of how to produce a new field of the possible out of the confrontation with the impossible. Therefore, he is mainly concerned with the historical turning points, when the coordinates of thinking about art were re-established. He has translated works by Djuna Barnes, Fernando Pessoa, Pier Paolo Pasolini, and César Vallejo into the Slovene language. In 2014, he was a grant recipient of the Igor Zabel Award for Culture and Theory.

Lev Kreft, PhD, is a professor of aesthetics at the University of Ljubljana. His research areas are contemporary art, historical avant-garde, struggles on the artistic left, Marxist aesthetics, totalitarian art and aesthetics, postmodern and post-socialist art, aesthetics of sport, and philosophy of sport. He is a member of the Slovene Society of Aesthetics, the British Philosophy of Sport Association, the International Association for the Philosophy of Sport, the International Society for the Social Sciences of Sport, and a founding member and ex-President of the European Association for the Philosophy of Sport (2008–2014). His recent books and chapters include *Aesthetician's Atelier* (in Slovene, 2016), "Avant-Garde, Retro-Garde, and Progress" (in *NSK from* Kapital *to Capital*, 2015), "The Radical Critique of Sport" (in *Routledge Handbook of the Philosophy of Sport*, 2015), *Left Hook: Essays in Philosophy of Sport* (2011 in Slovene, 2013 in Serbian). He was a researcher at The Peace Institute, Ljubljana, which was a grant recipient of the Igor Zabel Award for Culture and Theory in 2010.

Aldo Milohnić, PhD, is an assistant professor of the history of theatre at the Academy of Theatre, Radio, Film, and Television, University of Ljubljana. He has edited and co-edited numerous anthologies of texts and special issues of cultural journals (*The Politicality of Performance*, *At the Crossroads of Cultural Politics*, *Artivism, Brecht/Gestus*, *Along the Margins of the Humanities*, etc.), and co-authored several books (*Culture Ltd.: Material Conditions of Cultural Production*, 2005; in Slovene *It's Time for Brecht!*, 2009, among others). He is the author of two books (in Slovene): *Theories of Contemporary Theatre and Performance* (2009) and *Art in the Times of the Rule of Law and Capital* (2016), as well as of numerous articles in academic journals. Over the last twenty years, he has been involved in many research projects dealing with the history and theory of performing arts and the sociology of culture. He was a researcher at The Peace Institute, Ljubljana, which was a grant recipient of the Igor Zabel Award for Culture and Theory in 2010.

Kirill Medvedev is a poet, translator, and political activist based in Moscow. He is the co-founder of the publishing house Free Marxist Press and Arkady Kots riot-folk band. The Free Marxist Press has published books and pamphlets on such topics as contemporary Marxist and critical theory, political art and poetry, the history of labour, socialism, feminism, minority rights, and antifascist movements, including works by Pier Paolo Pasolini, Bertolt Brecht, Charles Bukowski, Adrienne Rich, Zlatan Dudov, Terry Eagleton, Jean-Luc Godard, and others. Medvedev has written several books of poetry, essays, and art actions in Russian (in English *It's No Good*, 2012). Kirill Medvedev, with the Free Marxist Press, was a grant recipient of the Igor Zabel Award for Culture and Theory in 2014. https://fm-books.wordpress.com/

Piotr Piotrowski (1952–2015), PhD, was an outstanding art historian, scholar of 20th-century art, and professor ordinarius at the Art History Department at the Adam Mickiewicz University, Poznan, which he chaired from 1999 to 2008. He is the author of several books, including *Meanings of Modernism: Towards a History of Polish Art after 1945* (in Polish 1999, 2011), *In the Shadow of Yalta: Art and the Avant-garde in Eastern Europe, 1945-1989* (2005, English ed. 2009), *Art After Politics: From Melancholy to Passion* (in Polish, 2007), *Art and Democracy in Post-Communist Europe* (2010, English ed. 2012), and *Critical Museum* (in Polish, 2011), as well as editor, co-editor, and co-author of many others. He was also the director of the National Museum in Warsaw (2009–2010), and visiting professor at Humboldt University Berlin (2011–2012), Warsaw University (2011, 2012-13), Hebrew University in Jerusalem (2003), and Bard College, USA (2001). He was a permanent research fellow of the Graduate School for East and South-East European Studies, Ludwig-Maximillians University, Munich and Regensburg University as well as a fellow at the Center for Advanced Studies in the Visual Arts, Washington D.C. (1989–90), Columbia University (1994), Institute for Advanced Study, Princeton, NJ (2000), Collegium Budapest (2005–06), and the Clark Art Institute, Williamstown, MA (2009), among others. Piotrowski received the Igor Zabel Award for Culture and Theory in 2010.

Jelena Vesić, PhD, is a freelance curator, art writer, editor, and cultural activist who lives and works both in Belgrade and abroad. She has been a co-editor of *Prelom – Journal of Images and Politics* (Belgrade, 2001–2009) and was a founding member of both the Prelom Collective (Belgrade, 2005–2010) and Other Scene, a network of independent organizations (Belgrade, 2005–present). She is also a co-editor of Istanbul-based *Red Thread: Journal for Social Theory, Contemporary Art and Activism* (2009–present) and a member of the editorial board of *Art Margins*. Jelena Vesić's research is dedicated to the politics of representation in art and visual culture as well as practices of self-organization and politicization of cultural work. Her recent curatorial projects include *Oktobar XXX: Symposium–Exposition–Performance* (KC Pančevo, 2012), *Against Art: Goran Djordjević: Copies 1979–1985* (Salon of the Museum of Contemporary Art, Belgrade, 2011), and *Political Practices of (post-) Yugoslav Art: RETROSPECTIVE 01* (Museum of Yugoslav History – Museum of 25th May, Belgrade, 2009). Jelena Vesić, with Prelom Kolektiv, received a grant of the Igor Zabel Award for Culture and Theory in 2008. www.prelomkolektiv.org

Raluca Voinea is a curator and art critic. Since 2012, she has served as co-director of tranzit.ro Association and runs the tranzit.ro space in Bucharest where she organizes exhibitions and discursive programmes that focus on the relationships between contemporary art and wider political and social determinations. One of the ongoing projects that she initiated at tranzit.ro/București is *Tranzit Garden*, an urban garden built on permaculture principles and also a means of linking the art space with different communities, the city, and current discussions about ecology. In 2016, Tranzit Orangerie was opened as an annex to the gallery and the garden, offering shelter for fragile plants and ideas. In 2013, she curated the Romanian Pavilion at the 55th Venice Biennale, bringing in the project *An Immaterial Retrospective of the Venice Biennale* by artists Alexandra Pirici and Manuel Pelmuș. Since 2008, she has been the co-editor of *IDEA arts + society* magazine. In 2010, she was a grant recipient of the Igor Zabel Award for Culture and Theory. http://ro.tranzit.org/en

What, How & for Whom / **WHW** is a curatorial collective based in Zagreb and Berlin that was created in 1999. Its members are Ivet Ćurlin, Ana Dević, Nataša Ilić, Sabina Sabolović, and designer and publicist Dejan Kršić. WHW organizes a range of production, exhibition, and publishing projects, and directs Gallery Nova in Zagreb. Since its first exhibition *What, How & for Whom: On the Occasion of 152nd Anniversary of the Communist Manifesto* in Zagreb in 2000, WHW has curated numerous international projects, including *Collective Creativity* (Kunsthalle Fridericianum, Kassel, 2005), the 11th Istanbul Biennial *What Keeps Mankind Alive?* (2009), and *One Needs to Live Self-Confidently...Watching* (Croatian pavilion at the 54th Venice Biennale, 2011). More recent projects include the festival *Meeting Points 7: Ten Thousand Wiles and a Hundred Thousand Tricks* (Zagreb, Antwerp, Cairo, Hong-Kong, Beirut, Vienna, and Moscow, 2013-2014), the exhibition *Really Useful Knowledge* (Museo Nacional Centro de Arte Reina Sofia, Madrid, 2014), and David Maljković *Retrospective by Appointment* (Gallery Nova and various venues in Zagreb, 2015). Currently WHW and Kathrin Rhomberg are preparing a series of exhibitions and discursive and performative programmes at various locations in Zagreb (November 2016–May 2017) that are based on the artworks from Kontakt: The Art Collection of Erste Group. The curatorial collective WHW was the recipient of the first Igor Zabel Award for Culture and Theory in 2008. www.whw.hr

Editors

Christiane Erharter is a curator and project manager based in Vienna. She graduated from the Academy of Fine Arts, Vienna, and holds a postgraduate degree in Critical Studies from the University of Lund. She has worked at the Office for Contemporary Art Norway in Oslo and at the Galerie im Taxispalais in Innsbruck. Since 2006, she has been working for the ERSTE Foundation conceptualizing and managing projects such as *Gender Check*, a research, exhibition, and publication project about femininity and masculinity in Eastern European art, and the Igor Zabel Award for Culture and Theory. Her recent curatorial work includes the exhibitions *Srebrenica Today* (2015), *Anna Jermolaewa: Good Times, Bad Times* (Zachęta National Gallery of Art, Warsaw, and Wrocław Art Center, 2015), *AT YOUR SERVICE: ART AND LABOUR* (Museum of Technology, Vienna, 2012, and Technical Museum, Zagreb, 2014). In 2012, she co-curated the exhibition *Rosa Arbeit auf Goldener Straße* on queer art practices; she is also the co-editor of *Pink Labor on Golden Streets: Queer Art Practices* (2015).

Rawley Grau, originally from Baltimore, USA, is a translator (from Slovene and Russian) and English language editor who lives in Ljubljana. His Slovene translations include works by Igor Zabel (*Contemporary Art Theory*, 2013) and Beti Žerovc (*When Attitudes Become the Norm: The Contemporary Curator and Institutional Art*, 2015) for the Igor Zabel Association; he has also translated and language-edited many texts for other Slovene art institutions, including the Moderna galerija, the Museum of Architecture and Design, and the International Centre of Graphic Arts. He was also a translator and language editor for *East Art Map: Contemporary Art and Eastern Europe* (2006), edited by Irwin. From Russian, he has translated essays by Boris Groys and Viktor Misiano. His literary translations from Slovene include the novels *The Succubus* by Vlado Žabot, *Dry Season* by Gabriela Babnik, and most recently, *Panorama* by Dušan Šarotar. His translation of the 19th-century Russian poet Yevgeny Baratynsky, *A Science Not for the Earth: Selected Poems and Letters*, was chosen by the online journal *Three Percent* as one of the ten best translated books of poetry in the United States in 2015. He teaches translation and English at the University of Primorska in Koper, Slovenia.

Urška Jurman is an editor, curator, project manager, art writer, and sceptical enthusiast in the field of contemporary art. She holds a degree in Art History and Sociology of Culture from the Faculty of Arts, University of Ljubljana. She has worked for and with various art institutions and initiatives in Slovenia (Škuc Gallery, SCCA-Ljubljana, hEXPO – Festival of Self-Organizing Cultural Forms, P74 Gallery). She is a co-founder and member of the Obrat Culture and Art Association, being active mainly in the field of critical spatial practices. She is a co-editor of the *PlatformaSCCA* magazine for contemporary art and theory (2000–2005), *Ready 2 Change* reader (2005), editor of *Sanja Iveković: Public Cuts* catalogue (2006), and of Beti Žerovc's monograph *When Attitudes Become the Norm: The Contemporary Curator and Institutional Art* (2015), among others. Since 2013, she has served as the programme manager of the Igor Zabel Association for Culture and Theory in Ljubljana.

IZA Editions
Publications series by the Igor Zabel Association for
Culture and Theory (Ljubljana) and Archive Books (Berlin).

Series editor
Urška Jurman

Extending the Dialogue
Essays by Igor Zabel Award Laureates,
Grant Recipients, and Jury Members, 2008–2014

Editors
Urška Jurman, Christiane Erharter,
and Rawley Grau

Language editors
Rawley Grau and Erica Johnson Debeljak

Design and layout
Ivian Kan Mujezinović / Ee

Printing and binding
Formatisk d.o.o.

1000 copies printed

The editors gratefully acknowledge Jutta Braidt,
Eda Čufer, Rainer Fuchs, Vít Havránek,
Magdalena Radomska, and Maria Zuk-Piotrowska
for their valuable assistance with this book.

Distribution

Anagram Books
contact@anagrambooks.com
www.anagrambooks.com

Les presses du réel
info@lespressesdureel.com
www.lespressesdureel.com

RAM Publications + Distribution Inc.
info@rampub.com
www.rampub.com

Ljubljana, Berlin, and Vienna, December 2016

© 2016 by the Igor Zabel Association for Culture
and Theory, ERSTE Foundation, and Archive Books.
Individual texts © 2016 by the authors.

All rights reserved. Except for brief quotations, this book,
or parts thereof, must not be reproduced in any form without
the written permission of the publishers or authors.

Published by

Igor Zabel Association for Culture and Theory
Trg Prekomorskih brigad 1
SI-1000 Ljubljana
info@igorzabel.org
www.igorzabel.org

Archive Books
Müllerstraße 133
DE-13349 Berlin
mail@archivebooks.org
www.archivebooks.org

ERSTE Foundation
Am Belvedere 1
AT-1100 Vienna
office@erstestiftung.org
www.erstestiftung.org

ISBN 978-3-943620-52-8

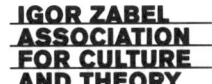 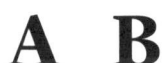 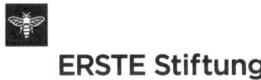

CIP - Kataložni zapis o publikaciji
Narodna in univerzitetna knjižnica, Ljubljana

7.01"20"(082)

EXTENDING the dialogue / essays by Igor Zabel Award laureates, grant recipients, and jury members, 2008-2014 ; [editors Urška Jurman, Christiane Erharter, and Rawley Grau]. - Ljubljana : Igor Zabel Association for Culture and Theory ; Berlin : Archive Books ; Vienna : Erste Foundation, 2016

ISBN 978-3-943620-52-8 (Archive Books)
1. Jurman, Urša
287279616